W. E. B. DU BOIS

Also by Rayford W. Logan

The American Negro: Old World Background
and New World Experience (*co-author with Irving S. Cohen*)
The Negro in the United States: A Brief History
The Betrayal of the Negro: From Rutherford B. Hayes
to Woodrow Wilson
Haiti and the Dominican Republic
Diplomatic Relations of the United States
with Haiti, 1776–1891
Howard University: The First Hundred Years, 1867–1967

W. E. B. Du Bois

A PROFILE

EDITED BY

RAYFORD W. LOGAN

AMERICAN PROFILES

General Editor: Aïda DiPace Donald

American Century Series
HILL AND WANG : NEW YORK

Contents

v

Introduction

The first topic at the opening session of the Eighty-Third Annual Meeting of the American Historical Association in New York City on December 28, 1968, was "W. E. B. Du Bois (1868–1968): In Observance of the One Hundredth Anniversary of His Birth." Three speakers discussed him as a "Sociologist," "Historian," and "Negro Nationalist." The last two topics were the subject of papers by Herbert Aptheker and Vincent Harding, respectively, and these essays are included in this volume.

A complete biography of Du Bois would have to include portrayal of him as a novelist, poet, and public speaker; author of two-score books and several hundred articles and pamphlets; editor of one of the most effective polemical magazines in the United States; scholar and teacher; leader of "The Talented Tenth," authentic American radical, pragmatist, and romantic; a founder and officer of the National Association for the Advancement of Colored People, socialist and Communist; pluralist, integrationist, and advocate of "voluntary segregation"; "nationalist" and Pan-Africanist; opponent of Booker T. Washington and Marcus Garvey. With the exception of Frederick Douglass, he was the greatest American Negro. The centennial observance, five years after Du Bois' death, suggests that many scholars consider him a great American. Yet some hold different views and emphasize his polemics, the contradictions in his tactics and goals, his final belief that communism was the salvation of American and other Negroes, his voluntary expatriation and the renunciation of his American citizenship for Ghanaian citizenship. Controversy followed him beyond the grave. Only after a bitter struggle did the town of Great Barrington, Massachusetts, authorize in 1969 a memorial park surrounding the site of the Du Bois family home.

"The Paradox of W. E. B. Du Bois," the title of one of August Meier's selections in this book, which ends with an excellent but incomplete summary of paradoxes, is the most common theme, implicit or explicit, of all the selections. Several contributors, for example, stress Du Bois' ambivalence on the issue of "race." Francis Broderick quotes a statement by Du Bois when he was a student at Fisk University, 1885–1888: " 'I am a Negro; and I glory in the name! I am proud of the black blood that flows in my veins.' " Even Vincent Harding, who pictures Du Bois as a "Black Messiah," concedes his "dividedness" on the question of race. But, in order to support his basic thesis, Harding distorts Du Bois' reasons for not marrying the blue-eyed German girl who wanted to marry him in 1892. In *Dusk of Dawn* (1940, p. 46), Du Bois told her that she would be unhappy in the United States and, besides, he had work to do. Harding links the romance with a general statement by Du Bois (*Dusk of Dawn*, p. 102) that in Europe "my friendships and close contacts with white folk made my own ideas waver." Harding interprets this statement to mean "Beware of close contacts with white folk!" On the contrary, Du Bois—in the sentence following the sentence Harding quotes—wrote: "The eternal walls between races did not seem so stern and exclusive." Moreover, Du Bois stated in his essay "My Evolving Program for Negro Freedom," in *What the Negro Wants* (1944, p. 42), that as a result of his European experiences, "I became more human; learned the place in life of 'Wine, Women, and Song'; I ceased to hate or suspect people simply because they belonged to one race or color." This was not a latter-day conversion—Broderick points out that as early as 1887 Du Bois had hoped that Negroes and whites of "taste and education could join hands to lead the ignorant of both races."

Writing in 1912 or 1913, William Ferris expressed his belief that he understood Du Bois because he too was a Negro (a view held today by some advocates of "Black Studies" who assert that only Negroes should teach courses about Negroes). Elliott Rudwick sharply criticizes Du Bois for his denunciation of white racism while being guilty himself of extreme Negro racism. Harold Isaacs observes that in Du Bois' view "race doctrine that was anathema when it was white became eloquent when it was black."

Another aspect of the ambivalence of Du Bois on race was his concept of "Two-ness," most fully developed by Meier. Du Bois first used the word in "Strivings of the Negro People," *Atlantic Monthly* (August 1897), and he repeated it, with minor modifications, in *The Souls of Black Folk* (1903). In the latter (pp. 3, 4), Du Bois wrote: "One ever feels his two-ness—an American, a Negro; two souls, two thoughts, two unreconciled strivings; two warring ideals in one dark body, whose dogged strength alone keeps it from being torn asunder. . . . He [the American Negro] simply wishes it possible for a man to be both a Negro and an American, without being spit upon by his fellows, without having the doors of Opportunity closed roughly in his face." In *The Conservation of Races* (1897), Du Bois wrote: "Am I an American or am I a Negro? Can I be both? Or is it my duty to cease to be a Negro as soon as possible and be an American?" Ferris expresses the dilemma in slightly different words. Without indicating the source, he quotes Du Bois as having said, "The black man has the same feelings and thoughts and aspirations as the white man."

Herein lies, I believe, the most important and most difficult of the Du Bois paradoxes. In *What the Negro Wants* (1944, p. 36), he stated that at Fisk in 1885 he had been tossed boldly into the " 'Negro Problem.' . . . Thereupon a new loyalty and allegiance replaced my Americanism; henceforward I was a Negro."

Of course, he was not. Two of the more intriguing instances of his two-ness are his famous editorial "Close Ranks" in the July, 1918, issue of *The Crisis,* and his willingness shortly thereafter to accept a commission as captain in the United States Army Intelligence. In "Close Ranks," Du Bois wrote: "Let us, while this war lasts, forget our special grievances and close ranks shoulder to shoulder with our own fellow citizens and the allied nations that are fighting for democracy." The editorial provoked such an uproar, including allegations that the editorial was a bribe in return for the offer of the captaincy, that it was withdrawn. In the September, 1918, issue of *The Crisis,* Du Bois asserted that "Close Ranks" had been in exact accord with the resolution adopted by thirty-one Negro newspaper editors shortly prior to the editorial. Charles Kellogg does not dispute this assertion, but Rudwick points out that the editors had not told anyone to " 'forget' " all grievances during the remainder of the war. Rudwick adds that Du Bois' "wartime accommodation strategy made him seem like an Uncle Tom and disillusioned some Negroes who were unfamiliar with his lifelong paradox by which he found value in some aspects of segregation."

In *Dusk of Dawn* (1940, p. 255), Du Bois wrote that he was less sure of the soundness of his war attitude; he doubted if "the triumph of Germany in 1918 could have had worse results than the triumph of the allies." Perhaps his reassertion of his Negroness in 1944 was due to his horror of the Nazi doctrine of a "master race" which, of course, excluded Negroes. In any event, his two-ness continued to bedevil him until, at the end of 1961, he ceased to be an American, an American Negro, and became an African Negro. Consequently, largely one-dimensional interpretations of Du Bois, such as Aptheker's portrayal that he was most significantly influenced by Marx and Marxism and Harding's that he was a "Black Messiah," are necessarily incomplete. Meier shows more perceptiveness when he finds a similarity between Du Bois' two-ness and cultural pluralism.

In some respects Du Bois' expatriation may be considered the culmination of his search for a career. As early as 1890 and 1891 (Broderick, see below, pp. 23–24), he deplored the inability of Ethiopia to be a worthy leader of the Negro world. On his twenty-fifth birthday, February 23, 1893, he wrote in his diary (Broderick, see below, p. 33): " 'These are my plans: to make a name in science, to make a name in literature and thus to raise my race. Or perhaps to raise a visible empire in Africa thro' England, France, or Germany.' " In his interview with Isaacs, probably in early 1959, Du Bois stated that a small museum at Fisk was responsible for his interest in Africa. Evidence is still lacking to show the origins of Du Bois' statement at the Pan-African Conference in London, July, 1900, which he repeated in *The Souls of Black Folk:* "The problem of the twentieth century is the problem of the color line—the relation of the darker to the lighter races of man in Asia and Africa, in America and the islands of the sea."

In a large measure, Isaacs is correct when he calls Du Bois a "romantic" as far as Africa was concerned (a view held also by the late Professor E. Franklin Frazier). But here again emerge paradoxes which pervaded nearly every aspect of his thinking. In his *Atlantic Monthly* article "The African Roots of War" (May 1915), he warned that, if lasting peace were to be achieved, "we must extend the democratic ideal to the yellow, brown and black peoples." Isaacs finds also in Du Bois' novel *Darkwater* (1920) a prophetic vision that World War I was not the end of world wars, partly because of the white man's despisings of " 'these savage half-men, this unclean canaille of the world—these [yellow, brown, and black] dogs of men.' "

On the other hand, Du Bois was a "romantic" when he apparently believed that the Pan-African Congresses which he initiated in 1919, 1921, 1923, and 1927 would result in a measurable improvement of the plight of indigenous Africans. Yet, like most present-day black militants, he was blind to obvious gross inequalities in Liberia, especially when he first set foot on African soil in 1923. But later when I was Du Bois' colleague at Atlanta University, 1933–1938, I tried in vain to have him call a Fifth Pan-African Congress. Had he become a "realist," disillusioned about the prospects for self-government in Black Africa? He was certainly convinced that American Negroes, especially the NAACP, which had defrayed a large share of the expenses of the Congresses through 1923, were more concerned about the quest for equality at home than the liberation of African colonies. It was probably World War II, which had impoverished Belgium, Britain, and France so that they could only with great difficulty maintain their imperium in Africa, that led to a revival of Du Bois' interest in the liberation of the colonies. He and Dr. Peter Milliard, a Negro physician from British Guiana practicing in Manchester, England, were co-chairmen of the Fifth Pan-African Congress in that city, October, 1945. Du Bois and Kwame Nkrumah wrote two declarations addressed to the colonial powers which asserted the determination of colonial peoples to be free. With perhaps some exaggeration, Nkrumah wrote twelve years later (*Ghana: The Autobiography of Kwame Nkrumah*, p. 54): "It was this Fifth Pan-African Congress that provided the outlet for African nationalism and brought about the awakening of African political consciousness. It became, in fact, a mass movement of Africa for the Africans." Many African nationalists and their Negro supporters in the United States and the West Indies deride today the influence of the "bourgeois American-dominated" first four Pan-African Congresses and agree with Nkrumah.

On the other hand, Isaacs states that Nkrumah in 1959—two years after Nkrumah's *Autobiography*—linked the names of Du Bois and Marcus Garvey as the pioneers who had " 'fought for African national and racial equality.' " Isaacs, writing in 1963, dismisses this idea. However much a romantic Du Bois was at times about Africa, "Du Bois had the imagination and intelligence to see, long before anyone else, that the meaningful slogan for beleaguered American Negroes as far as Africa was concerned was not [Garvey's *Back to Africa* but *Africa for the Africans* [Isaacs' emphases]." Although Isaacs concludes that Du Bois' Pan-African Congresses were a failure, he points out that at the Ghana Republic Day celebrations in July, 1960, Du Bois was much honored as the " 'father of Pan-Africanism.' "

Imprecise terminology, which some persons think is a product of the "Black Revolution" of the 1960's, is of ancient vintage.

Du Bois, like Frederick Douglass for instance, used almost interchangeably the three terms, *Negro, black,* and *colored.* For example, Du Bois wrote in his novel *Dark Princess* (1928, pp. 110–111): "He [a Chicago politician] replaced white ward heelers with blacks who were more acceptable to colored voters and were themselves raised from the shadow of crime to well paid jobs; some even became policemen and treated Negro prisoners with a certain consideration."

Ignoring Du Bois' inconsistent terminology, Harding endows him with a Messianic vision of "black" people in America and adds: "Du Bois was likely the most significant voice to prepare the way for this current, new stage of 'blackness.' " Harding distorts also Du Bois' role as a leader by stating that he "is the proper context for an understanding of Malcolm [X], of [Frantz] Fanon, of Stokely Carmichael and Martin Luther King [Jr.]." After Malcolm X's visit to Mecca in 1964, he ceased to be a Messiah of "blackness" and espoused the religious idea of brotherhood. Fanon had fought in the ranks of the "brown" Algerian revolutionists against France. Carmichael was still advocating "Black Power." Despite some inconsistencies, Dr. King generally preached and practiced interracial cooperation. Finally, it is impossible to equate Du Bois' "Black Messianism" with Harding's more accurate emphasis on Du Bois' "tripartite dedication: to truth, to the world's good, and to the good of his people."

Aptheker's discussion of Du Bois as an historian is another example of casting Du Bois in the writer's own image. The essay would have been more valuable if it had not devoted so much space to *Black Reconstruction in America.* Surely *The Suppression of the African Slave-Trade to the United States of America: 1638–1870* (1896), the first volume in the Harvard Historical Series, deserves more than Aptheker's brief comments about the original edition and Du Bois' "Apologia" in the 1954 edition. Aptheker does not discuss *The Philadelphia Negro* (1899) which Du Bois, with something of his own acknowledged conceit, said in *Dusk of Dawn* (pp. 58–59) was "so thorough that it has withstood the criticism of forty years." As for the Atlanta

University Publications, also ignored by Aptheker, Du Bois (in *Dusk of Dawn,* p. 59) did not greatly exaggerate when he wrote that between 1896 and 1920 there was no study of the race problem in the United States which did not depend in some degree upon them. I add that many are useful today; they have been reprinted by the Arno Press and *The New York Times.*

Aptheker's most perceptive remarks about *Black Reconstruction* relate to differences of opinion about whether Du Bois was a Marxist and to the question of land for the freemen and the freedmen, an issue which deserves fuller treatment. I cannot accept the assertion that "Du Bois' extraordinary career manifests a remarkable continuity." Aptheker modified this categorical statement later by pointing to Du Bois' varied political affiliations or affinities, and then added: "These were, however, political choices and not defining marks of his philosophical approaches. All his life Du Bois was a radical democrat." I disagree even with this judgment, as do all the other contributors.

One change in Du Bois' political affiliations or affinities was based on a new philosophical approach. In November, 1961, he publicly applied for membership in the American Communist party. In his essay in *What the Negro Wants* (1944), Du Bois wrote (p. 61): "I did not believe that the Communism of the Russians was the program for America; least of all for a minority group like the Negroes; I saw that the program of the American Communist party was *suicidal* [my emphasis]." In his *Autobiography* (1968), edited by Aptheker, this quotation is repeated verbatim except that "inadequate for our plight" has replaced "suicidal." Aptheker's paper at the American Historical Association in December, 1968, reproduced here, would be more valuable if he had explained the reasons for the change in the language between 1944 and 1955–1956 when the basic draft for the *Autobiography* was written and somewhat revised by Du Bois in 1960. What is even more necessary is an explanation for the reasons why Du Bois, "a radical democrat" all his life, became a Communist. Harding does not attempt to answer this question in 1968, probably because his concept of Du Bois as a "Black Messiah" would hardly be accepted as a tenet of communism.

Although Booker T. Washington died on November 14, 1915, what Basil Mathews called "The Continuing Debate" between the followers of Washington and Du Bois was still acrimonious when Mathews' biography of Washington was published in 1948. In 1970, some aspects of the controversy and the debate have still not been fully explored. Neither Mathews nor any of the other contributors, including Meier, the most authoritative writer about the Du Bois-Washington controversy, mentions what I have called Washington's "apostasy" in his famous Atlanta Address of September 18, 1895. Washington, in a speech in Boston on January 27, 1889, to the Women's New England Club, excoriated Henry W. Grady of Atlanta for his glorification in New York, 1886, of "The New South." But in 1895, Washington painted an even more glorious picture of "The New South," probably in order to establish himself as "the leader of his people." Nor do any of the contributors mention the observation by James Creelman, a well-known reporter for the New York *World,* that at the end of Washington's speech, "most of the Negroes in the audience were crying, perhaps without knowing just why." * Ferris, the only contributor who wrote prior to Washington's death, is perhaps correct when he accuses Washington of "saying the things the Georgia white man desired him to say."

The controversy between Du Bois and Washington did not immediately erupt after the Atlanta Address. As Du Bois recalled in *Dusk of Dawn* (p. 55), he wrote to the New York *Age* suggesting that the Atlanta speech might be the basis of "a real settlement between whites and blacks in the South, if the South opened to the Negroes the doors of economic opportunity and the Negroes co-operated with the white South in *political sympathy* [my emphasis]." Ferris oversimplifies the differences between Du Bois and Washington in the early days when he writes that Dr.

---

* Logan, *The Betrayal of the Negro: From Rutherford B. Hayes to Woodrow Wilson* (New York: Collier Books, 1965), pp. 281, 344–345.

Washington had clearly seen "the economic and industrial phase of the race problem; Dr. Du Bois the moral and political phase." Ferris was closer to the truth when he calls Washington later in the controversy "the educational and political boss and dictator of the Negro race of ten million human beings."

Meier presents in sharp focus both the dichotomies of "Radicals and Conservatives" and Washington's attempts to control the Afro-American Council, the Niagara Movement founded by Du Bois in 1905, the NAACP, the Negro press, the disbursement of philanthropic funds, and the appointments of Negroes. Both he and Mathews make clear that Du Bois' temperate essay "Of Mr. Booker T. Washington and Others" in *The Souls of Black Folk* soon gave way to resentment against the "Tuskegee Machine." President John Hope of Atlanta Baptist College (later Morehouse College) was the only college president who dared attend the second meeting of the Niagara Movement at Harpers Ferry in 1906. Later, President Hope found it so difficult to obtain funds from the General Education Board, endowed by John D. Rockefeller, and from Andrew Carnegie, that in "desperation," according to Ridgely Torrence in *The Story of John Hope* (1948, p. 159), Hope asked Robert R. Moton, Commandant of Cadets at Hampton Institute and Washington's successor as Principal of Tuskegee Institute, to intervene with Washington in 1909. "Then, as if by magic, things began to happen. Carnegie made a gift; the General Education Board made a gift; the [American Baptist Education] society in New York voted a large sum." There is more agreement on Du Bois' resentment of the "Tuskegee Machine" than on any other point in "The Continuing Debate," except for agreement on the differences between the goals of Du Bois and Washington. Mathews (see below, p. 206) expresses the conviction that Washington "from the outset had in his mind the ultimate goal of political and social as well as economic equality." Du Bois (*The Souls of Black Folk,* p. 57), praised Washington for sending letters to the Louisiana (1898) and Alabama (1890) constitutional conventions opposing attempts to disenfranchise Negroes while allowing equally unqualified whites to vote. On the other hand, Du Bois in the same essay (p. 53) insisted that Negro leaders should no longer remain silent but ask for the right to vote and for civic equality. One fact is incontrovertible and should have been known to Mathews, namely that by 1910 all the Southern states had, by amendments and legislation, deprived practically all Negroes of the right to vote. In addition, segregation was expanding to cover practically every phase of Negro-white relations in public.

While Du Bois, like Washington, did not plow a straight furrow, there remained a fundamental difference between them, according to Meier (see below, p. 74): ". . . all that really remained to make the two men irreconcilable ideological opponents was for Du Bois to advocate the importance of protest rather than accommodation." At times, however, Du Bois was an accommodationist, in World War I and in his advocacy of "voluntary segregation" in the 1930's, for example. On the whole, however, Meier's observation is correct.

There is, of course, no complete analogy between 1896–1915 and 1960–1970. It is none the less true that a debate continues between the "accommodationists," now led by Roy Wilkins, of the NAACP, and (until his death in early 1971) Whitney M. Young, Jr., of the National Urban League, on the one hand, and such advocates of protest as Stokely Carmichael and LeRoi Jones, on the other hand. The "accommodationists" of 1970 are, in large measure, the intellectual heirs of Du Bois; some of the "Black Militants" proclaim themselves the followers of Frantz Fanon, Kwame Nkrumah, Mao Tse-tung, and the disillusioned expatriate Du Bois. The "Tuskegee Machine," moribund when Democrats under Woodrow Wilson replaced the Republicans upon whom Booker T. Washington relied for most of his support, is dead.

To date, there is no "definitive" biography of Washington or of Du Bois. Even though the acrimonious controversy about them has largely ceased, a scholarly biography about Du Bois may have to await a quiescence of the "Black Revolution" and of the turmoil in American foreign policy and domestic affairs. Meanwhile, neither the South nor the rest of the Nation is willing to grant the Negro the equal rights sought in different ways by Booker T. Washington and W. E. B. Du Bois.

RAYFORD W. LOGAN

William Edward Burghardt Du Bois, 1868–1963

William Edward Burghardt Du Bois (pronounced "Du Boyce") was born in Great Barrington, Massachusetts, on February 23, 1868, of French Huguenot, Dutch, and Negro ancestry. Shortly after his graduation from the town high school in 1884, the death of his mother left him an almost penniless orphan. The quiet insistence of the principal, Frank Hosmer, however, encouraged him to seek a college education. His small salary as a time-keeper in a Great Barrington mill and a scholarship from Fisk University (Nashville, Tennessee) enabled him to enroll there in the fall of 1885. After his graduation in 1888 with an A.B. degree, he entered Harvard College as a junior. Summer work, a Price Greenleaf Aid scholarship of $250, and thrift carried him through to graduation, A.B., *cum laude,* in 1890. He earned his M.A. degree in 1891; after two years at the University of Berlin, aided by a belated Slater Fund grant, he completed his dissertation, and became in 1895 the first Negro to receive, from Harvard, the degree of Ph.D. (in sociology). From 1894 to 1896, he was Professor of Greek and Latin at Wilberforce University, Ohio; during 1896–1897, Assistant Instructor in Sociology, University of Pennsylvania; and Professor of Economics and History, 1897–

1910, at Atlanta University, Atlanta, Georgia. In 1905, he was one of the founders of the Niagara Movement, a forerunner of the National Association for the Advancement of Colored People, which he helped to establish, 1909–1910. In the latter year, he became its Director of Publicity and Research as well as Editor of the Association's monthly organ, *The Crisis*.

He was a participant in the Pan-African Conference held in London in 1900, and in the First Universal Races Congress also in London, 1911. He organized the First Pan-African Congress, Paris, 1919; the Second in London, Brussels, and Paris, 1921; the Third in London and Lisbon, 1923; and the Fourth in New York City, 1927.

His public support of "nondiscriminatory segregation" led to his resignation, 1934, from the NAACP. From 1933 to 1943, he was Professor of Sociology at the new Atlanta University, the first graduate institution primarily for Negroes. Named Professor Emeritus in November, 1943, he was retired as of June 30, 1944, with a year's salary of $4,500 and a small life pension. In 1940, he founded and was Editor, 1940–1944, of *Phylon, The Atlanta University Review of Race and Culture*. From the latter year to 1948, he was Director of Special Research for the NAACP; conflicts over the interpretation of his functions led to his dismissal as of December 31, 1947.

In 1945, he and Walter White, the Executive Secretary of the NAACP, were accredited as Consultants to the San Francisco Conference which organized the United Nations. Later in the same year, Dr. Du Bois was a Co-chairman at the Fifth Pan-African Congress, Manchester, England. From 1949 to 1954, he was Vice Chairman of the Council on African Affairs, a private organization which gathered and disseminated valuable information about the "black" African colonies.

In 1950, he was an unsuccessful candidate for United States Senate from New York on the left-wing Progressive Party ticket. His increased interest in the Soviet Union and organizations to promote world peace resulted in his indictment, by a New York City grand jury on February 9, 1951, on the charge of being an "unregistered agent" of a foreign principal (Russia), the Peace Information Center of which he was Chairman. During his arraignment in Washington, February 16, 1951, he was briefly handcuffed. The ensuing months until the trial, November 8–20, 1951, were, he wrote, "a gruesome experience." Though Judge Matthew McGuire gave a directed verdict of acquittal because of the failure of the Department of Justice to prove the charge, Du Bois and his supporters were convinced that the real purposes of the indictment and trial were to prevent public criticism of American capitalism and imperialism, "and above all to crush Socialism in the Soviet Union and China." [1]

He became increasingly embittered with life in the United States and enthusiastic about the Soviet Union and Communist China as the best hopes for world peace and the liberation of colored peoples. During his fifteenth trip abroad, 1958–1959, he made extensive journeys to the Soviet Union and Communist China, where he received many signal honors. In 1961, he publicly announced his application for membership in the American Communist Party. Later that year, he accepted an invitation from President Kwame Nkrumah of Ghana to reside at Accra, and in 1963 he became a citizen of Ghana. Until the eve of his death in Accra, August 27, 1963, he devoted most of his time to a projected Encyclopaedia Africana. He was given a state funeral and buried in Accra.

Dr. Du Bois was married on May 12, 1896 to Nina Gomer, whom he met in Wilberforce, Ohio. She bore him two children: Burghardt Gomer, who died some time before 1903, and Nina Yolande, born in 1900 or 1902. His daughter's marriage, to Arnett Williams, gave Du Bois his only granddaughter, Du Bois Williams, born in 1932. After the death of his first wife, Du Bois married in 1951 Shirley Graham, A.B. and M.A., Oberlin College, 1934 and 1935, respectively. She is the composer of folk operas and the author of several biographies.

1. W. E. B. Du Bois, *In Battle for Peace: The Story of My 83rd Birthday* (New York: Masses & Mainstream, 1952), pp. 68, 70, 71, 118, 141, 151.

Du Bois was elected an alumni member of the Fisk University chapter of Phi Beta Kappa in 1958. He was awarded the following honorary degrees: LL.D., Howard University, 1930; Litt.D., Fisk University, 1938; L.H.D., Wilberforce University, 1940; Dr. Sci. of History, Charles University (Prague), 1950; Econ.D., Humboldt University (East Berlin), 1958; L.H.D., University of Sofia, 1958; and Dr. Sci. of History, Lomonosov University (Moscow), 1959. He was also a Fellow and Life Member, American Association for the Advancement of Science; Member, National Institute of Arts and Letters; Knight Commander of the Liberian Order of African Redemption. He received the International Peace Prize and the Lenin Peace Prize.

The Search for a Career

After his birth in Great Barrington, Massachusetts, in 1868, Will Du Bois took twenty-six years to settle on a career. A black man in a white culture, he learned that the barrier of color created two worlds: a dominant white society and a separate Negro community. Alert and sensitive, he became a part of both worlds. In the process, nothing impressed him so much as the intensity of the hostility between them, yet he came to see in each the roots of reconciliation: among white men, a commitment to Christianity, democracy, and truth; among Negroes, a wealth of undirected talent avid for leadership. Here was the task for a young man's lifetime: to set his talents as the mediator between two cultures. With that goal in view, young Will Du Bois, bright pupil and high-school orator, moved on to his career as Dr. W. E. Burghardt Du Bois, historian, sociologist, teacher, and missionary to both races.

DOING THE GROUNDWORK

A mulatto of French Huguenot, Dutch, and Negro ancestry, Will Du Bois—the name is pronounced "Du Boyce"—was born

Reprinted from *W. E. B. Du Bois: Negro Leader in a Time of Crisis* by Francis L. Broderick (Stanford, Calif.: Stanford University Press, 1959), pp. 1–32, with the permission of the publishers, Stanford University Press. © 1959 by the Board of Trustees of the Leland Stanford Junior University.

1

into Great Barrington's small Negro community, perhaps fifty strong in a town of five thousand.[1] It was a confined, provincial group. It kept in touch with the colored families in the nearby town of Lee, but as a rule its world did not stretch beyond the Berkshires. When the National Convention of Colored Men met in Louisville, Kentucky, in 1883—a meeting which attracted Frederick Douglass, the best-known spokesman for the race, and other leaders from twenty-four states—Great Barrington Negroes took no interest except to disapprove of this sort of concerted action. These same older, established families also looked down their noses at "contraband" Negroes immigrating from the South and breaking in on their comfortably settled society.

The Burghardts, Will's mother's family, had been in the community since Revolutionary days; Will's maternal great-grandfather, born a slave, had been manumitted after fighting briefly for the colonial forces. Ever since, the family had had small farms in nearby Egremont Plains. Will's father's family lived farther east. His paternal grandfather, Alexander Du Bois, had been a steward on a ship on the West Indies run, and Will's father, Alfred, had been born in Santo Domingo. When the family settled down in New Haven, Connecticut, Alfred fled from his stern parent and found his way west to Great Barrington to ply his trade as a barber. There he married Mary Burghardt. When Will was still quite young, his father wandered away and did not return, and the young lad and his mother moved to grandfather Burghardt's farm.

When Will reached school age, his mother left her father's

1. This account of Du Bois' early life is based on unpublished material in the W. E. B. Du Bois Papers in Herbert Aptheker's possession, and on his published autobiographical accounts, especially *Dusk of Dawn: An Essay Toward an Autobiography of a Race Concept* (New York, 1940); *The Souls of Black Folk: Essays and Sketches* (Chicago, 1903), especially Chap. VI; *Darkwater: Voices from Within the Veil* (New York, 1921), pp. 5–23; "My Evolving Program for Negro Freedom," in Rayford W. Logan, ed., *What the Negro Wants* (Chapel Hill, 1944), pp. 31–70; *A Pageant in Seven Decades, 1868–1938,* pamphlet, n.p., n.d.; "From McKinley to Wallace: My Fifty Years as a Political Independent," *Masses and Mainstream,* I (August 1948), vi., 3–13; and various newspaper columns written during the course of a long life.

farm and came to town, determined to give her son every possible educational opportunity. In town he could attend the public school regularly. If she could get him a good education, then success, she was sure, was just a matter of sacrifice and hard work. Ambitious for her son, she gave him her sense of purpose, and in turn enjoyed his little successes as her own. Her brother, also a barber, shared their cramped tenement and helped with their expenses. She pieced out their income by occasional domestic service; some unobtrusive charity added a little more; and, as Will grew older, he helped a bit with boyish chores: splitting kindling, mowing lawns, firing a stove in a millinery shop.

For young Will it was a happy life. In an unpublished short story written some years later, Du Bois, under a thin disguise, recalled his boyhood as almost idyllic: a "demure" town with its winding Housatonic River searching out the way from the Great Hoosac Range to the Taconic Hills; skating by moonlight on Mansfield Pond, coasting down Castle Hill (where the railroad added the spice of real danger), and playing Indians during the summer. There was a brook running through the little yard in front of his house. There were the sweet eyes and filmy dresses of his landlady's niece.

The white community found room for him in its social life, for in this Northern region the color line was faint. Years later, he could recall "almost no experience of segregation or color discrimination." [2] His schoolmates, mostly white, welcomed him readily in their activities and in their homes, and when occasional quarrels grew into pitched battles, they followed boyish logic rather than the color line. Like the richer white children, whom Will "annexed" as his "natural companions," young Will felt the native's patronizing scorn for the overdressed children of summer colonists. Social divisions were defined more clearly by class than by color. When the influx of an Irish and South German working class into the town's manufacturing plant added an alien element to the homogeneous community of Americans of English and Dutch descent, the Burghardts, resident in the neighbor-

2. Du Bois, "My Evolving Program for Negro Freedom," p. 32.

hood for several generations, associated themselves with the established families rather than with the newcomers. For his part, young Will "cordially despised" the mill workers as a "ragged, ignorant, drunken proletariat, grist for the dirty woolen mills and the poor-house." [3] From his companions, as well as from his mother, he learned the capitalist ethic of late nineteenth-century America: "Wealth was the result of work and saving and the rich rightly inherited the earth. The poor, on the whole, were to be blamed. They were lazy or unfortunate, and if unfortunate their fortunes could easily be mended by thrift and sacrifice." [4]

Du Bois' own experience in school confirmed this philosophy: without financial resources, he achieved success on his ability alone. He took the standard "classical" college preparatory course: four years of Latin and three of Greek; arithmetic, algebra, and geometry in three of the four years; one year of English; a year of ancient and American history; and scattered bits of geography, physiology, and hygiene. In addition, like every other student, he presented compositions, declamations, and recitations, and performed occasional exercises in reading, spelling, and music. Competing with the children of the town's leading families, he matched his talent against theirs and usually won. Du Bois recalls that while they struggled to perform well for visitors, he answered glibly, tauntingly. His high-school principal, Frank A. Hosmer, encouraged him to plan for college and even helped to provide the necessary textbooks. Will rewarded Hosmer's confidence by completing the high-school course with high honors, along with various extracurricular distinctions such as the presidency of the high-school lyceum. (Many years after Du Bois' school days at Great Barrington, Du Bois wondered what would have happened if Hosmer had been "born with no faith in 'darkies.'")[5]

Several decades later, as Du Bois recalled these experiences

3. Du Bois, *Darkwater,* p. 10; "Harvard and Democracy," typescript of speech, n.d., Du Bois Papers.
4. Du Bois, *A Pageant in Seven Decades, 1868–1938,* p. 2.
5. Du Bois, *Darkwater,* p. 17.

with wonder, he realized that if the high school had had fraternities, honor societies, and dances, there might have been more color discrimination. As it was, however, the color line only faintly crossed his educational experience. When students differed, it was merely a difference in levels and types of talent: Art Gresham could draw caricatures for the *High School Howler*; Du Bois could express his meaning better in words; Mike McCarthy, a perfect marble player, was dumb in Latin. Will was inferior in ball games but could lead the pack in exploring, story-telling, and planning intricate games. He happened to have a lively intellect—he accepted the fact and reveled in it. At the home of Maria Baldwin, a teacher at the high school, he would make himself the center of argument: this was, as he says himself, his "hottest, narrowest, self-centered, confident period, with only faint beginnings of doubts," when he knew most things "definitely" and argued with a "scathing, unsympathetic finality that scared some into silence." [6] The important fact was that neither the argument nor the silence arose from color. Indeed Miss Baldwin, herself a Negro instructor of hundreds of white children, effectively symbolized Great Barrington's apparent indifference to race.

In the Negro community Du Bois came to hold a special place. As a member of one of the oldest families, as the only Negro in his high-school class of twelve, as one of the two or three students who would go on to college, and as the local correspondent for a Negro newspaper, he took on seriousness and self-importance all out of proportion to his sixteen years. Already Du Bois was fascinated by the record of his own intellectual development. At the age of fifteen, he was gathering and annotating his collected papers. In the same year, he had started to use his newspaper column in the New York *Globe* as a running critical commentary on the internal activities of the Negro community. The *Globe* (later the New York *Freeman*) was a pioneer newspaper published by T. Thomas Fortune to serve as a chronicle for Negroes of the Northeast. It gave much space to national news, but it kept

6. *The Crisis* (New York), XXIII (April 1922), 248.

its local touch through short columns of items supplied by dozens of local correspondents. Few reporters were as young as Will, yet there was probably no one in the neighborhood of Great Barrington better equipped by education and interest. The reporter quickly became a social critic. The services at the African Methodist Episcopal Church he found "interesting," though not as fully attended as they might have been. He recorded the general regret among "our people" that they had no local businessmen. On another occasion, "those intending to replenish their libraries" were advised "to consult the *Globe* correspondent before so doing." He encouraged the suggestion of forming a literary society in the colored community as the "best thing" for people there. He condemned "another wrangle" in the Negro church at Lee as a "shocking scene." During the Christmas season of 1884, the Sons of Freedom, of which Du Bois was secretary-treasurer, decided to take up the history of the United States at its next meeting and "pursue it as far as possible." Two weeks later he reported that it had been pursued with profit. The citizens of the town formed a law-and-order society to curb the sale of liquor; Du Bois said it would be a "good plan" for some colored men to join. Alarmed by the numbers of Negroes absent from town meeting, he warned his readers sternly that they took too little interest in politics to protect their rights. He even proposed a caucus to line up a solid bloc of Negro votes. Little escaped his interest. Week by week, he awarded gold stars to the local Negro community, or turned himself into the village scold.[7]

Toward the end of his high-school course, he escaped the sheltered valley, and as he visited the larger Negro concentrations in Connecticut and Rhode Island, he felt overwhelmed by the full grandeur of the race. At New Bedford he met his grandfather, old Alexander Du Bois, a formidable figure—short, thick-set, taciturn; curt but civil with his grandson; awesome with the dignity of eighty years. At Rocky Point, Rhode Island, where Will wit-

7. New York *Globe,* April 12, 1884, October 20, 1883, May 17, 1884, May 3, 1883, June 2, 1883; New York *Freeman,* December 27, 1884, January 10, 1885; New York *Globe,* April 14, 1883, September 29, 1883.

nessed an unusually large congregation of Negroes "of every hue and bearing," he was "transported with amazement and dreams." Noting nothing of poverty and degradation, he saw only "extraordinary beauty of skin-color and utter equality of mien." [8] Characteristically, in his reports on these trips he balanced satisfaction and regret: he found evidences of industry and wealth but not enough literary societies, which "of all things ought not to be neglected." [9]

During that time Du Bois sensed little slights which he associated with his color. Among the older girls with whom he had played for years, coolness developed when strangers or summer boarders came to town. One summer visitor cut Will by refusing his "visiting card" in a juvenile (and therefore very serious) burlesque of a custom of their elders. In school he came to sense an aloofness rooted in something other than resentment of his superior academic ability. In politics the color line was more perceptible. On the one hand, the *Globe* recorded that Negroes took part in town meetings as a matter of course and marched in political parades without being "tucked in the rear nor parcelled off by themselves." [10] But, on the other hand, when the Republican town committee selected a white Democrat for night watchman over a Negro Republican, Du Bois could not doubt that racial bias had dictated the appointment. When the town determined to push Will's career along, he was characteristically shunted off to Fisk, a Negro college in Tennessee training young Negroes to lead their own people, rather than prepared directly for Harvard, the goal of his ambitions, or for Amherst or Williams, closer at hand. His Negro friends resented his being sent off to school in the South (among "his own people," as his white supporters put it), for the South had an "unholy name" in Du Bois' community, and his family and his colored friends regarded the citizens of Great Barrington, not the Southern Negroes, as "his people." Yet, as Du Bois himself noted later, Great Barrington could not expect

8. Du Bois, "My Evolving Program for Negro Freedom," p. 35.
9. New York *Globe*, September 8, 1883.
10. New York *Globe*, October 18, 1884.

that a colored person of his talents would find an adequate role in the local social system.

Despite these occasional hints that New England was not altogether color blind, Du Bois left Great Barrington in the summer of 1885 with little first-hand awareness of discrimination. The town had accepted him as a person, admitting him to its select society and sharing with him its disdain for the newcomers who worked in the mills and worshipped in the Catholic church. It had trained him. It had encouraged him to higher education, and had even contributed to his college expenses.

Young Will set out for Tennessee in the fall of 1885. Seventeen years old, slight in build, he had a handsome bronze skin, dark hair, sharp features. He moved and spoke rapidly—a young man in a hurry. His mother died just before he left, too soon to see his exciting career develop, but not too soon to see him well launched upon it. A simple and untutored woman, she had left young Will her pride in a family free since Revolutionary times, her ambition for his success, and her determination to make every sacrifice necessary for that success. To his credit, Du Bois remembered this legacy with deep gratitude each time he reflected on his early years. The mature Du Bois linked her name with William James in describing the formative influences crucial for his development.

During his three years at Fisk—the quality of his work at Great Barrington admitted him to sophomore standing upon entrance— he found himself in a very different world. Later he would recall the experience:

I was tossed boldly into the "Negro Problem." From a section and circumstances where the status of me and my folk could be rationalized as the result of poverty and limited training, and settled essentially by schooling and hard effort, I suddenly came to a region where the world was split into white and black halves, and where the darker half was held back by race prejudice and legal bonds, as well as by deep ignorance and dire poverty.[11]

11. Du Bois, "My Evolving Program for Negro Freedom," p. 36.

Yet what resources appeared to meet the problem! When Will was set down at Fisk among two hundred students from all parts of the South, a new world opened up to him—not a little lost group, but "a world in size and a civilization in potentiality." At Great Barrington high school, he had been almost alone. But at Fisk, thirty-five Negroes were registered in the college department. Here, he thought, was the advance guard of the Negro civilizing army; here the yearning for truth which would bring the Negro race abreast of modern civilization; here the variety of hue in both sexes which showed the immense physical richness of the Negro mass; here the difference in background, a catalog of Negro experience in nineteenth-century America. To Will, who had never been south of New Haven, fellow students from Georgia, Alabama, Mississippi, Louisiana, and Texas, for the most part five to ten years older than he, "could paint from their own experience a wide and vivid picture of the post-war South and of its black millions. There were men . . . who knew every phase of insult and repression." [12] Du Bois' two summer sessions of teaching in Wilson County introduced him to the Southern rural Negro, whose poverty made every day spent in school during the summer months a financial drain, but who nonetheless sought out education for himself and for his children.

As Du Bois saw them all, his spirit took possession of them, and his ambition told him to lead them. In a "public rhetorical" he told his Fisk classmates, "ye destined leaders of a noble people": "I am a Negro; and I glory in the name! I am proud of the black blood that flows in my veins. From all the recollections dear to my boyhood have I come here, not to pose as a critic but to join hands with this, my people." He spoke with passion of the "mission of the black orator of the 20th century" to raise his people by the power of truth.[13] Almost sixty years later, Du Bois could still remember the fervor of those days: "The excellent and earnest teaching, the small college classes; the absence of distractions, either in athletics or society, enabled me to re-arrange and

12. *Ibid.,* p. 36; *Dusk of Dawn,* p. 24.
13. Du Bois, Ms. of untitled, undated oration at Fisk, Du Bois Papers.

rebuild my program for freedom and progress among Negroes. I
replaced my hitherto egocentric world by a world centering and
whirling about my race in America. . . . Through the leadership
of men like me and my fellows, we were going to have these
enslaved Israelites out of the still enduring bondage in short
order." [14]

Along with similar colleges, such as Atlanta and Howard, Fisk
had been founded after the Civil War to help train Negro youth
as a leaven of intelligence for the race as a whole. Supported
largely by Northern white philanthropic organizations or by de-
nominational groups, and at one time aided financially by the
Freedmen's Bureau, these colleges drew students from all parts
of the South. Fisk itself, founded and supported by the American
Missionary Society, spoke of its purpose in its catalog for 1884–
1885: "Fisk University aims to be a great center of the best
Christian Educational forces for the training of the colored youth
of the South, that they may be disciplined and inspired as leaders
in the vitally important work that needs to be done for their race
in this country and on the continent of Africa." The college hoped
"to thoroughly establish among the colored youth the conviction
of the absolute necessity of patient, long-continued, exact and
comprehensive work in preparation for high positions and large
responsibilities." [15]

Within the walls of the university, accepting and accepted by
the all-white teaching staff, Du Bois had three enriching years. In
his first year, he studied the *Iliad,* the *Odyssey,* and the Greek
Testament, conic sections and the calculus, rhetoric, French grammar and literature, and botany. In junior year, he read Livy and
Tacitus along with Demosthenes' *Oration on the Crown* and
Sophocles' *Antigone,* studied German grammar and translations,
and found time for physiology, hygiene, and astronomy. Finally
in his senior year, he and six classmates studied "mental sciences,"
using John Bascom's *Science of Mind* and James McCosh's *Laws
of Discursive Thought.* Ethics, political economy, English litera-

14. Du Bois, "My Evolving Program for Negro Freedom," p. 37.
15. *Catalogue of . . . Fisk University . . . 1884–1885,* Nashville, 1885.

ture, and a laboratory course in chemistry rounded out a heavy schedule. The university explicitly rejected industrial education as part of its formal curriculum, but, as the catalog put it, "manual labor is dignified and made honorable." [16]

Almost forty years later, on the occasion of a commencement address at Fisk, and perhaps under the influence of the occasion, Du Bois recalled those three years of "splendid inspiration" and "nearly perfect happiness" with teachers whom he respected, amid surroundings which inspired him. The ten years after Fisk he chronicled as "a sort of prolongation of my Fisk college days. I was at Harvard but not of it. I was a student of Berlin but still the son of Fisk." [17] At Fisk, Adam Spence taught him Greek, and Frederick A. Chase the natural sciences. Du Bois came to think of these two, along with William James and Albert Bushnell Hart at Harvard, as the persons outside his own family who had influenced him most. With a missionary commitment to the uplift of the Negro race, this devoted band, headed by President Erastus Cravath, spurred Du Bois on by judging his skills and knowledge without attention to his color. When, at the end of three years at Fisk, Du Bois looked North to Harvard, they endorsed his application with praise beyond the usual platitudes of letters of recommendation. Though Fisk did not have a regular marking and ranking system, President Cravath spoke of Du Bois' high rank, noted his "unusually quick, active mind," and could hardly fail to mention that Will was ambitious. Other teachers referred to his manliness, faithfulness to duty, earnestness in study, and excellent scholarship. Chase in the physical sciences gave a more revealing picture by recording that in addition to his regular assignments, Will had done outside work in anatomy, and, though he never overworked and had a remarkable capacity for sleep, he achieved "first grade" in scholarshp. Chase admitted that Du Bois might give the impression of being some-

16. *Catalogue of . . . Fisk University . . . 1887–1888,* Nashville, 1888.
17. Du Bois, "Diuturni Silenti," Ms. of speech, 1924, Du Bois Papers; reprinted in the *Fisk Herald,* XXXIII (1924), 1–12.

what conceited, but added that this trait would not prevent faithful work.[18] In Du Bois' mind, this encouragement from his Fisk teachers did something to compensate for the discriminatory pattern of Southern life.

They had much to redeem. Away from Fisk, Du Bois was not a promising student, but simply a Negro; and thus the "race question" at last became an intimate experience pressing in on him daily. The move toward legal segregation and Negro disfranchisement had not yet gained ground in the South, but informally enforced etiquette and extralegal coercion made personal affronts routine. In a generous mood, Du Bois could explain the South's attitude in terms of ignorance or misunderstanding: in an unpublished short story written in these years, he tells of a young Negro teacher who recognizes, after a conversation with two white men in a village store, that the white South's intentions are good and that its prejudice would yield to education. But how long could patience and generosity mask the hostile white world which, this hot-tempered Negro boy was sure, rejected black men as "aliens, strangers, outcasts from the House of Jacob—niggers." [19] In his own person, he saw the kind of teacher and the sort of education which Tennessee was giving to the Negro—a college student who for two months in the summer worked for $28 or $30 in an antique shack in Wilson County to bring culture to Negroes who had had only one other school session since the Civil War.

In his junior or senior year, Du Bois put together a full statement of the Negro's grievances. In "An Open Letter to the Southern People," [20] written about 1887, Du Bois assailed the arbitrary line between the white man and the Negro in the South; they were,

18. These letters are in the "W. E. B. Du Bois, Class of 1810" folder in the Harvard University Archives—[1810 should be 1890—ed.].

19. Du Bois, "What the Negro Will Do," Ms. of unpublished article, February 4, 1889, Du Bois Papers; written in reply to George Washington Cable, "A Simpler Southern Question," *Forum,* VI (December 1888), 392–403.

20. The letter, now in the Du Bois Papers, was probably never published.

respectively, patrician and plebeian, capitalist and laborer, Democrat and Republican. He pointed to an anomaly: while justifying disfranchisement by Negro ignorance, the white South refused equal educational opportunities. Trial by peers, a free ballot, free entrance into the various callings of life—all had been denied to the Negro. The white South placed the Negro at the level of a dog or a horse. He warned that Negroes, forced into the galley, the hovel, and the Jim Crow car, responded with hatred, which retarded the progress of both races. Yet there was hope: if the "best of you" in the white South would lay aside race prejudice and make common cause with educated Negro leaders, together they could give direction to the masses. This appeal was directed at Southern white conservatives who, as C. Vann Woodward says, held to "an aristocratic philosophy of paternalism and *noblesse oblige*" and who felt more comfortable with mannerly colored men than with what a Charleston paper called "unmannerly and ruffianly white men." [21] Du Bois rejected their paternalism, for he felt that he, and educated Negroes like him, shared this *noblesse*; yet he was anxious to work with them, for he hoped that the black and white men of taste and education could join hands to lead the ignorant of both races. Needless to say, this appeal went unheeded—the walls rarely come tumbling down in response to manifestoes by college students.

About the same time that Du Bois was urging enlightened white men to join hands with educated Negroes, he made a dramatic appeal to Negroes as well. Speaking at an intercollegiate convention of Negro students, the fiery young orator told them to throw off their "political serfdom" in the Republican party and to vote on issues, specifically issues important to the Negro, like federal aid to education, civil rights, and lynching. If Negroes voted thoughtfully, he said, "gratitude for services rendered would be due not to the party but to the principles upon which it stands. When it leaves those principles, it leaves it[s] right to your suf-

21. C. Vann Woodward, *The Strange Career of Jim Crow* (New York, 1955), p. 30.

frages. Too often have men forgotten the substance *principle* and gone after the shadow *party*. . . . Neglecting the sacred duties of citizenship more sacred in a Republic than elsewhere, they have given up the manipulation of parties into the hands of political bosses and ward machines who represent no principles but those of dishonesty and avarice; then taking a ballot labelled with the name of their patron saint they march to the ballot box." Republicans, he said, had abandoned the principles of Lincoln; therefore, they had no right to Negro votes. Du Bois longed for a Negro Parnell dangling a bloc of votes between the two great parties; but if not a Parnell, at least an independent vote responsive to political wooing.

Neither party, he said, liked Negroes, but both wanted votes, and Negroes should be willing to bargain with Democrats,[22] especially since the recent administration under Grover Cleveland had, much to the Negro's surprise, treated him like a man. Times had changed: the South of slavery was dead. Du Bois denied that the outrages of caste prejudice could be laid at the door of the Democratic party: "They arise from the blind race prejudice which, however reprehensible, is nevertheless natural when a horde of ignorant slaves are suddenly made the equals of their one-time masters." Then he added, very significantly in view of his later development: "We ourselves make the color line broader when in defiance of our principles and best interests we vote in opposition to the people of this section *because* they're *white* and we're *black*. Our interests are not antagonistic, they are one and the same, and to blind you[r]selves to any party in spite of these

22. The idea for this switch to the Democrats probably came to Du Bois through the influence of T. Thomas Fortune, editor of the *Globe* and the *Freeman* (the papers to which Du Bois contributed Great Barrington news) and author of *The Negro in Politics* (New York, 1885), where the idea of "*Race first; then party*" (p. 38) is developed at length. Du Bois has never acknowledged this influence, for he and Fortune feuded in later years. But the parallels between Fortune's ideas and Du Bois', their close relationship through the newspaper, and Fortune's substantial prestige in the Negro community as a pioneer newspaper editor lend support to this assumption.

bonds of mutual interest . . . [is] to keep alive the smoldering coals of Race antagonism." [23]

Though it had no political significance—Du Bois himself, aged nineteen or twenty, could not even vote—this notion had some plausibility, for in the late 1880's the Democratic party, both in the South and under the national administration of Cleveland, was making efforts to woo the Negro vote away from its sentimental Republican moorings. (Frederick Douglass said he would as soon divide the Negro vote "between light and darkness, truth and error, Heaven and Hell" as divide it between Republicans and Democrats.[24]) Not raised in slavery and therefore less responsive to the appeal of the party of Lincoln, Du Bois wanted Negroes to respond calculatingly. He looked for a level of independent judgment and political maturity that colored men had not yet attained. Therefore, the first step in Negro emancipation was a program to train Negroes to overcome their prejudices. He was proud that the "heart of Africa" was broader than its mind; but now the mind must gain equal breadth.

It would be a long struggle. Du Bois saw himself leading it.

HARVARD AND BERLIN

The years at Fisk left Du Bois with a sense of the "absolute division of the universe into black and white." [25] In this state of mind he approached Harvard. The admissions office wanted to know his "special reason for wishing to enter Harvard College." His blunt reply, which someone at Fisk intercepted and revised before it went out in the mail, was: "I have very little money and think I can get more aid there than elsewhere." [26] He never de-

23. Du Bois, "Political Serfdom," Ms. of speech at Fisk, *ca.* 1887, Du Bois Papers.
24. Quoted in Benjamin Quarles, *Frederick Douglass* (Washington, D.C., 1948), p. 235.
25. Du Bois, "Harvard and Democracy."
26. "W. E. B. Du Bois, Class of 1890," folder.

veloped any affection for the university. Glorying in his isolation and eschewing Harvard life except as a "laboratory of iron and steel" where he could extend his knowledge, he came to think of Harvard as a library and a faculty, nothing more. He found himself a corner room at 20 Flagg Street, a ten-minute walk from the Yard and a block or so from the Charles River. He boarded at the common refectory in Memorial Hall his first year, but finding it too expensive he took modest meals in his room, or in town, or at an inexpensive eating club. For four years he commuted from his room to his classes and to the library without ever feeling himself a part of the university's social community.

Du Bois' academic plans were fluid. Fisk had given inspiration but not direction. Du Bois had already rejected President Cravath's suggestion of the ministry as a career. Trained in a Congregational Sunday school, he had during his first year at Fisk proudly joined the Fisk congregation and asked for the prayers of his Great Barrington Sunday school to "help guide me in the path of Christian duty." He approved of a recent revival which had won forty converts.[27] But during the next three years, organized religion ceased to be meaningful: he believed too little in Christian dogma to become a minister. In his autobiography Du Bois attributed this attitude to the heresy trials, especially those controversies over "higher criticism" of the Bible which eventually led to the suspension of Charles A. Briggs from the Presbyterian Church, and to the insistence of the local church at Fisk that dancing was a sin. Furthermore, the compulsory "book of 'Christian Evidences' "[28] struck him as a "cheap piece of special pleading."[29] Rejecting Christianity as dogma, he also became distrustful of Christian ethics, for he could find scant ethical commitment on the race issue in Christian churches. At the first symptoms of higher longings among Negroes, Du Bois said the year

27. Du Bois to Evarts Scudder, February 3, 1886, Du Bois Papers.
28. The reference is probably to William Paley, *A View of the Evidences of Christianity* (London, 1794), a text written in the spirit of rationalism to prove the truth of Christian doctrines. It was widely used in the nineteenth century.
29. Du Bois, *Dusk of Dawn,* p. 33.

after he left Fisk: "There is no devil in Hell that would countenance more flagrant infringements upon Human Liberty, to crush
the rising genius of a People, than the average deacon of the
Methodist Church South." [30]

What career, if not the ministry? It took Du Bois several years
to decide. His diary for the Harvard years shows him tussling with
the problem. On occasion he saw himself the tragic hero—"What
care I though death be nigh?" he asked; sometimes as an epic
poet; again as a philosopher, author of "A Philosophy by Me";
or as an orator sending light into civilization. Whatever the role,
the underlying motive remained constant: to develop himself as a
Negro leader who would use his talents to improve the condition
of the race as a whole. In a course paper for William James, Du
Bois wrote that the fundamental question of the universe, past
and future, was Duty. [31] In preparation for duty, "Work is but
play with an end in view." Such an attitude invested every action
with high seriousness. On a trip to New York, he wrote, one must
see Brooklyn Bridge, Central Park, the Statue of Liberty, the
Battery, and Broadway, for these were "the *only* things to really
repay such a visit." [32]

In later years Du Bois reconstructed his education as a straight-
line preparation for the life's work which in shadowy form he had
planned from his youth. Actually the decision came relatively late
as the terminal point of desultory intellectual meandering. [33] His
preliminary inquiry to the secretary of the university spoke of
study leading to a Ph.D. in political science, with political econ-

30. Du Bois, "What the Negro Will Do."
31. Du Bois, "The Renaissance of Ethics: A Critical Comparison of
Scholastic and Modern Ethics," Ms., 1889 (James Weldon Johnson Collection, Yale University Library).
32. Du Bois, account book and diary, 1888–1890, and scrapbook fragment, *ca.* 1891, Du Bois Papers.
33. This discussion of Du Bois' academic work at Harvard is derived
from successive issues of the *Harvard University Catalogue* (Cambridge,
Mass., 1888–1892); Registrar's Records, "Record of the Class of 1890,"
p. 314; the "Record of the Graduate Department, 1888 [*sic*]," at the office
of the Graduate School of Arts and Sciences; and the "W. E. B. Du Bois,
Class of 1890," folder.

omy as a special field. Six months later, in his application for scholarship aid, he proposed to give "especial attention to the sciences and Philosophy" as preparation for a postgraduate course, probably in philosophy. At Harvard, where he repeated the junior and senior years of college, his first-year courses favored the sciences. In addition to a prescribed course in English composition, a half course in "earlier English Ethics," and an economics course, he concentrated on scientific subjects: qualitative analysis based chiefly on laboratory work, a beginner's laboratory course in geology, and a more advanced geology course given by Nathaniel Shaler. Though he scored A's in all his science courses, the following year the exact sciences disappeared from his schedule without explanation. Perhaps chemistry and geology seemed too remote from Negro problems and deprived Du Bois of an adequate outlet for what he regarded as his talent for creative writing.

In the second year, the bulk of his work was in philosophy— George Santayana's French and German philosophy, William James's logic and psychology, and F. G. Peabody's ethics of social reform. To these he added the senior composition course; a half course in elocution; an economic survey of railroads and bimetallism; and Albert Bushnell Hart's Constitutional and Political History of the United States from 1783 to 1861.

This philosophical schedule was more appealing. There was inspired teaching by Santayana and James. Furthermore, Du Bois' admission into the realm of speculative ideas allowed him to see himself as a Negro at the frontiers of knowledge, working under the developing philosophy of pragmatism and participating in the most advanced developments of modern thought. Du Bois thoroughly enjoyed jousting with ideas. His account book and diary for this period is full of random sentences reflecting his current notions about basic questions. "The very conception of the Caused carries with it the conception of the Uncaused." "The Infinite—that specious invention for making something out of nothing." "I hold it Truth: that every argument rests on an unprovable postulate which contains *implicit* the whole conclusion."

"Science is Mathematics. Mathematics is Identity. Science is Identity."

Yet philosophy did not hold Du Bois either, and in graduate school he shifted to political economy and history. The reason for this second change is only slightly clearer than for the first. Years later Du Bois recalled that James, like Chase at Fisk, had urged him away from philosophy: "It is hard to earn a living with philosophy." [34] Perhaps Du Bois' recollection of James's advice was milder than the original. James, famous for his gentleness in dealing with his students, may have preferred this way of saying that Du Bois' talents were ill suited for the logical and speculative disciplines. Perhaps the two B's which Du Bois received in senior year from James and Santayana compared to the A-plus from Hart in constitutional and political history of the United States indicated that the latter was a field better oriented to his talents. Perhaps the inductive study of social problems such as charity, divorce, labor, prisons, and temperance under Peabody impressed Du Bois as more germane to Negro problems than French philosophy or James's logic. Maybe the explanation is simpler: he may have regarded the natural sciences and philosophy as basic equipment; having surveyed them, he was ready to turn to the more specialized social sciences which had figured prominently in his early plans. In any case, by the spring of 1890, when Du Bois applied for a graduate fellowship, he had decided to pursue the Ph.D in social science "with a view to the ultimate application of its principles to the social and economic rise of the Negro people." Having canvassed the catalog thoroughly, Du Bois bombarded the graduate school with applications for every type of aid even remotely connected with his project and finally received the $450 Rogers scholarship for the study of ethics in relation to jurisprudence or sociology.

For the next two years Du Bois dug into political and constitutional history. The historians of the generation of Hart and

34. Du Bois, *Dusk of Dawn*, p. 39.

Herbert Baxter Adams sought to understand the present through
a study of the development of institutions; Hart's course, which
Du Bois had already taken, was devoted almost exclusively to this
type of history, and little else was included in Harvard's history
offerings. Hart had helped to introduce the German universities'
research seminar into Harvard's history department a few years
before Du Bois entered the graduate school. Du Bois joined Hart's
"seminary" and, following the methodology of his mentor, combed
the statutes of the United States, colonial and state laws, the *Congressional Record,* executive documents, and "contemporary
sources" for material on the African slave trade. It was slow,
painstaking research: by March, 1891, he reported to the faculty
that he had located 146 pertinent statutes on the period from 1638
to 1788. At the same time he was carrying a full course load: in
his first year, another course in history, one in English composition, one in political economy, and one in Roman law; in his
second year, four half-year courses in history and one in political
economy. Once in a while he took time out to compete for a prize
in a field related to his work. But as a rule his research had first
claim; indeed it consumed so much of his time that his course
work suffered. Eventually his hours in the library stacks gave him
the material for his doctoral dissertation and his first book.

In general, Du Bois' record at Harvard justified the confidence
of his friends at Fisk, though it did little to increase his modesty.
His five A's and one C (in English composition) in junior year,
four A's and three B's in senior year, and honorable mention in
philosophy at graduation constituted a creditable showing, and
his A-plus in History 13 led Hart to scribble a note of recommendation of Du Bois as a good candidate for a graduate fellowship. In two years of graduate school residence he was awarded
five A's and five B's, and though the completion of his degree took
somewhat longer than he intended, his thesis, *The Suppression of
the African Slave-Trade to the United States of America, 1638–
1870,* was published in 1896 as the first volume in the *Harvard
Historical Studies.*

Will found other successes outside the classroom. When he gave an address, "Jefferson Davis as a Representative of Civilization," to the commencement audience at Harvard at the end of his senior year, *The Nation* recorded his distinct personal triumph. "Du Bois not only far excelled Morgan [Clement Morgan, the other orator, also a Negro] in mere delivery, but handled his difficult and hazardous subject with absolute good taste, great moderation, and almost contemptuous fairness." In contrast to the type represented by Davis—the white "Teutonic" ideal of "stalwart manhood and heroic character" badly smeared with "moral obtuseness and refined brutality"—Du Bois set up "the patient, trustful, submissive African as a type of citizen the world would some day honor," *The Nation* continued. "For the moment the audience showed itself ready to honor this type as displayed in the orator." [35] Here was the way to a hearing in the white world: a Negro abreast of modern civilization and devoted to truth could make people listen. Heartened, Du Bois returned the following year to argue that the Negro problem could be solved if the spirit of Harvard, "that spirit of intellectual breadth and liberty that seeks Truth for Truth's sake," prevailed over misunderstood economic principles in the South.[36] That winter, a joint meeting of Harvard's history and political-economy seminaries* heard a preliminary summary of Du Bois' research on the slave trade, and when Du Bois repeated this report at one of the early meetings of the American Historical Association, Herbert Baxter Adams praised it as a "scholarly and spirited paper." [37]

Successful as a student, Du Bois felt that he had to share his education; as he later expressed it himself, he "tried to take culture out into the colored community of Boston." [38] He pro-

* Seminars [ed.].

35. Du Bois, "Jefferson Davis as a Representative of Civilization," Ms., 1890, Du Bois Papers; *The Nation,* LI (July 3, 1890), 15.

36. Du Bois, "Harvard and the South," Ms. of commencement "part," June 1891, Du Bois Papers.

37. Herbert B. Adams, "The American Historical Association in Washington," *Independent,* XLIV (January 7, 1892), 10.

38. Du Bois, *A Pageant in Seven Decades, 1868–1938,* p. 8.

moted local plays: he took a part in a production entitled "Samp-
son and Delilah, or the Dude, the Duck and the Devil," a burlesque of the Negro hair-tonic business. Six months later, on
Thanksgiving night, he was at it again, this time with the *Birds*
of Aristophanes at the Charles Street Church.

One long address—"Does Education Pay?"—written in 1891
when Du Bois was a first-year graduate student, carried the burden
of his message, and incidentally revealed a good deal about the
speaker, whose lack of tact later became a Negro legend. Speaking
to the National Colored League of Boston,[39] Du Bois reported his
alarm that "a people who have contributed nothing to modern
civilization, who are largely on the lowest stages of barbarism in
these closing days of the 19th century," were unfitting themselves
for modern life by neglecting education, even high-school education.[40] At the moment of basic economic and political change, he
said, Negroes were throwing away the road to truth, beauty, and
virtue by ignoring the wisdom of man's past experience. By doing
this, he warned, they disqualified themselves for a part in the future
of mankind and, indeed, destroyed their only legitimate reason for
existence.

He especially defended college life as a time of leisure to study
under a faculty gathered to guide work. He dismissed the usual
criticisms of higher education—that it was irreligious, snobbish,
and expensive. The charge that college made a man irreligious he
mocked as "mere fol-de-rol": if religion were not true, men should
not believe it; if it was true, college would confirm it. "A religion
that won't stand the application of reason and common sense," he

39. The occasion and date of this speech are marked on the manuscript
in the Du Bois Papers. But Du Bois failed to show up for a scheduled
speech about that time, and this may have been the occasion.

40. Du Bois' prose in this period is worth sampling: "With a coldly
critical world looking on, when every passion, every precedent is calling
for the strained nerve & master hand, when this battle of life never offered
dearer booty, when the blanched face of the coward should never mock
our lines, when the blood of our fathers is shrieking from the soil, to
cheer a battle as much nobler than other battles as the moral and intellectual is nobler than the dust—This day, I have seen—I have seen an army
throwing away its arms."

said, "is not fit for an intelligent dog." Nor was the charge of snobbery a fair criticism, he went on, for no thoroughly educated man
ever turned his nose up at a fellow human being, though "on the
other hand, as long as one man is lazy, and another industrious,
you will, you *must* have social classes." On the matter of cost,
Du Bois cited his own expenses to prove that any boy "with grit
and average ability" could get through without a penny.[41]

Du Bois complained that Boston Negroes ("you people," he
called them) were neglecting existing facilities for a rich cultural
life. He found Negro ideas of recreation stunted: amusements
lacked literary achievement; churches in condemning respectable
dances, card parties, and decent fun of any kind as immoral drove
Negro youth into less reputable establishments. There were other
complaints: churches contributed nothing to practical social work
or to manly character; sermons never contained thoughtful discourses of any kind; and revivals concealed deviltry instead of saving souls. To meet a real need, Du Bois outlined a complete
program for Negro Boston's social life: libraries, lectures. Chau-
tauqua circles, literary societies, and churches that stood for "education and morality." According to his estimate, the Boston community spent $5,000 a year on amusements. If that were true, he
said, the money should be concentrated in an amusement center
which would provide cultural uplift and still have a surplus to
support some students at Harvard.

The Negro world, he continued, lacked the leadership worthy
of the race. Ethiopia, he asserted, "is calling for the strong man,
the master-felt man, the honest man, and the man who can forget
himself." And in return she has received a "reign of the coward"
—scamps among the politicians, rascals among the leaders, "a
time-server for our Moses and a temporizer who is afraid to call
a lie a lie." [42] Even the great mass of the Negro people, though

41. Income: summer work, $125; scholarship, $200; tutoring, $50;
monitorships, $10; prizes, $45—total, $430.
    Expenses: tuition, $150; books, $25; room, $22; board, $114; fuel, light,
$11; clothes, $60; washing, $18; sundries, $30—total, $430.
    42. In a poem mourning Douglass' death in 1895, Du Bois softened this
judgment: the death of "our mightiest" is as a "watchfire/Waving and

honest and generous, he said, seemed afraid to take a stand for
"truth, honor, and grit," though they saw the rottenness. The
whole race must become dutiful and moral: "No Negro can afford
to stoop to an Anglo-Saxon standard of morality."

This type of speech did little to ingratiate Du Bois with the
Boston community. On his arrival at Harvard, the established
Negro urban communities had opened their social life to him. His
English themes record various evenings with girls—one at which
the girls took advantage of the privileges of leap year, another at
which two young ladies "apparently did not notice me." One girl
teased this self-conscious intellectual until he decided in despair:
"She is a thorough trifler in philosophy—a still better explanation
perhaps . . . a woman." His fantasy carried him even further: a
short story written in this period describes the adventures of four
young blades who courted two sets of girls the same evening and
had to steal a trolley to make proper connections.

But the longer he stayed, the less welcome he became. During
Du Bois' undergraduate years, the Boston correspondent for the
New York *Age* had praised his scholastic accomplishments and
noted that, popular and genial, Du Bois had made many friends in
and out of school. As he entered graduate school, the praise
leveled off to perfunctory notice, and then dipped into criticism.
His failure to appear for a scheduled speech was reported. His
dramatic efforts were unappreciated and resented. When he went
to Europe, criticism followed him. His letters to the *Age* about
his European adventures led the Cleveland *Gazette* to comment:
"Much of W. E. B. Du Bois' letters from Europe published in the
New York *Age* make one very tired. 'I, I, I, I, Me, me, me, Black
bread and butter,' *Scat!*" [43]

Du Bois' own memory of these years conjures up nothing but
a parade of successes. Actually, there were distinct disappointments. Toward the end of his first term of graduate school, his

---

bending in crimson glory" which "Suddenly flashes to the mountain and
leaves/A grim and horrid blackness in the world."
    43. Cleveland *Gazette*, November 4, 1893.

English 12 instructor summarized Du Bois' work sharply: "Unthinking seems to me the word for your style. With a good deal of emotional power, you blaze away pretty much anyhow. Occasionally, a sentence or a paragraph, and sometimes even a whole composition, will be fine. Oftener there will be a nebulous, almost sulphorous indistinctness of outline. As for reserve of power, it is rarely to be found. More than most men, you need . . . an appreciation of good literature." [44] The graduate school, at the end of his second year, apparently felt some reservation about his progress, for his application for a fellowship for the third year, preferably to be taken abroad, was not approved, and the defensive tone of Du Bois's application suggests that he was under criticism for inattention to course work and for his slow progress toward his doctoral examinations.

In general, however, Du Bois could regard his academic career at Harvard with satisfaction. His sampling of courses in the first two years gave breadth to his education; his specialization in graduate school gave depth in a single subject. He had heard applause from scholarly and popular audiences.

Not so much can be said, however, for his life in the white community surrounding the classrooms. He never felt himself a part of his class or of the college, and he deeply resented the color line, which proved to be more obvious around Cambridge than it had been at Great Barrington.

There were occasional breaks in the pattern. A program for a class dinner at the Parker House during Will's undergraduate years is preserved in his papers. He at least bought a ticket to Class Day exercises in the Yard during his senior year. Robert Morss Lovett, a contemporary at Harvard, recalls long hikes with him (one to Quincy to see "drumlins and dunes") and says he never thought of Du Bois as a Negro until Du Bois achieved some honor as a prize orator.[45] But these were the exceptions. When Du Bois

44. Instructor's note on Du Bois, "Hunted Mouse," December 11, 1890, Du Bois Papers.
45. Robert Morss Lovett, "Du Bois," *Phylon,* II (3rd Quarter 1941), 214.

met a fellow undergraduate on the trolley into Boston, an inquiry
about the "race's statistics at Harvard" served to remind him again
of his color—as he was regularly reminded, he observed, by 90
per cent of the visitors to the college. He generally lived apart
from college life. Even marginal organizations such as the Graduates Club, with mingled social and intellectual interests, were
closed to him.[46] He trained himself, as most Negroes who circulated among white men had to train themselves, to ignore stares
as he sat down to a meal. He stayed with his books and was
satisfied with his reputation as a "grind." He pitied the absence of
purpose among his white contemporaries and mocked the pageant
of Harvard: seeing an anachronistic portrait of Jared Sparks, the
nineteenth-century historian, in a toga, Du Bois looked for Socrates in wig and top boots, or Minerva in a corset.

Early in his career at Harvard, Du Bois drew a distinction between the treatment of the Negro in the North and in the South.
In the South, he said, the Negro sustained positive outrage as liberty was throttled by prejudice and fear. In the North, he went on,
conditions stung the pride of the ambitious and educated—i.e.,
himself—but Negroes had grown up in the hope that obstacles
would finally disappear. Now, however, after noble hearts like
Garrison, Sumner, and Phillips had helped raise the Negro from
slavery, the Negro "arisen, educated and willing, fired by memory
of the past," found no door open save that to the dining room and
the kitchen.[47]

The church seemed especially at fault. To help defray the expenses of his education, Du Bois gave "readings" to church groups
for an admission charge of twenty-five cents, shared by the church
and the orator. In the scrapbook for his first year at Harvard, he
chronicled a recent trip to see the rector of "—— church." On the

46. Thomas E. Will, a classmate, later told Du Bois that he, Will, had
declined membership in the Graduates Club because Du Bois was "said to
have been blackballed because of your color." Will to Du Bois, January 1,
1906, Du Bois Papers.
47. Du Bois, "What the Negro Will Do."

way everyone stared, for it was the God-given right of American ladies, he said, to eye a social inferior from head to foot without losing their self-respect. The domestic at the rectory was astonished to see a Negro calling, but the lady of the house was cordial. She made a show of how nice she could be to colored people, mentioned casually the vast debt owed to the Anglo-Saxon race because of the great interest "her" people had in "your" people and the pile of clothing sent to Tuskegee the previous winter. In turn, Du Bois gave her an account of the "extraordinary" fact that he was at Harvard, and "a verbal census of all other such past and future anomalies." Then the rector rejected the reading project; rejected politely, but rejected. So Du Bois returned to Flagg Street: "Mind not, little heart," he wrote in his diary, "if the world were you I could love it. And so we have spent a sample day. We are disappointed. And yet I have spent the happiest hours of my life when I have come home in the twilight with a life plan in my bosom smashed—and alone—sturdy man, forsooth: laid my head on my table, and wept." [48] Evidence of a recurring hostility to the white Christian church appears time after time. He writhed at what he called the Anglo-Saxon's "high Episcopal Nicene creed" which justified the white man in putting his heel on the neck of the man down. He commented on the text: "Ethiopia shall in these days stretch forth her hands to God." That may be, Du Bois wrote, but "the spectacle [of] the venerable colored dame in this rather unbalanced position in regard to the Anglo-Saxon god has become somewhat nauseating to the average young Negro of today." [49] Only the "self-forgetful Quakers," he said, still remembered God.[50]

By the end of his Harvard years, the range of Du Bois' hostility to American white society had broadened considerably. Despite some exceptions such as Lovett (even this exception is recorded

48. Du Bois, "A Vacation Unique," Ms. dated June 1889, Du Bois Papers.
49. Du Bois, account book and diary, 1888–1890.
50. Du Bois, "A Vacation Unique."

by Lovett and not by Du Bois), rejection by the white world
evoked in Du Bois a mounting bitterness against it. In response
to exclusion, he countered with an exclusiveness which frequently
reduced him to a group of one. The four years in Cambridge had
given Du Bois his fill of social slights, of coolness from Harvard
organizations, of patronizing wives, and of fellow students who
saw him as a Negro rather than as a classmate.

The Harvard faculty departed dramatically from this pattern
of discrimination. Shaler, who taught Du Bois in several courses,
was sensitive to, if not particularly informed about, the Negro
problem. Barrett Wendell flattered Du Bois by reading a part of
one of his themes to a crowded class. Hart not only guided his
work, but helped him secure successive Harvard scholarships and
probably arranged for his appearance before the American Historical Association. A "smoker" of history professors, instructors,
and graduate students included Du Bois as a member. William
James, to whom Du Bois refers as "my favorite teacher and my
closest friend" and "guide to clear thinking," welcomed him to his
home "repeatedly" and encouraged his work.[51] James commended
Du Bois' long course paper, "The Renaissance of Ethics: A Critical Comparison of Scholastic and Modern Ethics," as very original, full of independent thought, vigorously expressed—an "ex-
ceptionally promising production." [52] George Santayana read
Kant privately with Du Bois. From Ephraim Emerton and Frank
W. Taussig, President Charles W. Eliot, Josiah Royce, and
Charles Eliot Norton came to call on specified evenings.

In short, at the top level of intellect and scholarship, Du Bois
found that he was being accepted, if not as a peer, at least as a
prospective peer. If his color entered into the appraisal of his work,
he did not know it; as far as he could see, the faculty at Harvard
was free from racial prejudice. Looking back, Du Bois could say:
"God was good to let me sit awhile at their feet and see the fair

51. Du Bois, "Comments on My Life," typescript, *ca.* 1943, Du Bois
Papers; *Dusk of Dawn*, p. 38; *A Pageant in Seven Decades, 1868–1938*,
p. 7.
52. The comment is on the paper, "The Renaissance of Ethics."

vision of a commonwealth of culture open to all creeds and races and colors." [53]

Meanwhile he had etched a clear picture of life behind the Veil. With a wonder tinted with sentimentality, he dwelt lovingly on the varied beauty of Negroes and on their patience, generosity, and submissiveness. As discrimination limited the extent of his identification with white culture, he took up this minority group passionately and defended it against its white critics. This group, he thought, could contribute much to American life.

On the other hand, it could receive much more: a vision of the panorama of modern Western culture. In an age requiring reason and education, Negroes languished in prejudiced ignorance. The fault, Du Bois thought, lay not with the Negro people themselves —their hearts and souls were sound; the fault lay with incompetent leadership unprepared to bridge the gap between the "lowest stages of barbarism" and modern civilization. In Du Bois' view, the first task for the Negro was to develop his cultural resources, to catch up with his white neighbors.

An unnoticed trap lay under this image of life behind the Veil. Du Bois assumed that the Negro's cultural advance would qualify him for a full part in modern civilization and presumably for integration in white society. Yet, ironically enough, cultural advance might actually confirm separation. An increase in Negro businessmen might broaden the Negro's range of achievement, presumably a cultural advance, but it would also set Negroes apart, because Negro merchants would for the most part serve customers of their own race. A larger turnout at a town meeting might symbolize Negro participation in American life; yet if Negroes met in caucus as a preliminary to bloc voting, as Du Bois suggested, they were separating themselves from the rest of the town. The notion of the Negroes as balance of power overlooked the possibility that such a political device might not compel white justice, but might invite the alternative of removing the Negro from politics entirely.

Du Bois' own experience in Great Barrington illustrated the

---

53. Du Bois, "Harvard and Democracy."

dilemma. The same academic success which gave impetus to his career disqualified him from a role in the town's social system. His mother might deny discrimination on account of color—"it was all a matter of ability and hard work" [54]—but Will's ability and hard work led to a scholarship at a Negro college, not at Amherst or Williams. The very process of catching up with modern civilization created obstacles to integration by exciting opposition among white men unable to conceive of the Negro at any but the most servile level. The cure was, to be sure, not worse than the condition, nor could the condition be met except by applying the cure. Yet this paradox of Negro progress did exist, and Du Bois at this stage of his career was unaware of it.

Two years at the University of Berlin gave Du Bois a chance to think objectively about the Negro's status and his own relation to it. In 1892, after two years of graduate study at Harvard, Du Bois went abroad on a grant—half gift, half loan—from the Slater Fund, a philanthropic foundation headed by former President Rutherford B. Hayes. Du Bois' travels in England, France, Italy, and Germany, his visits to Vienna, Cracow, and Budapest, and his studies at Berlin released him from his consuming preoccupation with color. "From the physical provincialism of America and the psychical provincialism of my rather narrow race problem into which I was born and which seemed to me the essence of life," he recalls, "I was transplanted and startled into a realization of the real centers of modern civilization and into at least momentary escape from my own social problems and also into an introduction to new cultural patterns." [55] He went to the theater every week and to the symphony now and again. He learned to regard an art gallery as a house for a single picture, all the others serving simply as a frame for it. As he sailed down* the Rhine, a German family took him under its wing, and a young Fräulein may even have fallen in love with him. Except where Americans had penetrated in some numbers, Du Bois found little in Europe to parallel the racial

---

* Up, since the voyage began at Rotterdam [ed.].
54. Du Bois, "My Evolving Program for Negro Freedom," p. 33.
55. Du Bois, "Comments on My Life."

discrimination inescapable even in the North. In the student beer halls he was as welcome as any other foreigner. When his exotic color was a cause for comment at all, it never created a barrier; if anything, it added to his welcome. During his vacations he traveled to the limit of his budget. He was fascinated by the rise of anti-Semitism in Germany: it "has much in common with our own race question," Du Bois said, "and is therefore of considerable interest to me." [56] In Prague he was surprised to find the surge of nationalism which led people to avoid the study of German. He made a long analysis of German socialism, which later apparently served as a lecture. At the University of Berlin, Heinrich von Treitschke lectured on the superiority of the Anglo-Saxon race and snarled at the backwardness of colored peoples, but he greeted Du Bois cordially on a casual meeting before vacation time. Those glorious months abroad made Du Bois realize that "white folk were human." [57]

At the university Du Bois observed that Harvard's red tape seemed paralyzing only because Americans had never seen the "deeper crimson" of Berlin's variety. To the newcomer Berlin's academic halls glistened with that "ethereal sheen which, to the fresh American, envelopes everything European," but by Christmas time the sheen wore off, and the young scholar settled down to his ambitious program in the social sciences.[58]

His work for the fall term of his first year, for example, included a course in politics under Treitschke; a study of the beginnings of the modern state; Rudolph von Gneist's Prussian state reform; theoretical political economy and "industrialism and society" un-

56. Du Bois to Daniel Coit Gilman, undated, *ca.* April 1893, Du Bois Papers. Du Bois appears to have absorbed some anti-Semitism himself. In his "Diary of my Steerage Trip across the Atlantic" (Summer 1895) he says that he had seen the aristocracy of the Jewish race and the "low mean cheating pöbel," but he had seldom seen "the ordinary good hearted good intentioned man." He found two congenial Jews on the trip, but he shunned the rest—"There is in them all that slyness that lack of straightforward openheartedness which goes straight against me."

57. Du Bois, *A Pageant in Seven Decades, 1868–1938,* p. 10.

58. Du Bois, "Harvard in Berlin," diary fragment, November–December, 1892, Du Bois Papers.

der Adolph Wagner; and Gustav Schmoller's Prussian constitutional history. In addition, he was admitted to Schmoller's seminar and, as at Harvard, spent the bulk of his time preparing a research paper, "The Plantation and Peasant Proprietorship Systems of Agriculture in the Southern United States."

The interlude at Berlin served several purposes. For one thing, Schmoller's cordiality reinforced Du Bois' conviction that intellectuals were above color prejudice. For another, Schmoller, with one of the brightest reputations in German economic thought, drew Du Bois away from history into a type of political economy which could easily be converted into sociology, and, at a more general level, encouraged him to a career devoted to scholarship. Again Du Bois could look back at a chapter with satisfaction. Though his plan to take a degree at Berlin never materialized, he brought back to America flattering testimonials from Schmoller and Wagner along with Schmoller's tentative commitment to publish Du Bois' Berlin research paper in his "yearbook."

On his twenty-fifth birthday Du Bois paused to take stock. Looking back over his education and forward to his career, he dedicated himself as the Moses of his people. After a "sacrifice to the Zeitgeist" of Mercy, God, and Work, and a curious ceremony with candles, Greek wine, oil, song, and prayer, he dedicated his library to his mother and then went on to compose a long note in his diary, speculating on his own place in the modern world:

I am glad I am living, I rejoice as a strong man to run a race, and I am strong—is it egotism is it assurance—or is it the silent call of the world spirit that makes me feel that I am royal and that beneath my sceptre a world of kings shall bow. The hot dark blood of that black forefather born king of men—is beating at my heart, and I know that I am either a genius or a fool. . . . this I do know: be the Truth what it may I will seek it on the pure assumption that it is worth seeking—and Heaven nor Hell, God nor Devil shall turn me from my purpose till I die. I will in this second quarter century of my life, enter the dark forest of the unknown world for which I have so many years served my apprenticeship—the chart and compass the world furnishes me I have little faith in—yet, I have none better—

I will seek till I find—and die. There is grandeur in the very hopelessness of such a life—life? and is life all? If I strive, shall I live to strive again? I do not know and in spite of the wild sehnsucht for Eternity that makes my heart sick now and then—I [grit?] my teeth and say I do not care. Carpe Diem! What is life but life, after all? Its end is its greatest and fullest self—this end is the Good. The Beautiful its attribute—its soul, and Truth is its being. Not three commensurate things are these, they [are] three dimensions of the cube —mayhap God is the founder, but for that very reason incomprehensible. The greatest and fullest life is by definition beautiful, beautiful—beautiful as a dark, passionate woman, beautiful as a golden hearted school girl, beautiful as a grey haired hero. That is the dimension of *breadth*. Then comes Truth—what is, cold and indisputable: That is *height*. Now I will, so help my Soul, multiply breadth by height, Beauty by Truth and then Goodness, strength, shall bind them together into a solid whole. Wherefore? I know not now. Perhaps Infinite other dimensions do. This is a wretched disguise and yet it represents my attitude toward the world. I am striving to make my life all that life may be—and I am limiting that strife only in so far as that strife is incompatible with others of my brothers and sisters making their lives similar. The crucial question now is where this limit comes. . . . God knows I am sorely puzzled. I am firmly convinced that my own best development is not one and the same with best development of the world and here I am willing to sacrifice. The sacrifice is working for the multiplication of (Truth × Beauty) and now here comes the question how. The general proposition of working for the world's good becomes too soon sickly sentimentality. I therefore take the work that the Unknown lays in my hands & work for the rise of the Negro people, taking for granted that their best development means the best development of the world.

This night before my life's altar I reiterate, what my heart has . . .

Here the manuscript breaks off, but it is resumed shortly thereafter:

These are my plans: to make a name in science, to make a name in literature and thus to raise my race. Or perhaps to raise a visible empire in Africa thro' England, France, or Germany.

I wonder what will be the outcome? Who knows? [59]

59. Du Bois, diary, February 23, 1893, Du Bois Papers.

This remarkable diary entry, inchoate, histrionic, but, above all, moving, reveals much of Du Bois' sense of himself as a person destined to redirect the history of his time. This personal assertiveness, however, was modified by a sense of duty: he would subordinate his personal ambition to the central purpose of elevating the Negro people. If occasionally duty coincided with personal ambition, that merely demonstrated the extent to which he had intertwined the two. When he asked the Slater Fund trustees to subsidize a second year abroad, he explained that the experience was absolutely necessary to the completion of his education. He went on to say: "I realize, gentlemen, the great weight of responsibility that rests upon the younger generation of Negroes, and I feel that, handicapped as I must inevitably be to some extent in the race of life, I cannot afford to start with preparation a whit shorter or cheaper than that deemed necessary to the best usefulness of my white fellow student." [60] Du Bois was ready to pay for the luxury of his duty, for he offered to renew his fellowship on the same basis as the original award, half grant and half loan, or as a full loan. Actually, the Slater trustees renewed his grant on the same terms, but even so, by the time he started teaching (on a salary of $800 a year), his education had saddled him with a debt of $1,125. In short, he mortgaged his future to prepare himself adequately for the task of serving his race.

A SENSE OF MISSION

The world of Du Bois' youth pointed the way to his career. If white men were guilty of race prejudice arising from ignorance, if black men were retarded, remote from the culture of the time, then Du Bois must teach both and reconcile them. He knew with conviction that he had the talent and the technique; his missionary sense of duty would permit him to do no less. He decided upon a life's work of teaching and research; as a college teacher he would

60. Du Bois to the Slater Fund Trustees, undated, *ca.* April 1893, Du Bois Papers.

dispel Negro ignorance by training other missionaries who could carry the gospel back to their communities; at the same time, his research would convert white America to a just appraisal of the Negro. His career would serve a third purpose as well: it would fill a genuine personal need. Among white intellectuals he had always found acceptance. As their peer he would continue to find it. In the Negro world he would be a liberator. Here was a career, a mission, which could consume many lifetimes.

This decision was never, to be sure, consciously plotted out. Yet Du Bois had been working toward a scholar's career for several years: from science through philosophy to history and economics.

With Du Bois' background in scientific courses, he found great appeal in James's pragmatism, for he assumed that pragmatism gave assurance that ethics, once freed of "scholastic dogma," could be based on empirical observation and on reason. In his paper for James, Du Bois traced the process by which ethics was "liberating" itself from ultramundane, theistic teleology that was "useless as a science." Scholasticism, with its "pernicious" substitution of dogma for faith, caused reason to be subjected to dogma, and ethics to be based on dogma instead of on facts. At the time of Descartes and Bacon, he went on, the separation of science from teleology and the conviction that only matter was capable of scientific treatment led to enormous advances in science, but left metaphysics bogged down in scholasticism. There it had stayed, he said, as unproductive from Kant to Royce as it had been from Abelard to Occam. Metaphysics would regain an equal place with science, he asserted, when it dropped inquiries into the categories of reason, space, perception, and authority of conscience, and systematically studied accumulated facts, as the physicist studied heat. With James and Royce, Du Bois continued, an attempt had been made "to base ethics upon fact—to make it a *science*." [61] Its method was to separate the "what" from the "why" on the way to the creation of an all-embracing science, "the beacon light of

61. James commented in the margin: "I doubt whether we do seek to make it a science—to me that seems impossible."

a struggling humanity to guide its knowledge of the Infinite." (As a side issue, Du Bois took a page or two to prove the necessary existence of objective reality, but James rejected the proof as begging the principal question of the whole idealist position.) Here then, according to Du Bois, was "the cornerstone of a world structure—first the What, then the Why—underneath the everlasting Ought."

Even after Du Bois abandoned his plans for a career in philosophy, these ideas showed their reflection in his work. James had expressed reservations about Du Bois' analysis—his failure to show the method of "real teleology" despite his assumption of its existence, the impossibility of making a science out of ethics, and the "oracular & ambiguous" nature of the conclusion that "truth is the one path to teleology, teleology is ethics." Yet, despite these reservations,[62] Du Bois continued to assume that the path to reform lay in the accumulation of empirical knowledge which, dispelling ignorance and misapprehension, would guide intelligent social policy. As he said succinctly in his diary: "The Universe is Truth. The Best ought to be. On these postulates hang all the law and the prophets."

As success in Hart's course turned Du Bois toward history, his diary noted: "What we want is not a philosophy of history but such a collection and . . . placement of facts physical and mental as to furnish material for a philosophy of man." For a Negro with a missionary sense, this suggested a study of the background of the Negro in America, a study of his "advance" since emancipation. The accumulation of adequate historical information for understanding the Negro, Du Bois thought, would pave the way for a just social policy. At Berlin, Schmoller confirmed this basic analysis, but redirected Du Bois' scholarly ambition to economics, and ultimately to sociology. In a letter to the Slater Fund trustees in 1893, Du Bois outlined his program after his return to America: to get a place in a Negro university (Howard University in Washington was his first choice) and to build up a department

62. These comments are all written on the paper, "The Renaissance of Ethics."

of sociology for two purposes: "1. Scientifically to study the Negro question past and present with a view to its best solution. 2. To see how far Negro students are capable of further independent study & research in the best scientific work of the day." [63]

Du Bois returned from Germany in the summer of 1894, his education complete (except for receiving his Ph.D. at Harvard in 1895). Conscious that he had received an education rare for any young American, black or white, he embarked on a mail campaign to secure a job. Eventually three offers came. He accepted the first, the chair in classics at Wilberforce University at Xenia, Ohio, at $800 a year. Shortly thereafter, the Lincoln Institute in Missouri offered $250 more, and even later, Booker T. Washington invited Du Bois to Tuskegee Institute in Alabama to teach mathematics. Du Bois stuck to his original commitment and, in the fall of 1894, started on a career of teaching and research, which, continuing for sixteen years, would include what he afterward characterized as "my real life work." [64]

63. See note 60, above.
64. Du Bois, *Darkwater,* p. 20.

★

"Radicals and Conservatives"[1]— A Modern View

At no time were Booker T. Washington's policies favored by all Negroes. Opposition to Washington existed from the time of the Atlanta Address, became more marked after 1900, and culminated in the founding of the National Association for the Advancement of Colored People.

While most articulate Negroes appear to have welcomed Washington's speech, it had a mixed reception among the elite of the national capital,[2] and a significant segment of the press was at first reticent and then broke into criticism. It was three weeks before the Cleveland *Gazette* mentioned the address, but once it had done so it reported receiving a torrent of abuse from other papers for its criticism, to which it replied by charging that Washington's actions

---

1. The title of this chapter was suggested by that of the opening essay in Kelly Miller's *Race Adjustment*, 3rd ed. (New York, 1910).

2. *Bee*, October 26, 1895; Booker T. Washington, *The Story of My Life and Work* (Naperville, Ill., 1900), pp. 203, 204; "Report of the Secretary of Bethel Literary and Historical Society, 1895–1896," Ms. in Cromwell Papers.

Reprinted from *Negro Thought in America, 1880–1915: Racial Ideologies in the Age of Booker T. Washington* by August Meier (Ann Arbor, Mich.: The University of Michigan Press, 1963), pp. 171–189, by permission of the University of Michigan Press. Copyright © 1963 by the University of Michigan.

were motivated by his desire for money and praise. The Washington *Bee* also failed to print the address and declared a few weeks later that "Prof. Washington's speech suited the white prejudiced element of the country." H. T. Johnson of the A.M.E. Christian *Recorder* expressed himself guardedly at first, but two months later said he believed the Tuskegeean's views to be incorrect.[3]

As the century drew to a close, support for Washington increased. W. E. B. Du Bois later recalled that criticism, at first widely voiced, largely disappeared. In those dreary years the advancing tide of segregation and disfranchisement made protest seem futile, and even some who, like the Grimké brothers, were later numbered among the Tuskegeean's most distinguished opponents, supported his program. Characteristically, the *Bee* was inconsistent in its attitude, but as early as 1897 the *Recorder* declared Washington "endorsed by his people" after a period of misunderstanding.[4]

Perhaps the extent to which Washington's philosophy was accepted among the articulate during the late 1890's was best illustrated by the conventions of the Afro-American Council, attended as they were by the most distinguished leaders. At the December, 1898, meeting, Alexander Walters, president of the Council, employing a judicious combination of militance and accommodation, seemed to sum up the thinking of the majority of leaders in that period of extreme discouragement. He insisted that there could be no real peace in America until Negroes were accorded equal rights, but he also thought the race would have done well if these were attained in a hundred years. He believed it would be unwise for Southern Negroes to withdraw from politics altogether, yet he did not object to educational and property qualifications for voting as long as the poor and illiterate of both races were disfranchised. He delivered a peroration on behalf of agitation, for to remain silent in the face of continued outrages

3. *Gazette,* December 7, 1895; *Bee,* October 18, 1895; *Recorder,* September 26, November 28, 1895.
4. Du Bois, *The Souls of Black Folk* (Chicago, 1903), pp. 42, 45; *Recorder,* August 9, 1897.

and discrimination would be advertising Negroes as unworthy of freedom, but he also counseled reliance on the school house, hard work and moral improvement, and the creation of a group economy. He approved all types of education, but criticized those who after the Civil War had avoided manual labor and entered the professions. In short, "Let us improve our morals, educate ourselves, agitate and wait on the Lord."

The speech's enthusiastic reception indicated that here was something that appealed to all sides and to that large middle ground of opinion that held to a broad spectrum of ideologies. Yet the meeting was marked by a sharp clash between the "conservatives" and "radicals" that was precipitated by Ida Wells-Barnett. In her talk on mob violence she charged that Washington was greatly mistaken in thinking that Negroes would gain their rights merely by making themselves a significant element in the nation's economy, and criticized President McKinley for failure to give attention to the matter of the race's rights. These statements naturally displeased Tuskegee supporters and federal office-holders—both chiefly from the South. Henry Plummer Cheatham, recorder of deeds, not only defended McKinley, but made a strong plea for conservatism and moderation, asserting that "hot-headed meetings in the North are making it impossible for the Negroes of North Carolina to live peaceably in their Southern home." Thus opened a contentious discussion on political activity in which the Southerners and officeholders were ranged against Northern agitators and opponents of the administration.

Some Northerners were scathing in their attack upon accommodating Southerners, and Dr. N. F. Mossell of Philadelphia denounced "the utterance made by a Southern Negro that the ballot had been given too soon, as the most damnable heresy." The convention's address to the country reflected a distinct compromise. It declared that no one method would achieve the desired ends, that in the North agitation and political activity were essential, while in the South education and internal development would pave the way for citizenship rights. It specifically affirmed that

Negroes claimed all rights guaranteed by the Constitution and contended that manhood suffrage was the most effective safeguard of liberty, but did not oppose "legitimate restriction" in the form of an educational or a property qualification, or both, applied to both races. It also attacked segregation, lynch law, and penal conditions and urged federal aid to education and both higher and industrial schools.[5]

Succeeding conventions displayed a similar view. Generally, as a New York daily reported, the Council was "conservative in all of its actions," though the Northern radicals continued to criticize Washington. At Chicago in 1899 a minority group vigorously attacked his political doctrines and charged that he favored industrial to the exclusion of higher education. At the Indianapolis convention in 1900 the conservative element won the day only after a committee report dealing harshly with Southern whites had been modified under pressure from Southern delegates, one of whom, R. R. Wright, Sr., denounced the report as "a lie." It should be noted, however, that a legal bureau, created early in 1899, within a year had taken up the work of testing the franchise provisions of the Louisiana constitution in the courts.[6] Subsequently, this bureau was responsible for most of the Council's significant work.

Meanwhile, Washington had been moving secretly toward control of the Council. During 1901 and 1902 he was anonymously making major financial contributions toward the legal bureau's work and was, in fact, clandestinely directing its course of action. At the rather stormy 1902 St. Paul convention the Washington group secured Fortune's election as president over determined opposition. The convention's manifesto was even more conciliatory than usual, and the elected officials were clearly almost

5. *Colored American,* January 7, 1899; *Gazette,* January 7, 1899.
6. New York *Sun,* August 30, 1900 (Hampton Clippings); *Colored American,* March 25, August 26, 1899, January 20, 1900, August 17, 1901; Cyrus Field Adams, *The National Afro-American Council* (Washington, D.C., 1902), p. 8; A.M.E. *Review,* XVI (October 1899), 272.

entirely in the Washington orbit. As Washington's secretary, Emmett J. Scott, said, "We control the Council now." Yet the situation was unstable. When the executive committee met in Washington in January, conflict was in the air. Both the committee's address to the country and the speeches by its chairman, Bishop Walters, and by James H. Hayes of the recently organized National Negro Suffrage League, had a decidedly radical tone. Hayes asserted that if the intolerable Southern conditions continued, Negroes "must resort to the torch," and both speakers ridiculed the notion that acquisition of wealth and education would solve the problem.[7]

As a matter of fact by 1903 it was evident that there had been a recrudescence of the opposition to Washington. In addition to the handful of older journals that generally criticized the Tuskegeean during the first years of the century—most notably the Cleveland *Gazette* and the Chicago *Conservator*—there appeared in 1901 the most famous of all the anti-Tuskegee papers, the Boston *Guardian,* edited by William Monroe Trotter. The son of Cleveland's recorder of deeds, James Trotter, and the first Negro elected to Phi Beta Kappa at Harvard, he had imbibed from his father—who would not live in a segregated neighborhood and who did not become a minister because he would not be a pastor in a segregated church—an uncompromising hatred of all forms of discrimination. The *Guardian*'s articles, editorials, and cartoons flayed Washington and Roosevelt. Trotter called Washington a "self-seeker" who had endorsed Jim Crow cars and disfranchisement, a "coward that . . . skulked all his life far from the field of combat." The Tuskegeean's antipolitical line was "a remarkable piece of deception in view of the fact that Mr. Washington is claiming in private that he, and he alone, is responsible for the president's Colored appointments, and his lily-white policy." When Washington contended that the revised constitutions of the

7. Correspondence of BTW with Jesse Lawson, 1901–1902; *Colored American,* July 19, 1902; *Age,* July 21, 1902 (Hampton Clippings); Scott to BTW, July 17, 1902; *Colored American Magazine,* VI (March 1903), 338.

Southern states had put a premium upon intelligence, ownership of property, thrift, and character, Trotter charged that Washington had deliberately made a false statement and had thus given a fatal blow to the Negro's liberty and political rights. Indeed, all the talk of education, wealth, and morality solving the problem was mere "twaddle." Actually, in the South Negroes with these things were disliked; and all the wealth and intelligence acquired by Negroes before the Civil War did less toward freeing the slave than did the agitation of the abolitionists.[8]

Boston in fact was the center of the most vehement agitation. Among Trotter's leading associates there were the lawyer and former minister to Santo Domingo, Archibald Grimké, president of the Massachusetts Suffrage League, and the attorney Clement Morgan, a holder of degrees from Atlanta and Harvard universities, and a member of the Cambridge City Council, 1896–1898. Other significant Northern centers of anti-Bookerite agitation were Chicago, where the two lawyers Ferdinand Barnett and E. H. Morris led a group organized around the *Conservator,* and Philadelphia, where Dr. N. F. Mossell, founder of Douglass Hospital, was a central figure. In New York, however, it appears that the influence of men like Fortune and later of Charles W. Anderson, collector of internal revenue, minimized anti-Tuskegee expression.

In the South protest activity had not entirely disappeared. Undoubtedly the best examples of it had been the boycotts organized in various cities against the Jim Crow streetcars. Between 1898 and 1904 citizens of Augusta, Atlanta, Columbia, New Orleans, Mobile, and Houston boycotted the streetcars. In Houston and in 1906 in Austin, Nashville, and Savannah, Negroes even organized their own shortlived transportation companies. In 1905 Jacksonville residents temporarily held the line by securing a court decision declaring the segregation ordinance illegal. And as late as 1910, the Reverend W. H. Steward of Louisville, editor of the

8. *Guardian,* February 28, 1903, December 6, December 30, November 1, 1902, April 14, 1903.

National Baptist, was credited with defeating an attempt to institute Jim Crow cars in that city.[9] Not unexpectedly, therefore, in a few places—chiefly Richmond and Atlanta—anti-Washington groups did appear. In Richmond, with its noted liberal arts college, Virginia Union University, the *Planet* for a few years had attacked the Tuskegeean, and James H. Hayes, an attorney who had carried the fight against disfranchisement in the Old Dominion to the Supreme Court, provided a focus of dissident activity through his Suffrage League. And in the intellectual atmosphere at Atlanta, with its half dozen institutions of higher learning, at least two leading figures, President John Hope of Atlanta Baptist College and W. E. B. Du Bois came out against Washington. Atlanta continued to be a stronghold of radicalism. In 1905 when the noted magazine the *Voice of the Negro* started to criticize Washington openly, Atlanta obtained its own radical journal. And in 1906 several hundred Georgia Negroes at a state convention in Macon, under the leadership of William Jefferson White, adopted a stirring address of protest and formed an Equal Rights Association.[10] Meanwhile, in the spring of 1903, there had appeared Du Bois' *Souls of Black Folk* with its critical essay about Booker T. Washington, an important work that helped to crystallize the anti-Tuskegee sentiment that became evident at the Afro-American Council meeting at Louisville in July of that year.

Fearful of a combination of dissidents from various cities coalescing around Hayes and Trotter, the Tuskegee circle had worked feverishly during the spring of 1903 to keep control of the Council and assure Fortune's re-election. As a matter of fact delegates from New York, Virginia, New Jersey, and New England held a rival meeting with Hayes's equal suffrage league, and only after much negotiation were they brought into the Convention. Washington was bitterly attacked on the floor of the convention by Trotter and two of his associates. Later, there was an undignified

9. *Gazette,* September 24, 1898, October 26, 1906; *Age,* July 5, 1900 (Hampton Clippings); A.M.E. *Review,* XX (April 1904), 409; *Bee,* August 12, 1905; *Freeman,* March 8, 1910.
10. *Voice of the Negro,* III (March 1906), 175–177.

struggle over the election of officers, though Fortune won easily. Trotter conceded that most of the resolutions he submitted were rejected. The Convention's "Address" tactfully deplored the influences at work throughout the country to destroy the "friendly" relationships that had always existed between the best people of both races. In Tuskegeean tones it pointed out that lynching was demoralizing to whites. And though it did assert that the disfranchisement laws, originally designed ostensibly to prevent only ignorant Negroes from voting, actually were now openly directed at all Negroes, it made the usual statement accepting restrictions on the ballot.[11]

Opposition editors now regarded the Council, which had been founded as a protest organization, as clearly dominated by Tuskegee. Washington himself felt that he had retained control.[12] But at the end of July more excitement occurred when Washington spoke at a meeting sponsored by the Boston Business League. Heckling and hissing interrupted the speakers, and when Trotter and a friend of his attempted to make Washington reply to questions from the floor, the uproar was so great that Washington was temporarily silenced. The police were called, the two men were arrested, and later they were sentenced to a fifty-dollar fine and thirty days in jail for their role in this "Boston Riot." While some were alienated by Trotter's tactics, to others, like Du Bois, he became a martyr.[13]

With the opposition active, Washington, as early as February, had been thinking of a conference of race leaders as a means of effecting an understanding. And it was high time he did so, for as acute an observer as Kelly Miller commented that "few

11. BTW to T. Thomas Fortune, February 17, 1903; Charles W. Anderson to BTW, June 8, 1903; *Colored American,* July 11, 18, 1903; *Guardian,* July 11, 1903; *Age,* July 4, 1903 (Hampton Clippings).

12. *Gazette,* July 11, 1903; *Bee,* August 8, 1903; *Guardian,* July 11, 1903; BTW to Emmett J. Scott, July 27, 1903.

13. *Guardian,* August 1, 8, 15, 1903; *Bee,* August 8, 1903; *Gazette,* August 8, 1903; Ruth Worthy, "A Negro in Our History: William Monroe Trotter, 1872–1934" (M.A. thesis, Columbia University, 1952), Chap. iv; BTW, *My Larger Education* (New York, 1911), pp. 122–125; Du Bois, *Dusk of Dawn* (New York, 1940), pp. 87–88.

thoughtful men espouse what passes as Mr. Washington's policy without apology or reserve." Finally, a secret meeting, called by Washington and financed by Andrew Carnegie, was held at Carnegie Hall, New York, in January, 1904. Some reports did leak out. The hostile *Bee* revealed that at the end of the conference Washington said that he favored "absolute civil, political and public equality," higher education, and the abolition of Jim Crow cars, and that Du Bois declared himself ready to work with Washington as long as he lived up to this statement. The confidential summary of the conference's proceedings, drawn up by Kelly Miller, also revealed a wide range of agreement among the leaders. They held that most Negroes should stay in the South, that Negroes should at all times work to protect and exercise their right to vote, that lawsuits should be instituted to secure "absolutely equal accommodations" in transportation and public facilities, and that Negro education should include both industrial and higher training.[14]

The Committee of Twelve for the Advancement of the Interests of the Negro Race, established by the Carnegie Hall Conference, existed for several years. Its first important effort was an unsuccessful attempt to negotiate with the Pullman Company in regard to the latter's complying with the separate-but-equal laws by excluding Negroes altogether. Du Bois soon withdrew because he felt that the committee's activities were being dictated by the chairman, Booker T. Washington. Subsequently, committee members, with money secretly supplied by Washington, discreetly employed a lobbyist to work against the proposed Warner-Foraker Amendment to the Hepburn Railway Rate Bill and worked to defeat disfranchisement in Maryland. The committee's work consisted chiefly of publishing a number of pamphlets, which were financed by Carnegie. Most of the pamphlets dealt with Negro

14. BTW to Du Bois, February 12, 1903; [Kelly Miller], "Washington's Policy," Boston *Transcript,* September 19, 1903; Correspondence of BTW and Carnegie, November 1903—January 1904; *Bee,* January 23, 30, 1904; "Summary of Proceedings, Conference of Colored Men, January 7, 8, 9, 1904," BTW Papers.

self-help and economic achievement or were reprints of speeches by distinguished, but conservative whites whom Washington regarded as sympathetically interested in the race problem. But the committee also published pamphlets on how to vote and obtain jury representation, and even one entitled *Why Disfranchisement Is Bad* by Archibald Grimké.[15]

Despite Washington's efforts, the rift grew wider. Directly after the Carnegie Hall meeting one of the conferees, E. H. Morris, precipitated an acrimonious debate at the Bethel Literary Society with an address in which he charged Washington with believing in Negro inferiority, racial segregation, and the relegation of the franchise to a secondary position. The speech caused considerable agitation in the Tuskegee circle, and in March, Washington spoke in the same church defending his program as the best way to achieve the higher aims of the race. But this and similar speeches to Northern audiences over the next few years failed to mollify the opposition.[16]

Meanwhile, at least as early as 1902, Washington had been utilizing his reservoirs of power to silence the opposition. He used personal influence to wean people away from the radicals, attempted to deprive opponents of their government jobs, where possible arranged to have his critics sued for libel, placed spies in radical organizations, employed his influence with philanthropists as an effective weapon in dealings with educators and others, deprived critics of participation and subsidies in political campaigns, and subsidized the Negro press to support him and to ignore or to attack the opposition.[17]

15. On Maryland, see BTW to Charles W. Chesnutt, January 2, 1906; in general, see correspondence of BTW with Hugh M. Browne, secretary of the committee.

16. *Gazette,* January 23, 1904; *Bee,* January 16, 1904; Adams to BTW, n.d., 1904; BTW, extracts from Ms. speeches of BTW, 1904–1906, at Tuskegee Institute Department of Records and Research.

17. For details of Washington's fight with the opposition, 1902–1915, see August Meier, "Booker T. Washington and the Rise of the NAACP," *The Crisis,* LXI (February 1954), 71–72, 117–122; see also Elliott Rudwick, "The Niagara Movement," *Journal of Negro History,* XLII (July 1957), 181–184, 186–187, 190, 196.

In spite of these tactics, some of Washington's critics formed a national organization—the Niagara Movement—in 1905. In response to a call issued by Du Bois, twenty-nine delegates from fourteen states attended the meeting at Fort Erie in July. All but five were from the North or from Washington and its environs. Most of the remainder were from the two chief Southern centers of anti-Bookerite sentiment—three from Atlanta and one from Richmond. The address adopted by this group insisted that Negroes should protest emphatically and continually against the abridgement of political and civil rights and against inequality of economic opportunity. It called for all types of education, including college training. It refused to allow the impression to remain that "the Negro-American assents to inferiority, is submissive under oppression and apologetic before insult." Above all, it stated, "We do not hesitate to complain, and to complain loudly and insistently."

The Niagara Movement, aiming to combat Washington's policy, made clear the split that was to cause the bitterest acrimony for over a dozen years. Washington was clearly upset by the movement and, as earlier, he exerted multifarious and even devious pressures against the movement and its members. Though the Niagara Movement created a considerable stir, its maximum membership was only about 400, and beyond agitation its accomplishments were relatively limited. At Boston in 1907, Du Bois exulted in the movement's sheer survival and reported helping the Brownsville soldiers* and winning a segregation case in which the

* In August 1906, three companies of the Twenty-Fifth Regiment of Infantry (one of the four Negro Regular Army regiments) were involved in a riot in Brownsville, Texas. Although only one citizen was killed, one wounded, and the chief of police injured, whites alleged that the troops had "shot up the town." After a hasty investigation, President Theodore Roosevelt dismissed the three companies without honor and disqualified the soldiers for service in either the military or the civil service of the United States. Some Negroes, who were proud of the record of the Regular Army troops, especially during the Spanish-American War, protested vigorously and were supported by a few white liberals. President Roosevelt revoked the civil disability of the discharged soldiers in January, 1907, but a majority of a Senate investigating committee sustained the President's

claimant had been awarded one cent in damages. Thereafter, the movement was in decline, its last meeting being held in 1909. Nevertheless, particularly in view of Washington's opposition, it was significant because, as Ray Stannard Baker reported, "it represents, genuinely a more or less prevalent point of view among many coloured people." [18]

Meanwhile, Du Bois and others had established first the *Moon* (published in Memphis, 1906) and then the *Horizon* (published in Washington, 1907–1910) as unofficial organs of the Niagara Movement. The latter, a sprightly tabloid, engaged in heavy-handed satire at the expense of "King Booker" and his allies, and in a more serious vein projected its own protest philosophy. In attacking Washington the magazine hit at a wide range of issues: the centering of race interests at Tuskegee, thus making the Institute "a kind of capital for the American Negro with Dr. Washington as king without constitutional limitations"; the fear people had of joining the Niagara Movement because of Washington's influence; Washington's alliance with Roosevelt and Taft and his subsidizing the Negro press. And there was ceaseless criticism of Washington's ideological viewpoint, well summed up in March, 1908:

If there is anything dominant in the South that Booker Washington is not a warm supporter of, either expressly, by words written and spoken, or implicitly, by silence kept and maintained, his friends would do well to point it out. He has accepted the revised constitutions . . . ; he has acquiesced in the "jim crow" car policy . . . ;

---

finding that the soldiers were guilty of causing the riot. Prodded by Senator Joseph B. Foraker of Ohio, Congress in 1909 established a court of inquiry which provided for the re-enlistment of soldiers eligible for re-enlistment as of the date of their discharge, the receipt of their salary and other allowances as well as other rights and benefits from the date of the discharge. This belated reversal of Roosevelt's precipitate action did not satisfy many Negroes, for during the three years white mobs had killed Negroes—notably in Atlanta and in Springfield, Illinois. In these cases the white rioters were not punished [ed.].

18. *Bee,* July 22, 1905; *Horizon,* II (September 1907), 4; Baker, *Following the Color Line* (New York, 1908), p. 223.

he has kept dumb as an oyster as to peonage . . . ; he has even discovered that colored people can better afford to be lynched than the
white people can afford to lynch them. . . .[19]

The radicals were not evenly distributed among all groups in
the population. They were more numerous in the North than in
the South. Ray Stannard Baker characterized the Northern radicals as being highly educated individuals who held themselves
aloof from the masses and tried to avoid or deny the existence of
the color line. "Their associations in business are largely with
white people and they cling passionately to the fuller life," he
observed.[20] Though the whole matter is extremely complicated,
it appears . . . that many radicals belonged to that older upper
class which believed in immediate integration because its roots
were to a large extent in the white community. The Niagara
Movement's members were drawn almost entirely from the ranks
of the college-educated professional men. Those attending its
meetings included Dr. C. E. Bentley of Chicago, Northern lawyers like Clement Morgan, F. L. McGhee of St. Paul, George H.
Jackson of Cincinnati, and George W. Crawford of New Haven;
ministers such as Byron Gunner of Newport, Reverdy Ransom of
Boston and New York, J. Milton Waldron of Jacksonville and
Washington, George Freeman Bragg of Baltimore, and Sutton E.
Griggs of Nashville; a handful of college educators like W. H. H.
Hart of Howard University, President J. R. L. Diggs of Kentucky
State College and John Hope; an occasional government employee, and a few editors like Trotter, Harry Smith and J. Max
Barber of the *Voice of the Negro*. Other radicals had a similar
background. In Baltimore, a stronghold of radical sentiment, the
leadership of the anti-Bookerite movement was in the hands of
men like the attorney W. Ashbie Hawkins, the high-school
teacher Mason Hawkins, and the Episcopal rector George F.
Bragg, and its supporters in that city seem to have been chiefly
a college-educated elite of ministers, high-school teachers, and

19. *Horizon*, II (November 1907), 15–16; III (March 1908), 12–13.
20. Baker, *Following the Color Line*, pp. 217–220.

lawyers. Yet . . . it is not possible to say that the majority of college graduates and professional men supported the Niagara Movement.

Although the Niagara Movement failed it did chalk up one significant victory against Tuskegee when it ousted Washington from control of the Afro-American Council. As early as 1905 the Council appears to have given up its support of a restricted franchise—in fact it urged Negroes toward collective action in testing the disfranchisement laws in the courts. At the October, 1906, convention in New York, it was clear that Washington's control was slipping. Though the majority of men elected to office were friendly with the Tuskegeean, and though Washington personally urged calmness and self-control, the delegates, stirred by the Atlanta riot* and other outrages, vigorously condemned ballot restrictions, Jim Crow, and mob violence. Walters, having flirted with both sides, had been returned to the presidency the preceding year, and now charged that "it is nonsense for us to say Peace! Peace! when there is no peace. . . . We use diplomatic language and all kinds of subterfuges, but the fact remains that the enemy

---

* Of the numerous race riots at the beginning of the twentieth century, that in Atlanta, September, 1906, a month after the Brownsville riot, was one of the most serious. Latent ill feeling was intensified by rumors and inflammatory newspaper articles, especially on September 22, a Saturday when large numbers of country people were in the city. Without provocation, whites attacked Negroes. New attacks on September 24 led many Negroes to seek refuge in Clark University and Gammon Theological Seminary, located in what was then a suburb of Atlanta. Officers of the law arrested some Negroes and fired into a crowd that had armed themselves in self-defense. They returned the fire, killing one officer and wounding another. Whites went on a rampage throughout the city and destroyed a number of Negro homes and killed four Negroes. For several days, the city was paralyzed. Some Negroes sold their homes and left the city. A group of white and colored citizens organized the Atlanta Civic League to improve conditions and prevent other riots. Nothing was done to the rioters. The assertion frequently made, as noted in Rudwick (*W. E. B. Du Bois,* p. 107), that Du Bois had fled to Alabama during the riot is unfounded; Du Bois, who was making a study of conditions in Lownes County, Alabama, heard the news of the riot and returned to Atlanta by the next train. On the way, he wrote his famous poem, "Litany of Atlanta" (Du Bois, *Dusk of Dawn,* p. 86) [ed.].

is trying to keep us down and we are determined to rise or die in the attempt."

In the following months the Niagara Movement came to play a significant role in Council affairs. The 1907 convention actually marked the end of Washington's power in the Council. The anti-Bookerites eliminated several Tuskegee stalwarts from positions of influence, and the outspoken "Report to the Country" not only lacked the usual tactful phrases that would have counterbalanced its attack on the increasingly "bitter and relentless race hatred and contempt," but condemned those Negroes in high places who were "base enough" to urge silence and patience "in obedience to American color-phobia." [21] But victory for the radicals resulted in disruption of the Council whose 1908 meeting was scarcely reported in the press, and no evidence was found to indicate that it even met in 1909.

Despite the increasing dissatisfaction among Negro leaders that this state of affairs undoubtedly represented, the parallel decline of the Niagara Movement made it clear that Washington's critics were not yet in a position to make themselves the ideological spokesmen of the race. Indeed, given the power structure and the nature of American race relations at the time, it was exceedingly unlikely that the Negro radicals, limited in funds and influence, would have been victorious alone against the Tuskegeean and his powerful white allies. It was in large part the fact that the radicals were able to enlist the aid of a small group of prominent white progressives that enabled them—even during Washington's lifetime—to achieve a significant measure of success.

Among this group two men especially stand out—John Milholland and Oswald Garrison Villard, and both were originally supporters of Washington. Milholland, a manufacturer of pneumatic tube equipment and a Progressive Republican with a variety

21. A.M.E. *Review,* XXII (October 1905), 183–184; *Age,* October 11, 1906; *Alexander's Magazine,* III (December 1906), 63–64; *Proceedings of the Ninth Annual Session of the National Afro-American Council . . . 1906* (Louisville, 1907), 13, 42, 15–16; A.M.E. *Review,* XXIII (January 1907), 289–290; *Bee,* July 6, 1907; *Horizon,* II (July 1907), 20.

of reform interests, was the leading spirit behind the interracial Constitution League which aimed to attack disfranchisement, peonage, and mob violence by means of court action, legislation, and propaganda. At first Milholland and Washington worked together informally on certain matters, but frictions arose, and in 1906 the Brownsville episode led to a permanent break. Washington had himself done all he could do to dissuade Roosevelt from discharging the accused soldiers, but once the President and Secretary of War Taft had taken their action, Washington remained loyal to them, on the ground that they had made a sincere, though unfortunate mistake.[22] Most Negroes, however, did not see the matter in this light. Consequently, while the Niagara Movement seemed to be declining the Constitution League (whose members included Walters and radicals like Ransom, Barber, and Trotter) kept the pot boiling, and in the Brownsville case it had an effective issue. As Washington worked to swing Negroes behind Taft in 1908 he found his chief difficulty was with the League. All in all it was a troublesome period for Washington, who came to admit that the initiative had largely passed from his hands into those of the "black-legs" and "schemers" on the payroll of the League, which he regarded as the headquarters of all the opposition to him.[23]

Villard had long been friendly with Washington and had raised over $150,000 for the Tuskegee endowment. But he was not isolated from Washington's critics, and he was not entirely satisfied

22. Andrew M. Humphrey to BTW, May 4, 1904; Humphrey to BTW, June 4, 1904; Correspondence of BTW and Anderson, 1905–1906. On the League's activity in Brownsville case, see Mary Church Terrell, *A Colored Woman in a White World* (Washington, D.C., 1940), pp. 269–277; Anderson to BTW, January 4, 1907; *Recorder,* August 8, 1907; *Preliminary Report of Commission of the Constitution League . . . on Affray at Brownsville . . .* , 59th Congress, 2nd session, Senate Document No. 107 (1906). On BTW's stand, see BTW to Oswald Garrison Villard, November 11, 1906; BTW to Taft, November 19, 1906; BTW to Anderson, November 7, 1906; Roosevelt to BTW, November 5, 1906 (copy in F.J. Garrison Papers).

23. BTW to Anderson, February 28, February 26, March 8, 1908; BTW to Ralph W. Tyler, April 26, 1908.

with current efforts for the advancement of colored people. In 1908 he disclosed to Washington his belief that a vigorous central defense committee was necessary. Not surprisingly, therefore, he willingly complied when three socialists—the writer William English Walling and the social workers Dr. Henry Moskowitz and Mary White Ovington—prompted by the Springfield, Illinois, riot of 1908, urged him to issue a call for a national conference on the Negro question to be held on Lincoln's birthday in 1909.

Washington declined Villard's invitation to attend the conference. Walters and radical leaders like Ida Wells-Barnett, Barber, and Du Bois came, and in their speeches stressed the importance of the ballot. The conference denounced outrages, persecution, and segregation; demanded academic and professional education for the gifted; and insisted on the right to vote. Out of a second conference a year later developed the formal organization of the National Association for the Advancement of Colored People.[24] The NAACP did not actually unite with the Niagara Movement or with the Constitution League, but most of their members joined the new movement. The interracial character of the NAACP was fundamental to its success, for it gave the agitation for Negro rights a wider audience, better financial support, and the prestige of the names of well-known white progressives like Villard, Milholland, Lillian Wald, Jane Addams, John Haynes Holmes, Franz Boas, Moorfield Storey, and Clarence Darrow. Except for Du Bois, all of the chief officials of the organization at first were whites. But the backbone of the organization, the branches and their membership, consisted chiefly of elite, college-educated Negroes. By 1914 the organization had 6,000 members in fifty branches, and a circulation for *The Crisis*, edited by Du Bois, of 31,540.[25] From the beginning largely a

24. Villard to BTW, January 27, 1908; Mary White Ovington, *How the National Association for the Advancement of Colored People Began* (New York, 1914), pp. 1–3, 6; *Proceedings of the National Negro Conference* (no imprint, 1909), *passim;* Flint Kellogg, "Villard and the NAACP," *The Nation,* CLXXXVIII (February 14, 1959), 137–140.

25. *Fifth Annual Report of the NAACP* (no imprint, 1914), p. 5.

legal-action organization, the NAACP achieved its first important victory just a few months before Washington's death, when the Supreme Court declared the Oklahoma grandfather clause unconstitutional.

Tuskegee was not slow in taking steps against the new organization, and the old pattern of using various forms of pressure was repeated. Officially, the Association was not anti-Washington. Villard, who continued to correspond with Washington, encouraged the efforts of R. R. Moton of Hampton Institute to effect an understanding between the two groups. Others, however, did not hesitate to attack Washington. In October, 1910, during Washington's lecture tour in England, a group headed by Du Bois circulated a statement in London criticizing the Tuskegeean. The signers contradicted the pleasant picture described by Washington, denied that the problem was being solved, and accused Washington of misrepresenting the truth because of his dependence on certain powerful interests for philanthropy.[26] Washington was deeply troubled by such attacks and even more by defections to what Charles W. Anderson referred to as the "Vesey Street crowd." But tensions were relieved considerably when Washington was severely beaten in New York in 1911, allegedly for approaching a white woman. All factions rushed to his defense, and an era of temporary reconciliation followed which included all but Du Bois. During 1913, however, new tensions arose and though Moton continued to negotiate, cordial relationships do not appear to have been restored before Washington died later in 1915.

But by that time various individuals friendly to Washington were working with the NAACP. Influential among them were middle-of-the-roaders like the noted Mary Church Terrell and Dean Kelly Miller of Howard University, both of whom had become associated with the organization rather early. Washington in 1914 might crow over the internal feuds in the NAACP, such as Walters' desertion, Mossell, Mrs. Barnett, and Trotter quarrel-

26. Circular entitled "Race Relations in the United States," copy in Chesnutt Papers.

ing with the others, and the split between Villard and Du Bois that later led to Villard's withdrawal from active participation. But the fact was that by 1914 two of Washington's most loyal supporters, S. Laing Williams of Chicago and John Quincy Adams of St. Paul, were officials of their local branches.[27] Washington's death helped to smooth things over, and the selection of Moton to succeed him at Tuskegee meant that a moderate who had long attempted to work with the opposition led the Hampton-Tuskegee group. In 1916 Joel Spingarn, the president of the NAACP, sponsored the Amenia Conference attended by representatives of all points of view ranging from Emmett Scott to Monroe Trotter. This conference reached virtual unanimity of opinion in regard to certain principles—the desirability of all types of education, the importance of the ballot, and the necessity of replacing ancient suspicions and factions with respect for the good faith and methods of leaders in all parts of the country.[28] And then, in the very same year, the NAACP played an ironic masterstroke in inviting the author and diplomat James Weldon Johnson, one of the most capable figures in the Washington orbit, to become its national organizer.

In spite of all that Washington did the opposition triumphed. Probably nothing Washington could have done would have prevented the rise of the NAACP. For the continued deterioration of conditions during the period of his ascendancy led to ideological disillusionment with his program, and this fact, coupled with the reform spirit of the Progressive Era, encouraged the rise of protest organizations. Undoubtedly also, the decline of Washington's political power after 1909 and especially after 1913 worked to lessen the support he received from other leaders; his death removed him entirely as an element in the power structure. Nothing could illustrate better than Johnson's selection as national organizer of the NAACP the large shift that had taken place in

27. BTW to Scott, January 6, 1914; *Fifth Annual Report of the NAACP,* p. 5.
28. Du Bois, *The Amenia Conference* (Amenia, N.Y., 1923), pp. 14–15.

the less than a dozen years since the founding of the Niagara Movement in 1905.

The radical Negroes were chiefly "radical" on the race question, and most of them remained "conservative" in their broader economic and social outlook. Yet it was among them that economic and social radicalism found something of a foothold. The Niagara Movement, at its 1906 meeting, asserted that "we want the laws enforced against rich as well as poor; against Capitalists as well as Labor; against white as well as black," and the *Horizon* expressed a broadly radical social view that only a few Negroes shared. As it said in November, 1909: "THIS IS A RADICAL PAPER. . . . It advocates Negro equality and human equality; it stands for universal manhood suffrage, including votes for women; it believes in the abolition of war, the taxation of monopoly values, the gradual socialization of capital and the overthrow of persecution and despotism in the name of religion."

True, this was not the first time a Negro advocated socialism. As early as 1897 the Niagarite orator the Reverend Reverdy Ransom had suggested that since the great majority of Negroes belonged to the proletarian class, it would be the socialists who, believing like Jesus "that the rights of men are more sacred than the rights of property," would bring about the solution of the race problem. Other Niagarites who espoused socialism included J. Milton Waldron, J. Max Barber, and, most notably, Du Bois. As he put it in the *Horizon* of February, 1907, he was a "Socialist-of-the-path," for while he did not favor the complete socialization of property, he felt that progress lay in more public ownership of wealth. After all the Negro's natural allies were not the rich, but the poor. In socialism therefore, he believed, with its "larger ideal of human brotherhood, equality of opportunity and work not for wealth but for weal," lay the best hope for American Negroes.[29]

In part because of Washington's close ties with Presidents

29. Du Bois, *Dusk of Dawn*, p. 91; *Horizon*, VI (November 1909), 1; Ransom, "The Negro and Socialism," A.M.E. *Review*, XIV (October 1897), 196–197; *Horizon*, I (February 1907), 7–8.

Roosevelt and Taft, in part because of the increasing disregard in which the Republican party held Negroes, and in part because they found the platforms of Bryan and Wilson more appealing than that of Taft on nonracial matters, the leaders of the rising protest movement were the source of a significant sentiment in the North that favored the Democratic party in the elections of 1908 and 1912.[30]

A few distinguished Negroes who were not "radicals" did, it is true, support the Democrats at times, as did Bishops Abraham Grant, W. B. Derrick, and Henry M. Turner in 1900, and Turner, as previously, continued to support the party as late as 1908 and 1912. Much of the sentiment leading Negroes to support the Democratic party in 1900 appeared to be its anti-imperialist stand. John B. Syphax, a prominent Washingtonian, speaking before the United Colored Democracy in Brooklyn, rang the changes on the treachery of the carpetbaggers, the imperialism of the Republicans, and their oppression of colored Filipinos.[31] An important source of Democratic support in the North was that in many instances Democratic politicians proved more sympathetic toward Negro aspirations than did Republicans. Thus, F. L. McGhee of St. Paul wrote Washington on September 14, 1904, that while he hoped to see Roosevelt re-elected, he would vote for the Democrats because in Minnesota they were better to Negroes than Republicans were. In Chicago and Boston Democratic machines courted Negroes with considerable success beginning in the middle 1890's, and in New York Tammany Hall made a gesture toward giving Negroes some political patronage through the establishment of the United Colored Democracy. In 1910 over a third of the Boston Negroes voted for the Democratic gubernatorial candidate, and Charles Anderson reported from New York that he had never before seen so many Negroes displaying Democratic badges.[32]

30. For more details and fuller documentation of material in the following pages, see August Meier, "The Negro and the Democratic Party, 1875–1915," *Phylon*, XVII (2nd Quarter 1956), 182–191.

31. Brooklyn *Citizen*, October 10, 1900 (Hampton Clippings).

32. Anderson to BTW, November 11, 1910.

With Roosevelt's second administration Negroes grew increasingly disillusioned with the Republicans. Even organs close to Tuskegee soundly berated Roosevelt for his stand on Brownsville and his message to Congress in 1906, and some were lukewarm toward Taft in 1908. George L. Knox, editor of the Indianapolis *Freeman,* and a good friend of Washington, had been irked in 1904 by the Tuskegeean's insistence that he not run for Congress lest he jeopardize Roosevelt's chances in Indiana. He therefore came to criticize the Negro's gullibility in politics, and for the next several years urged independence at election times.[33]

By 1908 substantial elements of the Niagara Movement had come out for the Democrats. At a stormy convention in April, Trotter, Walters, and the radical clergymen S. L. Corrothers and J. Milton Waldron of Washington emerged as the group that came to be the backbone of the National Negro American Political League organized in June. This group, reported to consist of representatives of organizations like the Afro-American Council, the Niagara Movement, and the Constitution League, took a strong stand against Roosevelt's policies. In fact a significant segment of thoughtful Negroes supported Bryan in 1908. The *Gazette* followed the other radical leaders in deserting "Mr. 'Disfranchisement, Jim Crow Car' Taft"; it urged its readers to vote for anyone else, and thus "preserve your self-respect, manhood, and race respect." [34]

Du Bois presented the best rationale of those economic and racial radicals who hoped that the Democrats might move toward both racial and economic justice. Though at first he said that Bryan was just as bad as Taft and that the Socialist party was the only one which treated the Negroes as men, he soon regarded Bryan's silence on the Negro as infinitely better than the statements of the "Coward of Brownsville." Northern Democrats treated Negroes better than did the reactionary Republicans who had sided with Southern Democrats in depriving Negroes of their

33. BTW to Knox, October 17, 1904; *Freeman,* August 25, 1906, October 24, 1908.
34. *Gazette,* October 31, 1908.

rights. Whether or not Bryan would appoint Negroes to office, Negroes would benefit from a Democratic victory, for the Democratic party stood for the regulation of corporate wealth, for freedom for brown and black men in the Philippines and the West Indies, for the rights of labor, and for the elimination of all special privileges. Negroes held a balance of power in twelve Northern states, and if they used their vote properly they had it in their power to end "the impossible alliance of radical and socialistic Democracy at the North with an aristocratic caste party at the South," and to make the Democrats truly the party of the working men of both races.[35]

After the election the National Negro-American Political League, rechristened as the National Independent Political League, remained active under the leadership of Walters and Niagarites like Waldron, Trotter, and Byron Gunner. In 1912 the Independents worked closely with the Colored National Democratic League, of which Walters was president, and published a series of pamphlets and broadsides which rehearsed the arguments about Republican hypocrisy, Cleveland's appointments, and the role of Negroes as a balance of power in key states, pointed to the appearance of segregation in the federal offices at Washington, and described Wilson as a Christian gentleman who had never harmed the race.[36] Du Bois, after toying with the idea of working with the Progressives, withdrew from the Socialist party in order to support Wilson. He rationalized his action:

As to Mr. Wilson, there are, one must confess, disquieting facts; he was born in Virginia, and he was long president of a college which did not admit Negro students. . . . On the whole, we do not believe that Woodrow Wilson admires Negroes. . . . Notwithstanding such possible preferences, Woodrow Wilson is a cultivated scholar and he has

35. *Horizon,* III (February 1908), 17–18; III (April 1908), 4–6; IV (July 1908), 6–7; IV (August 1908), 2–4; IV (September 1908), 4–6.
36. National Independent Political League, *Pamphlet No. 3* ([1912]); J. Milton Waldron and J. D. Harkless, *The Political Situation in a Nutshell* (Washington, D.C. [1912]), pp. 3, 11, 16, 17.

brains. . . . We have, therefore, a conviction that Mr. Wilson will treat black men and their interests with farsighted fairness. He will not be our friend, but he will not belong to the gang of which Tillman, Vardaman, Hoke Smith and Blease are the brilliant expositors. He will not advance the cause of an oligarchy in the South, he will not seek further means of "jim crow" insult, he will not dismiss black men wholesale from office, and he will remember that the Negro . . . has a right to be heard and considered, and if he becomes President by the grace of the black man's vote, his Democratic successors may be more willing to pay the black man's price of decent travel, free labor, votes and education.

Du Bois felt that Debs was the ideal candidate but that Wilson was the only realistic choice.[37]

Despite some misgivings the anti-Roosevelt, anti-Taft, anti-Tuskegee group swallowed Wilson upon his own profession of being a Christian gentleman and his promise of fair dealings, even though he refused to make a forthright statement. Only a minority went along with the Walters-Du Bois-Trotter-Waldron group. The Cleveland *Gazette,* for example, though it was a decidedly radical organ, and though it had supported Bryan in 1908, felt that Taft was the least of the three evils that had a chance of winning. Yet, though not all of the radicals favored Wilson, outside of the professional Democrats, it was among this group that the party found its chief supporters.

The majority of Negroes, perhaps 60 per cent, voted for Roosevelt, the remainder being about evenly divided between Wilson and Taft. Kelly Miller represented the political outlook of many in his discussion of this state of affairs. He exulted in Negro independence from the Republican party, which he believed little different from the Democrats on radical matters. He was sympathetic toward the Progressive party, for as the most disadvantaged group in America, Negroes had the most to gain from its program. He explained away evidence of Roosevelt's opportunism in regard to the Negro as political maneuvering that was intended in the

37. *The Crisis,* IV (August 1912), 181.

long run to bring Negroes a square deal. "In any event," concluded Miller, "the black man's political emancipation is now
complete." Never again would he be regarded as indissolubly
linked to any party.[38]

Miller's enthusiasm was premature. The Progressive party col-
lapsed and disillusionment with Wilson set in quickly, so that
Negroes drifted back to the Republican fold. Walters, feted as the
successful leader of the Colored Democracy, soon found that the
President evidently did not intend to appoint many Negroes to
office. Wilson even failed to keep his promise of awarding the
traditionally Negro posts of minister to Haiti, register of the
Treasury, auditor for the Navy, and recorder of deeds to colored
men. So bad were conditions that when Robert H. Terrell was
renominated by Wilson and confirmed by the Senate, after a
difficult battle, the event was hailed as a major victory for the
race. Under Wilson also the policy of segregation in federal offices
was greatly broadened. In 1914 matters came to a head on this
issue when a delegation headed by Trotter obtained an audience
with the President. The conference closed unpleasantly when
Wilson ordered Trotter out of his office for what he deemed insulting language.[39] Thus, by at least tacit approval of the " 'Jim
Crow' insult," by "dismiss[ing] black men wholesale from office,"
and by seemingly failing "to remember that the Negro has a right
to be heard and considered," Wilson had almost step by step
refuted Du Bois' campaign estimate of him. So ended the honey-
moon between the radical Negroes and the Democrats. The paradoxical union of office seekers and anti-Bookerites, disillusioned
Republicans and economic radicals, was unable to weather the
chilling realities of the Wilson administration, in which Southern
whites played such a large role.

Actually, few Negroes—indeed only a few of the radicals on
racial matters—ever embraced socialism, and only a minority ever

38. Miller, "The Political Plight of the Negro," *Kelly Miller's Mono-
graphic Magazine*, I (1913), 1, 6, 8, 10, 11, 14–17, 21.
39. *Bee*, November 21, 1914; A.M.E. *Review*, XXXI (January 1915),
309–318; *The Crisis*, IX (January 1915), 12–13.

favored the Democrats. Negroes remained by and large conservative in their political and economic orientation during the Progressive Era of the Square Deal and the New Freedom. In fact, in the
face of increasing trade-union discrimination they were becoming
more rather than less hostile to organized labor. In spite of some
exceptions, most remained at least lukewarm Republicans in their
allegiance. Only the temporary swing toward the Progressives in
1912 gave any indication that "left-of-center" reformism would
some day have a profound impact upon the Negro vote and upon
Negro thought.

The Paradox of W. E. B. Du Bois[1]

If, of the great trio of Negro leaders, Frederick Douglass best expressed the aspirations toward full citizenship and assimilation, and Booker T. Washington the interest in economic advancement, it was Du Bois who most explicitly revealed the impact of oppression and of the American creed in creating ambivalent loyalties toward race and nation in the minds of American Negroes. As Du Bois said in 1897:

One feels his two-ness—an American, a Negro, two souls, two thoughts, two unreconciled strivings, two warring ideals in one dark body. . . .

The history of the American Negro is the history of this strife,—this longing to attain self-conscious manhood, to merge his double self into a better and truer self. . . . He would not Africanize America for America has too much to teach the world and Africa.

1. All works cited are by Du Bois unless otherwise stated. The Du Bois Papers have been closed to scholars for some years. All references to letters to and from Du Bois and all references to manuscript materials by Du Bois are to the notes on these materials made by Francis L. Broderick and placed on file at the Schomburg Collection of the New York Public Library.

Reprinted from *Negro Thought in America, 1880–1915: Racial Ideologies in the Age of Booker T. Washington* by August Meier (Ann Arbor, Mich.: The University of Michigan Press, 1963), pp. 190–206, by permission of the University of Michigan Press. Copyright © 1963 by the University of Michigan.

He would not bleach the Negro soul in a flood of white Americanism, for he knows that Negro blood has a message for the world. He
simply wishes to make it possible for a man to be both a Negro and
an American, without being cursed and spit upon. . . .

More than any other figure Du Bois made explicit this ambivalence—an ambivalence that is perhaps the central motif in his
ideological biography. Even Du Bois has described himself as
integrally a part of European civilization, and "yet, more significant, one of its rejected parts; one who expressed in life and action
and made vocal to many, a single whirlpool of social entanglement
and inner psychological paradox." [2]
A proud and sensitive youth reared in a western Massachusetts
town, Du Bois had occasion to know the sting of prejudice and
early realized that "I was different from others; or like, mayhap
in heart and life and longing, but shut out from their world by a
vast veil." Subsequently he therefore found the segregated community of Fisk University, which he attended from 1885 to 1888,
an enriching experience. Though he yearned for the full recognition of his American citizenship, he was also, he later recollected,
"thrilled and moved to tears," and recognized "something inherently and deeply my own" as a result of his association there
with a "closed racial group with rites and loyalties, with a history
and a corporate future, with an art and a philosophy." By the
time he received his A.B. from Fisk and entered Harvard as a
Junior in 1888, "the theory of race separation was quite in my
blood," and the lack of social acceptance he experienced at Harvard, he recalled later, did not disturb him. Yet it certainly was
his sensitivity to discrimination that led him at this time to view
Negroes as a "nation"—Americans, but rejected in the land of
their birth. [3]
Meanwhile, Du Bois had been expressing himself on other sub-

2. "Strivings of the Negro People," *Atlantic Monthly,* LXXX (August
1897), 194; *Dusk of Dawn* (New York, 1940), p. 2.
3. "Strivings of the Negro People," 194–195; "Public Rhetoricals,"
Fisk University, Ms. [1885–1888]; *Dusk of Dawn,* pp. 23–24, 101, 136; "A
Vacation Unique," Ms., 1889; "What Will the Negro Do?" Ms., 1889.

jects. As a correspondent for Fortune's New York *Globe* during the early 1880's and as editor of the Fisk *Herald,* he displayed an interest in industriousness and ambition. Furthermore, as a student at Fisk and at Harvard—where he received his Ph.D. in 1895— and as a professor at Wilberforce University (1894–1896), Du Bois proved more than willing to meet Southern whites half way. He told both Fisk students and his white associates in the Tennessee prohibitionist movement that the interests of the two races were essentially the same. To his Fisk audience he proposed the admittedly unorthodox idea that Negroes should divide their vote in order not to exacerbate race relations. He assured Southern whites that they could depend on the friendship of Negroes if only the whites would grant them citizenship rights and adequate educational facilities. Since the Negro's condition was such as to encourage prejudice, for their part Negroes must stress duties as well as rights, and work for their own advancement. At both Harvard and Wilberforce he could, in a single speech, lash out at America's immoral and un-American treatment of Negroes (and at Harvard suggest that Negroes would revolt if other means failed) and at the same time adopt a conciliatory position. Since Negroes had not yet achieved what it took the Anglo-Saxons a millennium to do, they were not yet equipped to vote. What he objected to was not the disfranchisement of the Negro masses, but of intelligent, law-abiding Negroes; and what he advocated was a franchise limitation fairly applied to both races along with adequate educational opportunities for all. In 1891 it was even reported in the *Age* that Du Bois had asserted that the whole idea underlying the Lodge Elections Bill* was wrong, for it was proposed on the assumption that

* In 1890 Representative Henry Cabot Lodge (R. Mass.) introduced a bill providing for the appointment of federal supervisors of federal elections. The supervisors, representing both parties, were to be appointed on petitions by a specified number of voters in any election district. They were to have power to pass on the qualifications of any voter challenged in a federal election and to place in ballot boxes ballots wrongfully refused by local officers. On July 2, 1890, the House approved the bill by an almost strict party vote. Although Mississippi adopted a constitutional

law can accomplish anything. . . . We must ever keep before us the fact that the South has some excuse for its present attitude. We must remember that a good many of our people . . . are not fit for the responsibility of republican government. When you have the right sort of black voters you will need no election laws. The battle of my people must be a moral one, not a legal or physical one.[4]

It was no wonder then that after Washington's address Du Bois wrote the *Age* suggesting "that here might be the basis of a real settlement between whites and blacks." [5]

Meanwhile, Du Bois was formulating his notion of leadership by a college-educated elite, which he regarded as necessary for the advancement of any group. In 1891 he deplored the South's effort to make common and industrial schools rather than colleges the basis of its educational system. For only a liberally educated white leadership could perceive that, despite the justification for overthrowing the Reconstruction governments, to permanently disfranchise the working class of a society in the process of rapid industrialization would, as socialists from Lassalle to Hindman had said, result in economic ruin. And only a liberal higher education could create an intelligent Negro leadership. Thus, while still a student at Harvard, Du Bois had suggested his theory of the talented tenth, foreshadowed his later concern with the working

---

amendment which denied the suffrage to most Negroes while permitting equally unqualified whites to vote, the Senate shortly thereafter, January, 1891, rejected the Lodge bill, which opponents had cleverly dubbed the "Force Bill." Fear that it might upset the economy of the South, and thereby keep out Northern investments, and the trading of votes by Republican senators from silver-producing states for Southern votes in support of their currency legislation helped defeat the bill. The principal reason, however, was the desire of some Republicans not to challenge the threat of Southern senators that enactment would prevent the further development of friendly relations between the North and South [ed.].

4. New York *Globe,* e.g., September 8, 1883; Fisk *Herald,* V (December 1887), 8 and V (March 1888), 8–9; "Political Serfdom," Ms., 1887; "An Open Letter to the Southern People," Ms., 1888 [?]; "What Will the Negro Do?"; "Hharvard and the South," Ms., 1891; "The Afro-Americans," Ms. [1894–1896]; *Age,* June 13, 1891.

5. *Dusk of Dawn,* p. 85. Unfortunately the files of the *Age* are not available for the early 1890's.

class, and adumbrated the thesis he later stressed so much—that without political rights Negroes, primarily a working group, could not secure economic opportunity. Furthermore, it should be noted that his educational views were not unrelated to his ethnocentric feelings. As he said at Wilberforce, the educated elite had a glorious opportunity to guide the race by reshaping its own ideals in order to provide the masses with appropriate goals and lift them to civilization.[6]

After two years at Wilberforce, Du Bois accepted a one-year research appointment at the University of Pennsylvania. Then in 1897 he became professor of sociology at Atlanta University, where he remained until 1910, teaching and editing the annual Atlanta University Studies on the American Negro.

At no time in his life did Du Bois place greater and more consistent stress upon self-help and racial solidarity than during the last four years of the century. Like many of his contemporaries he fused this emphasis with one on economic advancement; and like a few of them he synthesized it with his educational program for the talented tenth. To Du Bois in fact, the race prejudice which isolated the Negro group and threw upon it "the responsibility of evolving its own methods and organs of civilization" made the stimulation of group cooperation "the central serious problem." [7]

It was his appointment to the University of Pennsylvania that provided Du Bois with his first opportunity to begin a scientific study of the race problem. He had long awaited such an opportunity because he believed that presentation of the facts derived from scientific investigation would go a long way toward solving the race problem. The resulting monograph, The Philadelphia Negro, leaned toward the blame-the-Negro, self-help point of view. Yet Du Bois did describe what it meant to be snubbed in employment and in social intercourse, and he judged that the Negro's participation in politics had been, in net effect, beneficial

6. "Harvard and the South"; "The Afro-American"; "The True Meaning of a University," Ms., 1894.
7. Some Efforts of American Negroes for Their Own Social Betterment (Atlanta University Publications No. 3, 1898), p. 43.

to the city and to the Negro himself. Above all, he felt that Negroes must uplift themselves, and by racial cooperation open enterprises that would provide employment and training in trades and commerce. Whites had their duty to help but society had too many problems "for it lightly to shoulder all the burdens of a less advanced people." Negroes ought to constantly register strong protests against prejudice and injustice, but they should do so because these things hindered them in their own attempt to elevate the race. And this attempt, Du Bois held, must be marked by vigorous and persistent efforts directed toward lessening crime and toward inculcating self-respect, the dignity of labor, and the virtues of truth, honesty, and charity.[8]

Like Washington, then, Du Bois combined an enthusiasm for racial solidarity with one for economic development and the middle-class virtues. In fact, he regarded a college education as "one of the best preparations for a broad business life" and for the making of "captains of industry." Likening Negroes to other nationalities, he chided them for being ashamed of themselves, and held that such success as had been achieved by other nations no larger in population than the American Negroes could be accomplished only through a badly needed cooperation and unity. In view of the poverty of the Negro and the economic spirit of the age, it was most important to achieve success in business. Because of race prejudice the major opportunity for such achievement lay in commercial activity based on Negroes pooling their earnings and pushing forward as a group. Though their collective capital be small, thrift and industry could succeed even under the handicaps of prejudice. Under the circumstances a penny savings bank would be more helpful than the vote. Negroes should patronize and invest their money in Negro-owned enterprises, even at a personal sacrifice. For "we must cooperate or we are lost. Ten million people who join in intelligent self-help can never be long ignored or mistreated." [9]

8. *The Philadelphia Negro* (Philadelphia, 1899), pp. 325, 388–391, Chap. XVII, and *passim*.
9. "Careers Open to College-Bred Negroes," in Du Bois and H. H.

It should be noted, of course, that Du Bois did not, during the *fin de siècle* years, give up all interest in political rights, though like the majority of articulate Southern Negroes of the day he was willing to compromise on the matter. He was among those who in 1899 petitioned the Georgia legislature not to pass the Hardwick disfranchisement bill, though like Booker T. Washington he was willing to accept an educational and/or property qualification as long as free school facilities were open to all.[10]

During this period Du Bois was more emphatic than at any other time about the value of racial integrity. Speaking on "The Conservation of Races" in 1897 he asserted that there existed subtle psychic differences, which had definitely divided men into races. Like his racist contemporaries, he was certain of the universality of "the race spirit," which he regarded as "the greatest invention for human progress." Each race had a special ideal—the English individualism, the German philosophy and science, and so forth. Therefore, "only Negroes bound and welded together, Negroes inspired by one vast ideal, can work out in its fullness the great message we have for humanity." To those who argued that their only hope lay in amalgamating with the rest of the American population, he admitted that Negroes faced a "puzzling dilemma." Every thoughtful Negro had at some time asked himself whether he was an American, or a Negro, or if he could be both; whether by striving as a Negro he was not perpetuating the very gulf that divided the two races, or whether Negroes "have in America a distinct mission as a race." Du Bois' answer was what is now called cultural pluralism. Negroes were American by birth, in language, in political ideas, and in religion. But any further than this, their Americanism did not go. Since they had given America

---

Proctor, *Two Addresses* (Nashville, 1898), pp. 7, 12; "The Meaning of Business," Ms., 1898; quotation at end of paragraph is from resolutions of the Fourth Atlanta University Conference, *The Negro in Business* (AUP No. 4, 1899), p. 50.

10. Du Bois and others, *Memorial to the Legislature of Georgia Upon the Hardwick Bill,* pamphlet, 1899, Du Bois Papers; "The Suffrage Fight in Georgia," *Independent,* LX (November 30, 1899), 3226–3228.

its only native music and folk stories, "its only touch of pathos and humor amid its mad money-getting plutocracy," it was the Negroes' duty to maintain "our physical power, our intellectual endowment, our spiritual ideas; as a race, we must strive by race organizations, by race solidarity, by race unity to the realization of the broader humanity which freely recognizes differences in men, but sternly deprecates inequalities in their opportunity of development." To this end, separate racial educational, business, and cultural institutions were necessary. Despised and oppressed, the Negroes' only means of advancement was a belief in their own great destiny. No people that wished to be something other than itself "ever wrote its name in history; it must be inspired with the Divine faith of our black mothers, that out of the blood and dust of battles will march a victorious host, a mighty nation, a peculiar people, to speak to the nations of the earth a Divine truth that should make them free." Washington, it should be pointed out, while advocating race pride and race integrity, did not glory so much in the idea of a distinctive Negro culture (though he was always proud of the spirituals or "plantation melodies"). Nor did he exhibit Du Bois' sense of identification with Africans, evident in Du Bois' advocacy of "pan-Negroism" in this same address.[11]

During the last years of the century Du Bois developed his educational theories at considerable length, attempting to construct "A Rational System of Negro Education" by reconciling the two widely diverging tendencies of the day—training for making a living and training for living a broad life. All agreed, he said, on the necessity of universal common school training, and on the contribution Hampton, Tuskegee, and the Slater Fund had made in stressing the building of an economic foundation, the freedmen's primary concern. But unfortunately only three or four

11. *The Conservation of Races* (American Negro Academy, Occasional Papers No. 2, 1897), pp. 7, 9–13. Nor was Du Bois averse to a considerable number of American Negroes migrating to Africa, uniting for the uplift and economic development of the continent. See "Possibility of Emigration to Congo Free State," Memorial to Paul Hegeman, Belgian Consul-General to the United States [1895–1897].

schools made broad culture their chief aim. Du Bois criticized the talk of rosewood pianos in dingy cabins, of ignorant farmers, of college graduates without employment, though he agreed that more stress had been placed on college training than the economic condition of the race warranted. But the vogue for industrial education had become so great that the colleges were hard-pressed for funds. This was particularly deplorable because the isolation of the Negro community demanded the creation of an indigenous leadership of college-trained captains of industry and scholars, who would advance the masses economically and culturally, and who could view the race problem from a broad perspective.[12]

There were remarkable similarities between Du Bois and Washington during the late 1890's—a period when more Negro leaders than at any other time adopted a conciliatory tactic. Both tended to blame Negroes largely for their condition, and both placed more emphasis on self-help and duties than on rights. Both placed economic advancement before universal manhood suffrage, and both were willing to accept franchise restrictions based not on race but on education and/or property qualifications equitably applied. Both stressed racial solidarity and economic cooperation. Du Bois was, however, more outspoken about injustices, and he differed sharply with Washington in his espousal of the cause of higher education.

The years from 1901 to 1903 were years of transition in Du Bois' philosophy, years in which he grew more critical of industrial education and more alarmed over disfranchisement. Writing in 1901 he engaged in sharp protest against the Southern race system, even while recognizing that Negroes must adjust to it. He denied that the "many delicate differences in race psychology" excused oppression. He complained of the economic discrimination that retarded the development of a substantial landowning and artisan class. He bemoaned the lack of contact between the races that increased prejudice by preventing the best classes of

12. "A Rational System of Negro Education," Ms. [1897–1900]; Du Bois, ed., *The College-Bred Negro* (AUP No. 5, 1900), p. 29.

both races from knowing each other. Yet he felt that, since Negroes must accept segregation, the road to uplift and economic improvement lay in the development of college-educated leaders: "Black captains of industry and missionaries of culture" who with their knowledge of modern civilization could uplift Negro communities "by forms of precept and example, deep sympathy and the inspiration of common kindred and ideals." But while Negroes would have to temporarily acquiesce in segregation, they could not acquiesce in disfranchisement. Du Bois did not object to "legitimate efforts to purge the ballot of ignorance, pauperism and crime," and he conceded that it was "sometimes best that a partially developed people should be ruled by the best of their stronger and better neighbors for their own good," until they were ready to stand on their own feet. But since the dominant opinion of the South openly asserted that the purpose of the disfranchisement laws was the complete exclusion of Negroes from politics, the ballot was absolutely necessary for the Negro's safety and welfare. Moreover, as European experience had demonstrated, workers under modern industrial conditions needed the vote in order to protect themselves; Negroes, laboring under racial discrimination, needed it even more.[13]

Du Bois developed further his educational views and the theme of the talented tenth. He agreed that it was most important to train Negroes to work, and he conceded that industrial schools would play an important role in achieving this end. He also approved of the compromise function of industrial education, which had brought together races and sections; and although industrial education would not solve the problem he asserted that "it does mean that its settlement can be auspiciously begun." Yet he had come to criticize the overinsistence of industrial schools upon the practical, the unfortunate opposition of their advocates toward colleges, the fact that industrial schools were preparing their students in obsolete crafts, and the fact that they produced few

13. "The Relations of the Negroes to the Whites of the South," *Annals of the American Academy of Political and Social Science*, XVIII (July 1901), 121–133; "The Case for the Negro," Ms., 1901.

actual artisans. Du Bois defended Negro colleges from charges
that they had erred in training school teachers and professional
men before turning to industrial training. He pointed out that
historically the European university had preceded the common
school, and that out of the liberal arts institutions came the backbone of the teaching force of the Negro common schools and of industrial schools like Tuskegee, where almost half of the executive
council and a majority of the heads of departments were college
graduates. All races, he held, had been civilized by their exceptional men; "the problem of education, then, among Negroes,
must first of all deal with the Talented Tenth." [14]

It is evident that Washington and Du Bois had come to disagree
not only in their educational philosophy, but also on the fundamental question of the immediate importance of the ballot. By
1903 Du Bois was not only pleading for higher education, but
had begun to criticize the work of the industrial schools. Both
men spoke of captains of industry, but where the Tuskegeean
emphasized economic skills, the Atlanta educator stressed a high
grade of culture. And unlike Washington, Du Bois had come to
believe that educational and property qualifications for voting
would not be equitably applied. True, Du Bois never gave up his
belief that, in the face of white prejudice and discrimination group
solidarity was necessary, especially in economic matters. But all
that really remained to make the two men irreconcilable ideological opponents was for Du Bois to advocate the importance of
protest rather than accommodation. This he did in his opening
attack on Washington in 1903.

During the 1890's Washington and Du Bois had been cordial in
their relationships. Upon returning to the United States from Germany in 1894 Du Bois accepted a position at Wilberforce, having
had to turn down a somewhat later offer from Tuskegee. Again
in 1896, 1899, and as late as 1902 Du Bois seriously considered

14. "The Talented Tenth," in Booker T. Washington and others, *The
Negro Problem* (New York, 1903), pp. 60–61; *The Negro Artisan*
(AUP No. 7, 1902), p. 81; "Of the Training of Black Men," *Atlantic
Monthly*, XC (September 1902), 291; "The Talented Tenth," 45, 33–34.

invitations to Tuskegee.[15] In his correspondence with Washington, through his articles and speeches, and by attending the Hampton and Tuskegee Conferences he exhibited his sympathetic interest in Washington's work. He had, it is true, mildly criticized the Tuskegeean in an article in 1901. In it he said that some of the most prominent men of the race regarded the Hampton-Tuskegee approach as only a partial approach to the race problem, in that they stressed the highest aspirations of the race, advocated college education, and believed that Negroes should enjoy suffrage equally with whites. But as late as July, 1902, the *Guardian* denounced Du Bois for siding with Washington at the St. Paul meeting of the Afro-American Council. "Like all the others who are trying to get into the bandwagon of the Tuskegeean, he is no longer to be relied upon," declared the editor, Monroe Trotter.[16]

Kelly Miller has asserted that Trotter wove a "subtle net" around Du Bois and captured him for the radical cause. It would be difficult to test the truth of this statement. Certain it is, however, that by January, 1903, Trotter was praising Du Bois as a brilliant leader who, despite temptations, "has never in public utterance or in written article, betrayed his race in its contest for equal opportunity and equal rights." Du Bois himself has recalled that he was gradually growing more disturbed after 1900—less by the ideological difference between him and Washington (which he remembered as mainly one of emphasis) than by the immense power over political appointments, over philanthropic largess, and over the press wielded by what Du Bois has labeled the "Tuskegee Machine." Du Bois found Washington's influence over the press especially deplorable, in view of the Tuskegeean's softpedaling of agitation on segregation and disfranchisement.[17] Yet

15. Samuel R. Spencer, Jr., *Booker T. Washington and the Negro's Place in American Life* (Boston, 1955), pp. 146, 148–149.

16. "The Evolution of Negro Leadership," *The Dial,* XXXI (July 1901), 54 (an article which anticipated in several significant respects Du Bois' discussion in "Of Booker T. Washington and Others"); *Guardian,* July 27, 1902.

17. Miller, *Race Adjustment,* 3rd ed. (New York, 1909), p. 14; *Guardian,* January 10, 1903; *Dusk of Dawn,* pp. 70–77.

whatever his actual motivation for criticizing Washington, his first public statement on the matter was confined to ideological issues.

This statement was Du Bois' famous essay, "Of Booker T. Washington and Others," in *Souls of Black Folk,* published in the spring of 1903. "Easily the most striking thing," began Du Bois, "in the history of the American Negro since 1876 is the ascendancy of Mr. Booker T. Washington." Others had failed in establishing a compromise between the North, the South, and the Negroes. But Washington, coming with a simple though not entirely original program of industrial education, conciliation of the South, and acceptance of disfranchisement and segregation, had succeeded. For with "singular insight" he had grasped the spirit of the age—"the spirit and thought of triumphant commercialism."

Du Bois went on to criticize the Tuskegeean because his policy "practically accepted the alleged inferiority of the Negro," allowed economic concerns to dominate over the higher aims of life, and preached a "submission to prejudice." Although Washington had made some statements about lynching and the franchise, generally his speeches purveyed the "dangerous half-truths" that the Negro's lowly condition justified the South's attitude and that the Negro's elevation must depend chiefly on his own efforts. Du Bois perceived paradoxes in Washington's attempt to make Negro workers businessmen and property owners when it was impossible for workers to defend themselves without the ballot; in his preaching self-respect while counseling accommodation to discrimination and in his advocacy of industrial and common schools while depreciating the colleges that supplied their teachers. Furthermore, Washington's propaganda had undoubtedly hastened the disfranchisement, the increased segregation, and the decreased philanthropic concern for higher education that accompanied his ascendancy.

Washington's popularity with whites, Du Bois held, had led Negroes to accept his leadership, and criticism of the Tuskegeean had disappeared. The time was ripe therefore for thinking Negroes to undertake their responsibility to the masses by speaking out. In addition to the few who dared to openly oppose Washington, Du

Bois thought that men like Archibald and Francis J. Grimké, Kelly Miller, and J. W. E. Bowen could not remain silent much longer. Such men honored Washington for his conciliatory attitude, and they realized that the condition of the masses of the race was responsible for much of the discrimination against it. But they also knew that prejudice was more often a cause than a result of the Negro's degradation; that justice could not be achieved through "indiscriminate flattery"; that Negroes could not gain their rights by voluntarily throwing them away, or obtain respect by constantly belittling themselves; and that, on the contrary, Negroes must speak out constantly against oppression and discrimination.

Du Bois had indeed moved away from his conciliatory ideology of the 1890's. Yet attempts at cooperation between him and Washington were not quite at an end. In the summer of 1903 Du Bois spoke at Tuskegee. The two men also continued their collaboration—begun in 1902—in an effort to prevent the exclusion of Negroes from Pullman cars. Nevertheless, after the "Boston Riot" * Du Bois was—with reservations—lining up with Trotter. He did not, he said, agree with Trotter's intemperate tactics, but he admired his integrity and purpose, which were especially needed in view of Washington's backward steps.[18] The Carnegie Hall Meeting of January, 1904, and Du Bois' appointment to the Committee of Twelve temporarily restored an uneasy working relationship between him and Washington, but he soon resigned from the Committee and in 1905 was chiefly responsible for inaugurating the Niagara Movement. Meanwhile, he has recollected, he found it increasingly difficult to obtain funds for his work at Atlanta, experienced criticism in the Negro press, and in other ways "felt the implacability of the Tuskegee Machine." [19] He was one of the most active members of the Conference on the Negro

* See above, p. 45 [ed.].

18. Spencer, *Booker T. Washington*, p. 157; Du Bois to Clement Morgan, October 19, 1903; Du Bois to George Foster Peabody, December 28, 1903.

19. *Dusk of Dawn*, pp. 82–83, 86, 95. On the embarrassment that Du Bois' stand caused Atlanta University, see Horace Bumstead to Du Bois, December 5, 1903 and January 26, 1905.

in 1909, and when the NAACP was organized in 1910 he became director of publicity and research and editor of *The Crisis*.

Thus by 1905 Du Bois had definitely come to the parting of the
ways with Washington. And it is in the Niagara Movement manifestoes and in the pages of the *Horizon* and *The Crisis* that one
can best observe Du Bois as the consistent agitator, the ardent and
brilliant fighter for integration and citizenship rights. For example,
he insisted that disfranchisement retarded the economic development of the Negro because the voteless could not protect their
property rights. He cited cases of persecution of prosperous
Negroes as evidence that Washington's program would not obtain
the respect of the white man and the rights of citizenship.[20] In
a typical editorial he pointed out that in spite of Washington's
conciliatory policy conditions had grown worse. True, as Washington said, Negroes had continued to accumulate property and
education, but how Washington could assert that discrimination
and prejudice were decreasing was incomprehensible to Du Bois.
Horrible as race prejudice was, it could be fought if faced frankly.
But "if we continually dodge and cloud the issue, and say the
half truth because the whole stings and shames . . . we invite
catastrophe." Elsewhere he insisted that opportunism was a dangerous policy that gave moral support to the race's enemies, and he
denounced the stress on sycophancy, selfishness, mediocrity, and
servility at the expense of the best education, the highest ideals,
and self-respect.[21] Naturally he criticized industrial schools. On
one occasion he attacked Hampton for its opposition to the work
of the Negro colleges, and described it as "a center of that under-
ground and silent intrigue which is determined to perpetuate the
American Negro as a docile peasant," lacking political rights and
social status. Du Bois was unequivocal in his stand on segregation. He scathingly denounced the separate-but-equal doctrine:
"Separate schools for Whites and Blacks, and separate cars for

20. E.g., *The Crisis,* VII (February 1914), 189–190; I (December
1910), 27.

21. *The Crisis,* II (June 1911), 63–64; *"The Forward Movement,"*
Ms., 1910.

Whites and Blacks are not equal, can not be made equal, and . . . are not intended to be equal." He charged that what the South wanted was not mere separation but subordination, and insisted that no "square deal" was possible as long as segregation existed. And unlike Washington he opposed a colored Episcopal bishop to work only among Negroes, even though this would have elevated a Negro to a high church office.[22]

It is evident from a reading of Du Bois' less publicized scholarly and nonpolemical statements that throughout these years he still maintained his interest in racial solidarity and self-help, in the group economy, and in the American Negro's ties to Africa. On occasion he was most explicit about his concept of economic nationalism. Just as a country can by tariffs build up its separate economy to the point where it can compete in international trade, so the Negro should create a group economy that would "so break the force of race prejudice that his right and ability to enter the national economy are assured." His enthusiasm for the group economy was indeed at times interpreted as implying a favorable attitude toward segregation, and in an exchange of letters on the subject with the editor of the Boston *Transcript,* Du Bois was finally prompted to declare that while opposed to physical separation he was prepared to accept for some time to come a "spiritual" separation in economic life that would involve Negroes trading only among themselves. True, he shifted his support from the creation of captains of industry who would exploit the Negro proletariat to the building up of a consumers' and producers' co-operative movement among Negroes. But inevitably he had to reconcile his espousal of a group economy with his demands for full integration. In 1913, replying to a communication which claimed it was hard to meet the argument that segregation forced Negroes to develop themselves, Du Bois agreed that undoubtedly thousands of Negro businesses, including *The Crisis,* had developed because

22. *The Crisis,* XVI (November 1917), 11; *Horizon,* II (October 1907), 16; *The Crisis,* I (February 1911), 20–21; *Horizon,* II (October 1907), 7–8.

of discrimination, capitalizing, in a sense, on race prejudice. But this did not make discrimination a "veiled blessing." While Negro enterprises had done creditable work under the circumstances, and although Negroes must make the best of segregation, turning even its disadvantages to their advantage, they "must never forget that none of its possible advantages can offset its miserable evils, or replace the opportunity . . . of free men in a free world." [23]

A similar paradox was involved in Du Bois' stand on intermarriage. Writing in the *Independent* in 1910 he held that a person had the right to choose his spouse, that the prohibition of intermarriage was not justified when it arbitrarily limited friendships, and that where satisfactory conditions prevailed, race mixture had often produced gifted and desirable stocks and individuals, such as the Egyptians, and Hamilton, Pushkin, Douglass, and Dumas. He believed, however, that for the present widespread intermarriage would be "a social calamity by reason of the wide cultural, ethical and traditional differences" between the races, and predicted that if Negroes were accorded their rights and thus encouraged to build up their racial self-respect, the two races would continue to exist as distinct entities, perhaps forever, and this not "at the behest of any one race which recently arrogantly assumed the heritage of the earth, but for the highest upbuilding of all peoples in their great ideal of human brotherhood." [24]

Nor was Du Bois consistent in his views on race differences. Earlier, while never accepting any idea of Negro inferiority, he had referred to Negroes as a backward, childlike, undeveloped race, and he had accepted the idea of inherent racial differences. But in March, 1908, he attacked the "glib" Darwinist interpretations about undeveloped races and the survival of the fittest. After

23. *Negro American Artisan* (AUP No. 17, 1913), pp. 128–129; E. H. Clement to Du Bois [December ? 1907], December 18, 1907; Du Bois to Clement, December 10 and 30, 1907; *Economic Co-operation Among Negro Americans* (AUP No. 12, 1907), p. 12; *The Crisis,* XV (November 1917), 9; *The Crisis,* V (January 1913), 184–186.

24. "The Marrying of Black Folk," *Independent,* LXIX (October 13, 1910), 812–813.

the Universal Races Congress in London in 1911 Du Bois enthusiastically reported its conclusion that there was no proven connection between race and mental or cultural characteristics. Yet in 1913 he harked back to the idea of inherent racial differences and described the Negro as primarily an artist, possessing a "sensuous nature . . . the only race which has held at bay the life destroying forces of the tropics," gaining thereby an unusual aesthetic sensitivity. This quality explained the artistic achievements of the Egyptians and the Ommiads, the literature of Pushkin, the bronze work of Benin, and the "only real American music." [25]

As a matter of fact Du Bois maintained his strong feeling of identification with other colored peoples, especially Africans. At one time he was secretary of a company which aimed to participate in the economic advancement of East Africa. Years before Melville J. Herskovits cited anthropological evidence for African origins of the culture of American Negroes, Du Bois held that their religious life and institutions, family life, burial and beneficial societies, the roots of economic cooperation, and the skill of Negro artisans all had their origins in Africa. Finally, *The Negro,* published in 1915, dealt with Negro history from ancient Egypt to the United States and was especially notable for its discussion of the history and culture of West Africa. In it he also adopted the Italian anthropologist Giuseppe Sergi's thesis that an ancient rather dark-skinned race spawned all of the ancient Mediterranean civilizations. Moreover, he predicted the emergence of a Pan-African movement, uniting Negroes everywhere, and a growing unity of the darker races against the intolerable treatment accorded them by the white man. Since the colored races were in a majority, the future world would probably be what colored men make it, and "in the character of the Negro race is the best

25. *Philadelphia Negro,* p. 359; "Relations of Negroes to the Whites of the South," 121–122; *The Souls of Black Folk* (Chicago, 1903), p. 50; *Horizon,* III (March 1908), 5–6; *The Crisis,* II (August 1911), 157–158; "The Negro in Literature and Art," in *The Negro's Progress in Fifty Years* (Annals of the American Academy of Political and Social Science, XXXIX [September 1913]), 233–237.

and greatest hope. For in its normal condition it is at once the strongest and gentlest of the races of men." [26]

A new theme in the pages of the *Horizon* and *The Crisis* was Du Bois' interest in the labor movement and in socialism. At one time he had viewed the white working class as the Negro's "bitterest opponent." By 1904 he had come to believe that economic discrimination was in large part the cause of the race problem, and to feel sympathetic toward the socialist movement. Three years later, he was writing favorably of the socialists in the *Horizon*. Elsewhere he advised the socialists that their movement could not succeed unless it included the Negro workers, and wrote that it was simply a matter of time before white and black workers would see their common economic cause against the exploiting capitalists. Though in 1908 Du Bois did not vote for the socialists because they had no chance of winning, in 1911 he joined the party. In a Marxist exegesis in the concluding pages of *The Negro,* Du Bois viewed both American Negroes and Africans, both the white workers and the colored races, as exploited by white capital which employed the notion of race differences as a rationalization of exploitation, segregation, and subordination. And he predicted that the exploited of all races would unite and overthrow white capital, their common oppressor.[27]

Du Bois' espousal of the cause of labor was so deep-seated that he had *The Crisis* printed by members of a union that did not admit Negroes, and in its pages he welcomed the rare signs that

26. Circular of African Development Company, March 1, 1902; Melville J. Herskovits, *Myth of the Negro Past* (New York, 1941); *The Negro Church* (AUP No. 6, 1903), pp. 5–6; *The Negro American Artisan,* p. 24; *The Negro American Family* (AUP No. 13, 1908), pp. 10–17; *Economic Co-operation Among Negro Americans,* pp. 12–14; *The Negro* (New York, 1915), Chap. II, pp. 241–242; Sergi, *The Mediterranean Race* (London, 1901).

27. *The Negro Artisan,* p. 25; Du Bois to I. M. Rubinow, November 17, 1904; *Horizon,* I (February 1907), 7–8; "A Field for Socialists," Ms. [1907–1909]; "The Economic Revolution in the South," in Booker T. Washington and Du Bois, *The Negro in the South* (Philadelphia, 1907), p. 116; Du Bois to Mr. Owens, April 17, 1908; Elliott Rudwick to author, July 17, 1954; *The Negro,* pp. 238–241. Note also his Marxist, economic interpretation in his first novel, *The Quest of the Silver Fleece,* 1911.

white and Negro workers might be getting together. In this regard he was certainly ahead of his time, and even he finally expressed discouragement after the 1917 East St. Louis riot* in which white unionists played such a striking role.[28] Thus Du Bois' attempts to woo union labor had succeeded no better than his related attempt to woo the Democratic party. . . . Du Bois never gave up his vision of a union of white and black workers creating a society of economic and racial justice. He had in fact shifted from pinning his faith on the intellectuals or talented tenth of professional and business men to pinning it on the actions of the black working classes, though quite likely they were to be led, as has been suggested, by a talented-tenth intelligentsia.[29]

In W. E. B. Du Bois then, the most distinguished Negro intellectual in the age of Booker T. Washington, we find explicitly stated most of the threads of Negro thought at that time. On the one hand he had a mystic sense of race and of the mission of the Negro, which made him sympathetic toward ideas of racial pride and solidarity as sentiments useful for racial uplift. On the other hand he held explicitly and constantly, especially after 1901, to the ideal of waging a struggle for full acceptance in American society. While at times he seemed to view segregated institutions as good in themselves, actually he regarded them as second-best instruments in the struggle for advancement and citizenship rights. He envisaged not amalgamation but cultural pluralism as the goal. He was inconsistent on the question of innate race differences, but he never admitted that Negroes were inferior. Above

---

* When white union workers at the Aluminum Ore Company in East St. Louis went on strike, the firm brought up a small number of Negroes from the Deep South to be used as strikebreakers. On July 2, 1917, fires engulfed the entire Negro residential area of the city, destroying $7,000,000 worth of property, driving 10,000 colored persons from their homes, and causing a number of deaths—estimated at 200 for Negroes and 8 for whites. Though President Theodore Roosevelt denounced the rioters, Samuel Gompers, President of the AFL, supported them by accusing capitalists of importing colored workers to supplant white labor [ed.].

28. *The Crisis*, XVI (1918), 216–217.
29. Elliott Rudwick to author, November 14, 1955.

all he insisted that Negroes wanted to be both Negroes and Americans, maintaining their racial integrity while associating on the freest terms with all American citizens, participating in American culture in its broadest sense, and contributing to it in fullest freedom.

It is notable that though Du Bois expressed the views held by most of the articulate Negroes of the age of Booker T. Washington, both in his stress on racial solidarity and economic cooperation and in his demand for full citizenship rights, nevertheless he frequently found himself in the minority. Few articulate Negroes exhibited the same extent of political independence; not many Northern Negroes agreed with his accommodating tactic of the late nineteenth century; relatively few championed the cause of liberal education as enthusiastically as he did; few either dared or cared to follow him in the extent to which he championed the protest movement during the first years of the twentieth century; and few embraced socialism or the cause of the black workers and interracial working-class solidarity. It is important to note, however, that many times people, who at heart agreed with his point of view, were not courageous enough to flout the power structure both within and outside of the Negro community as he did.

Of the great trio of Negro leaders, Douglass was the orator, Du Bois the polished writer, and Washington the practical man of affairs. Like Douglass, Du Bois has been known primarily as a protest leader, though he was not as consistent in this role as Douglass. Like Douglass, too, he exhibited a marked oscillation in his ideologies—in fact his was more marked than that of Douglass. Like Douglass he clearly stated the ultimate goals which Washington obscured. Yet Du Bois displayed more of a sense of racial solidarity than Douglass usually did. Nor did he envisage the degree of amalgamation and the loss of racial consciousness that Douglass regarded as the *summum bonum.* On the contrary he, like Washington, emphasized race pride and solidarity and economic chauvinism, though after 1905 he no longer championed support of the individualist entrepreneur but favored instead a cooperative economy. Where Washington wanted to make Negroes entrepreneurs and captains of industry in accordance with the American economic dream (a dream shared with less emphasis by Douglass), Du Bois stressed the role of the college-educated elite and later developed a vision of a world largely dominated by the colored races which would combine with the white workers in overthrowing the domination of white capital and thus secure social justice under socialism. All three emphasized the moral values in American culture and the necessity of justice for the Negro if the promise of American life were to be fulfilled. But of the three men it was Douglass who was pre-eminently the moralist, while Washington and Du Bois expressed sharply divergent economic interpretations. Where Douglass and Washington were primarily petit-bourgeois in their outlook, Du Bois played the role of the Marxist intelligentsia. Where the interest of Douglass and Washington in Africa was largely perfunctory, Du Bois exhibited a deep sense of racial identity with Africans. Above all, though only Douglass favored amalgamation, all three had as their goal the integration of Negroes into American society.

Scholar and prophet; mystic and materialist; ardent agitator for political rights and propagandist for economic cooperation; one who espoused an economic interpretation of politics and yet emphasized the necessity of political rights for economic advancement; one who denounced segregation and called for integration into American society in accordance with the principles of human brotherhood and the ideals of democracy, and at the same time one who favored the maintenance of racial solidarity and integrity and a feeling of identity with Negroes elsewhere in the world; an equalitarian who apparently believed in innate racial differences; a Marxist who was fundamentally a middle-class intellectual, Du Bois becomes the epitome of the paradoxes in American Negro thought. In fact, despite his early tendencies toward an accommodating viewpoint, and despite his strong sense of race solidarity and integrity, Du Bois expressed more effectively than any of his contemporaries the protest tendency in Negro thought, and the desire for citizenship rights and integration into American society.

✪

The Emerging Leader*—
A Contemporary View

Many believe that Du Bois will loom up in colossal enough proportions to completely wrest the scepter of Negro leadership from [Booker T.] Washington. Thus far the movement against Washington's leadership has centered and focused around no single commanding personality. In 1901, William Monroe Trotter and George Washington Forbes were the brave warriors who donned plumed helmets and ventured forth as lone, chivalrous knights to battle for Negro rights. They hurled a dreaded mace, the Boston *Guardian*. In the spring of 1903, Du Bois was the David who attacked the Goliath of race prejudice. His *Souls of Black Folk* was his sling and five pebbles. Then the gifted Grimké brothers and the able lawyer E. H. Morris and Professor W. H. H.

* The first part of this selection has been rearranged, and the titles of Ferris' chapters have been shortened and made headings. Portions of the sections called "Booker T. Washington, Du Bois, and the Niagara Movement" and "Other Colored Leaders and Du Bois' Place in History" have been omitted because they are extraneous. The deleted sections are indicated by points of ellipsis [ed].

Reprinted from *The African Abroad; or His Evolution in Western Civilization, Tracing His Development under the Caucasian Milieu,* 2 vols., by William H. Ferris (New Haven: Tuttle, Morehouse & Taylor Press, 1913), I, pp. 273–277; II, pp. 183–200, 909–920.

Hart sharpened their swords. But they all fought as individuals. The Niagara Movement means that the opposition to Mr. Washington's leadership has crystallized around Du Bois.

Du Bois is gifted with a more powerful intellect than Washington, is a more uncompromising idealist, and is a more brilliant writer. On the whole, his is the more impressive personality. But Washington is a more magnetic speaker and more astute politician, a greater humorist, and less of an aristocrat. It remains to be seen whether the Niagara Movement, headed by Du Bois, will sweep Washington and his theories from the field. This is not a personal fight, but a battle of ideas, a struggle for the supremacy of rival theories.

There have been many instances in history where men, through their military or political genius, through their gift of speech or the magnetism of a fascinating personality, have forged to the front, challenged the admiration and compelled the homage of their fellows. Such men were Samuel Adams, George Washington, Abraham Lincoln, Frederick Douglass, James G. Blaine, Theodore Roosevelt, Daniel O'Connell, Parnell, Cavour, Garibaldi, Mirabeau, Bismarck, Napoleon, and Caesar. But Du Bois is one of the few men in history who was hurled on the throne of leadership by the dynamic force of the written word. He is one of the few writers who leaped to the front as a leader and became the head of a popular movement through impressing his personality upon men by means of a book. He had no aspiration of becoming a race leader when he wrote his *Souls of Black Folk*. But that book has launched him upon a brilliant career.

It will be observed that the best productions of the most gifted colored writers have dealt with various phases and aspects of Negro character and Negro life. The colored writers have not grappled with any of the great world problems nor related the so-called race question to the various theological, literary, political, or social questions which interest thoughtful men and women. But what the colored writers lose in breadth they gain in passion, what they lose in cosmopolitanism they gain in intensity. Then, again, it is natural that the thought of the reflective colored writers should turn upon themselves and their peculiar relation to their environment. The colored man lives in two worlds. He is regarded as a man, and yet an impassable gulf separates him from other men. He is an American citizen and yet is deprived of the civil and political rights which the most illiterate and ragged foreigner can have for the mere asking. And this paradox of the Negro's position in this country impresses every colored man, who thinks at all. . . .

And now we come to the great Du Bois. Both Dunbar* and Chestnutt† have artistically uncovered to our gaze the inner life of the Negro, but Du Bois has done this and something more. He has not only graphically pictured the Negro as he is, but he has brooded and reflected upon and critically surveyed the peculiar environment of the Negro, and with his soul on fire with a righteous indignation, has written with the fervid elo-

---

* Paul Laurence Dunbar, 1872–1896, was born in Dayton, Ohio, where he completed his formal education with graduation from high school. His *Lyrics of Lowly Life* (1896), for which William Dean Howells wrote a a commendatory preface, helped to make him a national literary figure. In spite of ill health, he wrote other volumes of poetry, in both formal English and in dialect, four collections of short stories, and four novels. For an excellent critique, see Sterling A. Brown, *Negro Poetry and Drama* (Washington, D.C.: The Associates in Negro Folk Education, 1937), pp. 32–36, 45–50 [ed.].

† Charles Waddell Chesnutt (1858–1923)—Ferris' spelling is incorrect here and again on page 94—was the first Negro writer to use the short story as a serious medium for literary expression. Born in Cleveland, he taught in North Carolina, the scene of his first collection of tales in dialect, *The Conjure Woman*. Professor Sterling Brown in 1937 accepted the view of a "careful critic" who stated that Chesnutt " 'was the first Negro novelist, and he is still the best.' " Chesnutt's first novel, *The House Behind the Cedars* (1900), is concerned like much of his writing with relations between white and colored people. His last novel, *The Colonel's Dream,* was published in 1905. In 1928, Chesnutt, "for his pioneering work as a literary artist depicting the life and struggles of Americans of Negro descent," received the Spingarn Achievement Award, a gold medal given annually to American Negroes who have made distinguished contributions in their chosen fields. His daughter, Helen M. Chesnutt, wrote *Charles Waddell Chesnutt: Pioneer of the Color Line* (Chapel Hill: The University of North Carolina Press, 1952) [ed.].

quence of a Carlyle. If one desires to see how it feels to be a Negro and a man at the same time, if one desires to see how a sensitive and refined Negro mentally and spiritually reacts against social, civil, and political ostracism, if one desires to see a Negro passing judgment upon his civil and political status, and critically dissecting American race prejudice as with a scalping knife, he must go to Du Bois.

I well remember the thrill and pleasure with which I read his *Souls of Black Folk*. It was an eventful day in my life. It affected me just like Carlyle's *Heroes and Hero Worship* in my sophomore days at Yale, Emerson's *Nature and Other Addresses* in my senior year, and Carlyle's *Sartor Resartus* in my graduate days.

The reading of these three books were epochs and crucial moments in my moral and spiritual life. Henceforth the world was a different world for me. They revealed to me my own spiritual birthright, showed that there was a divine spark in every soul, and that God was manifest in every human soul and breathed his own nature into every human soul. Du Bois' *Souls of Black Folk* came to me as a bolt from the blue. It was the rebellion of a fearless soul, the protest of a noble nature against the blighting American caste prejudice. It proclaimed in thunder tones and in words of magic beauty the worth and sacredness of human personality even when clothed in a black skin.

Du Bois is a literary artist who can clothe his thought in such forms of poetic beauty that we are captivated by the opulent splendor and richness of his diction, while our souls are being stirred by his burning eloquence. His style is not only graphic and picturesque, he can not only vividly describe a county, in his brilliant chapter upon the Black Belt, but there is a dreamy suggestiveness to his chapters "Upon our Spiritual Strivings," "The Wings of Atalanta," and "Alexander Crummell," a delicate literary touch, which entitles Du Bois to a place in the magic circle of prose poets. As a literary genius he ranks with Newman, Ruskin, Renan, and Taine, and he has come to a self-realization of the ideals of his own race.

What then does Du Bois lack? As Dunbar lacks a grasp of

the problems that interest and perplex the modern mind, so Du Bois seems to ignore the unity of human history. He is the voice of one crying in the wilderness, "The black man has the same feelings and thoughts and aspirations as the white man." It is a voice that has caught the ear of this country, and made its appeal to the American conscience. But it is a lone, solitary voice. It is Du Bois, an individual, crying out in righteous indignation and piteous wail, because he and his race, in the valley below, are prevented by the walls of American caste prejudice from climbing to the heights of Mt. Olympus and banqueting with the other immortals there. It is a Pilgrim, goaded and hurt because his race alone is shut out from the paradise of equal civil and political rights and equality of opportunity. It is not a prophetic voice, freighted with a message from the eternal, speaking, not with human force and emphasis, but with a "Thus saith the Lord" assurance and authority.

I understand the book because I am a Negro. White people put it down, surprised that a colored man's soul should be so sensitive to slights and insults.

But suppose Du Bois had gone back to Father Abraham, and showed that Abraham, Moses, Elijah, Elisha, and Isaiah championed the idea of the sovereignty of God, that they believed that he breathed into the nostrils of man the breath of life, and that man became a living soul, and that Christ completed this conception and revelation by declaring the brotherhood of man; suppose Du Bois saw in the religious faith of the Dark Ages, in the wresting of the Magna Carta from King John, in the Protestant Reformation in Germany, in the Puritan Reformation in England, in the American Revolution and the French Revolution, nothing but stages in the practical application to life of Christ's disclosure of the sacredness and worth of human personality; suppose that he saw in the anti-slavery struggle and the Negro's emancipation, not only the recognition of the Negro as a man but the application to him of Christ's divine revelation, and the culmination of the history of fifty centuries—then Du Bois' argument would have swept the country off its feet, because the tidal wave of five thousand years of history would have backed his argument with its irresistible movement, and would have carried his argument along with its resistless roll.

Then the Americans would not have seen in Du Bois a Negro chafing because he and his people have been caged and fettered, but a Daniel who reads the handwriting on the wall, and sees the hand of the Almighty in the progressive movement of human history. Matthew Arnold, the doubter, saw in human history "an eternal power not ourselves that makes for righteousness." Yes, what is human history but man's coming to self-knowledge, man realizing his own spiritual birthright, man realizing the moral and spiritual meaning and significance of life, man realizing that the same human soul pulses and throbs in men of all ages and races and colors.

Just as we cannot explain that impulse in grass and flower and seed that transforms the world into a fairyland every spring, save as we see that it is the Divine Mind and Life breaking into expression, so we cannot understand righteous indignation at wrong, and the impulse in man toward a nobler life and a saving faith in humanity, save as we see in it the stirring within human nature of God, the World Spirit, who is constantly uttering himself in nature and human nature. If Du Bois had grasped these truths as Carlyle and Emerson and Browning did, then he could say, "It is not I, Du Bois, who speak, but God, the World Spirit, in whom I live and move and have my being, speaking in me." As it is, *The Souls of Black Folk* is the protest of Du Bois, the individual, and not the protest of the universe against caste prejudice.

But it may be that if the subjective and personal note was not so clear and strong in *The Souls of Black Folk*; if instead of having for its keynote a despairing wail, it had rung with the buoyant faith of a Browning, the book might not have caught the ear of the age in the way that it has. Perhaps just such a pessimistic view of the race question was needed to arouse the American mind out of its lethargy, awaken the American conscience to its duty to the Negro, and acquaint the world with the

unrest and dissatisfaction of colored men and women, who faced
a blighting and blasting caste prejudice.

That Du Bois' *Souls of Black Folk* has become the political
bible of the Negro race, that he is regarded by the colored people
as the long-looked-for political Messiah, the Moses that will lead
them out of the Egypt of peonage, across the Red Sea of Jim
Crow legislation, through the wilderness of disfranchisement and
restricted opportunity, and into the promised land of liberty of
opportunity and equality of rights, is shown by the recent Niagara
Movement, which has crowned Du Bois as the Joshua before
whom it is hoped the Jericho of American caste prejudice will fall
down. In July, 1905, colored men from thirteen different states,
representing graduates from Harvard and Yale Universities, professors in Howard University, Washington, D. C., and some of
the most prominent colored educators, preachers, lawyers, and
businessmen of the South and West, assembled at Niagara Falls,
issued the declaration of Negro manhood and hailed Du Bois as
the standard-bearer of Negro rights and Negro liberty.

BOOKER T. WASHINGTON, DU BOIS, AND THE NIAGARA MOVEMENT

From the period when I, a boy of twelve, about a score of years
ago, read the *Life and Times of Frederick Douglass,* up to the
present time, I have been a close and serious student of the race
problem. Two racial phenomena have impressed me, as I have
marked the rise and progress of the recently emancipated race—
one was the rise and decline of Booker T. Washington; the other
was the origin and growth of the Niagara Movement.

That a man who was born a slave, and a member of a pro-
scribed and despised race, could reach a position of commanding
eminence and world-wide fame; could, for a time, win the confidence of the businessmen of the country, the respect of the
educators; could, for a while, dine with the aristocratic Wana-
maker and with the President of the United States; could finally

so send the prestige of his name and the splendor of his achievements across the Atlantic that next to President Roosevelt he became the best known American in the world—seems to me to be one of the crowning miracles of Negro history. Then as we read the steps by which he built up this world-wide fame and international renown, we seem to be reading of another Aladdin and his lamp. How he walked his way to Hampton, sleeping under a sidewalk; how he struggled to get an education; how a quarter of a century ago he went down into the black belt of the South and started a small school in an old church and dilapidated shanty in Tuskegee, Alabama; how he organized and marshalled his forces at Tuskegee; how he developed a magnificent industrial plant there and really built up a Negro school community there with over 2,000 pupils and lands and buildings valued at a quarter of a million dollars, and secured an endowment fund of nearly two millions; how he captured the heart of the South, won at first the confidence of the North and the ear of the President of the United States, until he became the educational and political boss and dictator of the Negro race of ten million human beings, is familiar to every schoolboy in the land.

That Dr. W. E. B. Du Bois, Editor William Monroe Trotter, L. M. Hershaw, F. H. Murray, Professor William H. H. Hart, Professor William H. Richards, Rev. R. R. Ransom, Rev. J. Milton Waldron, Professor W. S. Scarborough, Mr. F. L. McGhee, Mr. J. R. Clifford, Mr. A. H. Grimké, Professor William Bulkley, Rev. Owen M. Waller, Rev. Frazier Miller, Rev. Dr. Bishop, Rev. Charles Satchell Morris, Lawyers E. H. Morris, Carter and Crawford, and Clement G. Morgan, Mr. G. W. Forbes, Rev. A. Clayton Powell, Bishop Alexander W. Walters, and other educated Negroes should dare to form and join the Niagara Movement, which promulgated ideas antipodal to those of Dr. Washington and removed the halo that surrounded the brow of a man who was firmly entrenched in the world's regard, strikes me as nothing less than marvelous—as the second miracle in Negro history.

I believe that natural causes are behind the Negro's desire for his civil and political rights. A hundred years ago today* every one of my ancestors except two were free people and they secured their freedom soon after the War of 1812. Sixty years ago today both of my grandfathers owned and paid taxes on the roof which sheltered them and their families. My father and three of my uncles fought in the Civil War. Today my relatives own nearly $50,000 worth of taxable property in the State of Delaware. None of them are wealthy, but a score of them have managed to secure a modest home. Now there are hundreds of colored men and women in the North and East and West and scores in the Southland, whose family record is similar to mine. The free colored people of America owned nearly twenty million dollars worth of personal property and real estate at the time of the Civil War.

Since the Civil War, colored boys have been class orators and commencement speakers, and colored girls valedictorians and salutatorians in high schools and academies; colored students have won literary and oratorical prizes and honors in Yale, Harvard, Amherst, Dartmouth, Brown, Williams, Boston University, Cornell University, University of Pennsylvania, and other New England and Northern institutions of learning. Du Bois and Kelly Miller won national and international renown as sociologists; Frederick Douglass, J. C. Price, Booker T. Washington, Rev. R. R. Ransom, R. C. Bruce, and William Pickens as orators; Dunbar and Braithwaite as poets; Locke as a Rhodes scholar; Chestnutt as a novelist; Tanner as an artist; Coleridge-Taylor as a musician; Crummell, Bassett, Greener, Grimké, and Bouchet as ripe scholars, and Blyden as a linguist, Arabic scholar, and interpreter of Mohammedanism. In a word, the black man dazzled the eye of mankind, because as soon as he was emancipated from bondage he began to aspire after and absorb and assimilate and appropriate the most advanced and most complex civilization that the world has yet seen. The North welcomed, encouraged, and pushed to the front every aspiring and ambitious colored youth.

* About 1813, for Ferris' book was published in 1913 [ed.].

But then, in the summer of 1895, came Dr. Washington's famous Atlanta speech, followed by other addresses in which he ridiculed the higher aspiration and spiritual strivings of his own people and asked his own people to cease contending for their manhood rights, which things the Anglo-Saxon race has held dear and sacred in its own history and for which he sacrificed ease and happiness, yea life itself. Did not President Eliot of Harvard University in his "America's Contribution to Civilization" mention "The Development of Manhood Suffrage" as one of the five American contributions to civilization? And yet Dr. Washington in his Atlanta speech said, "We began at the Senate instead of at the plough. . . . The wisest among my people realize that agitating questions of social and political equality is the sheerest nonsense, etc." In that celebrated Atlanta speech we behold the spectacle of a Negro leader saying the things the Georgia white man desired him to say. The South hailed him as the Moses of his people. Then Dr. Washington lectured in Northern churches and imported into the North the South's estimate of the Negro. He minimized the intellectual achievements of the Negro and cut the foundation from under his civic privileges and political rights. The North soon began to think and feel that it had forced the higher education and civil and political rights upon the black man before he was ready for it and silently acquiesced in the South's practically undoing the work of Sumner, Garrison, Phillips, Thaddeus Stevens, Roscoe Conkling, and George Boutwell. What more natural than that the dammed-up waters of Negro striving and Negro aspirations should burst the dam erected by the Alabamian and swell into a formidable protest against the stifling and smothering teachings of Booker T. Washington.

The opposition to Booker T. Washington's leadership experienced difficulty in making headway for two reasons. First, the opposition produced no personality as resourceful and masterful, as tactful, strategic, and diplomatic as himself. And any movement that does not center and group itself around some great and commanding personality breaks to pieces.

Again, Trotter and the Niagara Movement underrated the weight of General Armstrong's* influence in this country. His philosophy of the Negro question embodied the fundamentals of civilization, because he advocated simple industry, settled habits of life, and simple home life. This latter fact drew around Washington, his pupil, the men who represented the financial bone and sinew of the country and were the molders of public thought and shapers of public opinion. And Trotter's campaign of condemnation and vituperation was powerless to convert his Anglo-Saxon friends. Had his critics recognized that his gospel of industrialism embodied the basic principles of Negro development, but that his industrial propaganda was not the entire program, they would have gone before the country with a stronger case. But since Dr. Du Bois has been elected secretary of the Society for the Advancement of Colored People he has gained in weight and influence. . . .

Empiricism claims that moral ideas are derived *a posteriori* from experience. Institutionalism claims that moral ideas are derived *a priori* from the innate functioning and forth-putting of the human mind. Materialism claims that mind states are epiphenomena, which are thrown off by the brain and caused by brain states. Idealism claims that something more than an excitation of nerve centers in the brain and a commotion in nerve tracts is needed to explain the poetic genius of a Shakespeare and Homer, the moral insight of a Kant and Paul, and the moral choice of a Caesar and Luther. In a word, idealism claims that while the life of the mind is connected with the life of the brain, the activity of the mind transcends the activity of the brain. The history of human thought shows that there is an element of truth in all of these views and that a true philosophy blends these scattered violet rays into the white light of truth.

Now, that is what I attempt to do in this history of the Negro race. Dr. Washington has clearly seen the economic and industrial phase of the race problem; Dr. Du Bois the moral and

* General Samuel Armstrong, the founder (in 1868) of Hampton Institute, and its principal until 1893, was Booker T. Washington's mentor [ed.].

political phase. General Armstrong's propaganda was basic and fundamental because the bread problem is the most important problem of life, and because in advocating simple industry, simple home life, and a settled mode of life, he was reaching the bedrock of modern civilization and grasping the fundamentals of civilization. I regard Dr. Du Bois' work as important and necessary, for he sees that the Negro is a member of the human family, belongs to the genus *vir* as well as to the genus *homo,* and has the same spiritual wants and needs that the rest of mankind has. He continued the noble work begun by Rev. A. F. Beard.*

Without industrial education and an economic basis, we would have a tree without roots, which would soon topple over. Without the higher education and the ballot, which confers dignity and self-respect upon an individual, we would have roots and a trunk but no leaves and branches upon our tree; we would only have an embryonic and not a developed tree. The first thought of a man should be to provide food, shelter, and clothes for himself and his family. His next thought should be the moral training of his children. The teachings of history show that no race that is without the ballot in a republic has ever been respected. The sciences of psychology and ethics show that pride, pride of self, pride of family, pride of race, and pride of ancestry are the bulwarks and props of feminine virtue. In a word, we say that the Negro is a moral personality of the genus *vir,* as well as a physical organism of the genus *homo.* Now to develop these ideas. . . .

Booker T. Washington is undoubtedly right when he says that a man who owns a bank, or a brick block, or a railroad line, or a steamboat company, is a potent factor in modern life. He is undoubtedly right when he preaches industrial education and urges the accumulating of property. In this history of the Negro race I assert that he is one of the industrial saviors of the Southern Negro, that he has solved the bread-and-butter problem for nearly

* Augustus Field Beard was the author of *A Crusade of Brotherhood: A History of the American Missionary Association* (New York, 1909) [ed.].

ten millions of toiling and struggling Negroes; but not the political and the moral problem. He has realized the necessity of making bread; but not the importance of making men. His philosophy of life has not rated character at its face value. He lacked General Armstrong's idealism. And that is why he has lost his grip on the world's attention.

But man is a metaphysical, religious, artistic, and moral being as well as a physical being, who needs to be clothed, sheltered, and fed. The late John Henry Newman, in one of his impassioned flights of eloquence, says, "Man is a being of genius, passion, intellect, conscience, power. He exercises these various gifts in various ways, in great deeds, in great thoughts, in heroic acts, in hateful crimes. He founds states, he fights battles, he builds cities, he ploughs the forest, he subdues the elements, he rules his kind. He creates vast ideas and influences many generations. . . . He pours out his fervid soul in poetry; he sways to and fro, he soars, he dives in his restless speculation, his lips drop eloquence, he touches the canvas and it glows with beauty; he sweeps the strings, and they thrill with an aesthetic meaning." . . .

Some students of history have regarded the wresting of the Magna Carta from King John by the English Barons at Runnymede as the true beginning of English history. Gray, in his immortal elegy, speaks thus:

> Some village Hampden here may rest
> Who with dauntless breast
> The petty tyrant of his fields withstood.

The philosopher Hegel says that all human history is but the struggle of the human spirit for personal freedom, the endeavor of the human personality to express itself, to develop its latent powers and capacities and to assert its latent manhood. History

* The correct stanza is:
> Some village Hampden, that with dauntless breast
> The little tyrant of his fields withstood,
> Some mute inglorious Milton here may rest,
> Some Cromwell guiltless of his country's blood.   [ed.]

shows unmistakably that the love of liberty is innate, that the desire for freedom is an inborn characteristic of the human soul. Such are the teachings of sociology and history.

But it may be objected that these are but the views of a doctrinaire or a political theorist, of a closet philosopher and bookworm. It is stated that the Negro is mentally and morally different from the Anglo-Saxon. It is true that the great race stocks which have made contributions to history have psychical and psychological qualities peculiar to themselves alone. The Hebrews were endowed with peculiar religious gifts; the Greeks were endowed with philosophic, artistic, and poetic gifts; the Romans were gifted with a genius for war and government; the Germans were gifted with a remarkable insight into philosophy and theology; the Anglo-Saxon possessed a genius for war and parliamentary government and a desire for simple home life and a settled mode of industrial life. So, too, in America the native Yankee, the Irish immigrant, the Italian, and the Jew have psychical and racial characteristics that are peculiar to themselves alone. So, too, the Negro has race traits and tendencies peculiar to himself alone. He is an emotional and happy and warm-hearted and sympathetic being. He has a gift for music and eloquence, a love and taste for dress and finery, and a humble and childlike trust and belief in the Almighty. But while this is true, still all the great race stocks, the Hebrew, Greek, Roman, German, and Anglo-Saxon, all the different races in America, the English, the Irish, the German, the Frenchman, the Italian, the Jew, the Indian, and the Negro have certain human characteristics common to all alike. All shudder at the mystery of death; all have an innate longing for life and liberty; all grope toward the Eternal and reach in their soaring aspiration the thought of some Great Mysterious Being, some Infinite Power, who is the creator of this universe; all strive to express and give utterance to what is deepest and most fundamental within them. In a word, the Negro is a member of the human family. We must recognize his humanity. And he desires those common rights that this country bestows so freely upon the priest and prophet, the prince and pauper, the beggar and king, who come fleeing from the persecution and oppression of his mother country or fatherland and knocks for admission to this country, which is an asylum for the oppressed and persecuted of every land and clime. For the Negro in America to be satisfied with less than is given to every ragged, dirty immigrant, every ignorant, illiterate, poverty-stricken, and bad-smelling foreigner, who comes to our shores, would be for him to be less than a man. If he would, without a protest or audible murmur, wear his color as the badge of his inferiority, he would lose the respect of the civilized world, and he would lose that self-respect and personal pride necessary alike for feminine virtue and manly self-reliance.

The world never puts a higher estimate upon a race or individual than that race or individual puts upon himself. If the Negro would voluntarily self-efface himself from politics and content himself with providing a living for himself, he would be despised by mankind and would justly be regarded as the most inferior of all the races. Then, again, it is true that the dynamic force of the ideal is the lifting power in human lives and the psychic uplift of the human race. Where, then, could come the inspiration for progress, if the Negro regarded himself as an inferior being, if he regarded his natural sphere as clinging to the lowest rounds of life's ladder, as vegetating in the lowest strata of human society?

Some pessimists say that the Negro will either be subjugated, exterminated, deported, or amalgamated; that the white man will never recognize his black brother as a full-fledged or full-orbed man. One distinguished Negro educator wrote me, "The original barbarity of the Teuton is mildly tempered with Christian hypocrisy."

A distinguished educator, who has the blood of so many races coursing in his veins that it is hard to tell which race he is identified with, wrote me, "I have lost hope for your people. I do not see how their condition can be bettered; indeed I am convinced that their condition will grow worse and worse instead of better, for reasons inhering in themselves as well as those outside of them. All the powerful forces of our civilization are coming more and more to be exerted against them—they are doomed."

But I must confess that dark and gloomy as is the outlook, at present, cheerless and hopeless as seem our prospects, I look forward to the future with hope. I believe that the Negro race will slowly and surely absorb and assimilate and appropriate the highest elements of the Anglo-Saxon civilization and embed the Anglo-Saxon ideals into the ground roots of its being, into the very fibres of its moral nature. And then, I believe that the innate and inborn sense of justice which slumbers in the Anglo-Saxon at times will reassert itself and welcome the black man into the brotherhood of the human family, into the circle of his politics. While the Anglo-Saxon will not share with us his *posterity* he will share with us his *prosperity*. If it were not so then is democracy a failure and Christianity a lie. Did not Emerson, the American Plato, say, "The Intellect is miraculous, who has it has the talisman. Though the black man's skin be as dark as midnight, if he has genius, it will shine through and be as transparent as the everlasting stars."

Some have regarded Emerson as a bookworm, a closet philosopher, and an impractical dreamer; but I believe that his insight into human nature, into the moral springs of conduct, was the truest and subtlest that the world has seen since that God-man, nineteen hundred years ago, by the Sea of Galilee, spoke as never man spoke before. Can we not trust the intuitions and divinations of such a prophet, seer, and sage as Emerson?

We must remember that for a thousand years Europe groped in darkness, intellectual and moral. The intellect was fettered and Europe ran riot with murder and bloodshed. Kings and queens killed each other and the rival claimants for the throne. The Feudal barons were but border ruffians and highwaymen on a colossal scale. It was unsafe to travel alone and unattended during the Middle Ages. What lifted England and Europe out of that dark and dismal night called the Dark Ages? It was the founding of universities in England and Europe and the revival of learning, the rediscovery of the Greek world, the Protestant Reformation, which emancipated the intellect and the soul, and the French Revolution, which ushered in modern democracy and bathed Europe in a sea of blood. Can the Negro, then, rise in civilization without the uplifting influences of education and political rights?

THE BLACK MAN'S STRIVINGS AND ASPIRATIONS

There are three attitudes which intelligent and thoughtful colored men assume toward the all-embracing and all-encompassing fact of American caste prejudice. Professor William H. H. Hart of the Law Department of Howard University says that we must ignore caste prejudice and live and act as if it did not exist; we must forget that we are colored men and live and work on the assumption that we are men the same as other human beings. Dr. Booker T. Washington, the founder of Tuskegee Institute, says that we must recognize American caste prejudice as a fact that cannot be striven against; but to which we must adjust and adapt ourselves just as we recognize the fact of gravitation as one of the immutable facts and laws of nature. To disregard it and jump from a tower or leap over a precipice is to court and meet certain death. So the colored man who clamors for his civil and political rights, who does not lie down, keep still, and remain quiet when the white man of the South tells him to, is as wise as the man who butts his head against a stone wall or as the bull who charges into a locomotive that is coming toward it at full speed, with steam up and throttle valves thrown back. Dr. Du Bois differs from Professor Hart and agrees with Dr. Washington in that he recognizes caste prejudice as a basic and fundamental fact of the black man's existence, which cannot be ignored or passed by, by our closing our eyes to it, just as the ostrich does not elude its pursuers by burying its head in the sand and thinking that because it does not see its pursuers, its pursuers cannot see it. On the other hand,

Dr. Du Bois differs from Dr. Washington and agrees with Professor Hart in holding that American caste prejudice can be overcome by the colored man's endeavoring to think and feel and act and live like a human being and an American citizen clothed in the full panoply of his constitutional rights.

There is an element of truth in each of these three attitudes. Professor Hart holds that the Negro is an imprisoned group, that he is confined on an island, as it were, and prevented by American caste prejudice from getting out into the sea of humanity that surrounds him upon all sides. He holds that it may be, confined and ostracised as he is, isolated in a group with a separate social and church life to himself, and developing within that group different social classes and building up an aristocracy of his own, the Negro may develop valuable race traits. But he also holds that if the Negro goes through life branding and libeling himself as a Negro, and thinking, feeling, acting as if he were a Negro, the country will take him at his own estimate and treat him as if he were a peculiar being. But if he regards himself as an American citizen and acts accordingly, the country will so treat him. Caesar saw that the only way to conquer the barbarians was to make incursions into Gaul. Hart holds that the Negro must accordingly transcend his Negro environment and participate in the national life. Hence he refused to go into a Jim Crow car in Maryland, refused to allow himself or wife to be written down colored or Negro on the marriage register, or his child to be written down colored or Negro on the birth register. As Hart's father was a white man of aristocratic lineage and his mother a refined mulatto, he is theoretically justified in his attitude. It is the only way to overcome race prejudice in the North or West; but if Hart were to carry out his principles South of the Mason and Dixon's line, he would suffer the experience of Bishop Phillips and wife and Dr. R. R. Ransom; the former were ejected from a sleeping [car], the latter from a Pullman palace car for refusing to remain in a Jim Crow car. So Hart's theory to ignore race prejudice and act as if it did not exist is the ideal attitude. But it cannot be lived out to the letter in the South.

Dr. Washington's policy is to recognize race prejudice as a fundamental fact, just as one recognizes the law of gravitation as the basic law of nature. His advice is to buckle down to hard work, don't make any fuss, and everything will come out right in the long run. It is a rash man who bombards Mr. Washington's theories with criticisms, for he has entrenched himself behind the impregnable walls of Tuskegee. Dr. Washington is something like Alcibiades. During the civic turmoils in Athens, Alcibiades would retire to the temple, where none would dare disturb him and molest him within those sacred walls, and he would there carry on his work. Now the sanctuary within whose sacred precincts Mr. Washington is safe against criticism is Tuskegee. He and his work are so indissolubly connected that to criticise his theories seems an attack upon his work. But we must distinguish between the vulnerability of his social and political philosophy and the utility of his work at Tuskegee; just as we do not accept Mr. Carnegie as an authority in orthography because he has been a successful financier and amassed a colossal fortune and has dotted the land with libraries. . . .

In his *Gospel of Work,* Mr. Washington has emphasized a basic law of human progress. But it has not been true in the past history of the race that all a man has to do is to toil and labor and save his money, and civic and political recognition will come to him. It has been true in the past history of Greece, Rome, England, America, Germany, and France that in order for men to secure civic rights, social and political privileges, they have usually been compelled to clamor and cry for them and sometimes strive and fight for them.

Men do not often give us the recognition that we deserve. They usually withhold that gift from cowards and bestow it on those who possess the courage to demand it. Then, too, in attempting to solve the race question with the Negrosaxon eliminated from politics, in solving the race question on the basis of the Negro-saxon being a hopeless and helpless social and political unit, Mr. Washington is running counter to the teachings of history. The race problem is practically the Negrosaxon's place in American politics. Everything hinges upon the ballot. It is the door which ushers one into the blessings of justice in the courtroom, educational oportunities, and civic privileges. It is the gate through which one enters the paradise of equality of rights and liberty of opportunity. Without the ballot the Negrosaxon is a helpless and hopeless pariah in society, absolutely at the mercy of a dominant prejudiced race. He is a member of a doomed race. He cannot demand anything like a man. He can only beg and plead, and weep and wail, and whine and cry for his rights.

Professor W. E. B. Du Bois sees that a man is not the slave of circumstances, but transforms his environment after the pattern of his ideals. He recognizes with Professor Hart that a man by his own attitude may transform the world's estimate of him. Whether Du Bois is right or wrong, he is following in the footsteps of Paul, Athanasius, Luther, Knox, Calvin, Cromwell, Milton, Hampden, Samuel Adams, Benjamin Franklin, Thomas Jefferson, Sumner, Garrison, and Phillips. What is human history but the attempt of man to reach out after the highest that he knows of and to struggle to express the deepest that is within him? Hence Du Bois is following after the saints and heroes, the sages and seers of all ages.

The same principle for which Martin Luther contended, when he nailed his ninety-five theses to the church door at Erfurt* and burned the Pope's bull; the same principle for which the Pilgrim Fathers contended, when they crossed the Atlantic in a frail bark and faced starvation and attacks by Indians and bore the rigors of a New England winter; the same principle for which Roger Williams contended, when he left the Massachusetts Colony; the same principle for which the Boston patriots contended, when they threw the tea overboard; these are the same principles for which the critics of Booker Washington contend, and that principle is the right of private judgment, the right of an individual to think for himself and to express his deepest thoughts and fundamental convictions. The critics of Booker T. Washington are the

* This should be Wittenberg [ed.].

twentieth-century champions of freedom of thought and liberty of conscience; they are the spiritual descendants of Martin Luther and the brave men and women who crossed the Atlantic in the *Mayflower*. The mantles of Samuel Adams and Wendell Phillips have fallen upon our shoulders.

Yes, all the ancient world sacrificed the individual to the State, and in Japan, which is the modern representative of Oriental ideals, it is not regarded as a terrible thing for a girl to prostitute herself to support a family. Education in the ancient world has to produce a certain type rather than develop the individual.

But in the spread of Christianity, which regarded the soul of everyone as of value in God's sight, and in the ascendency of the noble Teutonic peoples, who reverenced their own personality as something sacred and divine, who craved for personal recognition, we see the emergence of the idea that the individual was supreme and of value for himself alone. For nearly a thousand years these ideas smoldered during the so-called Dark Ages. They undermined Roman slavery and medieval serfdom. Then came the Renaissance, which emancipated the intellect of Europe from the domain of the medieval schoolmen; the Protestant Reformation, which emancipated the conscience of the individual believer from the authority of the infallible Pope; the French Revolution, which toppled over the doctrine of the divine right of kings and [led to] the democracy of the nineteenth and twentieth centuries. And I believe that the grand Anglo-Saxon has been the modern champion of the doctrine of liberty and independence, and of the worth and sacredness of human personality. The fact that Napoleon, the son of a revolution, could elect himself as emperor over a republic which had dethroned and beheaded a king; the fact that Louis Napoleon, his nephew, could, in December, 1851, transform the Second Republic into a Second Empire; the fact that the French people lean to socialism, shows that for them the state idea is more supreme than the idea of individual development. The German believes in method. Bismarck welded the army into a perfect fighting machine. He understood the German nature and made the soldier a part of a machine. But in England and America we see the aggressiveness of the Anglo-Saxon.

So we may say that the meaning of human history is the growth and spread of the conception of personal freedom; freedom to express one's personality and manifest one's individuality; freedom to think one's thoughts and utter one's deepest longings and cravings; freedom of thought, speech, and action in religion, politics, and civil life.

The difference between ancient and modern history is that in the ancient Oriental world the individual was ignored, while in the modern Occidental world he is recognized. In China and Japan the family was supreme; the individual was nothing. In Hindu philosophy the individual was lost and swallowed up and absorbed in the absolute. In Persia, Egypt, and Babylon, the individual was nothing; the monarch was supreme. Even in Greece, where the individual expressed his freedom in the realm of art and literature; and in Rome, where the right of private property and freedom in willing such property was recognized, the individual existed for the sake of the State, and not the State for the sake of the individual. That was the dream of Plato's republic. Aristotle was the first ancient thinker who clearly recognized the importance of the individual.

The Athenian democracy and the Roman republic meant that the development of personality and the assertion of individuality applied to all free citizens but not to the slaves. The growth and dissemination of Christianity, the rise of the Teutonic races, the abolition of serfdom in the Middle Ages, the revival of learning and the rediscovery of the Greek world, the Protestant and Puritan reformations, the American and French revolutions, meant that the development of human personality, the assertion of human individuality applied to all white men and women. And the twentieth century will witness the application of the ideals of personality, the conception of individuality, to the darker races. It will witness the embracing of the darker races within the brotherhood of the human family. It will mean that the Negro will be regarded as a person and not as a thing. It will see the sons and daughters of Ham attaining to selfhood. As Du Bois, the Emerson and Thucydides of the Negro race, says, "The problem of the twentieth century [is] the problem of the color line." I wonder if the Anglo-Saxon will ever realize that deep in the soul of the Negro divine impulses are stirring and are longing to break into expression in song and story and eloquent speech; that his revolt against some of the teachings of the Tuskegee sage express his desire to enter into the spiritual inheritance of the human race.

The most pathetic spectacle about the attitude of the American mind toward the Negro is not the facts of lynching, disfranchisement, and the enacting of Jim Crow, laws, for there are some vicious and boisterous Negroes who ought to be Jim-Crowed and disfranchised, but the fact that the higher courses have been eliminated from the State colleges and the higher schools for Negroes in the South; the fact that the Northern philanthropists are now refusing to aid the schools and colleges for the higher education of the Negro; the fact that the self-reliant, the self-supporting class of colored people are Jim-Crowed. As I read the daily press, the weekly and monthly magazines, I discover it is not the illiterate, vicious Negro who is the recipient of the most abuse and vituperation and villification; but it is the colored man who desires to become cultured and strives also for the bread of spiritual life. And the Niagara Movement is a protest against this low estimate of the Negro. It says Booker Washington is right in urging Negroes to become an agricultural, industrial, and economic factor in the country; but the colored man needs to aspire after the highest things in the American civilization, needs the ballot, whose possession exalts an individual and makes him a man. The Niagara Movement is but the world impulses of thought and feeling manifesting themselves in the Negro consciences. It is but the *zeitgeist* affecting Negro minds, it is but the stirring within the Negro's soul of the Immanent World Ground, the welling up within human nature of the Immanent World Spirit. It shows that the Negro is human and sensitive to slights and insults.

The Niagara Movement is but the surging up into the soul of the Negro of that Immanent World Spirit, who has been weaving at the loom of time for centuries, of whom the Apostle Paul said, "In him we live and move and have our being." It will be victorious, because it is in harmony with the tendencies of this democratic age and the genius of Christianity. It will become true of it that the stone that the builder rejected will some day become the head of the column; it will galvanize the Negro with the electricity of hope. From the Great Lakes to the Gulf, it will send the thrill of life throughout the Negro race. It will start a tidal wave of sentiment that will move mountain-high from the Atlantic to the Pacific, lifting the Negro out of the valley of the Shadow of Death to the Mount Ararat of Hope.

What William Roscoe Thayer, in his *Dawn of the Italian Independence,* says of Italy may well be said of the American Negro: "We must look for signs of progress in the aspirations rather than in the achievements of anything conspicuous. For this movement was inward and subtle; and its outward expression in deeds was stubbornly repressed. For no man can speak the truth that is in him when the hand of the oppressor is on his throat."

This being true, an epical grandeur is attached to the forces working unseen beneath the surface, which like the forces of nature, asserting themselves in budding spring, are slowly transforming the thought, life, and character of the Negro. And that is why the Niagara Movement has an epical significance and why Du Bois is the hero in the battle for spiritual freedom and Negro manhood.

There is one thing in the attitude of the American mind toward the Negrosaxon that I question and that is the leveling tendency, which acts upon the principle "all coons look alike to me," and which links all Negrosaxons indiscriminately together, good, bad, and indifferent, in a mass. President Roosevelt erred this way, when he in his annual message of December, 1906, intimated that the good Negrosaxons sympathized with and shielded Negro criminals. He erred again when he took it for granted that a whole battalion of the Twenty-fifth Infantry entered into a conspiracy of silence to shield the dozen who are said to have shot up Brownsville. New England philanthropists erred again when they intimated that the colored graduate of Yale and Harvard ought to go South to be a missionary and apostle of culture to his people, instead of hovering around Boston, New York, Philadelphia, Washington, and Chicago.

The mass of Southern Negroes are so densely ignorant, and so averse to learning and so hostile to scholarship and culture, that it will be at least twenty-five years before a colored scholar will be appreciated at his face value in the South. At present, the attitude of the Southern Negro to the Northern-born colored graduate of Yale and Harvard is one of hostility, distrust, and suspicion, of cynical, carping criticism rather than one of sympathetic appreciation. . . .

OTHER COLORED LEADERS AND DU BOIS' PLACE IN HISTORY

I heard Dr. Du Bois lecture upon John Brown a few years ago and I now regard him not only as the most gifted writer our race in America has yet produced, but as one of the greatest living American Negroes. The masterly way in which he described the decay of feudalism in Europe; the attempt at the same time to revive feudalism, the doctrine of a servile class, in America; the growth of the eighteenth-century ideas of the rights of man and the consequent undermining of the structure of human slavery, in the introduction to his address; the masterly manner in which he showed how the invention of the cotton gin and the demand for cotton gave a new impetus to slavery; the masterly way in which he analyzed the forces that made John Brown the man that he was, and his graphic picture of the Prometheus of the nineteenth century, all this shows that Du Bois possesses a philosophic and comprehensive grasp of great movements in history and a light, graceful touch in making the past live again before our eyes, quite an endowment for a literary man.

And then Du Bois' personality as a speaker shows that he possesses the note of personal ascendency that makes one an effective speaker and a leader of men, as well as unique gifts as a writer and historian. Cardinal Newman was one of the few literary men of the nineteenth century who possessed the masterful personality that makes one a leader of men. And I believe that it is the blending of philosophic and literary qualities, the blending of literary gifts with the strenuous will that makes one a leader of men that constitutes Du Bois' unique greatness. Is he then an orator and a born leader of men as well as a philosophic historian and prose poet?

Du Bois is not a mob orator who can set an audience crazy with excitement, cause men and women to run up and down the aisles, jump over benches, faint away into a swoon or trance, rise in their seats and then fall on the floor in hysterics and convulsions. But Du Bois can hold the attention of an audience and impress his thought upon it. As I looked at his Shakespeare, Sir Walter Raleigh, or Cardinal Richelieu type of head and face, as I saw mentality and intellectuality stamped upon that brow, and an imperial will, a royal and regal nature written upon that face; as I noticed his self-possession and perfect command of himself upon the platform and observed his quiet, easy manner of speaking, his well-modulated voice and his delightful flow of words, I realized then why some of the men who represent the brains, culture, and manhood of the Negro race look to Du Bois as their spokesman and champion.

I suppose that his peculiar genius as a writer and historian resides in the fact that he combines the psychological insight and philosophical grasp of an Edward Freeman and George Burton Adams with the imaginative touch and the delicate grace of a George William Curtis and Donald G. Mitchell.

The Niagara Movement, organized in July, 1900,* meant that the mantle of Frederick Douglass had fallen upon Du Bois and that the educated men of the race rallied around him with the

* 1905 [ed.].

fidelity of Scottish clansmen. But he lacked the magnetism to gather the οἱ πολλοί* of his race around him, lacked the fire and the force to electrify vast crowds, and lacked the generalship to bind the masses together.

Dr. Du Bois possessed the critical but not the constructive and creative faculties. He was more successful in pointing out the defects and shortcomings in Mr. Washington's personality and teachings than in building up a personal following and machine of his own. While splendidly endowed as a scholar and writer, Dr. Du Bois lacked the ability to size up and appraise men at their face value, and to discern that this man has a peculiar fitness for this task and that man for that task, which Toussaint L'Ouverture possessed, and which the great leaders of men, the great generals of history, the great captains of industry have ever possessed.

He possessed a dignity and manliness of character and polish of manner, but lacked the magnetic personality of a Samuel Ringo† Ward, a Frederick Douglass, and a J. C.. Price, which makes one a popular idol. And that is why the Niagara Movement, which embodied the highest racial ideals, could never get a grip upon the masses of men, became a cult instead of a crusade, and spent its force within five years. But it kindled a fire in the hearts of the Negro that is burning still, crystallized the opposition to Booker T. Washington's leadership, and taught the world to respect the strivings of men of color. And that is why I have so frequently referred to it. . . .

Then Hon. John E. Milholland, Editor Oswald Garrison Villard, Miss Mary White Ovington, author of that splendid monograph, *Half a Man,* Mr. William Walling, Hon. Moorfield Storey, Hon. A. E. Pillsbury, and other prominent men and women of both races organized the Society for the Advancement of Colored People; elected Hon. Moorfield Storey as president; selected Du Bois as secretary, with headquarters in New York City; and interested such public-spirited citizens as Rabbi Stephen S. Wise,

---

* In English, hoi polloi, the masses, the general populace [ed.].
† Ringgold [ed.].

Dr. Newell Dwight Hillis, Rev. John Hayes Holmes, Mr. Jacob H. Schiff, Mr. Henry Morgenthau, and Professor Spingarn in it; then Du Bois forged ahead of Mr. Washington and became one of the recognized spokesmen of his race.

Frederick Douglass became a conspicuous figure in 1850, when he and Samuel Ringo* Ward turned the tide at the celebrated Rynder's meeting in New York City; and he remained the most distinguished colored man in America until his death in the fall of 1894.† A few colored men essayed to fill his place. One of them, Booker T. Washington, was solidly backed by a group of Northern philanthropists and Southern statesmen and the Associated Press of the country. At first he swept everything before him like a mountain torrent. But he welcomed no other colored deities to the Olympian height of fame on which he dwelt. And he, with his colored political and educational machine, having its headquarters in the national capital, and the cordon of colored newspapers which he helped when they were in financial straits, removed from his path those who seemed capable of growing into colossal enough proportions to wrest from him the scepter of racial leadership or divide the supremacy with him.

His method was simple and easy; namely, to prevent their securing educational, political, ecclesiastical, and editorial jobs; to prevent his powerful white friends from aiding institutions, churches, and publishing enterprises they represented, and, if possible, to knock them out of the positions that they already held. He showered his favors upon the mediocre men in the Negro race and attempted to starve the powerful men into submission. In a word, he became a Jupiter Tonans,‡ who attempted to lord it over the other black gods and reduce them to submission. He and his followers checkmated a few Yale and Harvard graduates and then branded them as failures.

Finally, we had the spectacle of a King John with rebellious

---

* Ringgold [ed.].

† February 20, 1895 [ed.].

‡ Jupiter, the principal ancient Roman sky god, had various descriptive names. Jupiter Tonans is the "thunderer" [ed.].

nobles and feudal lords, of a Zeus with the other gods on Mt. Olympus warring against him, and with the colored mortals below divided in their sympathies. Dame Fortune or Divine Providence favored the rebellious nobles and the warring gods, and the Tuskegee sage finally lost his Jovian power, so that now the throne of Negro leadership is vacant again.

The question now is, will Dr. Du Bois, the Mars who was so conspicuous in the struggle that resulted in the downfall of Jupiter Tonans, fill the vacant throne?

Dr. Du Bois has some things in his favor. I read his *Souls of Black Folk* with eagerness. I admired the gorgeous imagery and poetic beauty of the book; I was swept off my feet by the lyric sway and cadence of its style. That book was scholarship speaking in the beauty and matchless cadence of a Newman; poetic beauty of style adding new charm and mystery to the hackneyed race question.

I think that as a literary craftsman, a magician in words and a verbal prestidigitator, Du Bois is the equal of the famous masters of English and American prose, and that his brilliant style has as its substratum solid learning. Indeed, his scholarship is equal to that of the average Yale or Harvard professor. He has the dignity, manliness, polish, and refinement that makes him show up to advantage in the drawing room, at a dinner party, or at a pink tea affair. No man in the race can show up better on social, semisocial, and semiliterary occasions as an example of a cultured and refined colored gentleman. But, on the other hand, Du Bois has a much more difficult task cut out for him than Douglass had. In the first place, he lacks Douglass' colossal physique, leonine countenance, thundering voice, and magnetic personality. Then, too, the educated colored men in Douglass' day were few and far between. Now they are numbered by the scores. Let us enumerate the list of colored men who rival or almost rival Du Bois in scholarship and leadership.

There are Rev. Dr. Francis J. Grimké and Hon. Archibald H. Grimké, who are aristocrats with a remarkable breadth of culture, common sense, force of character, and power of expression;

President W. S. Scarborough of Wilberforce University, a Greek scholar, a polished and dignified gentleman with a genial personality; Professor Kelly Miller, who has a wonderful analytical mind; Professor William H. H. Hart, a scholar who has a genius for oratory and politics; Professor John Wesley Cromwell and Mr. George Washington Forbes, learned almost as Samuel Johnson, blending scholarship with common sense; Professor William H. Richards, almost a match for Du Bois in scholarship, dignity, and polish; Dr. William V. Tunnell, a scholarly gentleman of dignified presence and unusual oratorical gifts, and Dr. William Sinclair, author of *The Aftermath of Slavery*. . . .

Of these men, Professor Hart, who desired the recognition of his white blood, Professor Miller, and Mr. Forbes are as rich in intellectual equipment as Du Bois. President Scarborough, Dr. Grimké, and Mr. Grimké are peers of Du Bois in every respect as scholars, men, and gentlemen.

The question is, can Du Bois give to each man his measure and due and by so doing maintain his ascendency?

If he becomes a Zeus, looking down from Mt. Olympus with mingled feelings of pity, sympathy, scorn, and contempt upon his benighted brethren in the vale below, he may find that uneasy lies the head that wears a crown. But if he essays to play the role of a Prometheus, who brought the divine fire of the gods down to the mortals in the valley below, he will be honored for generations by his own race and find a place in his country's history.

Thus far he has been an unknown quantity as a leader of vast bodies. His failure to make the Niagara Movement move should be no criterion by which to judge Du Bois, because it was his first attempt at racial leadership and he is now an older and a more experienced man. Let us give him the benefit of the doubt. Perhaps he may learn to size up men and appraise them at their face value.

Despite the thought of Mr. Booker T. Washington and the colored editors and educators who follow him, that an educated Negro should be an educational jack-of-all-trades, Nature is not prodigal in her gifts to man. She very rarely bestows all of her gifts upon any one individual. The ability to manipulate vast bodies of men and lead vast hosts is the rarest of all her gifts. Few men are endowed with the magnetic personality of Samuel Ringo* Ward, Frederick Douglass, and J. C. Price. Few men are endowed with the generalship of a Napoleon, George Washington, Abraham Lincoln, U. S. Grant, Count Von Moltke, and James G. Blaine.

Of our brainy colored men, George Washington Forbes of Boston pre-eminently showed the latter quality during the two years and three months in which he wrote the *Guardian* editorials and mapped out the campaign against Booker T. Washington. The way in which he pressed men of diverse temperaments into service and selected different men for different tasks and utilized means to realize an end indicated that he possessed some of the intellectual gifts that made his namesake famous.

The one thing that the natural-born leaders of men invariably do, some of the colored leaders rarely do. The former draw a man out by conversing with him and hence know him at first hand. The latter accept the popular estimate of a man, take the estimate formed of him by others, and hence know the man at second hand. The natural-born leader of men does not ask to see your letters of introduction or recommendations, or accept the estimate formed of you by the general public, by some society leader or head of a department in some college or university; but he looks you through and through; asks you a few searching and pointed questions, hears what you have to say in your own vindication, and then when he has heard both sides of the case renders his decision and issues his edict.

The natural-born leader of men is a judge who never renders a decision until he has heard both the plaintiff and defendant. The quasi leader of men asks, "Who weigh socially the most and who stand the highest officially?" He either dismisses the case or condemns the defendant accordingly as the plaintiff or defend-

* Ringgold [ed.].

ant stands the highest in the social, educational, ecclesiastical, and business world. The natural-born leader of men asks, "What are the *facts* in the case?" The quasi leader of men asks, "Which one of the parties has the most business prestige or highest social standing?"

If Abraham Lincoln had been a man of the latter type, he would not have retained Grant as commander-in-chief of the Union forces. If Napoleon had been a man of the latter type, he would not have shown such wisdom in selecting his marshals and generals of division.

Now this ability to size up and appraise men, which Jesus of Nazareth, Socrates, Napoleon, and Lincoln possessed can rarely be acquired by a man who is a born aristocrat. It can only be acquired by a man sprung from the οἱ πολλοὶ or by a chivalric aristocrat, whose sympathies go out to a self-reliant personality who is struggling against overwhelming odds; by a man whether born in the palace or hut, whether of patrician or plebeian birth, who sees into the heart of things, who looks beneath the clothes, the exterior, and the surface impression to the soul of the man, who detects qualities and capacities in a man which escape the superficial observer.

Perhaps Dr. Du Bois has this genius, this inborn quality of the soul, latent in him, only waiting contact with men on a large scale to bring it out. If such be the case, he will succeed where Mr. Washington failed, and become the real leader of the colored race in America, by virtue of his grip upon the hearts of his race.

But success intoxicates a man. It so intoxicated Napoleon that he thought of invading England, ordered the executions of Duc d'Enghien and the German printer, Platen, and caused him to lose the flower of the French army in the reckless, fruitless, and foolishly executed Moscow campaign. It so intoxicated Booker T. Washington that he imagined that he could corral and dominate the entire colored race in America as easily as he corralled and dominated the Negroes of the black belt of Alabama. It is to be hoped that his marvelous success as a scientific compiler of Negro statistics and Negro data, as a poetic voicer of the black man's striving aspiration and soul hunger, and as a polished and cultured representative of the race in literary and social gatherings, will not cause Du Bois likewise to attempt the impossible and believe that welding heterogeneous forces into a homogeneous unity is a holiday task.

But I am not quite sure whether this polished and refined scholar is endowed with the combination of qualities which make one a leader of men. He has the keen intellectual perceptions, the sensitive aesthetic perceptions, which cause one to be a superb literary, musical, and art critic and social arbiter. But that very intellectual and aesthetic sensitiveness causes him to be hypersensitive of a jar or discord, and hypercritical. And the leader of men, while conscious of the defects and limitations of a man, sees in him material at his disposal to be utilized as means to realize an end. Thus, they told Abraham Lincoln that Grant drank. Lincoln replied, "But he fights. I wish more of my generals drank of the same brand." They told him that Sherman was crazy, but Lincoln recognized his brilliancy, courage, and energy.

I believe that there is more of the Walter Pater than of the Thomas Carlyle in Dr. Du Bois. I can conceive of his writing *Marius the Epicurean, Imaginary Portraits,* and *Plato and Platonism.* I can even conceive of his writing a book like Emerson's *Representative Men,* but I do not know whether he could write a book like Carlyle's *Heroes and Hero Worship.* The characters of Odin, Mohammed, Luther, Knox, Cromwell, and Samuel Johnson might not have appealed to a sensitive, finely attuned nature like Du Bois. I am afraid that he would have found John the Baptist and the Apostle Paul rather boresome, and I am not quite sure that he would have found Diogenes and Socrates very entertaining, had he been a contemporary of theirs.

There is no doubt that Dr. Du Bois is endowed with rare and unique intellectual gifts, that he possesses an inborn manliness and refinement of character, and a superb self-possession, but the question is, "Does he possess that combination of traits and qualities which makes one a born ruler and leader of men?" Dr. Du Bois has admirably performed his part as a critic on the side lines and in the press gallery. But the world is more interested in the hero who crossess the line for a touchdown. He is the Ernest Renan of the Negro race. But the Mirabeaus have been the makers of history. And while I, as a student of psychology, regard Dr. Du Bois as an intellectual giant, with the aesthetic sensibility of an artist or poet; as a student of human history, I cannot predict that he will evolve into a leader with faith in God, faith in man, and faith in himself, who will breathe his own buoyant, hopeful, and heroic spirit into the minds and hearts of his followers; a leader who will fill individuals in his race with the thought that they, too, can climb the mount of human achievement; a leader who will inspire his race to do great things as Oliver Cromwell inspired the Ironsides, as John Wesley inspired the Methodists, as Theodore Parker inspired the Unitarians, as Bishop Wilberforce inspired the friends of abolition, as Mirabeau inspired the French Assembly, as Napoleon inspired the French soldiers by telling them that from the heights of yonder Pyramids forty centuries looked down upon them.

I realize that the race problem in America is one that requires the tact and good sense, the wisdom and discretion, the caution and patience of an Abraham Lincoln; but still it is true of any race that no man can dominate the race unless he is able to rouse the ambition, hope, and enthusiasm that slumbers in every man.

But we should not pronounce a man a failure simply because he cannot become a second Abraham Lincoln, Toussaint L'Ouverture, Frederick Douglass, and J. C. Price. We should remember that great leaders of men like Hannibal, Alexander, Caesar, Charlemagne, Cromwell, Napoleon, Peter the Great, Frederick the Great, Mirabeau, Bismarck, Chatham, Gladstone, Webster, Sumner, Washington, Lincoln, John Wesley, Bishop Phillips Brooks, Toussaint L'Ouverture, and King Menelik do not grow upon every briar bush. Then, too, we should remember that the Negro educator who propounded the doctrine that every educated colored man should be an educational jack-of-all-trades himself succeeded admirably in a large task of industrial leadership of a certain section of the country and failed in the more colossal task of national leadership, because he couldn't awaken the dormant manhood of his race and kindle the flames of aspiration in the hearts of the youth of his race, although he continuously for a period of nearly eighteen years concentrated his time, energy, and surplus funds upon that task.

The men of universal genius like Julius Caesar, who was a society gallant, a grammarian, an orator, a politician, a statesman, a jurist, a general, a ruler, an architect, an engineer, a historian, and a poet, are as rare in human history as are the Aristotles, the Newtons, the Bacons, and the Shakespeares.

I believe that Caesar even would have failed had he attempted to play Aristotle's role. The latter would have failed had he attempted to play Caesar's role. Cromwell would have lost out had he attempted to write the "Paradise Lost"; John Milton would have lost out had he attempted to command the armies of the Commonwealth. Newton would have cut a sorry figure had he attempted to write the plays of Shakespeare; and Shakespeare would have floundered had he attempted to write the *Principia*. Gladstone would have struck a snag had he attempted to write the *Origin of Species,* and Darwin would have waded beyond his depth had he attempted to become a parliamentary leader. Similarly we cannot expect any one Negro to be omniscient and omnipotent. And we cannot expect to find any one colored man who will be an Aristotle and a Julius Caesar rolled into one; or a Cromwell and John Milton rolled into one; or a Newton and Shakespeare rolled into one; or a Darwin and Gladstone rolled into one. The gifted individuals in the race like Toussaint L'Ouverture, Frederick Douglass, J. C. Price, Booker T. Washington, and Dr. W. E. Burghardt Du Bois are especially endowed to perform a few but not all and every task well.

The history of civilization shows that the type of personality represented by Montaigne, Ernest Renan, Mark Pattison, Coventry Patmore, Walter Pater, and Dr. Du Bois has played a part and an important one in the cultural history of mankind. But their very fineness and sensitiveness of organization prevented their swaying the masses and thus becoming dynamic factors and forces in human progress. The history of human thought shows also that the doubting Thomases act as a sort of brake or check to optimists and idealists and that they are society's safety valves. They have a place, and by no means an insignificant one, in the economy of the universe. But it is men with the crusading zeal of Paul, Mohammed, Peter the Hermit, Luther, John Wesley, General Booth, John Calvin, John Knox, Oliver Cromwell, Bishop Wilberforce, Samuel Adams, and William Lloyd Garrison and David Livingston who have launched the world movements in human history and set in motion currents of thought and feeling that are flowing still.

So we may conclude our discussion of Dr. Du Bois by saying that while his is a remarkable personality, in fact one of the most remarkable personalities thus far evolved by the colored race, it is not such a powerful personality that it holds the destiny of the colored race in its hands.

Casely Hayford, barrister-at-law at Secundi, West Africa, and author of *Gold Coast Native Institutions,* refers to Dr. Du Bois as seeking to promote the black man's "social enfranchisement amid surroundings and in an atmosphere uncongenial to racial development." And Du Bois has been criticized for desiring the social as well as the civil and political recognition of the colored man.

As a matter of fact, the Negro desires social, civil, and political recognition because he is human, and because every human being desires social, civil, and political recognition. Every true man desires first to be a man and then desires his fellows to recognize the fact that he is a man. Every human being who has tastes and desires above the brute, desires to be somebody, and desires other human beings to recognize the fact that he is somebody. And the desire of Dr. Du Bois, which is so passionately and eloquently expressed in *The Souls of Black Folk,* is for the world to recognize the humanity of the black man. But there are a few things that colored men who are striving for recognition should bear in mind.

✪

The NAACP and *The Crisis*

The name of the Association caused dissastisfaction and led to frequent discussion and debate during the first six or seven years. From March, 1909, to March, 1910, the founders spoke of themselves as the Committee on the Negro, the Committee on the Status of the Negro, or (after the first conference, May–June, 1909) as the National Negro Committee. The Committee on Permanent Organization headed by Oswald Garrison Villard proposed the name "National Association for the Advancement of Colored People," and this was accepted by the second annual conference in May, 1910. . . .

The active leaders of the "New Abolition Movement," like their contemporaries who led the Progressive Movement, were young men and women.[1] According to Mary White Ovington, the average age of the five incorporators was thirty-five.[2] Complementing the young leaders were the elder statesmen, whose

1. Richard Hofstadter, *The Age of Reform: From Bryan to F.D.R.* (New York, 1955), pp. 166–167.
2. Mary White Ovington, *The Walls Came Tumbling Down* (New York, 1947), p. 107.

Reprinted from *NAACP: A History of the National Association for the Advancement of Colored People, Volume I, 1909–1920* (Baltimore: The Johns Hopkins Press, 1967), pp. 89–115, by Charles Flint Kellogg, by permission of The Johns Hopkins Press. Copyright © 1967 by The Johns Hopkins Press.

lives embraced the two abolition movements. They were the Garrisons, Fanny Garrison Villard, the second William Lloyd Garrison (who died shortly after the first conference), Francis Jackson Garrison, Moorfield Storey, and Albert E. Pillsbury.

It was Pillsbury who drew up the bylaws for the Association, which were presented to the first meeting of the incorporators on June 20, 1911, and unanimously approved.[3] The bylaws provided for a Board of thirty directors to be elected at the first meeting of the corporation in January, 1912. Officers of the corporation were to be elected from the Board: a president, two or more vice presidents, a chairman of the Board, a secretary, and a treasurer. Thus, the Executive Committee was supplanted by a Board of Directors.

The Board was authorized to appoint a Director of Publicity and Research and other officers, and provision was made for committees on finance, legal redress, publications, and memberships, as well as a general advisory committee.[4]

The first meeting of the Board of Directors was held immediately following the incorporators' meeting and the three present, Villard, Miss Ovington, and Walter Sachs, constituted the quorum. (Later the quorum was changed to six.) They proceeded to nominate as officers: Moorfield Storey, president; John E. Milholland and Bishop Alexander Walters, vice presidents; Villard, chairman of the Board; Mary White Ovington, secretary; and Walter Sachs, treasurer. W. E. B. Du Bois was appointed Director of Publicity and Research.[5]

On January 4, 1912, three meetings were held. First the old

3. "First Meeting of the Incorporators of the NAACP," June 20, 1911, in Board Minutes, NAACP (now in manuscript Division, Library of Congress). Miss Ovington, Villard, and Walter W. Sachs were present, and Du Bois and John Haynes Holmes sent proxies. The Articles of Incorporation were drawn up and signed on May 25, 1911. They were approved June 9, and filed in the office of the Secretary of the State of New York on June 16, and with the County Clerk of New York County on June 19, 1911.

4. Bylaws of the National Association for the Advancement of Colored People, in Board Minutes, NAACP, June 20, 1911.

5. Board Minutes, NAACP, June 20, 1911.

Executive Committee met and presented a slate of thirty Board members for nominations and adjourned. Then the Board (authorized by the incorporators) met and voted that members of the General Committee (Committee of One Hundred) should be asked to serve on the new Advisory Committee. Finally the Annual Meeting of Members was held, and the thirty Board members were elected. Villard presided at all three meetings. There were at that time 329 members of the Association.[6]

At the first regular meeting of the Board in February, 1912, the officers who had been nominated at the time of incorporation were elected, and two vice presidents were added, the Reverend John Haynes Holmes and the Reverend Garnett R. Waller. Martha Gruening, a volunteer social worker, and Paul Kennaday were appointed as assistant secretaries.[7]

INTERNAL STRIFE

Dissension within the organization caused a great deal of trouble for the new Association. Though internal organizational conflict is not unknown in institutional life, there were times when Negroes and whites alike blamed the disruptive element on race. Booker T. Washington once expressed regret that all his friends could not seem to work harmoniously and naïvely commented, "In this respect white people excel us very much." Villard, when he first started working with the Negro problem, was distressed by the "way the colored people fight among themselves." Moorfield Storey was concerned with the differences among colored leaders and frequently tried to stop William Monroe Trotter from emphasizing points of difference.[8]

It is true that there were few places of prestige open to Ne-

6. Board Minutes, NAACP, January 4, 1912.
7. Board Minutes, NAACP, February 6, 1912.
8. Washington to Daniel Murray, March 6, 1904, Booker T. Washington Papers (Manuscript Division, Library of Congress); Villard to Garrison, October 23, 1906, Villard Papers (Houghton Library, Harvard University); Storey to Trotter, April 11, 1911, Storey Papers (in possession of Mr. Charles Storey, Boston, Mass.).

groes, and the rivalry for status was keen. The most extreme
individualists occasionally withdrew. Mrs. Ida Wells-Barnett felt
slighted when Villard called a meeting of the Chicago branch at
Hull House without notifying her. She complained that Villard
and Du Bois wanted Jane Addams to "mother" the movement,
although she had neither the time nor the strength to lead this
new crusade. Mrs. Wells-Barnett resented the patronizing assumptions of the academic few who wanted to keep the organization in their own hands. She had been given to understand at
a meeting of the Executive Committee in New York that she was
not expected to do anything save to be a member. For this reason she limited her active participation in the development of the
Chicago branch. Even Miss Ovington came in for denunciation.
Mrs. Wells-Barnett declared that Miss Ovington's attitude was
all right theoretically, but that she was not in sympathy with the
colored people as a whole. She accused Miss Ovington of having
special pets and claimed that her restrictive policy of admission
by ticket had limited the number of people attending the New
York annual meeting in 1912—in marked contrast to the Boston
conference, where there were no restrictions. On the other hand,
Mrs. Wells-Barnett counted William English Walling and Joel
Spingarn among her few real friends in the movement; they had
the "truest conception" of the work.[9]

William Monroe Trotter, always jealous of any invasion of
his National Equal Rights League, remained a member of the
NAACP until 1913, but by 1914 he had drifted out of the
NAACP and was attacking both Du Bois and Washington with
equal fury.[10]

If Negro leaders were inclined to be as temperamental as

9. Ida Wells-Barnett, "The National Association for the Advancement
of Colored People," *Fellowship* (organ of the Negro Fellowship League of
Chicago), January 17, 1912, n.p., clipping in Du Bois Papers (now in
the possession of Mrs. W. E. B. Du Bois, New York City); Ida Wells-
Barnett to Joel Spingarn, April 21, 1911, J. E. Spingarn Papers (Howard).
10. Garrison to Villard, November 5, 1911, Villard Papers; Trotter to
Spingarn, January 2, 1913, J. E. Spingarn Papers (Howard); Storey to
Bumstead, March 10, 1914, Storey Papers.

prima donnas, each seeking his own place in the limelight, the rank and file tended to be apathetic, indolent, and supine. Jessie Fauset, the novelist, felt that the average colored man was "too near the traditions of slavery not to esteem nominal freedom and fleshpots above their real value." Francis J. Garrison thought it would take five to ten years for the prosperous Negroes to assume their moral and financial obligation of supporting the Association, but he was confident that in time they would accept the responsibility of fighting for their own freedom.[11]

Even Negro intellectuals could not see the problem in its entirety at times. John Hope admitted that, shut off as Negroes were, they were apt to take an isolated and very personal attitude toward their problems. He acknowledged his debt to Joel Spingarn and Charles Edward Russell for helping him to see what he called the bigger, world side and the human significance of the Negro.[12]

Jessie Fauset urged Spingarn to "prod us, prick us, goad us on by unpleasant truths to ease off this terrible outer self of sloth and acceptance. . . . Some of us need to be told that we should be men. . . . Teach us, hammer into us that expediency is not all, that life is more than meat. And don't give us up. . . . For we are worth it." [13]

But the causes of friction within the Association were by no means confined to one race. White and Negro members were involved equally. In March, 1911, Miss Blascoer, disagreeing vehemently with Du Bois on all issues, resigned as "secretary" of the Association and became a member of the Executive Committee. A short time later she accepted an appointment to field work. Storey provided $1,200 for her salary for the first six months and the Association underwrote her expenses. As organizer, she was to spend a month each in Boston, Philadelphia, and Chicago,

11. Jessie Fauset to Spingarn, February 12, 1913, J. E. Spingarn Papers (Howard); Garrison to Villard, January 29, 1913, Villard Papers.
12. John Hope to Spingarn, February 28, 1913, J. E. Spingarn Papers (Howard).
13. Jessie Fauset to Spingarn, February 12, 1913, J. E. Spingarn Papers (Howard).

working with the branches. She became dissastisfied, however, with the arrangements concerning her expenses and before the middle of May gave up the work and returned to New York. According to Villard, she refused to be governed by simple business rules in regard to her expenses. She had already clashed with Du Bois over *Crisis* finances, refusing to show him the vouchers when their accounts did not balance.[14]

Miss Blascoer was apparently ill at this time. Villard spoke of her as a trying person to work with, though the first year of their association had been pleasant. Arthur Spingarn later recalled that she had a mental breakdown from which she never recovered. Her resignation was accepted but she remained on the Executive Committee for one more month. When she sent word that she could not attend meetings, she was asked to remain on the Committee of One Hundred.[15]

Miss Ovington took over the secretarial work without pay. To Villard, she was a perfect official, always unruffled, a "most ladylike, refined and cultivated person." Because of her other obligations on behalf of colored people, Miss Ovington was able to give only part time to the secretarial work. In May, 1912, she resigned and was elected a vice president of the Association. May Childs Nerney, a young woman of executive ability, a former librarian who had worked in the State Library in Albany and in the Newark Public Library, was hired to take over the secretarial duies.[16]

Friction in the national office continued. After less than a year, Miss Nerney threatened to resign, accusing Du Bois' secretary of insolence and impertinence. According to Villard, this young woman had for a long time merited dismissal, but Du Bois, pre-

14. Minutes, Executive Committee, March 7, 1911, April 11, 1911, May 2, 1911, in Board Minutes, NAACP; Garrison to Villard, April 8, 1911; Villard to Garrison, May 12, 1911, Villard Papers; Du Bois to Villard, April 11, 1911, Du Bois Papers.

15. Villard to Garrison, May 12, 1911, Villard Papers; A. B. Spingarn to writer, September 5, 1958; Minutes, Executive Committee, May 16, 1911, June 6, 1911, in Board Minutes, NAACP.

16. Villard to Garrison, May 17, 1911, March 21, 1912, Villard Papers; *The Crisis,* IV (July 1912), 125.

occupied with other matters, refused to let her go. Villard thought the only solution was to move Miss Nerney to separate quarters.

Villard got along with Du Bois by letting him go his own way, but he became irritated with the Negro leader when he discovered he was writing a book on NAACP time. He also resented Du Bois' attitude toward *The Crisis,* which Du Bois, according to Villard, considered his own property and his own creation. They clashed over Villard's suggestion that *The Crisis* publicize crimes perpetrated by Negroes as well as those committed against them. The Board straddled the issue by voting that Du Bois could publish information on the crimes of Negroes as he saw fit.[17]

Following this clash, Du Bois wrote to Villard, stating that he considered the Board of Directors his authority, and himself a fellow officer, not a subordinate receiving orders. He admitted the right of a Board member to criticize his work and to offer suggestions, but he resented Villard's implication that his independence of action was a breach of discipline or a personal discourtesy.[18]

Villard, however, thought of the chairman of the Board as *the* executive of the Association, with authority over paid employees, whether editors or clerks. He disclaimed any personal animosity toward Du Bois; the situation was the result of putting a paid employee on the Board of Directors. He left it to the Board to determine the relationship between officers of the Association, but he proposed that Joel Spingarn should soon succeed him as chairman of the Board.[19]

Du Bois cheerfully withdrew anything offensive he might have said in the heat of the argument, but a month later in April, 1913, there was another clash at the Board meeting and as a result Villard asked Du Bois to remove his name from the list of contributing editors of *The Crisis.*[20]

17. Villard to Garrison, February 7, 1913, February 11, 1913, Villard Papers; Board Minutes, NAACP, March 11, 1913.
18. Du Bois to Villard, March 18, 1913, Villard Papers.
19. Villard to Spingarn, March 20, 1913, Villard Papers.
20. Du Bois to Villard, March 18, 1913, Villard Papers; Villard to Du Bois, memorandum, April 2, 1913, in Board Minutes, NAACP. See

In an attempt to secure greater efficiency and better cooperation a committee, consisting of Miss Ovington, Charles Studin,
Francis Batchelder,[21] and Walter Sachs, was constituted to in-
quire into the functioning of the national office. In addition, a
Crisis advisory committee was appointed, consisting of Joel Spingarn, Dr. William Henry Brooks, and Miss Ovington.[22]

The friction continued, however, and to these personal irri-
tations of Villard's was added a feeling that other Board members were not shouldering their responsibilities. Villard was also
impatient with the Philadelphia members and complained of having to struggle "with the colored people and their easily hurt
feelings," not only in NAACP work but also at Board meetings
of the Manassas School.* Working so close to Association headquarters meant that he was frequently called on four and five
times a day, and his work for the *Evening Post* suffered accordingly.[23]

In November, 1913, Bishop Walters, a Board member, resigned because Villard publicly accused of him of advocating
segregation, and Sachs resigned as treasurer.[24]

THE CRISIS OVER THE CRISIS

Further trouble with *The Crisis* precipitated Villard's resignation
as chairman of the Board. Du Bois had remained defiant and in-

---

also Du Bois to Villard [April 3, 1913]; Villard to Du Bois, April 3, 1913,
Du Bois Papers.

21. Francis Batchelder, a certified public accountant, audited the Association's books from the time of incorporation for many years. He
was the brother of Margaret Batchelder, Miss Ovington's secretary, who
became an officer of the New York branch.

22. Board Minutes, NAACP, April 1, 1913.

* The Manassas Industrial School in Manassas, Virginia, was one of
several schools founded at the turn of the century [ed.].

23. Board Minutes, NAACP, May 6, 1913; Villard to Garrison, February 7, 1913, March 14, 1913, October 23, 1913, Villard Papers.

24. Villard to Garrison, September 23, 1913, Villard Papers; Board
Minutes, NAACP, November 6, 1913; New York *Age,* November 6, 1913.

subordinate in regard to *The Crisis,* and Villard had accused him of refusing to recognize it as an organ of the Association. Villard reluctantly put up with Du Bois' independence because Du Bois was a Board member, but he was unable to accept the same attitude from a subordinate, Augustus G. Dill, business manager of *The Crisis,* who refused to obey official instructions.

Villard was no longer willing to continue as chairman unless the functions of that position were clearly defined. He recommended that the staffs of *The Crisis* and the Association be promptly separated. To Miss Ovington he expressed a fear that he might eventually be carrying the organization alone, since he had had no support whatever on the financial side from other members of the Association.[25]

Miss Ovington hinted that he took too much of the burden on himself and suggested that he leave all the executive work to Miss Nerney. To Mary White Ovington, Villard's withdrawal meant "a confession to the world that we cannot work with colored people unless they are our subordinates. . . . It puts us back five years." [26]

Du Bois met with Miss Ovington and Joel and Arthur Spingarn, to try to iron out the difficulties concerning *The Crisis* and the Association. He suggested three plans for the possible reorganization. Under the first, *The Crisis* would be completely separated from the NAACP and operated by an independent organization, The Crisis Associates, and Villard would continue as chairman of the Board. If this arrangement should go into effect, Du Bois promised a complete and thoroughgoing effort at cooperation with Villard and the Board. The second plan proposed that Miss Ovington become chairman of the Board and that a

---

Sachs resigned from the Board in 1914. Board Minutes, NAACP, October 6, 1914.

25. Villard to Board of Directors, November 19, 1913; Villard to Ovington, November 21, 1913, Villard Papers.

26. Ovington to Villard, November 21, 1913, November 25, 1913, Villard Papers.

young colored man be selected as secretary and organizer. Du Bois would be under legal contract with the Board to edit and manage *The Crisis*; his other work would be voluntary, as in the case of other members of the Board. The third plan, which Du Bois professed to like least of all, proposed that the offices of Director of Publicity and Research and of Secretary be combined; Du Bois would become "executive secretary" working under the Board, and under the chairman between meetings. He proposed hiring an organizer, a managing editor for *The Crisis,* and with the first increase in revenue, a lawyer and an advertising agent.[27]

Du Bois envisioned *The Crisis* as a separate entity with himself in charge, although his third plan, by way of contrast, was suggestive of the proposal at the 1910 conference to bring him into the Association as executive secretary, a proposal which had been defeated by Villard and Miss Blascoer. In spite of his protestations to the contrary, his failure to be appointed executive secretary may well have been the basic cause of Du Bois' friction with the Association.

The Board, however, did not accept any of Du Bois' proposals and as a first step in countering his moves to withdraw *The Crisis* from the aegis of the Association they adopted a resolution that each issue of the magazine should clearly and prominently state the aims and objectives of the NAACP, and the duty of *Crisis* readers to become members of the National Association. This was followed by steps to copyright *The Crisis* and its contents in the name of the Association.[28]

In January, 1914, Villard retired as chairman of the Board and became treasurer and chairman of the finance committee. In spite of past differences, Du Bois complimented Villard in *The Crisis,* saying that no other person had done more for the

27. "Memorandum to Mr. J. E. Spingarn, Mr. A. B. Spingarn, and Miss Ovington from W. E. B. Du Bois," n.d. [November 1913], Du Bois Papers.
28. Board Minutes, NAACP, December 2, 1913, February 3, 1914; Nerney to Du Bois, February 6, 1914, Du Bois Papers.

new abolition movement: "He took it when it was nothing but an idea and left it a nation-wide movement, with 24 branches and 3,000 members, out of debt, aggressive and full of faith." [29]

Villard's retirement and the election of Joel E. Spingarn as chairman of the Board failed to bring peace to the Association. All through the year 1914 one episode followed another. Du Bois' comments in *The Crisis* antagonized both individuals and groups. One source of friction was Du Bois' failure to give general recognition to what Trotter and his associates in the National Independent Political League were doing in the battle against segregation during the Wilson Administration. Moorfield Storey was so concerned over the resulting disharmony that he wrote at length to Villard and Spingarn in an attempt to get *The Crisis* to take a broad and catholic view of all that was being done for the common cause. At Spingarn's behest, Du Bois printed an explanation of the omission, but Trotter considered the explanation inadequate and far from convincing. [30]

Early in 1914, the NAACP moved into larger quarters in the "educational building" at 70 Fifth Avenue. [31] Although Du Bois insisted that there would be no additional expense in the move, which gave *The Crisis* more room and convenience, running expenses at the new office increased $700 a year at a time when *The Crisis* was still not self-supporing. Villard, however, was relieved and glad NAACP staff were no longer his tenants, for they had been "hard to please." [32]

To Villard, the new chairman of the Board, Joel Spingarn, was

29. Board Minutes, NAACP, January 6, 1914; *The Crisis,* VII (February 1914), 188.

30. Storey to Villard, January 8, 1914, January 13, 1914; Storey to Spingarn, January 15, 1915, Storey Papers; Trotter to Spingarn, January 28, 1914, J. E. Spingarn Papers (Howard).

31. Nerney to Charles T. Hallinan, December 22, 1913, NAACP Files (formerly in NAACP offices, New York; now in Manuscript Division, Library of Congress).

32. Spingarn to Du Bois, October 24, 1914, Joel Elias Spingarn Papers (James Weldon Johnson Collection, Yale University; hereafter referred to as the Johnson Collection). Villard to Garrison, March 1, 1914, Villard Papers.

a firebrand who started off with a violent attack on Booker T. Washington. Villard had no faith in Miss Nerney's ability to carry on the executive work. He complained that Du Bois had again irritated many on the Board with a wanton attack on *The Survey,*[33] and that the mounting expenses made the Association's financial outlook appear ominous. Unwittingly, he gave a clue to his own personality (and to one cause of the clash with Du Bois) when he wrote of *The Nation,* "It is going to be a broad, fine paper with O. G. V. as absolute dictator of the policy." [34] But Villard was entirely correct when he predicted that Du Bois was precipitating an inevitable crisis with *The Crisis.* Within the next few months, Du Bois was to attack not only Trotter but the Negro press, white philanthropy, the colored clergy, and Negro higher education.

A number of Negro editors showed deep resentment when Du Bois said that Negro papers were poorly written and the Negro press as a whole was unreliable, incomplete, and venal.[35] Was this his method of guiding them "towards better methods and ideals?" [36]

Du Bois' harsh criticism of Robert C. Ogden, at the time of his death, was interpreted by the New York *Age* as an ungrateful attack upon white philanthropy. Du Bois wrote that "a self-con-

33. Villard to *The Crisis* Committee, January 23, 1914, NAACP Files; *The Crisis,* VII (February 1914), 187. *The Survey* was published by the Charity Organization Society of the City of New York and was sympathetic to the cause of the Negro. *The Survey* had asked Du Bois for an article, but had refused to accept it. Du Bois claimed Villard and Miss Nerney had "discredited" him behind his back, and he took a "last fling at the Survey" which disturbed Board members anxious to keep *The Survey* open to material about the Association. Du Bois to Spingarn, October 28, 1914 (Johnson Collection).

34. Villard to Garrison, March 1, 1914, Villard Papers.

35. *The Crisis,* VII (March 1914), 239–240. The New York *Age,* March 12, 1914, includes reprints from the Atlanta *Independent* and the Richmond *Planet.* The Washington *Bee* counterattacked the "insult to the Negro press" by accusing *The Crisis* of clipping its news from the Negro weeklies. Washington *Bee,* March 7, 1914.

36. Du Bois, Memorandum to Board on Objects and Methods of the Organization, n.d. [1913], Du Bois Papers.

scious, self-helping Negro was beyond Mr. Ogden's conception.
. . . He wanted Negroes to be satisfied and do well in the
place . . . he was sure they . . . ought to occupy." In spite of
Ogden's sincerity and unselfishness, he had become a captive of
the white South, and the activities of the Southern Education
Board had become a movement for white people only.[37]

Du Bois also aroused a storm of protest from W. S. Scarborough, president of Wilberforce University, by his article on "The
New Wilberforce," in which he praised the new state-supported
college and indirectly criticized the older church-related school.
Scarborough claimed that the article through misrepresentations
and distortions had greatly stirred up the alumni.[38]

The colored clergy were criticized and denounced in a "Church
Number" of The Crisis. The Negro church was censured for not
reaching the mass of middle-class Negroes and for not choosing
honest and efficient leaders. Alexander Walters, Bishop of the African Methodist Episcopal Zion Church and an NAACP Board
member, was embarrassed because The Crisis reported that his
was the only one of the four leading Negro churches which had
not responded to a request for an article for the "Church Number." Du Bois' comment on the need for radical reform in the
financial affairs of the Zion Church enraged Bishop Walters
and probably contributed to his rapprochement with Booker T.
Washington.[39]

The president of the Baltimore NAACP branch reported to

37. New York Age, April 23, 1914; The Crisis, VII (April 1914), 274–
275. For a discussion of Ogden and the Southern Education Board, see
the excellent study by Louis R. Harlan, Separate and Unequal: Public
School Campaigns and Racism in the Southern Seaboard States 1901–
1915 (Chapel Hill, 1958), pp. 75–101.
38. The Crisis, VIII (August 1914), 191–194; W. S. Scarborough to
Villard, September 8, 1914; Villard to Scarborough, September 10, 1914;
Nerney to Spingarn, September 11, 1914; Scarborough to Spingarn,
September 18, 1914; Spingarn to Scarborough, September 19, 1914, in
J. E. Spingarn Papers (Howard).
39. The Crisis, IV (May 1912), 24–25, 28–33; R. W. Thompson to
E. J. Scott, April 18, 1913, Washington Papers.

national headquarters that the position of *The Crisis* had caused much trouble and urged the Association to court, rather than criticize, the Negro press and ministry. This Du Bois would not do, and a Boston member urged Spingarn to do his best to eliminate from *The Crisis* "those bitter and sarcastic expressions that have created so many enmities." [40]

In an attempt to overcome these problems, a new policy was hammered out by the Association through the spring and summer of 1914. A new constitution and bylaws drawn up by Charles Studin were approved by the Board in July, 1914.[41]

Although the duties of officers were defined, Villard was not satisfied with the way the office of treasurer was presented and again found himself up against Du Bois. The new bylaws provided that the treasurer should receive regular reports, inspect the books, and audit the accounts of all departments and bureaus. Villard thought the treasurer should supervise all the financial affairs of the organization, including *The Crisis*. Failure to run the magazine in an efficient manner meant that the Association had to pay part of the expenses as well as the editor's salary. Villard thought *The Crisis* should produce a profit, which could be used to extend the work of the Association. His business experience in the publishing field made him conscious of the need for a trained business manager, and for accurate advertising records or statements to show the exact cost per issue and the exact returns. Information concerning the number of agents in arrears, totals of bad debts, and analysis of paper costs was also needed.[42]

During the discussions of the proposed bylaws, Du Bois offered a resolution further defining the duties of officers and this was accepted as an amendment to the constitution being evolved.

40. Dr. Francis N. Cardozo to Spingarn, December 18, 1914; George G. Bradford to Spingarn, December 2, 1914, J. E. Spingarn Papers (Howard).

41. Board Minutes, NAACP, April 17, 1914, April 28, 1914, July 7, 1914.

42. Board Minutes, NAACP, July 7, 1914; Villard to Spingarn, April 16, 1914, J. E. Spingarn Papers (Howard).

The treasurer, according to Du Bois, should, with the advice and cooperation of the Finance Committee, raise funds for the support of the Association. This made the treasurer the money-raising officer of the Association with little or no policy-making functions and with no control in financial affairs.

The chairman of the Board was also shorn of executive powers. The Du Bois resolution provided for an executive committee, consisting of the chairman of the Board, the treasurer, the secretary, and the Director of Publications and Research (a change of title from "Director of Publicity and Research").[43] This executive committee was to have general supervision over the work and finances of the Association and all its departments and was to report to the Board. Though the chairman was to have general control and supervision of the Association between meetings, his decisions and appointments were subject to the approval of the Board and the executive committee.[44] The secretary was to be limited in authority and function to keeping records, supervising the branches, the annual meetings and annual conference, conducting the press and lecture bureau, acting as secretary of the executive committee, and collecting and disbursing dues and general funds of the Association.

The Director of Publication and Research, with the advice and cooperation of the Publication Committee of the Board, was

43. This "executive committee" was a committee of the Board in contrast to the "Executive Committee" which was the governing body of the Association before incorporation.

44. This procedure is in direct contrast to a report on "methods of organization and administration" submitted in 1912 by an unidentified "Mr. Morgan." In order to avoid and overcome "many of the difficulties which have been encountered in the past," Morgan divided the organization into three functional areas: the advisory function, the executive function, and machinery for carrying out details. He recommended as "fundamental" to a successful organization that the executive function should be in the hands of one person, and that this director "must be the same person who follows it up and sees that it is done." This work could not be done by a Board of Directors or an Executive Committee. "Memorandum by Mr. Morgan of Organization Work," August 23, 1912, Du Bois Papers.

given power to edit and manage *The Crisis,* collect and disburse *Crisis* monies, make reports to the treasurer, edit and issue all other publications of the Association, and direct the Bureau of Research and Information.

Villard's opposition to Du Bois' plan found support in Florence Kelley, who thought the carte blanche proposed for his department was staggering. Nor could she accept his idea of the duties of the secretary, commenting that no sane person would undertake the task as Du Bois had outlined it.[45]

Nevertheless, the Board adopted Du Bois' resolution, along with the article naming the officers. The chairman of the Board did not become the center of authority that Villard had maintained was necessary. The secretary was in no sense an executive officer, and all power and authority, save that which it chose to delegate, lay with the Board of Directors and its subordinate executive committee.[46]

In so defining the duties of the officers, the Board at this time upheld Du Bois' contention as to his role as an equal on the Board with the chairman, the treasurer, and the secretary. The Board, in refusing to subject the finances and business management of *The Crisis* to the scrutiny and control of the treasurer, also defeated another move by Villard for control over Du Bois' activities. Villard's vision of a single, autocratic, efficient executive officer lost out to Du Bois' reliance on consensus of the group, over which he could wield influence.

Miss Ovington wrote Spingarn that she had warned Du Bois of the strong desire of some Board members to get rid of him. She had cautioned him against Villard, who had "always been opposed" to their choice of Director of Publicity and Research, and against Miss Nerney, who seemed also to be opposed to his being there. She told Spingarn of pleading with Du Bois not to give any of his opponents the slightest handle against him, and

45. Florence Kelley to Spingarn, June 8, 1914, J. E. Spingarn Papers (Howard).
46. Board Minutes, NAACP, July 7, 1914.

not to go to extremes in his speaking or writing in any way that would endanger his position.[47]

THE "COLOR LINE"

Though Villard would have denied it vehemently, to Du Bois the conflict between them was one more evidence of the color line. This becomes clear in an exchange which developed between Du Bois and Joel Spingarn, whom he later called a knight.[48] As chairman of the Board, Spingarn, too, found it difficult to work with Du Bois. This time it was Du Bois who felt the tension and made what was for him an exceptional effort at reconciliation. He felt that the new chairman doubted his honesty and did not meet him in a straightforward manner but approached him "warily and cautiously watching for his dodging and deception." Hoping it was only his imagination, Du Bois, who rarely confided his inmost thoughts, confessed in a letter to Spingarn that the feeling had become so poignant that it demanded—and almost forced—an expression.[49]

Perhaps this was the opening which Spingarn had been waiting for. In any case, he took the opportunity to write a frank letter, assuring Du Bois that there was no question of his honesty, but that he had an extraordinary unwillingness to admit a mistake and that he would find or even invent reasons and quibbles to prove that he was not wrong. This was nothing, however, compared with the atmosphere of antagonism surrounding Du Bois, not just with Villard, Miss Nerney, and the Board, but in the whole colored world, where even his best friends felt a mingled affection and resentment. Spingarn went on to accuse Du Bois of mistaking obstinacy for strength of character. Many were sure that he, Du Bois, was the only source of the disorder

47. Ovington to Spingarn, November 7, 1914, J. E. Spingarn Papers (Howard).

48. Du Bois, *Dusk of Dawn: An Essay Toward an Autobiography of a Race Concept* (New York, 1940). The dedication is "To keep the memory of Joel Spingarn, scholar and knight."

49. Du Bois to Spingarn, October 23, 1914 (Johnson Collection).

and lack of unity in the organization, and that for the Association to work together effectively and without friction, Du Bois must be eliminated. Though Spingarn disagreed with that point of view because of his faith in Du Bois' character and talents and because he believed it was a matter of temperament, he agreed that Du Bois' talents must be subordinated to the general welfare of the organization. He made it clear that the rift between the departments was closed. "There can be no Crisis, no non-Crisis; the war of dividing our work has failed; both must be one." Without this cooperation, Spingarn concluded, the Association was doomed.[50]

A few days later Du Bois replied to Spingarn. He denied that he was obstinate. He blamed his temperament on the peculiar education and experiences to which he had been subjected because of his color and asked for a chance to work unhampered. He looked upon *The Crisis* as one of the world's great journals, a means of educating and training the Negro masses. Not until the journal achieved a circulation of 100,000 would the machinery of the NAACP be perfected.

Here again was the conflict as to whether they should first perfect the organization or should proceed at once with widespread propaganda. Du Bois believed that the "great blow—the freeing of ten million" would not be possible until the support of the Negro masses had been enlisted. Internal friction within the NAACP was a minor matter for which he refused to take the blame. His explosion over the matter of publicizing Negro crimes had been the result of piled-up slights and unkindnesses on the part of Villard. Two weary years of that had put his nerves on edge. He had had little disagreements with Miss Nerney over office regulations, but Miss Nerney had a violent temper and was depressingly suspicious of his motives. She had elbowed him out of all connection with the general work of the NAACP, and he had been right in refusing to allow her to interfere with *The Crisis.*

50. Spingarn to Du Bois, October 24, 1914 (Johnson Collection).

The basis of all this friction, Du Bois explained to Spingarn, was the "color line." There was not a shadow of the thing in either Spingarn or Miss Ovington. As for Miss Nerney, though she had no conscious prejudice, "her every step [was] unconsciously along the color line." Du Bois found Villard even worse. (It is true that Villard's letters, in spite of his good intentions, often show a patronizing attitude toward the Negro. It was something that Booker T. Washington could tolerate, but it must have been extremely trying to Du Bois, who was sensitive enough to observe every "shadow.")

No organization of this type, Du Bois continued, had ever succeeded, because it became either a group of white philanthropists helping the Negro or a group of colored folk freezing out their white co-workers by insolence and distrust. Since everything broke along the so-called color line, Du Bois tried to evolve a scheme whereby Negroes and whites could work together on the same level of authority and cooperation by having two branches of the same work, one with a white head and one with a colored. In short the Association would work best with a white secretary, or chairman, while Du Bois kept complete control of *The Crisis*.

He recommended that, first of all, the rift of the color line be fully recognized. Secondly, he demanded a chance to complete his work without chains and petty hampering. He asked to be trusted with power, and to be allowed the same right as a white man to succeed or to make mistakes on his own merits. Then if the Association should decide that he was standing in the way of its success, he would leave.[51]

Spingarn brought the matter into the open at the November, 1914, Board meeting, a move which distressed Miss Ovington, who had worked steadily for five years to prevent this lining up of personalities. She became very angry when Spingarn claimed that the friction centered about a single individual, whom he described as childish and insubordinate. To Spingarn's charge that she idolized Du Bois, she answered that she did worship

51. Du Bois to Spingarn, October 28, 1914 (Johnson Collection).

genius. The other Board members were able journeymen, but Du Bois was the master builder. She defended Du Bois' criticism of Miss Nerney's temper, admitting that she had confined herself to working on *The Crisis* because of Miss Nerney's ill will toward her in the office.[52]

As a result of these events, Du Bois sent a new proposal to Spingarn, suggesting that the office and his salary as Director of Publication and Research be abolished and that he give full time to *The Crisis,* which would continue as the official organ of the NAACP. A committee would exercise a veto over editorials and have the right to publish in each issue five pages of material concerning the Association.[53]

To gain support for his proposal Du Bois went to Boston and discussed the plan with Storey. Storey wrote Villard that Du Bois had created *The Crisis* and should be permitted to carry it on, although privately he was doubtful that Du Bois would be able to succeed alone.[54]

BYLAWS AND REVISIONS

At the December, 1914, meeting the Board reversed its July decision. The executive committee was abolished and the chairman of the Board was made the executive officer, with full authority over heads of departments between meetings of the Board. Employees, however, were subject to the authority of heads of departments and not to the chairman of the Board. Department heads were to be hired and fired only with the consent of the Board. The Director of Publication and Research, having the rank of a department head, was to be responsible for the administration of the *Crisis* Fund and formulation of policy

52. Ovington to Spingarn, November 4, 1914, November 7, 1914, J. E. Spingarn Papers (Howard).
53. Du Bois, "Memorandum to Mr. J. E. Spingarn and Mr. O. G. Villard," November 10, 1914 (Johnson Collection).
54. Storey to Villard, November 19, 1914, November 21, 1914, Storey Papers.

for *The Crisis*, limited only by the advice of a *Crisis* committee, consisting of the chairman of the Board and two others. He was to report monthly to the Board. Voting with Du Bois against the majority report were Kennaday, George W. Crawford, Verina Morton-Jones, and Mary White Ovington. Twenty were present at the meeting.[55]

Further revisions of the bylaws gave the Board chairman greater control and full authority over all officials and employees between Board meetings. In spite of Du Bois' efforts, the Association had not relinquished control of *The Crisis*. Not only did his attempt to reduce the power of the Board chairman fail, but the chairman regained some control of *The Crisis* by means of his mandatory position on the *Crisis* committee. Steps were taken to incorporate *The Crisis* and the committee decided a lawyer should edit the legal notes appearing in the journal.[56]

The new bylaws also tightened control of nominations of directors, requiring that the nominating committee submit nominations sixty days before the annual meeting, and that they be published in *The Crisis* at least thirty days prior to the meeting. Independent nominations required the signature of at least fifteen members to be turned in sixty days in advance and published in *The Crisis*.[57] The original bylaws had permitted nominations from the Board ten days before the annual meeting and nominations from the membership twenty days before.[58]

In 1915, with Florence Kelley as chairman, the nominating committee established a policy that new Board members be "selected on grounds of substantive services to the colored race" and in particular to the NAACP. They decided that present mem-

55. Board Minutes, NAACP, December 1, 1914. Dr. Morton-Jones was head of the Lincoln Settlement in Brooklyn, and one of few Negro women physicians. She was elected to the Board in 1913 to fill the unexpired term of Mrs. Mary Dunlop Maclean. Board Minutes, NAACP, January 21, 1913.

56. Board Minutes, NAACP, February 2, 1915.

57. Board Minutes, NAACP, December 1, 1914. Some changes in bylaws were adopted at the October 6, 1914, Board meeting. Others were tabled and adopted at the December 1, 1914 meeting.

58. Bylaws, in Board Minutes, NAACP, June 20, 1911.

bers should be continued unless they wished to withdraw, had moved too far away to be available, or for reasons obvious to the Board had become useless or injurious. They refused to elect L. M. Hershaw because he was a government employee and in danger of suffering reprisals if he should protest Administration policies.[59]

In 1917 it was decided that at least sixteen Board members must live in the vicinity of New York so that they could easily attend Board meetings. It was also stipulated that the nominating committee be biracial. Again the question of service and active work for the Association was emphasized.[60]

In 1918 a move got under way to increase the Board from thirty to forty and this amendment was added to the bylaws at the 1919 annual meeting.[61] A standing nominating committee was appointed to recommend names from time to time until the ten extra places should be filled.[62]

In 1919, John E. Milholland was dropped from the list of vice presidents, because he had not been an active Board member for some time. Though the office was largely an honorary position, policy required usefulness to the Association.[63] Also in 1919, in response to pressure from the members for greater representation, the whole constitution came under review again. A study was undertaken of the relationship of branches to the national Board and to the nominating and electing of officers. Following this re-evaluation, the nominating committee sought to add strength to the Board by asking the Chicago branch to recommend someone of national reputation from that area.[64]

59. Board Minutes, NAACP, September 13, 1915; Kelley to Spingarn, October 23, 1915, J. E. Spingarn Papers (Howard).

60. Minutes, Annual Meeting, January 2, 1917, in Board Minutes, NAACP.

61. Board Minutes, NAACP, November 11, 1918; Minutes, Annual Meeting, January 6, 1919, in Board Minutes, NAACP.

62. Board Minutes, NAACP, February 10, 1919. The committee consisted of Holmes, Morton-Jones, and Charles H. Studin.

63. Board Minutes, NAACP, January 6, 1919.

64. Minutes, Annual Meeting, January 6, 1919, in Board Minutes, NAACP; Board Minutes, NAACP, November 10, 1919.

FINANCIAL MATTERS

Another item of business at the December, 1914, meeting was the adoption of the "retrenchment program" which had been presented by Villard in October. Adding to the interoffice tension that existed throughout the early years was the continual state of crisis created by the precarious financial condition of the Association. As the program expanded, expenses increased. Though some Board members contributed generously, Villard fretted because the Board as a whole did not assume its financial obligations. As chairman and later as treasurer, he often went "begging" for money at the end of the month to meet the bills, the rent, and the salaries, complaining to his uncle that he was carrying the whole Association on his shoulders, an opinion probably not shared by some other Board members.[65]

Throughout 1913 and 1914, salaries and bills were often unpaid. Villard frequently made loans, as did Spingarn, and money was borrowed from the various special funds. The retrenchment program adopted in December, 1914, was a six-month plan to reduce expenses, while Board members increased their efforts to raise money. These measures were so successful that Villard, in February, 1915, could speak of a "nest egg" for the summer and a reserve in the bank for operating expenses.[66]

Although the largest contributions to the NAACP ranged from $500 to $2,000, they were small when compared to the typical philanthropies of the day. For instance, Julius Rosenwald gave

65. Board Minutes, NAACP, October 6, 1914, December 1, 1914; Minutes, Annual Meeting, January 21, 1913, in Board Minutes, NAACP; Villard to Garrison, February 20, 1911, September 21, 1911, Villard Papers.
66. Villard to Garrison, January 28, 1913, October 6, 1914, January 15, 1915, February 26, 1915, Villard Papers; Board Minutes, NAACP, April 1, 1913, September 2, 1914, October 6, 1914, December 1, 1914; Treasurer's Reports for March, June, and December 1913, and for May, June, July, September, October, and November 1914, in Board Minutes, NAACP.

$1,000 in 1915,[67] but in 1912 he had donated $5,000 to Tuskegee Institute and later became a major contributor to education for Negroes in the South.[68] In 1914, more than half the income of the NAACP came from eighteen individuals, but by 1918 the bulk of support came from small contributions. From 1912 to 1917, annual income ranged between $11,000 and $15,000. In 1919, when more than 62,300 persons contributed to the Association, it was over $44,000.[69]

A SPATE OF RESIGNATIONS

In the fall of 1915, trouble over *The Crisis* and its editor flared up again. Villard took offense at an item in the magazine, and Walling challenged Du Bois' expense account. In November another move was made to limit Du Bois' activities to the editing of *The Crisis*. A committee was appointed to bring in a plan defining and delimiting the work of executive officers, and the entire problem was made the special order of business for the December, 1915, meeting—just one year after the last analysis of executive functions.[70]

Du Bois took advantage of the fifth anniversary of *The Crisis,* in

67. Board Minutes, NAACP, July 12, 1915.
68. John Hope Franklin, *From Slavery to Freedom: A History of American Negroes,* 2nd ed. (New York, 1965), p. 380.
69. *The Crisis,* IX (April 1915), 297–298; XVII (November 1918), 18; XIX (April 1920), 320; V (November 1912), 39; NAACP, *Third Annual Report 1912* (New York, 1913), pp. 31–32; "Fifth Annual Report 1914," *The Crisis,* IX (April 1915), 298; "Seventh Annual Report 1916," *The Crisis,* XIII (February 1917), 167; *Eighth and Ninth Annual Reports 1917–1918* (New York, 1919), pp. 13, 14, 73–75; *Tenth Annual Report 1919* (New York, 1920), pp. 84–86; *Eleventh Annual Report 1920* (New York, 1921), pp. 73–74; *Twelfth Annual Report 1921* (New York, 1922), p. 80; *Thirteenth Annual Report 1922* (New York, 1923), pp. 59–60; *Fourteenth Annual Report 1923* (New York, 1924), pp. 47–48.
70. Ovington to Villard, August 10, 1915; Villard to Ovington, August 11, 1915, Villard Papers; Board Minutes, NAACP, October 11, 1915, November 8, 1915.

November, 1915, to publicize his version of the relationship between the magazine and the Association.[71] It certainly must have
enraged Villard to read Du Bois' statement that though the Association was the journal's legal owner, it had never expended a
single cent for its publication. The Association, claimed Du Bois,
had undertaken no financial responsibility; he, as editor, had been
personally responsible for every debt, and had used his own salary
and borrowed money to meet emergencies;[72] therefore, there were
both precedent and moral right that legal ownership, in whole
or in part, should reward such financial risk. What Du Bois failed
to mention was the fact that *The Crisis* had been subsidized from
the beginning, since the Association had paid his salary and allowed him to devote the greater part of his time and efforts to it.[73]

Du Bois, by this move, had taken the fight to the *Crisis* readers
and to the Board members directly, in an attempt to enlist sympathy and support for himself. He not only wanted complete personal control of *The Crisis,* but he also wanted to be an executive
officer on a level with other Board members in directing the work
of the Association. Yet his personal antagonisms prevented his
working with most Board members and staff. As various solutions
to the problems were proposed, he appeared to acquiesce, but
there was trouble again and again.

The Board was ambivalent, trying at times to limit Du Bois'
activity to *The Crisis,* and at other times to force him to give more
of his energy to the NAACP program. Because of the tremendous
influence of his writings and his philosophy, they were unwilling
to let personal antagonisms bring about a complete break from
the Association. Villard, on the other hand, came to the conclu-

71. *The Crisis,* XI (November 1915), 25–27.
72. Du Bois to Spingarn, October 20, 1915 (Johnson Collection); copy
of signed personal two-year note for $484.05, bearing 4% interest, Du Bois
to Mrs. Frances E. Hoggan, M.D., London, England, December 14, 1912,
in *Crisis* material, Du Bois Papers; copy of signed personal three-year
note for $250.00, bearing 5% interest, Du Bois to Mary W. Ovington,
August 5, 1913, in *Crisis* material, Du Bois Papers.
73. *The Crisis,* XI (November 1915), 27; Minutes, Annual Meeting,
January 3, 1916, in Board Minutes, NAACP.

sion that the "National Association will never do its duty to itself until it removes a man of Dr. Du Bois' spirit from all connection with it!" [74]

The report of the 1915 committee to delimit the work of executive officers recommended specifically that Du Bois' activities be limited to *The Crisis* and Association business. Any other activity should require permission of the Board, although this was tempered with a policy "to allow all possible freedom of action consistent with the needs of the Association's work." The finances of *The Crisis* were to be assigned to a business manager selected by, and directly responsible to, the Board. In a startling move, however, the Board voted that it was inexpedient to approve the committee's report.[75] The refusal of the Board to adopt the report led Spingarn and Villard to announce their intention to resign. Miss Nerney wrote that the treasurer's resignation had been received "nine hundred and ninety-nine times"; she was distressed that the epidemic had spread, and that Spingarn was now playing with the idea of resigning.[76]

Miss Ovington, writing to Spingarn, conveys the tension of the meeting and the division among friends: "Now that this vote is over, won't you forgive us all around? It's dreadful to have you come in and turn away from our section of the room as though we were under suspicion." According to Miss Ovington, the only possible replacement for Spingarn as chairman would be a radical. Joseph Loud of the Boston branch unwittingly agreed with her when he wrote Spingarn that it would be disastrous if Milholland or Miss Ovington should come to the fore as a result of his resignation. He was afraid that the withdrawal of Spingarn and Villard would bring about complete collapse of the organization.[77]

74. Villard to Spingarn, November 3, 1915, J. E. Spingarn Papers (Howard).

75. Board Minutes, NAACP, December 13, 1915.

76. Villard to Garrison, December 31, 1915, Villard Papers; Joseph Loud to Spingarn, December 24, 1915; Nerney to Spingarn, n.d. [1915], J. E. Spingarn Papers (Howard).

77. Ovington to Spingarn, December 13, [1915]; Loud to Spingarn, December 24, 1915, J. E. Spingarn Papers (Howard).

Loud believed that Negroes should direct the affairs of the Association and he considered Archibald Grimké the Negro best qualified for chairman,[78] but he doubted that Grimké would be able to work with Du Bois any better than the others. He firmly opposed Du Bois as chairman of the Board, or a figurehead under Du Bois' control, and he did not believe that Du Bois could serve effectively as both secretary and Director of Research, as Du Bois himself had proposed. Yet he recognized that Du Bois was making a signal contribution to the work of the Association and that a way must be found of allowing him as much freedom as in the past, limited only as to the general policy as adopted by the Board. (Miss Ovington also urged that a way be found to use Du Bois and his "obstinacy" under conditions where he could work naturally and happily.)

The Association, thought Loud, was at a critical period of its existence, and he agreed with Miss Nerney that a program of constructive work must be formulated and put into action lest internal dissension result in loss of interest in the NAACP and its objectives.

Other members protested when they learned that Villard and Spingarn planned to refuse re-election at the end of their three-year terms. Butler Wilson pointed out the progress made by the Association, its growth of membership, and the publicity brought by its opposition to the motion picture "The Birth of a Nation." He appealed to Spingarn's idealism, reminding him that the "cause is human justice. The task is tremendous. What cause is more

78. Archibald and Francis Grimké were sons of Henry Grimké of South Carolina and Nancy Weston, "a beautiful family slave." When their father died, they were cared for by their white half-brother and their aunts, Sarah Moore Grimké and Angelina Emily Grimké, the antislavery crusaders. Archibald graduated from Lincoln University and from Harvard Law School. His brother Francis was a clergyman in Washington, D.C. Edward M. Hinton, "Archibald Henry Grimké," in Allen Johnson and Dumas Malone (eds.), *Dictionary of American Biography,* VII, (New York, 1931), pp. 632–633. Both Archibald and Francis were members of the original Committee of Forty. *Proceedings of the National Negro Conference 1909* (New York, May 31 and June 1), p. 225; New York *Evening Post,* June 2, 1909.

worthy of any man's steel? Who better than you to lead it? My friend, you must not quit us now. Never mind if the colored people have not rallied as you have reason to believe they should. Give them time. They are sure to come and we are sure to win." [79]

From the Deep South, William Pickens, a Negro educator who had graduated from Yale with Phi Beta Kappa honors, wrote Spingarn of his distress at learning of the proposed resignations. Dr. William A. Sinclair of Philadelphia wrote that Springarn had "the talent, tact, temperament, character, enthusiasm, earnestness and a happy combination of conservatism and radicalism—conservatism on non-essentials and radicalism whenever principle is involved—the qualities so necessary in a great leader in a great propaganda." [80]

Meanwhile Du Bois was busy rallying support for himself. He elicited from Moorfield Storey assurance, as he had the year before, that if *The Crisis* were to become self-supporting, Du Bois would take entire charge and sever all nominal connections with the Association. [81]

Using as an excuse that certain members of the Board were unable to attend meetings regularly and thus were not fully informed, Du Bois sent out a "Statement" to the Board in December, 1915, asserting that the real basis of the difficulties within the NAACP was the question of power and control. He had come to the Association with the understanding that he was to be an executive officer, responsible directly to the Board, and that he was to have as much freedom as possible in working for the Association. He had consistently refuted the contention that the chairman was chief executive officer and that the editor of *The Crisis* was responsible to him. The new chairman, the statement went on to say, had reasserted the idea of the executive function

79. Ovington to Spingarn, November 7, 1914; Loud to Spingarn, December 24, 1915, J. E. Spingarn Papers (Howard); Butler Wilson to Spingarn, December 28, 1915.

80. Willam Pickens to Spingarn, January 11, 1916, J. E. Spingarn Papers (Howard); *The Crisis,* XIX (April 1920), 334–336; Sinclair to Spingarn, January 4, 1915, J. E. Spingarn Papers (Howard).

81. Storey to Du Bois, December 27, 1915, Storey Papers.

of the chairman, but this time an agreement had been reached whereby Du Bois was assigned the specific work of editing and publishing *The Crisis*, together with some general duties, while the chairman was given general supervision over all other areas of the Association. Du Bois interpreted this action of the Board to mean that the chairman was "a sort of arbiter in cases of dispute . . . or where the whole machinery of the organization must act as a unit." He claimed to have abided by this agreement, but suddenly, to his great surprise, came a series of recommendations aimed at still more radical changes in his duties and in his relations to the Board. This proposal would have removed most of his control over *The Crisis* and still further subordinated him to the chairman.

The recommendations had been rejected by a vote of twelve to two, but this had not solved the problem. Du Bois, claiming to have been on the verge of resigning four times, demanded a clear understanding that he was an executive officer, independent of other executive officers, and responsible directly to the Board. This time, he insisted in his statement, the editing and management of *The Crisis* must be recognized as his job, and any other duties he performed would be on the same voluntary basis as the work of other members of the Board.[82]

The January, 1916, annual meeting was an airing of grievances from all sides. Spingarn paid tribute to Du Bois' work outside the Association, his books, articles, and activities in other organizations such as the Races Congress, the New York Emancipation Exposition, and the Horizon Guild. But while these activities indirectly stimulated interest in the cause, Spingarn held that the Association would profit by receiving more of the time of its most highly paid official. He blamed the Board for failing to make clear the understanding on which Du Bois had been induced to come to New York—a point on which Du Bois himself, incidentally, was perfectly clear.

Spingarn acknowledged Du Bois' role in creating without initial

82. Du Bois, "A Statement," n.d., [December 1915], Du Bois Papers.

capital a magazine with a circulation of over 30,000, reaffirming that *The Crisis* was the official organ of the NAACP, and that the editorials were necessarily the expressions of the personality that gave them shape. But Spingarn admonished Du Bois (and warned the membership as well) when he said that the editor must "interpret our cause nobly [and] never sink to the level of petty irritation, insulting personalities or vulgar recrimination [or] meet insult with insult and injustice with injustice."

In rebuttal, Du Bois reported that he considered his main usefulness to the objectives of the Association was forwarding certain pioneer movements and general methods of uplift. Three times he had prepared general programs for the guidance and reorganization of the Association. Because funds had not been made available he had been unable to establish what he had planned in the way of research and publication in the name of the NAACP. He now proposed a Publications and Research Fund of $2,500, implying that *The Crisis* would then be self-supporting and that the money which had been used to pay his salary would go to this fund. With it, he would publish a number of small bulletins.

Miss Nerney's report at the January, 1916, meeting was also full of complaints. She worried about the lack of activity of committees of the Board, especially the Publications and Research Committee, which had never met. She compared her own work of expanding the organization with that of Du Bois. Publishing a magazine, she said, had offered subscribers an immediate and steady return on their money, whereas the most she could offer to an American public which had not yet developed a social consciousness was lofty principles. White people were either ignorant of, or antagonistic to, her work; the masses of colored people did not know the organization; and the words "Civil Rights," "Democracy," and "The New Abolition" meant nothing to them. She warned that unless some great crisis should arise, they could not hope for material results for a long time. Though she offered no reason for her resignation, the heavy work of the secretary's job as well as the unsettled status of the officers caused a great strain on her. (She was irritated to learn later that Du Bois, the cause

of much of her problem, had suggested she was leaving because
of her health, and wrote Spingarn, "That's putting effect for
cause.")[83]

Villard, too, presented his formal resignation from the Board
in January, but despite lengthy discussion, the annual meeting
took no action on the resignations. At the Board meeting on
January 10, 1916, Miss Ovington once again became acting secretary, replacing Miss Nerney, but Spingarn, Storey, and Du Bois
retained their posts, and Villard was unanimously re-elected treasurer.[84]

The job of finding a new secretary was not easy. Miss Nerney,
who believed that Negroes should be given positions of leadership
in the Association, proposed Jessie Fauset and several others. A
white man, however, Royal Freeman Nash, became the new
secretary and remained in that post until he left for war duty in
1917.[85]

In another move to tie *The Crisis* to the Association, the *Crisis*
committee suggested that a list of officers and a statement of the
purposes of the Association be printed in a prominent place opposite the first page of reading material.[86]

VILLARD OR DU BOIS?

The compromises resulting from the January "resignations"
were only temporary. By April, 1916, Du Bois was once more
in trouble, this time with the proper Bostonians for using what
they called an unpleasantly suggestive cover on *The Crisis*. When
Villard protested the misuse of the cover, Du Bois "calmly left the

83. Minutes, Annual Meeting, January 3, 1916, in Board Minutes,
NAACP; Nerney to Spingarn, January 6, 1916, J. E. Spingarn Papers
(Howard).
84. Board Minutes, NAACP, January 10, 1916.
85. Nerney to Spingarn, January 6, 1916, J. E. Spingarn Papers
(Howard); Board Minutes, NAACP, February 14, 1916, March 13, 1916,
May 8, 1916, September 17, 1917. Miss Ovington called Nash "a writer."
Ovington, *The Walls Came Tumbling Down*, p. 147.
86. Board Minutes, NAACP, March 13, 1916.

room without excusing himself . . . a fine attitude for an employee of the Association." The Board voted its disapproval but referred the matter to the *Crisis* committee for action, a move which guaranteed no action at all.[87]

It was equally difficult to control Du Bois in other matters. When a *Crisis* supplement was issued describing a particularly atrocious lynching at Waco, Texas, Du Bois reluctantly altered his text to meet the objections of Charles Studin, chairman of the Legal Committee. Arthur Spingarn considered the pamphlet libelous, however, and it was necessary for the secretary to appeal to the chairman of the Board for a ruling before Du Bois would agree to additional changes. Nor was it possible for Du Bois to avoid rancor and personal thrusts in his editing of *The Crisis,* and letters continued to come to Spingarn urging a spirit of unity and a concentration of effort in the fight against "the real enemy." [88]

At the 1917 annual meeting, Miss Ovington revealed that Du Bois had a number of times made editorial changes to conform to what the *Crisis* committee considered to be the best interests of the Association. In reply to criticisms she explained that the policy of the committee had been to strike a balance between editorial freedom and restraint, lest the editor become a rabid propagandist and convert no one. Nevertheless, she praised Du Bois' work and commented that the yearly increase in the readership of *The Crisis* was the best comment on its management. The committee recommended that his salary be increased, a move approved by the Board, after postponing it for more than a year because of financial difficulties and continued friction.[89]

87. Garrison to Villard, April 27, 1916; Villard to Garrison, April 28, 1916; Villard to Garrison, May 10, 1916, Villard Papers; Board Minutes, NAACP, May 8, 1916.

88. Royal F. Nash to Joel Spingarn, June 14, 1916; George W. Cook to Spingarn, December 19, 1916, J. E. Spingarn Papers (Howard).

89. Minutes, Annual Meeting, January 2, 1917, in Board Minutes, NAACP; Board Minutes, NAACP, November 13, 1916; "Report of Committee delimiting the work of Executive Officers," in Board Minutes, NAACP, December 13, 1915.

The new secretary, meanwhile, was not measuring up to his responsibilities. Royal F. Nash had begun work in February, but by the middle of November he was still without a program, apparently lost in office routine. He was undecided as to whether the greatest need of the Association was for a lawyer or a publicity man, a matter which chilled Villard and Studin when they conferred with him.[90] Moreover, the Board found his plan for a financial campaign unsatisfactory and wasteful. Nash then requested the Board to appoint a committee to aid him in drawing up a program for 1917. On this committee were Miss Ovington, John Haynes Holmes, Villard, Du Bois, and James Weldon Johnson, who was hired in November as field secretary, the new title for "national organizer." [91]

Though Villard had accepted re-election as treasurer at the time of the annual meeting, a week later at the regular Board meeting he asked to be relieved of his duties as treasurer and Board member because of ill health. Meanwhile, his uncle, Francis Jackson Garrison, died in December, 1916, ending the twenty years of correspondence between the two men which reveals so much of the inner history of the NAACP, Villard's attitudes, and his work in behalf of the colored people. In May, 1917, Paul Kennaday agreed to serve as assistant treasurer to relieve Villard of some of his duties.[92]

The perennial question confronting the Board was: Villard or Du Bois? Villard frequently made it clear that if Du Bois were out of the way he would again be available as chairman of the Board, a possibility against which Miss Ovington and Du Bois were constantly on guard. In May, 1917, Spingarn and Nash entered officers training camp, leaving Miss Ovington as acting chairman and James Weldon Johnson as acting secretary. When Spingarn talked of resigning, Du Bois observed that Villard had

90. Villard to Spingarn, November 20, 1916, J. E. Spingarn Papers (Howard).
91. Board Minutes, NAACP, December 11, 1916; Cook to Spingarn, January 16, 1917, J. E. Spingarn Papers (Howard).
92. Board Minutes, NAACP, January 8, 1917, May 14, 1917; Loud to Spingarn, December 15, 1916, J. E. Spingarn Papers (Howard).

his eye fixed upon a possible vacancy. Miss Ovington warned
Spingarn that it was evident Villard wanted to return to control
things.[93]

In September, 1917, Nash, who had been on leave since May,
sent in his resignation and it was necessary to find a new secretary. Roger Baldwin was ruled out because he was a pacifist and
looked on with disfavor by the government. This action irritated
Villard because he considered himself even more a pacifist than
Baldwin and very much out of favor with the government. (An
unspoken reason for Baldwin's rejection by the Board may have
been that he and Villard were old friends and had once been
schoolmates.)[94]

As a member of the selection committee Villard then proposed
Owen Lovejoy, general secretary of the National Child Labor
Committee, but Miss Ovington objected to Lovejoy. She feared
he would assume command and alienate the colored people, who
had been won with such great effort. She observed that white
members of the Board received little support from Negroes who
resented direction. She looked forward to the day when a Negro
capable of the secretaryship would become available. She considered James Weldon Johnson a man of excellent ideas, but not
aggressive enough. She thought he needed someone to keep him
stirred up. On the other hand, any white man selected as secretary would need great tact and the ability to work with his colleagues on a basis of equality.[95] This was an obvious reference to
Villard, the autocrat, and to the type of person he himself would
choose as secretary. Miss Ovington had scolded him for his crit-

93. Board Minutes, NAACP, May 14, 1917; Du Bois to Spingarn,
September 25, 1917 (Johnson Collection); Spingarn to Board of Directors,
May 1, 1917; Ovington to Spingarn, November 24, 1916, September 26,
1917, September 29, 1917, J. E. Spingarn Papers (Howard).

94. Board Minutes, NAACP, September 17, 1917, October 8, 1917;
Villard to Ovington, October 6, 1917; Villard to Garrison, March 14, 1913,
Villard Papers.

95. Ovington to Spingarn, July 5, 1917, September 26, 1917, September
29, 1917, J. E. Spingarn Papers (Howard); Ovington to Villard, October 5,
1917, Villard Papers.

icisms at a time when he was not actively in touch with the work, and he had again lashed out at Du Bois and threatened to resign as treasurer. Conscious of his own prestige, Villard had said he would not lend his name to the organization unless it were efficient. "The first step toward that efficiency and public confidence," he reiterated, would be "the removal of Dr. Du Bois as editor." [96]

At the January 7, 1918, meeting Lillian Wald and Florence Kelley presented the name of John R. Shillady, an experienced social worker who had been employed in the Department of Charities and Corrections in Westchester, New York, and the Board voted to engage Shillady as secretary. As assistant secretary it selected Walter White, an active member of the Atlanta branch who worked for an insurance company. Both men were to contribute new vigor to the Association.[97]

Villard's contention that the Association could use a well-trained social worker was borne out by the efficiency demonstrated by the new secretary in organizing the work. Shillady was engaged with the stipulation that he must raise money. At the first Board meeting he attended he brought plans for a membership drive—the Moorfield Storey drive—which turned out to be the catalyst in a startling increase in membership. James Weldon Johnson later wrote of Shillady's great ability as a systematizer and organizer, and Miss Ovington commented on his businesslike manner. Walter White also lost no time in proving his fitness and adaptability for the work.[98]

In 1918, Spingarn again asked to be released as chairman, and Du Bois suggested that he propose Miss Ovington as his successor in order to evade "the usual unpleasant candidate" (meaning Villard). Miss Ovington was elected January 6, 1919, in time to

96. Villard to Ovington, October 6, 1917, Villard Papers.
97. Board Minutes, NAACP, November 12, 1917, January 7, 1918; *The Crisis*, XV (March 1918), 219; Walter White, *A Man Called White: The Autobiography of Walter White* (New York, 1948), pp. 28, 33–40.
98. Board Minutes, NAACP, January 14, 1918, February 11, 1918; James Weldon Johnson, *Along This Way* (New York, 1933), p. 329; Ovington, *The Walls Came Tumbling Down*, p. 148.

face another crisis over *The Crisis*. The irrepressible Du Bois had published an issue without first submitting its editorials to the *Crisis* committee, and even Miss Ovington found it necessary to discipline the editor after having defended him for so many years. When the committee met with Joel Spingarn as its new chairman, it decreed that *Crisis* matters should be discussed at the weekly staff conferences instituted by Shillady. The committee reaffirmed that its function was to approve the editorials and to pass on all matters of policy affecting *The Crisis*.[99]

The recurring crises over the Association's journal were too much for Oswald Garrison Villard. He finally resigned as treasurer and as Board member, giving as his reasons the pressure of his duties on the *Evening Post* and *The Nation*. They were legitimate reasons, but it is clear that Villard saw no end to Du Bois' career in the Association now that Miss Ovington had "come to the fore." In October, 1919, the Board elected Joel Spingarn treasurer in his place and made Villard a vice president, after praising him for his long service.[100]

99. Du Bois to Spingarn, January 12, 1918, August 15, 1918 (Johnson Collection); Board Minutes, NAACP, January 6, 1919, May 12, 1919.
100. Shillady to Spingarn, May 21, 1919, J. E. Spingarn Papers (Howard); Board Minutes, NAACP, October 13, 1919.

ELLIOTT M. RUDWICK

★

An Accommodationist in Wartime

With Washington's death, there seemed a possibility that a reconciliation might finally be attained, and leaders of the race might really "close ranks." The NAACP scheduled its annual conference for February 11, 1916, but, after the Tuskegeean's friends announced that on the same day they intended to hold a memorial service for their departed chieftain, Du Bois advised Association officers to postpone their meeting in order to avoid the charge of sponsoring "a counter attraction." The *Crisis* editor, although still suspicious of "certain elements," suggested a "get together meeting" with the leaders of all large Negro organizations, including Tuskegee Institute. NAACP officers agreed immediately. The Association, however, was not seeking alliances because of weakness. The membership had grown rapidly to about 9,000 in 1916, and the monthly circulation of *The Crisis* during the years was between thirty-five and forty thousand.[1] Already, the organization had some success in the field of legal redress.

1. *The Crisis,* XI (1915–1916), 255; James E. Pierce, "The NAACP— A Study in Social Pressure" (M.A. thesis, Ohio State University, 1933), p. 49.

The NAACP claimed "partial victories" in New Jersey where its lawyers attacked the practice of detaining Negro suspects without adequate evidence, and in Maryland where the courts ruled against the residential segregation ordinance. The Association proclaimed its "greatest triumph" in the 1915 United States Supreme Court decision declaring the "grandfather clause" unconstitutional.

When Robert R. Moton succeeded Booker T. Washington as head of Tuskegee Institute, *The Crisis* hoped for "a new era of union and understanding" based upon the race's right to first-class citizenship, and to all the perquisites (political, civil, educational, and social) which accompanied it. In an open letter to Moton— parts of which were condescending—Du Bois acknowledged that the Southern educator "substantially" subscribed to these principles; however, the *Crisis* editor expressed his "deepest solicitude" that Moton would not participate in a conciliation-at-any-cost program.[2] Du Bois was troubled by the undenied reports that the new Tuskegee principal had instructed Mrs. Moton to shun Pullman cars in the South—so whites would not be offended. The *Crisis* editor seemed incredulous when he quoted an account from the New York *Sun* praising the educator for having "respected the feeling of the objectors to Mrs. Moton's presence." [3]

Privately, Du Bois admitted to Joel Spingarn that the "direct frontal attack" did not pay off too well. He agreed "true equality" would not be achieved "for several generations"—in the meantime the race was compelled to endure segregation while making clear the nature of its ultimate goals. In his opinion, it was unnecessary for all Negro leaders "to work in the same lines or for the same things," if they were confident of each other and determined to create a "solid structure." Spingarn also judged the time was propitious to press for a united front and invited influential Negroes of various persuasions to meet at his home in Amenia, New York. Over fifty men and women gathered for the Amenia Conference, which was held from August 24 to August 26, 1916. Among those who attended were Tuskegeeans Emmett J. Scott,

2. *The Crisis,* XII (1916), 136.
3. *Ibid.,* p. 185.

Robert R. Moton, and Fred Moore; middle-of-the-roaders Mary
Church Terrell, Kelly Miller, James Weldon Johnson, and R. R.
Wright, Jr.; and Radicals William M. Trotter, William Sinclair,
and W. E. B. Du Bois.[4]

Although the conferees "arrived at a virtual unanimity of
opinion," they decided it was not in the race's best interest to
reveal what transpired. Almost immediately the decision was
reconsidered and the Amenia resolutions were published. The
participants recognized no conflict between industrial and college
education. The race required "complete political freedom," which
could be obtained through "a practical working understanding
among the leaders of the colored race." The delegates concluded
that Northern leaders should make a better attempt at compre-
hending the special problems of those Negroes who helped to
guide the race in the South. The conferees departed from Amenia
resolving to sponsor annual meetings.[5]

The New York *Age* believed an "epoch" had been reached.
Fred Moore, the paper's editor (and one of the conferees), wrote:
"It marks the birth of a new spirit of united purpose and effort
that will have far-reaching results." [6] Recalling the Amenia Conference, Du Bois wrote in 1925: "It not only marked the end of
the old things and the old thoughts and the old ways of attacking
the race problem, but in addition to this it was the beginning of the
new things. Probably on account of our meeting the Negro race
was more united and more ready to meet the problems of the
world than it could possibly have been." [7]

John Hope Franklin, the distinguished historian of the Negro
race in America, concluded in the same vein: "It was a happy
prelude to America's entry into the war. With a calm but firm
unanimity of opinion among the Negro leaders of the United
States, the black citizens of the Western republic could pursue

4. *Amenia Conference,* pamphlet, 1916 (Howard University Library).
5. "Amenia Report," Ms., August 26, 1916 (Howard). Final draft
published in New York *Age*, September 7, 1916.
6. New York *Age*, September 14, 1916.
7. W. E. B. Du Bois, *The Amenia Conference,* pamphlet (Troutbeck,
N.Y., 1925), p. 17. See also *The Crisis,* XL (1933), 226.

more intelligently and relentlessly the democracy which the allies were seeking to extend to all the world." [8]

Actually, the Amenia Conference has been overrated. Perhaps the conclave sowed a few seeds of understanding—which required years to germinate. Certainly, it was useful for the leaders to confer in the hope that the backbiting and backyard criticism would cease, but such disruptions did not fade away. No real division of labor was worked out and, although the group was supposed to meet once a year, its members never did. (When the second Amenia Conference was held in 1933, few of the old conferees were invited to participate.) Leaders of both wings remained bitter for some time to come. For example, Emmett J. Scott, in a 1917 biography of Booker T. Washington, referred to Du Bois' Talented Tenth in this manner:

This numerically small and individually unimportant element of the Negroes in America would hardly warrant even passing mention except that the always carping and sometimes bitter criticisms of these persons are apt to confuse the well-wishers of the race who do not understand the situation. . . . A number of these persons [the Talented Tenth] make all or a part of their living by publicly bewailing the wrongs and injustices of their race and demanding their redress by immediate means. . . .[9]

Scott then attacked Du Bois, although not naming him, as the "chief exponent" of the Talented Tenth who broke faith with Booker T. Washington.

Probably Du Bois more than any other racial adviser violated the Amenia principle of peaceful coexistence. He minimized the social pressure which was placed upon Southern Negro leaders and still blamed them for failing to propagandize on behalf of reforms he favored. Therefore, he continued to deprecate their projects and programs. For example, in the winter of 1917 Tuskegee Institute sponsored a conference on Negro migration. Southern newspapers commended the participants for discouraging Negroes from going

8. Franklin, *From Slavery to Freedom,* p. 447.
9. Scott and Stowe, pp. 24–25.

North. Du Bois examined the content of these Tuskegee resolutions inch by inch and found one-third of the space was devoted to advising colored people to stay South, while one-sixth dealt with imploring the region to be kinder to its Negroes. An additional one-fourth discussed the theme of interracial cooperation, while only one-thirtieth was concerned with the need for improved police protection and law enforcement. The *Crisis* editor fumed, "We do solemnly believe that any system of Negro leadership that today devotes ten times as much space to the advantages of living in the South as it gives to lynching and lawlessness is inexcusably blind." [10]

Du Bois' own views on migration were rather interesting.[11] He recommended immediate migration to resourceful Negroes who cared anything about living in "civilization." For years, he encouraged mass departure as a practical protest against Southern racism, but he demonstrated an inadequate comprehension of the sociological problems arising from such an exodus. He simply asked Northern Negroes to open their hearts to the migrants, whose presence he admitted would create further hardship for the long-time residents of the communities.

Contrary to the Amenia resolutions, he maintained his open war on industrial education. During the months following Amenia, the *Crisis* editor proclaimed Negro high schools and colleges were "ten times" more effective than Tuskegee or Hampton Institutes. He asserted that the Phelps-Stokes Fund was about to issue a report which, in effect, favored the death sentence for higher education. The report was also "dangerous" because it asked leaders of Southern Negro schools to cooperate with the whites.[12] Actually, the Phelps-Stokes survey, while praising the Tuskegee type of education, placed a high value upon secondary and college education. However, the observers noted that since most Negro colleges were small and inadequate, the race would be best served

10. *The Crisis,* XIII (1916–1917), 219.
11. *The Crisis,* XII (1916), 270; XIII (1916–1917), 115; XIV (1917), 8, 63.
12. *The Crisis,* XIII (1916–1917), 111; XV (1917–1918), 173–177.

by properly equipping several regional institutions instead of scattering resources. Also recommended was a curriculum change which placed more emphasis upon physical sciences, economics, sociology, and history; and less stress upon the traditional Latin and Greek.[13]

Du Bois blasted away at Hampton Institute and allied himself with "educated Negroes" who charged that this "educational blind alley" was doing incalculable harm. He contended that Hampton was not preparing its students for higher education or the professional schools; he accused the institution of an "illiberal and seemingly selfish attitude toward other colored schools." According to the *Crisis* editor, Hampton Institute was still the pawn of the Northern and Southern racist exploiters.[14] Du Bois' simple remedy: the school should place itself under the tutelage of the Talented Tenth. (If Hampton was a helot of the white supremacists, it is difficult to appreciate how the institution could have accepted his cure. It must also be asked how Negro education in the South could have been operated without cooperating with the whites of the region.)

In view of these attacks *after* the Amenia Conference, one may speculate about the basis for the belief that the conclave was the sunny shedding place of old suspicions and the bedding place of happy unity. Du Bois and the other conferees went to Amenia with strong hopes, and in their great need to *want* a reconciliation they thought they got one. They were only bewitched by the magic of resolutions. Since 1904 there had been fervent talk about a rapprochement, but no one could agree specifically and practically on whose terms it was to take place. Nevertheless, intraracial harmony was a goal around which to rally—nobody was against it in principle. But Booker T. Washington's death did not suddenly remove the suspicion which was nourished over the years. The conferees did not hammer out "a practical working understand-

13. *Negro Education, A Study of the Private and Higher Schools for Colored People in the United States,* Bulletin, 1916, Nos. 38–39 [Washington, D.C., 1917].
14. *The Crisis,* XV (1917–1918), 10–12.

ing" in Myrdal's sense of a functional interacting division of labor. For example, such an "understanding" would have permitted Southern leaders to stress industrial education while Northerners like Du Bois could have emphasized secondary-college education. Neither group would have tried to demolish the other but simply would have attempted to push its own program. Thus, the race would have achieved as much as possible. But old animosities did not die and old dogmas prevailed. Du Bois and the Radicals were emotionally blinded to a fact of life: Southern Negro education required the cooperation of whites in order to survive. Nor did the *Crisis* editor comprehend that a relatively small proportion of educational funds was warranted for high schools and colleges since most of the Negro youngsters attended grammar schools and industrial schools. Furthermore, because the majority of Negroes did not go beyond grammar school, vocational subjects occupied a justifiable place in its curriculum.

While it is true that the Amenia resolutions gave conservative Negro leaders a rationalization for doing little to propagandize on behalf of suffrage and civil rights, nevertheless these men had attended the reconciliation meeting at Amenia and their fears of the NAACP were lessened considerably. Du Bois should have courted them instead of antagonizing them with hostile editorials.

The Amenia conferees themselves injected the myth of "unanimity," and as such it was preserved by race historians like John Hope Franklin. Actually, the leaders cooperated more closely a few years after Amenia, and the change was due to more earthy reasons than a conference, i.e., World War I, the increase in urbanization and education within the race, *et al.* Undoubtedly, historians used Amenia to signify the place and time at which the schism was healed because it was difficult to know exactly when the rapprochement occurred. It must not be forgotten that a few of the conferees wrote their own historical accounts, and they wished to think their actions were directly responsible for achieving so desirable a goal as intraracial harmony.

Oswald Garrison Villard, who believed in the workability of the Amenia resolutions, was annoyed by the antagonistic *Crisis* editorials following the conclave. He had never given up his profound interest in industrial education and was certain that such training would be even more beneficial to the race if the NAACP and *The Crisis* encouraged the cooperation of "enlightened Southerners." [15] (It seemed to him that Booker T. Washington had been a major obstacle to such an arrangement, and when the leader died the white journalist saw beckoning opportunity.) Of course, such views created another clash with Du Bois. The same Phelps-Stokes report which the *Crisis* editor had described as "dangerous," Villard contended was "remarkable . . . the most useful and important thing of the kind that has been made." However, for the time being, Du Bois retained his near-absolute control of the magazine and Villard could only fume. Clearly, the tumultous January, 1916, meeting of the NAACP board had solved nothing—the white journalist still regarded Du Bois as an "employee," and at a board session in 1917 the Negro editor stomped out of the room just as Villard was preparing to criticize him. In view of the differences between the two men, the editor of the New York *Evening Post* talked once more of resigning from his position as NAACP treasurer unless Du Bois departed from the organization.[16]

But the Negro editor was too well entrenched to be discharged. His valuable support still came from Joel Spingarn and Mary White Ovington. During the early days of 1917, after Du Bois underwent a critical operation, Spingarn wrote:

I walked out of the hospital, thinking of all that it would mean for 12 million people if this champion of theirs were not permitted to live. Others would take up the gauge where he threw it down; others might wield brilliant pens; others would speak with something of his quiet eloquence. But never again could these millions find another leader exactly like him.[17]

15. O. G. Villard to Mary White Ovington, October 6, 1917, Villard Papers.

16. Villard to F. J. Garrison, May 10, 1916 and Villard to Ovington, October 6, 1917, Villard Papers.

17. *The Crisis,* XIII (1916–1917), 163–164.

Miss Ovington also publicly observed Du Bois and *The Crisis* were indispensable to the NAACP. Undoubtedly with the help of his two friends, Du Bois convinced the board that *The Crisis* was a journal "of general circulation" and should not be required to publish NAACP matters which were too parochial. In December, 1916, the Association decided to place material about the organization and the local branches, *not* primarily in *The Crisis,* but in a special *Branch Bulletin.*

The Spingarn-Ovington wing of the NAACP also believed in the value of the Amenia resolutions, but could not bring themselves to stop Du Bois' bitter pen. (However, in 1917 Miss Ovington reported to the directors that Du Bois must not possess too much freedom or he would destroy his effectiveness by becoming "rabid.")[18] The interference of these two officers with the work of the *Crisis* editor was infrequent, not only because they had a great deal of affection and admiration for him, but also because they agreed that some of the Southern Negroes did deserve an editorial thrashing now and then.

Since the board recognized, however, that other leaders within the Negro race must be conciliated to some degree, and since it was apparent that Du Bois could not or would not do the job, plans were made to give the task to someone else. Even before the Amenia Conference, the board searched for a middle-of-the-road Negro to serve as its executive secretary. In January of 1916, Du Bois proposed John Hope, his old associate in the Niagara Movement. Hope, who was president of the Atlanta Baptist College, declined the offer.[19] Spingarn considered James Weldon Johnson, and the board chairman was delighted by the thought of capturing one of the few Negro intellectuals associated with the Tuskegeeans. Johnson was the author of *Autobiography of an Ex-Colored Man*

18. Annual Report of the Chairman of the *Crisis* Committee to the NAACP Board, contained in Minutes of the NAACP Board of Directors, January 2, 1917.
19. Ridgely Torrence, *The Story of John Hope* (New York, 1948), p. 199.

and had been a United States consul in Venezuela and Nicaragua. Joel Spingarn viewed the appointment as an absolute "coup d'état" for the Association—if only it could be brought off. Roy Nash, a white associate in the NAACP, also favored Johnson: "He is not academic, is a good mixer with a social bent that Du Bois and Hope lack, he is free from the stigma of religion, is a good talker, and would offend no group nor any audience." [20]

Since Johnson had been friendly to the Booker Washington group, Spingarn especially requested the reactions of Du Bois and Miss Ovington. The latter called the candidate "hopelessly reactionary on labor and other problems," while Du Bois found him "entirely desirable." Amusingly, the leftist *Messenger* magazine was also interested in evaluating Johnson and termed him the choice of "radical opinion." [21]

The *Crisis* editor attempted to persuade Johnson to think seriously about Spingarn's offer and reminded him of an earlier conversation in which they discussed the possibility of forming a "secret organization": "There is no telling what your wide acquaintance as an organizer, etc., might not lead to. We might be able to tie a durable knot to insure the permanency of the main organization." [22]

It is not clear what Du Bois meant, and, in reply to a recent inquiry, he stated that he was unable to recall the plans for his "secret" structure. However, it is probable that he wanted to establish a Negro auxiliary to indirectly influence the white-dominated NAACP. The organization could have been kept in readiness to take over the Association machinery should the whites have withdrawn as a result of personality-power clashes, or because of some serious disagreement over policy. Apparently, no such group was created. In November, 1916, Johnson accepted

20. The following letters are from the Spingarn Papers (Howard): Spingarn to Roy Nash, October 21, 1916 and Nash to Spingarn, October 27, 1916.

21. *Messenger* (December 1920), 163.

22. W. E. B. Du Bois to James Weldon Johnson, November 1, 1916, Johnson Papers (Yale University Library).

the NAACP offer and Spingarn suggested in a "confidential" memorandum that the new executive secretary seek out Du Bois for immediate discussions.

Just as Du Bois sought to improve the race's bargaining position by cooperating for a short period with the Negro conservatives, when World War I came he pursued the same goal and gave his support to the Allied cause. In both instances he joined with erstwhile enemies; discomfort and dilemmas awaited him.

Until the United States entered the war, Du Bois seemed completely confused. At the start, he claimed that race prejudice, manifesting itself in the coveting and capturing of the black colonies by imperialistic nations, was the major cause of World War I. As he viewed it, white workers, once having achieved political power, rebelled against the system of exploitation which was unleashed by the industrial revolution. European capitalists were then forced to look beyond their home countries for huge profits, and turned to the African colonies. Rapacity brought about the slaughter of natives and inevitably one European nation challenged another in a struggle over spoils. Thus World War I began. Du Bois, untroubled by consistency, sided with the Allies against the "barbarous" Germans. For him, the Germans were now superracists who gloried in their suppression of the African natives, while the English and French were conscience-stricken atoners—after they recognized to what degradation their race prejudice and greed had led them. Besides being naïve, Du Bois was inconsistent. His commitment to the Allies seemed contradictory, after he had declared the whole "European civilization has failed," and that the war was not the temporary perversion of the cultures of Europe—it was "the real soul of white culture." The next step was an indictment of American society, "the daughter of a dying Europe." [23]

23. *The Crisis*, IX (1914–1915), 28; X (1915), 28; Du Bois, "African Roots of War," *Atlantic Monthly*, CXV (1915), 707–714; *The Crisis*, IX (1914–1915), 29; X (1915), 81; XI (1915–1916), 186; XII (1916), 216–217.

Du Bois stripped the world's whites of all moral resources and was also prepared to divest them of technological contributions, since he wished to arraign them as completely effete and rotten. In accomplishing this task, he returned to an old racist theme—civilization was the product of "the colored races." White civilization had borrowed just about everything without acknowledgment:

The iron and trade of black Africa; the religion and empire building of yellow Asia; the art and science of the "dago" Mediterranean shore east, south and west as well as north. And where she has builded securely upon this great past and learned from it she has gone forward to greater and more splendid human triumph; but where she has ignored the past and forgotten and sneered at it she has shown the cloven hoof of poor crucified humanity; she has played, like other empires gone, the world fool.[24]

And the other side of the coin of racism was the glorification and superiority of Negroes. The Negro race was noble and "can stand before Heaven with clean hands." Having been deluded, demoralized, and destroyed, Negroes were called upon to return to "old ideals . . . old standards of beauty . . . not the blue-eyed, white-skinned types which are set before us in school and literature but rich, brown and black men and women with glowing dark eyes and crinkling hair . . . that harks back to the heritage of Africa and the tropics." [25]

For a long time Du Bois had denounced white critics for racism, but it was clear he learned a few lessons from them.

Simultaneously he presented another recurrent and related theme in 1917—Negroes could not survive in the United States unless they united economically. He was aware the ideology smacked of self-segregation, and attempted to make a distinction between "Teamwork" and "Jim Crowism." As he embraced his

24. W. E. B. Du Bois, "Of the Culture of White Folk," *Journal of Race Development*, VII (1917), 438.
25. *The Crisis*, XII (1916), 216–217.

teamwork vision of Negro men aspiring to be "consecrated" workers instead of millionaires, he predicted capitalists and politicians would oppose it. He realized many "consumers" could buy very little because of insufficient funds, but he did not consider any of these roadblocks impenetrable. Instead, he emphasized that wartime migration had created a Negro concentration in the prosperous North, thus making race identification stronger. He also believed that a cooperative Negro economy was more easily attainable because socioeconomic class disparity was smaller than in the white group.[26]

During the same year he introduced a motion at the NAACP board sessions, asking the Association to embark upon a program of teaching Negroes the value of forming buyers clubs which operated on principles of economic cooperation. Although he wanted the project to be initiated "as soon as possible," the board did not indicate any appreciable interest. In 1918 he met with a group of people and formed the Negro Cooperative Guild. The organization wished to convince various clubs to study economic cooperation and hoped to encourage converts to open cooperative stores under its direction. The *Crisis* editor informed the NAACP board about the recent deliberations of the Guild and the board minutes fail to note any overt antagonism either to Du Bois' profusion of editorials on the racial economy or to his presentation at the September, 1918, meeting.[27]

And so, before the United States entered the war, Du Bois deliciously anticipated the promise of vigorous "race predilections" and had an unabashed desire to "revel in them." He proclaimed the majority of the world's population was "colored" and these people would very likely determine the future of mankind. There was no doubt in his mind that the planet would be in good hands, since the Negro race is "the strongest and gentlest of the races of

26. *The Crisis*, XIV (1917), 165–166, 215, 284. See also *The Crisis*, XV (1917–1918), 9. W. E. B. Du Bois, "The Passing of 'Jim Crow'," *Independent*, XCI (1917), 53–54.

27. Minutes of the NAACP Board of Directors, October 8, 1917. *Ninth Annual Report of the NAACP*, 1918, p. 50. *The Crisis*, XVI (1918), 215, 268. Minutes of the NAACP Board of Directors, September 9, 1918.

Men: 'Semper novi quid ex Africa!' " [28] Contradictorily, he also
foresaw the inevitable dissolution of the caste line and the arrival
of "true Socialism." [29] He predicted the expansion of the American
democratic ideals; yet only a few months before, he rather imagined the United States might become a substantial "race exploiter"
on an international scale.

Du Bois' contradictions and floundering were the marks of a
man's frustration at being in a no-man's-land and groping des-
perately for an exit. His paths in the maze seemed endless and
repetitious, frequently tinged with unreality. There was almost
nobody inside or outside his race he trusted completely and no
political leaders or party to whom he could give his unreserved
allegiance. At the 1916 Republican convention, the NAACP
requested approval of planks advocating: (1) use of the size of
voting population as a basis for Congressional representation, (2)
a national anti-lynching law, (3) no discrimination in interstate
commerce, (4) "repeal of all statutory recognition of race for
residents of this country." Receiving no satisfaction, Du Bois and
other NAACP officers tried and failed to secure any promises
from Charles Evans Hughes. Within weeks of the election the
Crisis editor reluctantly considered the establishment of a Negro
party and recognized that some would condemn him for advocating segregation. Nevertheless, he advised readers to support
only friendly Congressional candidates, and if none could be
found, to nominate Negro party candidates. In order to avoid
being duped by politicians of both races, Du Bois recommended
that NAACP branches assume responsibility for a program of
"political education." [30] The *Crisis* editor had been burned badly
in 1912 and he did not intend to publicly endorse Presidential
candidates for a long time to come. William F. Nowlin, examining the political activities of Negroes, observed that, although
nothing was done to promote Du Bois' Negro party proposal, "the
suggestions appear to have motivated Negroes in working up their

28. W. E. B. Du Bois, *The Negro* (New York, 1915), p. 242.
29. *The Crisis,* XII (1916), 216–217.
30. *The Crisis,* XII (1916), 135, 268, 269.

own political organizations in centers of colored population." [31]

After the United States joined the Allies in April of 1917, it began to seem that Du Bois had at last found an exit from the maze. Once more "the white world" was no longer the monster. The *Crisis* editor asked American Negroes to participate in the war effort wholeheartedly, and he was especially mindful that the conflict would present tremendous industrial opportunities. While he affirmed his loyalty, he still demanded equal rights.[32] Du Bois' cooperation with the American government may seem sudden when it is recalled that, as late as April of 1917, he termed it "impotent" and described Woodrow Wilson's 1916 victory as a "fraud." But even at that time—despite the harsh words—he added that the United States was "our country and the land of our dreams." [33] His accommodation to the American war effort is also understandable when his long-time interest in a segregated system is considered. Rapid strides—even on a separate basis were desirable. Beyond that, his new line was a reflection of the deluge of democratic propaganda which was unleashed after the American entry into the war. And his affection for Joel Spingarn was also an important factor in accounting for the change.

Spingarn believed it imperative that Negroes show whites they were capable of leadership and he recommended the establishment of a segregated officer candidate school. He disavowed segregation in all areas of American life but knew the army would not permit Negroes to enter white officer schools. He pushed the project as an individual—not in the capacity of NAACP board chairman. The Association prudently decided to take no official stand, in view of the controversy which the segregated camp aroused within the race.[34] Newspapers such as the Boston *Guard-*

31. William F. Nowlin, *The Negro in American National Politics* (Boston, 1931), p. 141.

32. *The Crisis,* XIV (1917), 165, 217.

33. *The Crisis,* XIII (1916–1917), 268.

34. Joel Spingarn to "The Educated Colored Men of the United States," February 15, 1917, Joel Spingarn Papers (James Weldon Johnson Memorial Collection, Yale University). See also *Eighth Annual Report of the NAACP,* 1917, p. 9.

ian and the Chicago *Defender* exerted pressure on the NAACP to repudiate the camp idea.[35] Spingarn, who denied he deviated from Association principles, offered to resign as chairman in order not to embarrass his organization.[36]

Since Du Bois administered *The Crisis* independently, he used the magazine to propagandize in favor of Spingarn's camp. As he interpreted it, the chairman and he were caught in the "Perpetual Dilemma." Segregation was an evil, but Negroes had always accepted it in schools, residential areas, and everywhere else. The alternative was to receive no facilities from the whites. Du Bois was charged with selling out to the whites, although he noted that the army privately opposed the camp. He was hurt and disgusted as the contention mounted:

Where in heaven's name do we Negroes stand? If we organize separately for anything—"Jim Crow!" scream all the Disconsolate; if we organize with white people—"Traitors! Pressure! They're betraying us!" yell all the Suspicious. If, unable to get the whole loaf we seize half to ward off starvation—"Compromise!" yell all the Scared. If we let the half loaf go and starve—"Why don't you *do* something?" yell those same critics, dancing about on their toes.[37]

The Crisis also declared many whites wished to bar the Negro from all military service because they knew that he would fight heroically at the front. Du Bois was absolutely enraged that he should have to beg the whites to permit his people to risk their lives for the country, and he sneered:

"We should worry."
If they do not want us to fight, we will work. We will walk into the industrial shoes of a few million whites who go to the front. We will get higher wages and we cannot be stopped from migrating by all the

35. Du Bois, *Dusk of Dawn*, p. 250; Ruth Worthy, p. 118. See also New York *Age,* March 1, 22, 1917.

36. Joel Spingarn Papers (James Weldon Johnson Memorial Collection, Yale): Spingarn to A. H. Grimké, April 3, 1917 and Spingarn to Mrs. J. E. McClain, April 12, 1917.

37. *The Crisis,* XIV (1917), 61. See also *The Crisis,* XIII (1916–1917), 270–271.

deviltry of the slave South; particularly with the white lynchers and mob leaders away at war. Will we be ousted when the white soldiers come back? THEY WON'T COME BACK!

So there you are, gentlemen, and take your choice—We'll fight or work. We'll fight and work. If we fight we'll learn the fighting game and cease to be so "aisily lynched." If we don't fight we'll learn the more lucrative trades and cease to be so easily robbed and exploited. Take your choice, gentlemen. "We should worry." [38]

The segregated officers' training camp was established at Des Moines and the NAACP officially "took active part" in the movement after May, 1917,* when the installation actually opened. However, there was some doubt among race leaders whether any of the men would be commissioned. This skepticism was heightened when the Negroes' highest ranking officer, Lt. Colonel Charles Young,† was involuntarily retired from active service. (Lt. Colonel Young told Du Bois and the NAACP that his physical condition was excellent.) In July of 1917, Du Bois sought without success an interview with Secretary of War Newton Baker.[39] By late summer, some of the officer candidates were restive and announced they intended to leave Des Moines and go home. NAACP leaders tried to persuade them to remain until the commissions came. Du Bois informed Joel Spingarn, who was then a major in the United States Army, that the Association was still trying to pressure the War Department. The editor's appointment with Secretary Baker was confirmed for early fall. In the interview, the cabinet officer "coldly" announced that the United States government was not at war in order to solve the race problem; the *Crisis* editor replied that racism delayed the successful prosecution of the war. A short time later, hundreds of Negroes received commissions and Joel Spingarn publicly praised

* The camp was opened on June 15, 1917 [ed.].

† Young was a full colonel. See Ulysses Less, *The Employment of Negro Troops* (Washington, D.C., 1966), p. 9 [ed.].

38. *The Crisis*, XIV (1917), p. 62.

39. Mary White Ovington to Joel Spingarn, July 5, 1917, Spingarn Papers (James Weldon Johnson Memorial Collection, Yale).

Du Bois for vigorous efforts on behalf of the camp. Since this issue was resolved to his satisfaction, the Negro editor was more certain than ever that his race would occupy a new and unprejudiced status in the United States. To prove his point he quoted from favorable comments on Negro soldiers which were written by Southern white editors.[40]

In his purveyor-of-hopefulness role, he produced a revealing editorial when the United States government assumed control of the railroads during the war. He interpreted the move as the probable beginning of the end of the capitalist system and the death blow to the segregated railroad car. According to his reasoning, if the government retained direction in the postwar period, railroad jobs would be placed under civil service and Negroes would receive new opportunities for employment.[41] Apparently he thought that after transportation, other basic industries would come under federal management.

Du Bois' line of accommodation was condemned by Chandler Owen, Negro coeditor (with A. Philip Randolph) of the leftist *Messenger,* which started publication in 1917. Du Bois was charged with supporting causes thwarting his avowed aim of integration. Owen blasted the *Crisis* editor's "superlative sureness" that the Negroes' military and industrial contributions in World War I would efface race prejudice. The *Messenger* editor represented a new breed of the Talented Tenth—consistently oriented toward Marxism and in rebellion against what he judged to be Du Bois' old-fashioned conservatism. Owen placed the *Crisis* editor in the same category with Robert R. Moton and Fred Moore. The *Messenger* was determined to prove Du Bois might even be an all-out reactionary and accused him of possessing an anti-union record. In the old days, critics had always deferred to him as a man of great learning, but Owen was not interested in following any long-established precedents. Eagerly he denounced Du Bois for showing no real understanding of economics, history,

40. *The Crisis,* XV (1917–1918), 61, 77–78.
41. *Ibid.,* p. 164.

or political science; Owen concluded that the race's new leaders must have "scientific education." [42]

Perhaps Du Bois was disturbed by the *Messenger's* pounding and the criticism of other newspapers; in early 1918 he returned to the protest motif. After thirteen Negro soldiers were executed for their crimes in the Houston race riot* he condemned the way of life in the United States which these men, and all other Negroes, had been forced to endure, and he reproached all whites (including President Wilson) who seemed to condone race oppression. Wilson was particularly censured for discussing democracy in Poland and Ireland while ignoring the American color problem. *The Crisis* also indicted the United States Civil Service Commission for racism. Du Bois returned to the case of Charles Young and accused the Adjutant General of discrimination. In May of 1918, the *Crisis* editor attacked the War Department for not enlisting large numbers of technically trained men in the segregated

---

* During World War I, by which the world was to be made "safe for democracy," many Negro troops refused to accept discrimination against them at home. Some whites who disliked seeing Negro troops in uniform, especially if they were in combat units, were determined to "keep Negroes in their places." Among the almost inevitable clashes, the most serious was the Houston, Texas, riot in September, 1917. There, police brutality and denial of public accommodations rankled members of the Twenty-Fourth Infantry, one of the Regular Army regiments. Their white commanding officers, fearing the use of arms by the troops to defend themselves, disarmed them. Some of the soldiers seized arms and killed seventeen white persons. Sixty-three soldiers were court-martialed on charges of murder and mutiny; thirteen were summarily hanged in December, 1917, without the right of appeal under a law which, according to the NAACP attorney, applied only to troops in action. Forty-one were sentenced to life imprisonment, four were given long prison terms, and five others were condemned to death. In a second court-martial, eleven more were sentenced to death. None of the white policemen were indicted, and none of the white officers in charge of the camp were brought to trial. After a review of the trial, by President Wilson, ten of the death sentences were commuted to life imprisonment and six more men were hanged. After a long campaign spearheaded by the NAACP, the last prisoner was finally released on July 20, 1938, by order of President Franklin D. Roosevelt. See Charles Flint Kellogg, *The NAACP . . . 1909–1920* (Baltimore: The Johns Hopkins Press, 1967), pp. 261–262 [ed.].

42. *Messenger* (January 1918), 23.

Ninety-Second Division, and he wondered if there were some government leaders working behind the scenes to prevent this Negro outfit from being a success.[43] He ran an advertisement in the magazine, calling upon skilled communications men and truck drivers to join the Ninety-Second.

About this time, the United States Department of Justice cautioned that his disparaging statements were harming the war effort, and under proposed legislation such expressions would be illegal. The Negro propagandist recognized prudence was imperative, and the NAACP board was so concerned about this warning that the head of the legal committee was assigned to *The Crisis* editorial board. The editor was instructed in the clearest terms that everything which appeared in the magazine must be submitted to the legal consultant prior to publication. At its June, 1918, meeting, the board ordered Du Bois to present only "facts and constructive criticism." [44] Beginning with the June issue, *Crisis* editorials presented a picture of unblemished optimism. With the Department of Justice and the NAACP board breathing down his neck, he was unusually careful about following instructions. For example, Du Bois, who received a poem in which the United States government was execrated for the deaths of the thirteen Negro soldiers, told the author he "would not dare" publish it in *The Crisis*. When the *Messenger,* which continued in hot pursuit, printed the poem some months later, the editors asked if the NAACP was "for the *advancement of colored people* or for the *advancement of certain people?*" [45]

In the summer of 1918, Du Bois published "Close Ranks," which became his most controversial editorial because of the following paragraph:

Let us, while this war lasts, forget our special grievances and close ranks shoulder to shoulder with our own fellow citizens and the allied

43. *The Crisis,* XV (1917–1918), 114, 165, 216, 218, 268; *The Crisis,* XVI (1918), 7.
44. Minutes of the NAACP Board of Directors, May 13, June 10, 1918.
45. *Messenger* (October 1919), 8, 25.

nations that are fighting for democracy. We make no ordinary sacrifice, but we make it gladly and willingly with our eyes lifted to the hills.[46]

According to the Washington *Eagle,* this piece "raised a storm—a sort of hurricane—among the radicals." Even the Norfolk *Journal and Guide* considered his advice "unfortunate" because "grievances" should be remembered and protests made to correct them. The District of Columbia branch of the NAACP called a special meeting to rebuke Du Bois for abandoning what they adjudged to be the traditional Association position, and the group warned such deviation would not be tolerated if he wished to remain the *Crisis* editor.[47]

The NAACP propagandist denied he had altered his course or that of the Association, whose leaders approved "Close Ranks" before publication. He argued that he never disavowed "full manhood rights," but had simply emphasized victory in the war took precedence over all other considerations. Nor was there any intention to imply "grievances are *not* grievances, or that the temporary setting aside of wrongs makes them right." [48] Du Bois claimed his counsel was no different from the conclusions of a recent Negro leadership conference which was held in Washington. the *Crisis* editor was inaccurate on this last point, although he had authored the Washington resolutions. The conclave, sponsored by the War Department and the Committee on Public Information, pledged "active, enthusiastic and self-sacrificing participation in the war." But the conferees pleaded for the settlement of "minimum" grievances, in order to increase Negro identification with the Allied cause. They asked for improved facilities in public travel and the end of lynching, among other things.[49] The general

46. *The Crisis,* XVI (1918), 111.
47. Washington *Eagle,* July 27, 1918; Norfolk *Journal and Guide,* July 27, 1918; and Chicago *Defender,* July 20, 1918, Hampton Clippings. See also *The Crisis,* XVI (1918), 218.
48. *The Crisis,* XVI (1918), 216.
49. W. E. B. Du Bois to Joel Spingarn, June 24, 1918, Spingarn Papers (James Weldon Johnson Memorial Collection, Yale); *The Crisis,* XVI (1918), 163, 232.

tone was almost as accommodating as "Close Ranks" but these leaders did not tell anyone to "forget" all grievances during the remainder of the war. Obviously, "Close Ranks" was a colossal blunder and Du Bois tried to squirm out of it.

On the heels of this controversial editorial, Du Bois was offered a commission in the United States Army Intelligence. If "Close Ranks" caused a "storm and hurricane," the announcement about the captaincy brought on "a cyclone of wrath and denunciation." According to the charges, the War Department bribed the NAACP propagandist, captured *The Crisis,* and demanded support for all government policies, no matter how much these suppressed Negroes.[50] A great deal of the discord resulted from Du Bois' request to retain "general oversight" of *The Crisis* while he was serving in the army. He also asked the NAACP for one thousand dollars a year to supplement his military pay because of the added living expenses in Washington. In the Negro leader's version of the affair, the "Close Ranks" editorial was written many days before the commission was discussed with him. He envisaged his army role as part of "a plan of far-reaching constructive effort to satisfy the pressing grievances of colored Americans." [51] Privately, he was "a little hazy" about the duties he was required to perform. It would appear that the United States Army Intelligence (persuaded by Major Joel Springarn) thought Du Bois might become its interpreter of accommodation to the Negro people.

At the July, 1918, NAACP board meeting, the *Crisis* editor told of his willingness to serve in Washington and stipulated the two conditions mentioned previously. The Association denied his requests—members feared a growing schism in the organization, and the District of Columbia branch was already in rebellion against the "turncoat" journalist.[52] The following week, the Washington branch held its "stormiest" session; Du Bois was

50. New York *Age,* July 13, 1918; Washington *Eagle,* July 27, 1918; Richmond *Planet,* September 7, 1918, Hampton Clippings.

51. *The Crisis,* XVI (1918), 215.

52. Minutes of the NAACP Board of Directors, July 8, 1918.

accused of "selfishness," of trying to draw two pay checks, and of other "endearing" terms—as the Chicago *Defender* put it. Joel Spingarn was present but was unable to pacify the local group. (One of the anti-Du Bois observers recorded that Spingarn's appearance "seemed to give us inspiration.") The branch delivered an ultimatum—if the journalist joined the army, he had better withdraw from *The Crisis*! The Washington *Eagle* sardonically congratulated "Captain Du Bois on his choice of Army life" and mockingly anticipated "that he may come out of the conflict as a Brigadier-General, at least." [53]

The *Crisis* editor reconsidered and came up with a compromise, offering to give his services to the government if the NAACP board guaranteed him "control" of the magazine after the Central Powers were beaten. Privately, he claimed he had wanted to retain power over the magazine while in the military service so that Oswald Garrison Villard would not have an opportunity to wreck the Association monthly. Since Joel Spingarn was instrumental in persuading Du Bois to seek the commission and was partially responsible for the Negro's tactical shift toward accommodation, he was saddened by the Association rebuff. In August, at the height "of this personal abuse," he thought of resigning from his position of leadership. Ironically, the army decided it was no longer interested in Du Bois; probably because of the thunderous complaints, the *Crisis* editor was written off as a liability.[54] Although he lost the fight, he played the martyr role with "unruffled serenity. . . . No one who essays to teach the multitude can long escape crucifixion."

Du Bois was hardly circumspect in proposing to control *The Crisis* while working for Army Intelligence. Certainly, it is conceivable that a clash of interest might have arisen. His army-*Crisis* relationship was, from the start, subject to misinterpretation. To his critics, Du Bois did not seem like a man who had decided

53. Chicago *Defender*, July 20, 1918; Washington *Eagle*, July 27, 1918, Hampton. See also Neval H. Thomas to O. G. Villard, September 13, 1918, Villard Papers.
54. Supplied by Mr. Arthur Spingarn in an interview, April, 1954.

sincerely to cooperate completely with the government, and had accepted the offer of a commission as the highest expression of this desire. His request for an NAACP subsidy was also questionable, since it was interpreted as proof of a close or binding association between what had long been a protest organization and the United States government, in which white supremacists possessed great power, if not absolute command.

Du Bois failed to gauge the strength of the clamor for equal rights among Negro intellectuals who had mistakenly identified him exclusively as a protest leader. But, after all, this was the first time in nearly thirteen years that he was not *primarily* concerned with producing protest propaganda demanding the immediate elimination of the color line. His wartime accommodation strategy made him seem like an Uncle Tom and disillusioned some Negroes who were unfamiliar with his lifelong paradox by which he found value in some aspects of segregation.

Until the Allies won he did not swerve from his "new Patriotism" and ringingly declared, "If this is OUR country, then this is OUR war." [55] His only slight concession to critics was the admission that there were "present grievances" about which it was proper to "grumble." For instance, he observed it was unfair to draft Negro physicians as privates, and calmly stated that Negroes would be happy if the government "will soon notice" this unjust practice. But he reminded readers that jobs were now plentiful and wages were high. Negroes were accepted as army officers, Red Cross nurses, and officials in the War and Labor Departments. Furthermore, the courts threw out residential segregation ordinances and President Wilson condemned lynching.[56] During the closing days of the war, Du Bois avidly seized a Wilson statement condemning the domination of the weaker peoples by the stronger. The *Crisis* editor realized the comment was "vague" but believed the President meant to reproach racists

55. *The Crisis,* XVI (1918), 164. See also *The Crisis,* XVII (1918–1919), 10.
56. *The Crisis,* XVI (1918), 217. See also *The Crisis,* XVII (1918–1919), 7.

everywhere, including the South. On this basis, Wilson's remarks were described as "one of the half dozen significant utterances of human history." [57] Du Bois cited other developments to show that the United States government cocked an ear for "just Negro public opinion." The War Service Commission and the Public Information Bureau sent Negro representatives to Europe, Liberia was to receive an American loan (he thought), and Haiti and Liberia "were prominently featured among the Allies during Liberty Loan weeks." Negro troops had finally gone overseas and were serving honorably. Du Bois published a letter from a French mayor, who described "a real brotherhood" between his community and the soldiers of the 349th Field Artillery Regiment. Most of the *Crisis* readers were probably just as satisfied with Negro progress, and it is doubtful if they paid much attention to the editor's critics.

Yet the great Du Boisian paradox appeared through the pages of the magazine. Without any evidence, he anticipated an integrated, Socialist postwar period, while simultaneously he proposed a segregated, socialized economy in the United States. He dreamed of carving out a large socialized African state and forming an international cooperative organization of Negroes. In the decade after World War I, he devoted attention to the Pan-African Movement.

57. *The Crisis*, XVII (1918–1919), 7.

The Continuing Debate:
Washington vs. Du Bois

A number of younger colored leaders became steadily more drastic in criticism of Booker Washington's policy and program during the first years of the twentieth century when he was pouring
all his energy into training a new leadership for "the man farthest
down," and winning for his projects white understanding and
support in the South as well as in the North.

Ever since his voice had reached the entire nation from the
platform of the Atlanta Exposition in 1895, a minority of black
as well as white intellectuals declared that he had "sold the pass"
for the Negro. For the most part men and women born, bred, and
educated in the North, they directly attacked him for accepting
social segregation, for not opening up aggressive political campaigns, and for concentrating almost all his educational effort
upon training the boys and girls of the Negro farmer and laborer
so that they could achieve economic stability by the acquisition of
skills and of land, houses, and tools. He had, they asserted,

* Portions of this selection have been omitted because they are extraneous. The omitted portions are indicated by points of ellipsis [ed.].

Reprinted from *Booker T. Washington: A Biography* by Basil Mathews
(Cambridge, Mass.: Harvard University Press, 1948), pp. 273–303, by
permission of The President and Fellows of Harvard College. Copyright
© 1948 by The President and Fellows of Harvard College.

deflected money from the "higher education" of the Negro; he had developed understanding between the white North and South in terms of using the Negro as an industrial tool for making the capitalists everywhere wealthier; he had failed to challenge and defy the Southern disfranchisement of the Negro. That formidable battery of criticism will continue to be deployed against him for a long time to come. . . .

The sharp divergence between Booker Washington's leadership and that of Du Bois leaps to the eye. The one was born a slave in the South, the other free in a North at that time devoid of race discrimination;* the one rooted in the soil and the Bible, the other saturated in the agnostic liberalism of *fin de siècle* Europe. Washington repeatedly said that objective tabulation of facts by a statistician at an office desk misses the vital essentials; Du Bois for decades pinned his faith to the publication of such surveys. Washington always linked the facts that he found on a farm or in a cabin with practical projects, training men's hands to grapple realistically with those facts. Du Bois brilliantly expounded facts and ideas, expecting men to act on them. Washington always interpreted the facts and his projects to men and women of means in order to win them and their money for building institutions to train leaders to achieve reform. Du Bois' efforts at money-raising were rare. Above all, with Washington thought and action were indivisible. Facts, ideas, and deeds were harnessed together in order to achieve change. Training hands in skilled work was integrated with training brains to handle ideas. Booker Washington, however burning his thought may at times have been, never expressed bitterness. Du Bois himself says that he could not break down his own "cold, biting, critical streak." When the Atlanta race riot blazed up, Washington hastened to the city and mobi-

---

* Mathews was mistaken. Conclusive evidence that the North was not devoid of discrimination is seen in the facts that the Civil Rights Act of 1875 was deemed necessary to prevent existing discrimination in places of public accommodations against any person on account of race or color and that five of the seven cases involved in the Civil Rights Decision of 1883 originated in the North [ed.].

lized all the forces of government and good will to repair and reconstruct; Du Bois also hurried thither to his family, writing en route his stirring and bitter *Litany of Atlanta.*

Events stung Du Bois into action on convictions that had for years been maturing in his mind and feeling. At the outset, as he said, "I was not overcritical of Booker Washington. I regarded his Atlanta speech as a statesmanlike effort to reach understanding with the white South. I hoped the South would respond with equal generosity and thus the nation would come to understanding for both races." About 1902 he had several interviews with Washington, who wished him to work at Tuskegee and offered him a larger salary than he was receiving at Atlanta. Du Bois' wife and other friends warned Du Bois that Tuskegee might cramp him; and their influence prevailed. He refused Booker Washington's invitation.

In 1903 Du Bois published *The Souls of Black Folk.* A chapter in it—"Of Booker T. Washington and Others"—contains a vigorous criticism of the older leader's policy and program. Du Bois had watched the South respond to Booker Washington's efforts, not with cooperation but with Jim Crow legislation to keep the Negro out of the white man's railway and street cars, restaurants, hotels, theaters, concert halls, libraries, universities, and schools; to relegate him to often unpaved, unlighted, undrained slum areas of cities; and to bar him in many states by devious methods from the ballot which the Federal Constitution said was the Negro's right. From 1890 to 1910 the South had hammered out a color caste system, making political discrimination against the Negro legal by state laws, against the intent of the post-war amendments to the Constitution. Washington's refusal to campaign in an all-out fight against these disabilities, and his concentration upon inciting the Negro to acquire property, led Du Bois to say:

Manly self-respect is more than lands and houses. A people who voluntarily surrender such respect or cease striving for it are not worth civilizing. . . . I hold these truths to be self-evident, that a disfranchised working class in a modern industrial civilization is worse than helpless. . . . It will be diseased, it will be criminal, it will be ignorant, it will be the plaything of mobs, and it will be insulted by caste restrictions.

As Du Bois saw it, the capitalistic industrial North was accumulating vast profits by using the cheap labor of the cotton- and tobacco-growing South as an economically dependent, quasi-colonial empire to feed the markets of the world. In his view, Booker Washington was employing this highly ambiguous motive to win money from the North in order to train Southern labor to be skilled and industrious but with the destiny of that labor ruled by the white financial magnates of the North and South. Washington's direction of the General Education Board, following on that of the Southern Education Board, impressed Du Bois as concentrating too exclusively upon elementary and technical training with a view to making the Negro a skilled tractable worker, thus diverting money from what is generally called higher education for the Negro.

In *The Souls of Black Folk* Du Bois showed that he has genuine respect for and admiration of Booker Washington. Thus, in 1905* Du Bois wrote, "to gain the sympathy and cooperation of the various elements comprising the white South . . . at the time when Tuskegee was founded, seemed, for a black man, well-nigh impossible." Washington not only achieved this but was, as Du Bois says, at the beginning of this century

the most distinguished Southerner since Jefferson Davis, and the one with the largest personal following, [and his] cult has gained unquestioning followers, his work has wonderfully prospered, his friends are legion, and his enemies are confounded. He stands as the one recognised spokesman of his ten million fellows, and one of the most notable figures in a nation of seventy millions. One hesitates, therefore, to criticize a life which, beginning with so little, has done so much. And yet . . . one may speak in all sincerity and utter courtesy of the mistakes and shortcomings of Mr. Washington's career . . . without being thought captious or envious, and without forgetting that it is easier to do ill than well in the world.

* This should read 1903 [ed.].

So far as Mr. Washington preaches Thrift, Patience and Industrial Training for the masses, we must hold up his hands and strive with him, rejoicing in his honors and glorifying in the strength of this Joshua called of God and of man to lead the headless host. But so far as Mr. Washington apologises for injustice, North or South, does not rightly value the privilege and duty of voting, belittles the emasculating effects of caste distinctions, and opposes the higher training and ambition of our brighter minds—so far as he, the South, or the Nation does this—we must unceasingly and firmly oppose them. By every civilized and peaceful method we must strive for the rights which the world accords to men who cling unwaveringly to those great words which the sons of the Fathers would fain forget: "We hold these truths to be self-evident: that all men are created equal; that they are endowed by their Creator with certain unalienable rights; that among these are life, liberty, and the pursuit of happiness." *

* Mathews did not quote exactly this passage from *The Souls of Black Folk*. It ended with a period after "personal following." Then followed a paragraph of fifteen lines which stated, *inter alia:* "And so thoroughly did he [Washington] learn the speech and thought of triumphant commercialism, and the ideals of material prosperity, that the picture of a lone black boy poring over a French grammar amid the weeds and dirt of a neglected home soon seemed to him the acme of absurdities." In the next paragraph, Du Bois wrote: "It is as though Nature must needs make men narrow in order to give them force." The passage continued: "So Mr. Washington's cult," etc. "Today" should precede "he stands," etc. After the end of the first paragraph quoted here, there follow several crucial pages, the basic points of which are these: "While, then, criticism has not failed to follow Mr. Washington, yet the prevailing opinion of the land has been but too willing to deliver the solution of a wearisome problem into his hands, and say, 'If this is all you and your race ask, take it.' " Du Bois added: "But the hushing of the criticism of honest opponents is a dangerous thing. . . . Mr. Washington represents in Negro thought the old attitude of adjustment and submission; but adjustment at such a peculiar time as to make his programme unique. . . . Mr. Washington distinctly asks that black people give up, at least for the present, three things,—
    First, political power,
    Second, insistence on civil rights,
    Third, higher education for Negro youth—. . ."
Recognizing Washington's letters to the Louisiana and Alabama constitutional conventions, his opposition to lynching and "sinister schemes, Du Bois stated: "Notwithstanding this, it is equally true to assert that

Dr. Du Bois, in correspondence with the author in 1947, said that he had not modified his judgment on Booker Washington in the intervening thirty years.

That chapter in *The Souls of Black Folk,* followed by *Darkwater*—written by Du Bois in prose of sensitive beauty and intellectual clarity, and glowing with prophetic zeal—provided the anti-Washington movement, for the first time, with a coherent argument. The opposition, therefore, grew, although Du Bois took no active part in it at that time.

A spectacular explosion of anger against Booker Washington and his policy took place in a colored church in Boston in 1905.* Three educated Negroes, one of them a Master of Arts named William Monroe Trotter, founder and editor of a fighting new weekly in Boston, led a group in vigorous hissing when Washington came forward to speak. They put questions to him on his attitude on the Negro's civil and political status and educational opportunities. Washington insisted that his duty was to speak on the subject before the meeting. They with others created an uproar. "Twenty-five policemen," William Ferris tells us in his *The African Abroad,* "were called in to quiet and subdue matters." Trotter was taken to prison. Du Bois strongly criticized the action of Trotter and his comrades in creating the uproar, but blazed with indignation at their imprisonment.† He had already aroused vehement resentment all across the Negro press and in many wealthy white supporters of Negro education by writing for

---

on the whole the distinct impression left by Mr. Washington's propaganda is, first, that the South is justified in its present attitude toward the Negro, because of the Negro's degradation; secondly, that the prime cause of the Negro's failure to rise more quickly is his wrong education in the past, and thirdly, that his future rise depends primarily on his own efforts. Each of these propositions is a dangerous half-truth. . . . The black men of America have a duty to perform, a duty stern and delicate— a forward movement to oppose a part of the work of their greatest leader." The omitted passages, preceding Mathews' second paragraph, indicate why Du Bois deemed it necessary to "unceasingly and firmly oppose" Washington's apologies [ed.].

* This should be 1903 [ed.].

† Only Trotter and one other person were fined and imprisoned [ed.].

Trotter's *Guardian* an article on the "venality" of Negro papers, which, he said, had "sold out" and "attacked viciously" every Negro who did not agree with Booker Washington. As he has said since, "I could not support this with concrete facts." His real resentment was against the methods of Tuskegee's press bureau, which sent advertisements of the Institute to Negro papers, special articles, "and other favors." As a result of Du Bois' attack, donations to Atlanta University, where he was on the faculty, decreased.

Du Bois was stung into action by all these events. He called a number of colored leaders together on the Canadian bank of Niagara Falls, and in 1906 the Niagara Movement, as it was called, met at Harpers Ferry (famous for John Brown's raid and death) and planned a direct attack upon Booker Washington's program. Their manifesto crisply defined the goal:

We shall not be satisfied with less than our full manhood rights. We claim for ourselves every right that belongs to a free-born American, political, civil and social, and until we get these rights we shall never cease to protest and assail the ears of America with the stories of its shameful deeds towards us. We want full manhood suffrage and we want it now. Second, we want discrimination in public accommodations to cease. Third, we claim the right of free men to associate with such people as wish to associate with us. Fourth, we want the laws enforced against rich as well as poor, against capitalists as well as laborers, against white as well as black. We are not more lawless than the white race; we are more often arrested, convicted and mobbed. Fifth, we want our children educated. The school system of the country districts of the South is a disgrace to civilization, and in few towns and cities are the Negro schools what they ought to be.*

* Again, as in his quotation from *The Souls of Black Folk,* Mathews' abridgment of the Harpers Ferry Resolutions is inaccurate. They begin with a brief statement of various aspects of discrimination. Mathews' first sentence should read: "We will not be satisfied to take one jot or tittle less than our full manhood rights." In the next sentence "single" should be inserted between "every" and "right"; this sentence should end with "America." After several lines, the Resolutions stated: "In detail our demands are clear and unequivocal."

"*First.* We would vote; . . . We want full manhood suffrage, and we want it now, henceforth and forever." Each of the succeeding demands is

Du Bois left Atlanta University in 1909 [1910] to become Director of Publications and Research of the newly-formed National Association for the Advancement of Colored People and founded the famous *The Crisis* magazine, which for decades absorbed his main energies, with intervals for travel to organize and attend interracial conferences and establish contacts in England, Belgium, France, Geneva, Spain, Portugal, Germany, Russia, Turkey, and Liberia; in the latter country he represented President Coolidge at the inauguration of President King in 1923.

Of the many speeches from different Negroes attacking Booker Washington during these years two may be quoted as characteristic. A colored New York pastor, the Reverend Charles Satchel Morris, said in Faneuil Hall in Boston on June 20, 1906: "I believe Booker T. Washington's heart is right, but that in fawning, cringing and groveling before the white man he has cost his race their rights and that twenty years hence, as he looks back and sees the harm his course has done his race, he will be brokenhearted over it."

The Reverend Richard Carroll of South Carolina, a popular

---

listed in a separate paragraph, with each of Mathews' sentences followed by an elaboration. Especially important are three omissions from Mathews' version. The fourth demand stated: "We want the Fourteenth Amendment carried out to the letter and every State disfranchised in Congress which attempts to disfranchise its rightful voters." The fifth demand stated: "We want the national government to step in and wipe out illiteracy in the South. Either the United States will destroy ignorance or ignorance will destroy the United States." Even more significant and timely is the closing paragraph:

> We do not believe in violence, neither in the despised violence of the raid nor the lauded violence of the soldier, nor the barbarous violence of the mob; but we do believe in John Brown, in that incarnate spirit of justice, that hatred of a lie, that willingness to sacrifice money, reputation, and life itself on the altar of right. And here on the scene of John Brown's martyrdom, we reconsecrate ourselves, our honor, our property to the final emancipation of the race for whose freedom John Brown died—August 15, 1906.

The complete, accurate statement of the Resolutions is in Howard Brotz, ed., *Negro Social and Political Thought, 1850–1920: Representative Texts* (New York and London, 1966), pp. 557–559 [ed.].

colored lecturer at that time, rebutted Washington's thesis in these cogent terms: "They teach, 'When the Negroes get property and money, persecution in the South will cease.' It will make it worse. The Jews in Russia have plenty of money and they are persecuted. It doesn't make any difference what Negroes get, how much land they own or how much money they have in the bank, the sentiment of the South as to social equality will remain."

Applauding that view, William Ferris in his *The African Abroad* argues:

We must produce a type of manhood and womanhood that the Anglo-Saxon will admire. Then and then only will the Negro no longer be despised, but he will be freely accorded his civil and political rights. The Negro must acquire culture, polish and refinement, he must acquire an aristocratic, high-bred feeling. We must improve the racial stock. We must produce a high-minded, high-spirited, high-toned race of men and women, who will walk with head erect, lift their feet and strike the ground with a firm elastic step. . . . We must make some contribution to civilization, must develop the intellectual, moral, and aesthetic sides of our nature—then we will no longer be a despised but an admired race.

Mr. Washington and I agree that it is up to the Negro to do something and work out his own salvation. But there the Tuskegee sage and I differ. He believes the Negro ought to be a millionaire before he demands to be treated as a man; I don't. He wants the Negro to begin at the foot of the ladder and remember his mission and destiny is to remain there. I, too, want him to begin at the bottom, but I also want him to climb to the dizzy heights of fame, to go higher and higher, cutting his way up niche by niche. I want him to reach up and write his name in letters of gold side by side with the scholars and scientists, the statesmen and orators, the poets and artists, the financiers and writers whom the world has long revered.[1]

The most coherent and serious critics of Booker Washington's policy and program must have been embarrassed by the degree to which the wild and whirling accusations of some of their colleagues prejudiced judgment on the reasonableness of their con-

1. William Ferris, *The African Abroad* (1913), I, 400–405.

tention. William Ferris, for example, as a climax to the foregoing incoherent and self-contradictory criticism of Washington, wrote that the creator of Tuskegee, "thinks the Negro ought to be content to be a race of Jim Crow, segregated, disfranchised and non-office-holding serfs and servants." The record of Washington's persistent pressure upon federal executives and state legislatures, as well as his public speeches and open letters attacking Jim Crow accommodation, and revealing the injustice of race discrimination in relation to the ballot box, together with the fact that he was responsible for securing government office for a greater number of leading Negroes of integrity than any other man of his time, shows the crude falsity of this charge. Nor does Ferris' accusation that Washington was content with industrial training for the Negro bear scrutiny in the light, for instance, of Washington's letter to President Taft in which he suggested the following policy with regard to higher education in words which Taft adopted as his own official speech (December, 1900):*

Since the Negro, in a very large degree, is dependent upon his own people for ministers, doctors, teachers and professional men, the Negro should not only have industrial training, but academic, college and university training as well, especially for those who are to become the advisers and leaders of the race.

Superficial observers like William Ferris led many people at the time to see in the Niagara Movement a head-on collision between two opposed policies incarnate in an older and a younger leader; and the possible elimination of Washington. Ferris wrote:

The Niagara Movement means that the opposition to Washington's leadership has crystallized around Du Bois.

Du Bois is gifted with a more powerful intellect than Washington, is a more uncompromising idealist, and is a more brilliant writer. On the whole his is the more impressive personality. But Washington is a more magnetic speaker and more astute politician, a greater humorist, and less of an aristocrat. It remains to be seen whether the Niagara

* 1908. This was in Taft's acceptance speech after his election in November, 1908 [ed.].

Movement, headed by Du Bois, will sweep Washington and his theories from the field. This is not a personal fight, but a battle of ideas, a struggle for the supremacy of rival theories.[2]

The debate, however, revolved around facts as well as ideas and persons.

Washington's policy of fighting hard to secure equal though separate facilities for colored and white citizens in the "Jim Crow" states is vehemently assailed on the ground, not only of principle, but that it has, in fact, proved to be futile.

The argument, which is powerful, runs on the following lines.

The Fourteenth Amendment to the Constitution of the United States, we recall, laid it down that no person shall be deprived of equal protection of the laws, or of his life, liberty, or property without due process of law. The Supreme Court had pronounced that segregation in street cars, buses, trains, waiting rooms, schools, libraries, and so on does not contravene that amendment as long as the separate facilities offered to the Negro are equal to those available to white persons. Booker Washington, as has been seen, worked in two ways to secure that transport facilities be equal; first, by direct pressure upon the railway and other transport companies, secondly, through the President. Continuously he also worked to persuade the different state administrations in whose hands education largely rests to raise the level of public education for the Negro. He did not fight for common use by both races of the same facilities.

Anyone who travels in the Southern states sees at once that the accommodation for the colored people is in general scandalously inadequate in quantity and wretchedly squalid in quality. All the pressure brought to bear by Booker Washington and others has produced but negligible results. The condition laid down by the Supreme Court in relation to the Fourteenth Amendment is thus defied.

Even more serious, from the point of view of the nation's general morale, is, in a number of states in the South, the atro-

2. Ferris, I, 276–277.

cious inequality of provision for the education of the Negro in schools, colleges, and universities supported by public funds.[3] In nine Southern states, a quarter of a century after the death of Booker Washington (that is, in 1940) the average expenditure for education per head upon white pupils was 212 per cent greater than that upon colored boys and girls. The real discrepancy was still more glaring, for in those states the white school term averaged 171 days as compared with 156 for Negroes. A white teacher received on the average $1,046 a year as compared with $601 for a colored teacher. Furthermore, where college education is concerned, we discover in those same states the following provision of colleges for white students: 17 in engineering, 15 in medicine, 4 in dentistry, 9 in social services, 14 in pharmacy, and 16 in law. From all of these colleges Negro students have been excluded. In all those states not a single publicly-supported college existed to train Negroes in those subjects, except one in law. It is not to be wondered at, then, that, taking the South as a whole, while a white doctor was available for every 859 persons, there was only one Negro doctor for every 5,300 colored persons.

These conditions reinforced the plea that Booker Washington's efforts on this line of approach have been largely frustrated. Critics go further and declare that this shows that his forecast was mistaken when he affirmed that, as the Negro rose in the scale of economic as well as intellectual attainment, he would be freely accorded advanced status by his white fellow-citizens. For such reasons as these the National Association for the Advancement of the Colored People came into being for more direct aggressive action. It sustains a steady succession of fights in the appropriate law courts, not simply for equal facilities for each race, but for common access by both races to educational and other facilities. That Association came into being in Booker Washington's lifetime, but not upon his initiative. Its origin in outline is as follows.

3. In one or two states, notably North Carolina, progress has been made in recent years.

An unexpected challenge from a white Kentuckian, William E. Walling, on the heels of race riots and the Supreme Court decision which affirmed that segregation did not violate the Fourteenth Amendment, spurred Du Bois, with Oswald Garrison Villard, then editor of the New York *Evening Post,* Mary White Ovington, the novelist, and some others, to call a national conference in May, 1909, to "renew the struggle for civil and political liberty." From that conference sprang the National Association for the Advancement of Colored People (NAACP), and its magazine, *The Crisis.* Its policy called upon black and white to cooperate to abolish forced segregation and to secure enfranchisement of the Negro, enforcement of the Fourteenth and Fifteenth Amendments, equal educational advantages for colored and white, with equality before the law, and an end to mob violence. Many have seen this as an implicit criticism of Booker Washington's policy. As outstanding an authority as Roy Wilkins of the NAACP, editor of *The Crisis* since 1934, argued in 1944 that the magazine and the organization really arose from Washington's "great work." "It was inevitable," he said, "that there should emerge, as the Negro made progress, a group which felt that the time had come for bolder words and more direct steps toward the goal." *

Just before the first issue of *The Crisis* appeared, under Du Bois' editorship, Booker Washington was in England, speaking before a distinguished group of British leaders at the dinner in London given in his honor by the Anti-Slavery and Aborigines Protection Society. In the course of that speech he laid emphasis on the progress made by the colored race in America during the forty-five years following emancipation. He also unfolded his own interpretation of the development of interracial relations in the

* Mathews distorted the relevant passage by Wilkins; see quotation below, p. 206. Washington also declined an invitation from Oswald Garrison Villard to attend the National Negro Conference in New York City, May 31 and June 1, 1909, that led to the organization of the NAACP in 1910. See Charles Flint Kellogg, *NAACP, A History of the National Association for the Advancement of Colored People, 1909–1920* (Baltimore: The Johns Hopkins Press, 1967), I, 19 [ed.].

United States and expounded his own program of cooperation
of black with white, of South with North, in educating the Negro.
An American, Mr. Milholland, with singular lack of timing,
issued a circular of protest against Booker Washington's presentation on the day *before* his speech was made. Oswald Garrison
Villard, whose pen has always been his eager sword, received
Milholland's circular at the NAACP headquarters and without
waiting for a report of Washington's speech, sent him a comba-
tive letter, hitherto unpublished, dated December 13, 1910, having already sent a still more drastic criticism to Major Moton at
Hampton Institute.

From my point of view [Villard wrote to Washington], your
philosophy is wrong. You are keeping silent about evils in regard
to which you should speak out, and you are not helping the race
by portraying all the conditions as favorable. If my grandfather [the
most famous of the Abolitionists, William Lloyd Garrison] had gone
to Europe, say in 1850, and dwelt in his speeches on slavery upon
certain encouraging features of it, such as the growing anger and
unrest of the poor whites, and stated the number of voluntary libera-
tions and number of escapes to Canada, as evidences that the institution was improving, he never would have accomplished what he did,
and he would have hurt, not helped, the cause of freedom. It seems
to me that the parallel precisely affects your case. It certainly cannot
be unknown to you that a greater and greater percentage of the intellectual colored people are turning from you, and becoming your opponents, and with them a number of white people as well.

In the course of a long letter in reply to Villard (January 10,
1911), Washington revealed clearly the sharp contrast between
his philosophy of construction and cooperation and that of aggressive attack; yet, in his restrained way, making an attack on
the knowledge and attitude of his opponents.

My speeches in Europe did not differ from my speeches in this
country. When I am in the South speaking to the Southern white
people, anyone who hears me speak will tell you that I am frank
and direct in my criticism of the Southern white people. I cannot
agree with you, or any others, however, that very much or any

good is to be gained just now by going out of the South and merely speaking about the Southern white people. . . . I think it pays to do such talking to the people who are most responsible for injustice being inflicted upon us in certain directions. . . .

There is little parallel between conditions that your grandfather had to confront and those facing us now. Your grandfather faced a great evil which was to be destroyed. Ours is a work of construction rather than a work of destruction. My effort in Europe was to show to the people that the work of your grandfather was not wasted and that the progress the Negro has made in America justified the words and work of your grandfather. . . .

You, of course, labor under the disadvantage of not knowing as much about the life of the Negro race as if you were a member of that race yourself. Unfortunately, too, I think you are brought into contact with that group of our people who have not succeeded in any large degree—dissatisfied and unhappy. I wish you could come more constantly into contact with that group of our people who are succeeding, who have accomplished something, and are not continually sour and disappointed. I keep pretty closely in touch with the life of my race, and I happen to know that the very same group of people who are opposing me now have done so practically ever since my name became in any way prominent, certainly ever since I spoke at the opening of the Atlanta Exposition. No matter what I would do or refrain from doing, the same group would oppose me. I think you know this. . . .

I cannot agree with you that there is an increasing number of intellectual colored people who oppose me, or are opposed to me. My experience and observation convince me to the contrary. I do not see how any man could expect or hope to have to a larger extent the good will and coöperation of the members of his race of all classes than I have, and it is this consciousness that makes me feel very humble.

I confess that I cannot blame anyone who resides in the North or in Europe for not taking the same hopeful view of conditions in the South that I do. The only time I ever become gloomy or despondent regarding the conditions of the Negro in the South is when I am in the North. When I am in the North I hear for the most part only of the most discouraging and disheartening things that take place in the South, but when I leave the North and get right in the

South in the midst of the work and see for myself what is being done and how it is being done, and what the actual daily connection between the white man and the black man is, then it is that I become encouraged.

You say that I ought to speak out more strongly on public questions. I suppose that means such questions as relate to our receiving justice in the matter of public schools, lynchings, etc. In that regard I quote you some sentences which I used only a few days ago in talking to the Southern white people here in Alabama concerning their duty toward the Negro: "I do not believe that the leading white people, and especially landowners of the Black Belt counties know how little money some Negro schools receive. I actually know of communities where Negro teachers are being paid only from $15 to $17 per month for services for a period of three or four months in the year. . . . More money is paid for Negro convicts than for Negro teachers. About $46 per month is now being paid for first-class able-bodied Negro convicts, $36 for second class, and $26 for third class for twelve months in the year. . . . One other element in the situation that drives Negroes from the farms of the Black Belt counties is this. In many of the Black Belt counties, when a Negro is charged with a crime, a mob of wild, excited and often intoxicated people go scouring through the country in search of the Negro. . . . In my opinion, if the Negroes understand that their public schools in the country districts are gradually going to be improved as fast as the state can do so, and that they will receive police protection in case they are charged with crime in the country districts, as they do in the cities, then the best colored farmers will cease moving from the country districts into the cities."

After giving one or two more cases of this kind Washington concluded his letter to Villard with "I am always glad to hear from you."

In reply to this letter Villard wrote a letter in which he endorsed the extracts from the addresses which Washington had been making in the South, saying, "They are good as far as they go, but do not go far enough to satisfy a Garrison!" Referring to the "Garrisonian temperament," Booker Washington replied on February 11, 1911:

No one has a higher appreciation of the work done for the Negro by William Lloyd Garrison than I. I have on numberless occasions spoken my word of appreciation. But is it not possible that those possessing the "Garrisonian temperament" may be disposed to be more impatient with others because they do not do as they would have them do, in contrast with what would probably be the attitude of Mr. Garrison himself if he were living?

I have found that, when I am in the South, talking with Southern people, I say quite as frankly as I know how to say those things which will help conditions, and that is the attitude which I believe Mr. Garrison would endorse. I could deal in epithet and denunciation as many of my own detractors do, but somehow it has never seemed to me that they got very far with that kind of thing.

Following this correspondence Booker Washington sought opportunity of personal talk with Villard. Evidently their conversation dealt to some degree with the development of the Association for the Advancement of Colored People. The Tuskegee files contain a telegram sent by Washington to Villard at Boston on March 30, 1911, saying:

Your telegram of March twenty-ninth received. Confirming the conversation we had in New York I would state that your lifelong interest and activities in behalf of my race urge me to repeat that I shall be glad to work in friendly cooperation with all the workers for the general advancement of the colored people especially in constructive directions.

It seems to me that while we necessarily may in the future as in the past work along different lines we still may work together in harmony, sympathy and mutual understanding. I am convinced that the time has come when all interested in the welfare of the Negro people should lay aside personal differences and personal bickerings and anything and everything that smacks of selfishness and keep in mind only rendering the service which will best promote and protect the whole race in all of its larger interests. In the last analysis I am sure that we all agree on more points than we disagree on. Further than this, the experience through which I have been passing convinces me that deep down in the heart of all of us there is a feeling of oneness and sympathy and unity. I am sure that all of my friends everywhere will happily cooperate with you in the directions I have mentioned. If your organization now in session can see its way clear to appoint two or more fraternal delegates to attend the next meeting of the National Negro Business League I feel quite sure that our organization will reciprocate in kind. It will be a happy day for my race when all of the forces and organizations while still remaining individually separate can sympathetically and heartily cooperate and work together for its larger good.

The NAACP went forward with its policy of direct attack and achieved remarkable successes in legal actions. As Du Bois said later, however, in his honest way, "We continued winning court victories and yet somehow, despite them, we did not seem to be getting far." [4]

A pungent comment upon the alternative attitudes which confront each other in this debate was made by Booker Washington in his book *The Story of the Negro,* at the end of a chapter upon slave insurrections, in language that clearly reflects bitter personal experience. He speaks of the type of Negro leader who

insists that, if he had the courage to stand up and denounce his detractors in the same harsh and bitter terms that these persons use toward him, in a short time he would win the respect of the world, and the only obstacle to his progress would be removed. . . . Any black man . . . willing either in print or in public speech, to curse or abuse the white man, easily gained for himself a reputation for great courage. He might spend but thirty minutes or an hour once a year in that kind of "vindication" of his race, but he got the reputation of being an exceedingly brave man. Another man, who worked patiently and persistently for years in a Negro school, depriving himself of many of the comforts and necessities of life, in order to perform a service which would uplift his race, gained no reputation for courage. On the contrary, he was likely to be denounced as a coward by these "heroes," because he chose to do his work without cursing, without abuse, and without complaint.[5]

A balanced and searching critic of Booker Washington's policy

4. "A Pageant in Seven Decades," an address delivered on his seventieth birthday in 1938.
5. *The Story of the Negro,* I, 190–191.

and program who certainly did not come under that scathing analysis was Dr. John Hope, president of Atlanta University until his death in 1936. While fighting battles alongside John Hope against racial exploitation and for interracial understanding, the author watched him in action in world conferences in North Africa, Nearer Asia, and Europe, as well as in America, and shared intimate discussions with him in the writer's own home in Geneva and in the home of the Hopes at Atlanta. He told the author that for him, as a Negro, life was already "a series of tricks, shocks, and fears when I was four years old," that is, in 1877.* He was an exquisitely sensitive and cultured Christian gentleman; indignation at the bitter tragedy and towering injustice of the colored people's situation in the Southern states smoldered in him with devouring heat. Where Booker Washington somehow sustained indestructible patience, John Hope burned with prophetic impatience, but without hate.

A characteristic incident took place when the president of the American Baptist Home Mission Society told John Hope in 1906, during the early struggling days at Atlanta, that Booker Washington would like to help him get money from Andrew Carnegie to put up a building there. Hope said that he was against the plan because he felt that it might mean agreement with Booker Washington's "social separation" compromise. That fear having been eliminated, the money was secured. A pleasant friendship grew up between the two men and their wives. At the same time Du Bois and Hope were intimately associated in the aggressive Niagara Movement with its strong criticism of Washington. Hope was the only college president at the Niagara Falls Conference.† He told Du Bois that he had accepted Washington's help in getting the money for Atlanta but hoped for Du Bois' continued trust. Du Bois replied that he disagreed with the action, but that he would certainly continue to trust him. Du Bois later accepted President Hope's invitation to join again the faculty of the greatly enlarged Atlanta University.

* Hope was born in 1868, the same year as Du Bois [ed.].
† Harpers Ferry Conference [ed.].

John Hope told the author that he felt that Booker Washington undoubtedly made a contribution to education in a practical way, adjusted to local circumstances; but that the conditions for support of that education meant keeping the Negro in his place of subservience. What Washington did for the Negro, he said, was useful when he did it. He helped to produce tolerance for the Negro, but at too great a price. He popularized the Negro in the field of industry when he was unpopular. He had not really brought the Negro better protection from violence and injustice. It was, Hope felt, tragic that there should be only one man to whom all white people in North America turned for advice about the Negro; for his leadership was always disputed by many Negroes. Washington was a shrewd politician; he could weigh up white people as well as black, and he used them both to forward his policy. In order to do that he said too many things capable of bearing, in the mind of the Southern white man, the wrong interpretation.

As will have been seen, much of the attack upon Booker Washington for his concentration upon industrial and agricultural training has been based on the contention that, in doing so, he accepted training for hand-labor as a special and perpetual racial function of Negro education, that he accepted a subordinate role for the colored people as a permanent condition. At least three considerations would appear to contradict that view.

First, Washington's view was not racial. He believed that similar training was needed for helping the "poor white" Southern sharecropper out of his morass of debt and dependence. He encouraged the extension of the mobile agricultural "school on wheels" to white farmers. He applied the Rosenwald school-building fund, the Jeanes Foundation, and the work of the General Education Board to the white rural world as well as to the colored. It is significant that, since his death, trade unions in the South with a membership of white and colored farmers have been formed across the color-line to work in interracial cooperation for the "second emancipation."

Second, his study of "the man farthest down," all across Europe from the North Sea to the Mediterranean, led him to similar conclusions with regard to education in rural and industrial skills for the elevation of the white peasant and miner on both sides of the Atlantic.

Third, he encouraged students who showed promise in cultural directions to go on to, say, Fisk University for special training.

In other words, Washington believed in specific types of education for different functions; he did not accept the view that the skilled performance of an agricultural or an industrial function is in essence lower than that of a white-collar worker or a member of one of the professions. He said truly that "to train the hand is to train the brain." He did not believe that any one set of functions belonged particularly to any one race more than to another. He was, however, confident, after a realistic study of priorities in the period following political emancipation and the tragedy of Reconstruction, that the outstanding and urgent need for the Negro in America at that time was to be equipped for owning and skillfully cultivating his own soil. He therefore concentrated upon those skills in Tuskegee. He did not attack any other educator for plowing a different furrow.* He started a specialized and needed type of educational institute. He rose, in doing so, to a pinnacle of national leadership of his race. This led superficial observers to the distorted view that Tuskegee expressed his whole policy, whereas he saw it as only one instrument, although a vital and essential one, in a work that equally needed other instruments that other leaders were shaping and using.

President Patterson, speaking in 1945 as head of Tuskegee, presents a masterly summary of the total perspective when he says:

It is clear to anyone who has read the autobiography of Booker T. Washington . . . that the objectives of Tuskegee Institute grew out of his dedication and that of his associates to the needs of the Negro people. This interpretation of need was based on a realistic concept

* For a different interpretation, see Kellogg, *NAACP*, I, 79–86 [ed.].

of the past, present and future of the Negro people as a minority group in a capitalistic nation of great natural wealth and abundant human resources. More than this, we are pleased to note that Dr. Washington used what is regarded as a completely modern approach to the development of an educational program—namely, a community survey to determine the actual needs before attempting to put into course form the type of program that was to be undertaken by this institution. Dr. Washington saw clearly that the situation which presented itself was not only one of administering to a need that was abundantly self-evident, but it also consisted of ruling out certain unrealistic notions on the part of those who were to receive an education as to what education was all about. It is also interesting to note that the type of program which was decided upon in 1881 attempted to accomplish a two-fold purpose, as our curriculum today is set up to accomplish a two-fold objective. Namely, that which has to do with the development of competence in terms of the technical skills of the communities from which the early students came, and, two, the development of wholesome integrated personalities capable of assuming the full responsibility of citizenship.[6]

If Booker Washington needed reinforcement from other minds in standing by his convictions under the spate of criticism, it frequently came to him from sources of high authority. It may be questioned whether the world, in the first decade of the twentieth century, held any more convinced exponent of democracy or more sagacious and informed mind on race relations in all continents than the British Ambassador to the United States, James (later Viscount) Bryce.* Writing from Washington on June 30, 1910, to Booker Washington, he first asked for the Principal's view on some material he had written, for the revised edition of his *American Commonwealth,* on the Negro question in the South, saying that he was anxious that any views he might state should not contain anything calculated to do harm in any quarter. He then went on to say that he had read Washington's

* Few readers of Bryce's *American Commonwealth* would agree with this statement [ed.].

6. Annual school opening address, 1945.

book[7] with great interest and that most of its facts were new to him, expressing his strong conviction that the right course for the colored people was to make the most of their own social life, standing on their own feet. He ended by sounding a note of hope for the future, based on a consideration of what had already been accomplished.

Not infrequently men who had bitterly assailed Washington came to more favorable conclusions on deeper reflection based on fuller knowledge. One of the most impressive conversions from criticism to support of Booker Washington's policy came from William Henry Lewis who, as Assistant Attorney General under President Taft, had become the foremost lawyer of the Negro race in America. As a fiery young politician and a famous Harvard football coach, Lewis had told Washington, at a dinner in Boston, "to go back South" and attend to his work and "leave to us matters political affecting the race." "I joined in with his most violent and bitterest critics," he recorded. A few months before Washington's death, Lewis said:

Fifteen years ago I was one of the critics, one of the scoffers, one of those who asked, "What does it amount to?" You have lived [he went on, addressing Booker Washington] to confute my judgment and shame my sneers. I am now making acknowledgment of my error. . . . While most of us were agonizing over the Negro's relation to the State and his political fortunes, Booker Washington saw that there was a great economic empire that needed to be conquered. He saw an emancipated race chained to the soil by the Mortgage Crop System, and other devices, and he said, "You must own your own farms"— and forthwith there was a second emancipation. He saw the industrial trades and skilled labor pass from our race into other hands. He said, "The hands as well as the heads must be educated." . . . He saw that, if the colored race was to become economically self-sufficient, it must engage in every form of human activity.

7. Probably the two volumes of *The Story of the Negro* published late in 1909 by the Association Press, New York, as volumes 3 and 4, in their series on The Race Problem in the South.

The conviction that has become increasingly strong in the mind of the author during the years of research and of weighing the evidence is that Booker Washington from the outset had in his mind the ultimate goal of political and social as well as economic equality; but that he could not possibly help his race to take the needed first steps if he alienated the white South by proclaiming that goal at a time of inflamed resentment after the wrongs of Reconstruction. He was able by supreme self-control and by his profound sense that the eternal purpose of God was with him to rise above bitterness and exercise both patience and persistence. A similar conviction was expressed in 1944 by Roy Wilkins, editor of *The Crisis*:

If it has seemed in the past that certain segments of the Negro population and certain leaders have demanded less than complete equality in the body politic, closer study will show that the goal has always been complete equality. There is considerable evidence that that master politician on the race question, Booker T. Washington, carelessly nominated as the "half-loaf" leader, envisioned complete equality as the goal for his people. A shrewd man, thoroughly in tune with his time, he *appeared* to be an appeaser and did his great work under that protective cloak.[8]

The longer one reflects upon Booker Washington's character and his hidden springs of action, the more deeply is one persuaded that his Christian faith gave him certainty that the way of constructive cooperation between races was in accord with the meaning of the universe and with the historic process. For the same reason he believed that high-pressure aggressive methods aimed at securing results swiftly by belligerent pressure were in the long run doomed to frustration.

Dr. Gordon Blaine Hancock has taken a similar position. A Negro born in South Carolina, with three degrees from Harvard University followed by study in England at Oxford and Cambridge and long experience as a Professor of Economics and Sociology at Virginia Union University, he holds that

8. R. W. Logan, ed., *What the Negro Wants*, p. 117.

The greatness of Booker T. Washington hinges about his common-sense approach to the question of race relations; and although his doctrines have been gainsaid by many who are unworthy to unlatch his shoes, his basic approach was sound. In advocating industrial education for his people, he hoped thereby to achieve their full-fledged citizenship in this country. He knew, as we have since learned, that the empty-handed knock in vain at the door of life. He reasoned that if the Negro could be made economically efficient he would stand a better chance of surviving even though his admittance to full citizenship be indefinitely postponed. This . . . above all else marked the great wisdom and common sense that make Washington probably the greatest Negro in history.[9]

Through those later years of challenge and testing Booker Washington moved on with ever more rigorous economy of time and energy to carry through toward fuller achievement the manifold projects that were all focused upon the central aim of his life. Counsels advising a slowing of the pace as physical breakdown became threatening failed to halt him. Through the summer of 1915 he kept going, although he felt increasingly the strain of activity. Against the advice of his physician and the wishes of his friends he spoke in August at the annual meeting of the National Negro Business League, which he had watched with so deep an interest since he brought it into being. A few days later he addressed the immense National Negro Baptist Convention in Chicago, a gathering which, at that time, represented as vast a multitude of colored people as any in the world. He had joined the Baptist Church as a youth at Malden and, within the wide setting of his Christian profession and practice, gave loyal service to his own denomination. On October 25 he spoke on Negro Education to the National Council of Congregational Churches in New Haven, Connecticut. A few days later, in a New York hospital, he was told by the physician that he had not many hours to live. "Take me home," he insisted, as he talked with his friend, Major Moton, the colored leader who was to succeed him as President of Tuskegee. "I was born in the

9. Logan, p. 222.

South, I have lived and labored in the South, and I wish to die and be buried in the South." They carried him aboard an express train. He was taken to Tuskegee and died a few hours after he reached there, early in the morning, on November 14, 1915.

The debate that has been surveyed upon some aspects of Booker Washington's policy and his program is likely to continue, for men will remain divided as to whether reform should be attempted in the main by denunciation and political pressure or by the flank approach of education, persuasion, and compromise. In relation to Washington's person and work we discover that, deep beneath the surface waves of criticism, lies an unswerving recognition by his critics of his sheer greatness. As attempts to express the quality of that excellence which marked him we may quote the words of those valiant critics Du Bois and Villard.

He was [said Du Bois at the time of his death] the greatest Negro leader since Frederick Douglass and the most distinguished man, white or black, who has come out of the South since the Civil War. His fame was international and his influence far-reaching. Of the good that he accomplished there can be no doubt; he directed the attention of the Negro race in America to the pressing necessity of economic development; he emphasized technical education and he did much to pave the way for an understanding between the white and darker races.[10]

Villard's fundamental view of Washington was expressed earlier in a characteristic outburst against two speeches by Mark Twain and Ambassador Choate who, he said, "spoke of Tuskegee with more or less reluctance." While they were speaking, said Villard,

I saw the man back of it; the earnest, inspired leader, modest, retiring, self-controlled and unsparing of self, too big to be affected by the snarling of the envious of his own race or insults offered by some of the other race. Never have I met anyone who has accomplished so much and connects himself with so little of it; nor have I

10. *Chicago Post*, December 13, 1915.

ever met a man of better poise in times fraught with danger and full of anxiety, not only for himself, but for his people. The Abolitionists would have rejoiced in him—would have found him a kindred soul, so bent on his work as to have lost all thought of personality in his devotion to his cause . . . Mr. Washington has had quite as many opportunities to display moral courage as they did . . . How happy it would make them to see him walking into dangerous places without bravado . . . with simple faith in the ultimate triumph of the right, no matter what his own fate. They would know how to admire and praise without stint one who stands so straight that with hundreds of thousands of enemies of his own race eager to see him make a mis-step, anxious to point out the slightest defect in his character, scandal and rumor and gossip are silenced and abashed.[11]

Whatever view any man may hold on Booker Washington's policy and program, all may take to heart the thought of a twelfth-century writer who said: "We are like dwarfs, sitting on the shoulders of giants, in order that we may see things more numerous and more distant than they could see, not, certainly, by reason of the sharpness of our vision or the tallness of our bodies, but because we are lifted and raised on high by the greatness of the giants."

11. *The Tuskegee Student,* April 28, 1906.

Pan-Africanism as "Romantic Racism"

Of all the writers of books who helped to shape the thinking of
the members of our panel,* none was mentioned more often than
Du Bois. His name recurred again and again as early memories
were summoned up of how each individual discovered his world
and the meaning of his place in it as a Negro. Mostly the Du

* Between 1958 and 1961, Isaacs explored the impact of world affairs
on race attitudes and behavior in the United States with a panel comprising one hundred seven Negroes. He interviewed and conversed with a group
of eighty in this country, sixteen in several West African countries, and
a group of eleven young men and women who had participated in a
student work-camp program in West Africa. Of the eighty, sixty-five were
leaders "or top achievers" in their fields as writers, scholars, educators,
businessmen, churchmen, key figures in important organizations. The remaining fifteen "occupied certain positions or places or were representative
of certain types, attitudes, or experience that might otherwise not have
been reflected in the report." The entire panel included eighty-five men
and twenty-two women. In the basic group of eighty, the ages ranged
from just under forty to well over seventy. Most of them came out of
poverty but would in 1962, the date when the manuscript was completed,
be classified as "middle class." Isaacs had extended interviews—often a
total of four to eight hours spread over two or three interviews—with
fifty-five members of the panel. These fifty-five people and the twenty-five
others with whom he had briefer interviews and conversations are listed
and identified in the Introduction to his book [ed.].

Reprinted from *The New World of Negro Americans* by Harold R.
Isaacs (New York: The John Day Company Inc., 1963), pp. 195–230, by
permission of The John Day Company Inc., Publisher. Copyright © 1963
by Massachusetts Institute of Technology.

Bois influence was associated with the issues of the struggle for rights in the society, but it was also a reflection of his impact that these issues were linked, much more often than not, with some kind of a rediscovery of Africa or an alteration in attitudes toward it. Here is the way some of these memories came up in our interviews:

I learned of Du Bois at my mother's knee, and she finished in a one-room four-year school in Markham, Virginia, and we were poor people. All the Negro intellectuals of my generation and those born up to 10 or 15 years later were his disciples. . . . The international aspect of his thought was very little noticed, however. It was a question of our posture vis-à-vis the whites . . .

I've known of Africa all my life, from Du Bois' *Souls of Black Folk,* from *Crisis.* . . . The way Du Bois presented Africa was beautiful and inspiring. . . .

Du Bois' history of the Negro in the 1920's gave me my first assured knowledge of the history of the Negro in Africa. . . . Du Bois is responsible for [changing attitudes on color]. . . . In one of his books he glorified the dark and the brown, used phrases "satin black, golden brown, warm ebony," and people can now find a black girl beautiful, whereas 40 years ago nobody would have . . .

I remember Du Bois from early girlhood. . . . Swallowed his work whole. I never thought he could be wrong about anything . . .

I first read Du Bois' *Souls of Black Folk* in my home, and his novel, *The Quest of the Silver Fleece.* . . . He writes, my father would say, but he doesn't lead anybody. . . . But my father also felt the evils of oppression and responded to Du Bois' lashing out at discrimination. It was a sort of catharsis; a way of going out and shooting all those white people . . .

It was very seldom a black person would admit he was "black." Du Bois used "black" deliberately to attempt to overcome this.

It seems like I have been aware of Du Bois all my life. I read him first at least 50 years ago. . . . I was in high school when I read in *Crisis* about Du Bois' Pan-African Conference in 1919. His name was a household word. His sentiments were those of my family, though my father didn't like Du Bois. He thought he was too cold, too aloof, not human enough with ordinary people.

I remember getting angry when I heard Du Bois speak to a packed house in Louisville in which he kept referring to Christianity as the bringer of all evils through the ages to so many people . . .

You couldn't discuss anything with Du Bois. You had to listen to him. If you challenged him he became indignant and showed it by becoming manifestly discourteous . . .

Du Bois was rude to Arthur Compton at my table and I never invited him again . . .

Du Bois was strapped in by his aristocratic stance. He appealed to the intellectual, but his intellectual quality was really quite low.

I think Du Bois would be very ill at ease in a contemporary discussion by Negro intellectuals about Africa. . . . He was a cocky and proud guy who could not pass on the one hand, or identify with the mass of colored people on the other . . .

These recollections come from some men in their seventies and some in their forties. Some go all the way back to 1903, some only as far back as 1933, but after that they fade, reflecting how Du Bois himself, in his last quarter century, has faded from people's minds. One of our panelists reported:

Three years ago I asked a class of students, "Who is Du Bois?" Nobody knew any more about him other than that he was a "great man." Some didn't know his name at all.

Let us have a look, then, at this man who occupies such a special niche in the minds of so many older Negroes, a lesser one among the young, and who among whites has remained throughout hardly known at all.

The lifetime of William E. Burghardt Du Bois, the most prolific of all American Negro writers and intellectuals, spans nearly the whole century back to Emancipation. He was born in 1868, had his first book published in 1896, and has been writing continuously ever since. His works include sociological studies, essays and sketches, biography and autobiography, history, novels, and poetry. As editor of several different series of scholarly papers and pamphlets and of several periodicals, he fathered still more words, especially in the volumes of *The Crisis,* which he founded in 1910 and edited until 1933, the period of his greatest personal impact on the affairs of Negroes in the United States. Never a successful leader or organizer or even a popular public figure, Du Bois with his words alone scratched deep, life-changing marks on the minds of a whole emergent generation of aspiring Negroes as it came to its youth and maturity in the first three decades of this century.

Du Bois' impact began in 1903 with the publication of *The Souls of Black Folk,* still his most famous and best-remembered book. In it he openly took issue with Booker T. Washington, until then the undisputed and unchallenged leader of American Negroes. Du Bois called upon Negroes to abandon the posture of submissiveness and modest aspiration that Washington counseled them to hold, and instead urged them to stand up to and fight for their rights as men and citizens in the American society. Instead of the limited system of education-for-work that Washington promoted at Tuskegee, Du Bois called upon Negroes to reach for the heights of all learning and to produce that famous "Talented Tenth" to lead Negroes to the full enjoyment of freedom. In 1905 he and a group of co-thinkers launched the Niagara Movement to promote these aims, and in 1910 he joined with a group of white liberals to found the National Association for the Advancement of Colored People, becoming its research director and the editor of its organ, *The Crisis.*

In the columns of *The Crisis* for the next twenty-three years Du Bois made himself the most eloquent tribune of the fight for civil rights and equality of opportunity for Negroes, lashing, arguing, cajoling, pontificating, fighting white injustices with slashing journalism, savage wit, and fierce polemics, and fighting black weaknesses with every weapon he could grasp. He fostered pride in Negro history, Negro achievements, and Negro good looks.

He coaxed out artistic talent, ran issues devoted to college graduates, budding writers and artists, and beautiful babies. And ever and always he set forth in his own articles and editorials his own strong views of issues big and small in the Negro's fight for equality. In addition, almost as an extracurricular activity to which even his Negro readers paid scant attention, Du Bois organized between 1919 and 1927 four Pan-African Conferences in an unsuccessful attempt to give world scope to the black man's struggle for freedom from the oppression of the white. But his editorial performance was spectacular enough, pushing *The Crisis* from an initial subscription of 10,000 to a top of 104,000, a figure small in looks but large in meaning because it included all Negroes who had set their faces upward and were pushing at the barriers for better education, political freedom, and better economic opportunity. It was a stormy editorship, because Du Bois, a prickly and vain man, was no easy associate. His object was to influence people, not to make friends, and he succeeded to a remarkable degree. Du Bois has written, sometimes sadly but more often complacently, of his special aloofness, and especially his aloofness from any personal contact with whites. From his earliest days he preferred to accept being glassed in—a figure of speech he has himself used. It was a withdrawal he liked to see as proud and austere, but it was really much more like the shrinking of a porcupine inside his armor of rising spines. A biographer will one day pursue this thread of self-separation through all the reams of Du Bois' writing about himself and about the world. It will help explain why, when he reached a time of despair after thirty years' struggle for integration and equality, he reverted to a program of self-imposed isolation for Negroes, a plan for growth-within-the-ghetto that took him all the way back into the shadow of Booker T. Washington.

In the same way, a biographer who seeks to put this man's parts together again will have to see the links and the spaces between his persistent elitism, his delight in elegance and aristocracy, his half-digested Marxism, his belief in power and authority and in a "Talented Tenth" to lead the slower-moving mass, and his slow gravitation toward the international Communist movement, ending in the last decades of his long life in a close embrace—indeed, a marriage—with totalitarian Communist world power. Over most of his active years Du Bois' attitudes toward the Soviet Union and the Communist party were conditioned, like everything else in his life, by considerations of race. He held the Communist party in rather scornful disdain most of the time for its gross ineptitude in the "Negro question," but he warmed to the Soviet Union early for its anti-colonialism and for what he believed to be its abdication of the color line. In the thirty years since he left the editorship of *The Crisis,* Du Bois moved first for a confused interval toward self-segregation and then more and more steadily into the camp of the Communists. In doing so he drifted into greater and greater isolation from Negroes in general, from most of those who still admired him for the great days of his past, and indeed from any significant contact with American or Western society. It is hardly accidental that Du Bois finally turned for his compensations and realizations to the emergent world of Communist power only when he could begin to see in it the verification of some of his prophecies of doom for the Western white world, the instrument for the defeat on the largest possible scale of the Anglo-Saxon dominators who were always his prime foes. In return, the Communist empire has given Du Bois the eminence and recognition of which he felt deprived in his homeland and even among his fellow Negroes in these last decades of his long life. In 1958–1959, Du Bois made a long journey across the Soviet half world from Prague to Peking, and he was showered with honors by Communist universities and leaders in country after country. Responding to encomiums offered on his ninety-first birthday on February 23, 1959, in a speech broadcast over the Peking radio, Du Bois gave his thanks and he said: "In my own country for nearly a century, I have been nothing but a nigger." [1]

Even a thumbnail introduction of W. E. B. Du Bois stretches

1. *The New York Times,* March 5, 1959.

from paragraphs into pages and thereby illustrates some of the difficulties of our task. He has already been the subject of a first book-length biography[2] which barely begins the task of telling his long story. I want here to try to show how Du Bois has dealt with the particular matter of the Negro relationship to Africa, but this by no means narrows the compass. For Du Bois, uniquely among the writers to be discussed in these pages, made Africa one of the central themes of his thought and his writings. On it he centered some of his most personal and some of his largest dreams. In the re-creation of Africa's past he saw the means of regaining for all Negroes the pride that he clung to so strongly in himself. For the reconstruction of Africa's own present and future he produced his vision of Pan-Africanism in a world of colonies reconquered by the nonwhite races from their white overlords. On these subjects he hammered away at his audience for year after year, re-educating some, stirring a few, but meeting most of the time that deep unresponsiveness to Africa which not even he, alone, could overcome.

Nor in dealing with Du Bois and Africa is it possible to deal any less with Du Bois and race, for, as he has put it himself:

In my life the chief fact has been race—not so much scientific race, as that deep conviction of myriads of men that congenital differences among the main masses of human beings absolutely condition the individual destiny of every member of a group. Into the spiritual provincialism of this belief I have been born and this fact has guided, embittered, illuminated and enshrouded my life.[3]

When Du Bois made the familiar boyhood discovery that to be a Negro in a white-dominated world was to be despised and rejected, his own reaction was to cut himself off for life from all but the most superficial personal contact with white people. But the problems of whiteness and nonwhiteness were part of some

---

2. Francis L. Broderick, *W. E. B. Du Bois, Negro Leader in a Time of Crisis* (Stanford, 1959).
3. *Dusk of Dawn,* pp. 139–140.

of the deepest issues of human society in times that were, as always, out of joint. Even while holding himself haughtily aloof behind that famous "veil" of which he wrote so often, he could put his gifts, glands, and powers to work to set things right, not for himself (he was above it, he always said) but for all. And this is what he set out to do. All that he has been and done in his life has been aimed to settle the score created by his racial identity and to do so in the largest possible arenas.

No matter what his subject or format, Du Bois has been writing autobiography all his life, and yet he has always managed to brush quickly past those episodes of his childhood that precipitated him into his life's struggle. He was born in Great Barrington, Massachusetts, and grew up there in a fatherless home. He shared the schooltime and playtime of his early years with white boys from the middle-class upper crust of the burgeoning industrial society of that small mill town. His natural impulse was to gravitate toward the top. He says he was in and out of their homes, "except [for] a few immigrant New Yorkers, of whom none of us approved." And again: "I cordially despised the poor Irish and South Germans who slaved in the mills, and annexed the rich and well-to-do as my natural companions. Of such"—he adds self-appreciatively—"is the kingdom of snobs!" His discovery that he in his turn was also despised came, he says, more slowly.

Very gradually—I cannot now distinguish the steps, though here and there I remember a jump or a jolt—but very gradually I found myself assuming quite placidly that I was different from other children. At first I think I connected the difference with a manifest ability to get my lessons rather better than most and to recite with a certain happy, almost taunting, glibness, which brought frowns here and there. Then, slowly, I realized that some folks, a few, even several, actually considered my brown skin a misfortune; once or twice I became painfully aware that some human beings even thought it a crime. I was not for a moment daunted—although, of course, there were some days of secret tears—rather I was spurred to tireless effort. If they beat me at anything, I was grimly determined to

make them sweat for it! Once I remember challenging a great, hard
farmer-boy to battle, when I knew he could whip me; and he did. But
ever after, he was polite.

As time flew I felt not so much disowned and rejected as rather
drawn up into higher spaces and made part of a mightier mission.
At times I almost pitied my pale companions, who were not of the
Lord's anointed and who saw in their dreams no splendid quests of
golden fleeces.[4]

Unsurprisingly, it was a girl who brought on the first great
climax in the discovery of his Negroness and set him on his way.
In a schoolhouse party one day the youngsters were gaily ex-
changing visiting cards and all was merry until one girl—a newcomer—"peremptorily, with a glance," refused Will Du Bois'
card.

Then it dawned upon me with a certain suddenness that I was
different from the others; or like, mayhap, in heart and life and
longing, but shut out from their world by a vast veil. I had thereafter no desire to tear down that veil, to creep through; I held all
beyond it in common contempt, and lived above it in a region of
blue sky and great wandering shadows . . .[5]

In another version of this episode, describing his flight from the
pettiness of individual slights and insults to the larger shapes of
things beyond, he gives it the literal form of a race to a hilltop:

Then I flamed! I lifted my chin and strode off to the mountains,
where I viewed the world at my feet and strained my eyes across the
shadow of the hills.[6]

His straining eyes began then to see all the other Negroes in
America, then all black men everywhere, and before long all the
nonwhites in the world. He stretched his view to all the great
continental arenas, America, Europe, Asia, Africa, and even, on

4. *Darkwater: Voices from Within the Veil* (New York, 1920), pp.
11–12.
5. *The Souls of Black Folk*, p. 2.
6. *Darkwater*, p. 11.

some of his steeper rhetorical flights, right up into the unwalled and gateless spaces of Heaven itself.

It is difficult to resist a parenthetical pause here to explore the beginning of this process a bit further, for Du Bois offers the biographer a striking example of one of the ways in which intensely personal and powerfully impersonal forces can combine to shape the drives that make a notable life. Erik Erikson, in *Young Man Luther,*[7] has described this process of score settling in a psychoanalytic framework, showing us some of the less obvious underpinnings of Luther's career. Luther became the one to shake and change his world because of a whole complex of historical circumstances which provided the opportunity and a whole set of uniquely individual gifts and drives which led him to seize it when it was offered. Erikson suggests that one of the deepest and most decisive of these drives came from his great outward push from the issue of his relations with his own father to the issue of the Christian's relations with his father, the Pope, and man's relations with his Father, God. The Du Bois story suggests a certain rearrangement of weights and measures in this kind of analytical outline.

A great reformer or world changer who comes out of a dominant group in society may acquire his score to settle in some intensely individual experience in the parental and family setting in his earliest years; the biographer alerted by Erikson will perhaps find such experiences in the lives of men like Franklin Roosevelt or Woodrow Wilson at depths he might otherwise fail to sound. But the world shaker who comes out of a despised caste or class has a score to settle even before he is born, before he has ever opened his eyes or first seen the faces or heard the voices of those first beings who hover over him. It is there in his situation, ready made and waiting for whoever, out of whatever unique combination of personality, history, time, or social circumstance, will seize upon it and meet his own deep need by

7. (New York, 1959.)

forcing society to meet the collective need of his fellows. This element is to be found in a Simon Bolivar's mixed blood and the stigma attached to it at the Spanish court, or in a Nehru, stung by his automatic subjection to British assumptions of superiority. The unique life experiences of such men help tell us why they became *the* men who did what they did; but the target for their energies had been there, waiting for them long before their fathers and mothers had combined to make them or tried, the one or the other, to break them. Every revolutionist or reformer has had a father to contend with, but that does not mean that all revolutions, all great reforms, have been at bottom against fathers.

In the case of a Negro coming up in American society, a host of common and special features appears in the making of each individual personality. In our present group, consisting almost entirely of men of considerable achievement, it would be a matter of no small interest to try to assemble some of these shaping factors: the presence or absence of a father in the early years, the nature of the father and mother and of their relationship, the special roles of grandparents, uncles and aunts, friends, and even of strangers so often called upon to play the roles of substitute parents. Then there is all that appears in their own adulthoods, the shape of their own life experiences, the making of their own families, the raising of their own children, or their childlessness. Many of these things, to be sure, gave many such men and women their uniquely personal scores to settle; the panel includes some notable examples of this. But it was rare that even these did not become entwined with all the elements of race imposed on each one's pattern of self-discovery and self-assertion—the items of color, of caste, and the great overhanging pressures of the white world. It was perhaps something about this ready-made and common identity, as well as the white world's myopia, that helped form that feeling, expressed by almost every Negro writer, that their Negroness had deprived them of their individuality, glassed them off from the world of men—as Du Bois put it—or made them "invisible"—as Ellison had it. Whether or not this became part of any one man's picture, the big score to settle was nevertheless always there for all of them, awaiting the challenge that some one man, given the gifts and opportunity, might try to solve in the larger areas of life.

Du Bois is hardly to be classed as a world shaker or world changer. Other Negroes have been far greater as leaders and played much larger historic roles. But he did reach for the larger role, and though he failed to grasp it, he did make an impact on men's minds and even perhaps on events. Both in its public and private dimensions his life story offers most of the standard materials for such a case study. He came up in a fatherless home, and he has written much about his grandfather and about his forebears and about his life to suggest all kinds of clues to the course of his development. But except by their own mixtures of racial backgrounds through which they passed on the great tangle of ambivalences and confusions with which the young Du Bois rose to wrestle, none of his forebears, immediate or remote, "made" the issue which guided and enshrouded his life and made him what he was.

Under the towering shadow of his racial subjection, the Negro child generally learned some way of accepting his fate, of turning his hatreds and frustrations upon himself, and in one way or another upon his fellow Negroes. But always out there, beyond himself, his family, his kind, was the great white world to fear and to hate, which he did, and to defy only if he dared. Whatever his sins or failings, or whatever his father's or mother's, they were—or could be seen as—part of the weight of the sins of society so heavily visited upon them all. I am sure that deep analysis of each individual case would eventually unravel all the inner connections, but I notice all the same that up to now in literature written by Negroes and in the autobiographies that have partly unfolded before me in so many of these interviews, it has been only rarely that a father has cast a larger or longer shadow across a youth's life than the larger, longer, more dominating, more threatening, and, until now, seemingly unchallengeable figure of the white man. Perhaps we must wait until the age of deprivation passes and this, too, appears more commonly among the gifts of tomorrow's freedom.

Du Bois, then, from his hilltop, linked himself to the whole world of nonwhiteness. In the beginning this meant regaining contact with Negroes. From the isolation of Great Barrington he did not go at first to Harvard, as he had dreamed of doing, but was content enough ("after a twinge, I felt a strange delight") to be deflected to Fisk, where he came into the company of other Negroes.

I was thrilled to be for the first time among so many people of my own color or rather of such various and such extraordinary colors, which I had only glimpsed before, but who it seemed were bound to me by new and exciting and eternal ties. . . . Above all for the first time I saw beautiful girls. At my home among my white school mates there were a few pretty girls; but either they were not entrancing or because I had known them all my life I did not notice them; but at the first dinner I saw opposite me a girl of whom I have often said, no human being could possibly have been as beautiful as she seemed to my young eyes that far-off September night of 1885.[8]

At Fisk he not only related himself to other Negroes and especially to beautiful young Negro girls, but with the same romantic idealism about race he also, for the first time, embraced Africa.

His great-grandmother ("black, little, and lithe") used to "croon a heathen melody" to her children, and the song came down in the family to become "the only one direct cultural connection" Du Bois ever had to his African background as a child. But his upbringing was "not African so much as Dutch and New England," and he came to Africa only after discovering that New England rejected him. He says this clearly:

My African racial feeling was then purely a matter of my own later learning and reaction; my recoil from the assumptions of the

8. *Dusk of Dawn*, p. 24.

whites; my experience in the South at Fisk. But it was none the less real and a large determinant of my life and character. I felt myself African by "race" and by that token was African and an integral member of the group of dark Americans who were called Negroes.[9]

When I interviewed the aged but crisp Du Bois in his Brooklyn home, I pressed him a little to look back down the years all the way to Great Barrington to see what else about Africa might have brushed him in his boyhood. He first again mentioned the African song that had come down in his family. No, he did not remember reading about Africa then, though he devoured everything the Great Barrington library had on its shelves. "The books I remember taking out were books on English history and such. If I had sought books about Africa there, I doubt that I would have found any."

"And in school?" I asked.

"I was tremendously incensed that there was nothing in the textbooks about Africa," he said. "Only pictures of white men, no pictures of colored or black men, and this began to get me curious."

Did he mean, I asked, that no pictures of people accompanied the mentions of Africa in those first textbooks? And here Du Bois came up with his own report of the familiar experience. "We did get pictures of the races of man," he said, "a white man, a Chinese mandarin, and the savage Negro. That was what the class got and it made me especially sensitive. I did not recognize those pictures in the book as being my people.

"Africa," he went on, "was not a major thing in my thought or any part of my experience. My first real acquisition of any of this was at Fisk, where they had the beginnings of an African museum, some pieces like that one up there—" and he pointed to a small carved figure of stone on his mantelpiece. "But Africa still never came to the center of my thought. It was something in the background. There was always a lack of interest, a neglect, a resentment at being classed as Africans when Negroes felt

9. *Ibid.*, p. 114 [and p. 115—ed.].

that they were Americans. Interest in Africa did not begin with
anyone until after 1880 or so. . . . I did not myself begin actively to study Africa until 1908 or 1910. Franz Boas really influenced me to begin studying this subject and I began really to
get into it only after 1915."

Du Bois' tie to Africa remained pure racial romance, whether
he related to it as an individual, as a propagandist for the greatness of the Negro's past, or as a geopolitician of race, a dreamer
of great dreams of Pan-Africanism as part of a general re-emer-
gence of the world of nonwhites brought together by their common history of slavery, discrimination, and insult. All of this
appears together in a single passage in his 1940 autobiography:

> As I face Africa, I ask myself: what is it between us that consti-
> tutes a tie that I can feel better than I can explain? Africa is of
> course my fatherland. Yet neither my father nor my father's father
> ever saw Africa or knew its meaning or cared overmuch for it. My
> mother's folk were closer and yet their direct connection, in culture
> and race, became tenuous; still, my tie to Africa is strong. On this
> vast continent were born and lived a large portion of my direct an-
> cestors going back a thousand years and more. The mark of their
> heritage is upon me in color and hair. . . . But one thing is sure
> and that is the fact that since the fifteenth century these ancestors
> of mine and their other descendants have had a common history,
> have suffered a common disaster, and have one long memory. The
> actual ties of heritage between the individuals of this group vary
> with the ancestors that they have in common and many others, Eu-
> ropeans and Semites, perhaps Mongolians, certainly American In-
> dians. But the physical bond is least and the badge of color relatively
> unimportant save as a badge; the real essence of this kinship is its
> social heritage of slavery; the discrimination and insult; and this
> heritage binds together not simply the children of Africa, but ex-
> tends through yellow Asia and into the South Seas. It is this unity
> that draws me to Africa.[10]

Du Bois could write that the "physical bond" was "least" and
that the "badge of color was relatively unimportant," while

10. *Ibid.*, pp. 116–117.

nourishing for all his life a near-obsession with color. He was hardly ever able to describe anyone without stress upon it, or to deal with many values far detached from it. On the lighter-brown side himself, he early set his face against the Negro color caste. In his Harvard days he "hotly championed the inclusion of two black schoolmates whose names were not usually on the invitation list to our social affairs." In Europe he turned away the proffered love of a white girl and back home even ended a courtship with a Negro girl who "looked quite white" and therefore might create misunderstandings that would embarrass him. In his writing he began to stress blackness as a positive virtue, and when he did eventually set foot himself in Africa, he positively swooned on its "black bosom."

This journey took place at the end of 1923, and William E. Burghardt Du Bois returned to his ancestral homeland as, of all things, Envoy Extraordinary and Minister Plenipotentiary of the President of the United States to the inauguration of the President of Liberia. This episode is described fully and lovingly by Du Bois himself.[11] There is first a sharp and wonderfully revealing vignette of Du Bois on shipboard, a day out of Africa, the land of so many dreams, reading his favorite author. His diary note, full text: "Tomorrow—Africa! Inconceivable! As yet no sight of land, but it was warm and we rigged deck chairs and lay at ease. I have been reading that old novel of mine—it has points. Twice we've wired Liberia. I'm all impatience." Then at the landing came the nearly orgasmic ecstasy he felt in his role, in the trappings and protocol and the snap of his military escort, the pomp of his reception at the presidential mansion, the bows of the assembled diplomatic corps, and the reading of his address as all respectfully listened. In calling this experience perhaps his greatest hour, Du Bois suddenly shows us a small man, shrunken inside the vestments of his golden words.

He goes on, from the story of the brief spurt of his enjoyment

11. *The Crisis* (April 1924), 248–251; *Dusk of Dawn,* pp. 122–125.

of the sensations of sovereignty, to the gushing, melting passion of joy over his reunion with the land of his black ancestry:

The spell of Africa is upon me. The ancient witchery of her medicine is burning my drowsy, dreamy blood. This is not a country, it is a world, a universe of itself and for itself, a thing Different, Immense, Menacing, Alluring. It is a great black bosom where the spirit longs to die. It is life so burning, so fire encircled that one bursts with terrible soul inflaming life. One longs to leap against the sun and then calls, like some great hand of fate, the slow, silent, crushing power of almighty sleep—of Silence, of immovable Power beyond, within, around. Then comes the calm. The dreamless boat of midday stillness at dusk, at dawn, at noon, always. Things move— black shiny bodies, perfect bodies, bodies of sleek unearthly poise and beauty. Eyes languish, black eyes—slow eyes, lovely and tender eyes in great dark formless faces . . .[12]

Du Bois walked out into the "bush" to visit a village. He wrote:

How shall I describe it? Neither London, nor Paris, nor New York has anything of its delicate precious beauty. It was a town of the Veys and done in cream and pale purples, still, clean, restrained, tiny, complete. It was no selfish place, but the central abode of fire and hospitality, clean-swept for wayfarers. . . . They gave our hands a quick soft grasp and talked easily. Their manners were better than those of Park Lane or Park Avenue. Oh, much better and more natural. They showed [us] breeding . . . These folk have the leisure of true aristocracy, leisure for thought and courtesy, leisure for sleep and laughter. They have time for their children—such well-trained, beautiful children with perfect, unhidden bodies. . . . Come to Africa and see well-bred and courteous children, playing happily and never sniffling or whining . . .[13]

He never saw a quarrel or fight, "nor met with a single lewd gesture." He saw "no impudent children or smart and overbearing young folk," and found everyone, old and young, uniformly polite and full of deference, tolerance, and affection for each other.

12. *The Crisis* (April 1924), 274.
13. *Dusk of Dawn,* pp. 126–127.

And always recurring, his special duet on bodies, one part in tropical rhapsody:

I believe that the African form in color and curve is the beautifulest thing on earth; the face is not so lovely, though often comely with perfect teeth and shining eyes—but the form of the slim limbs, the muscled torso, the deep full breasts! [14]

And the other, in shrill New England tenor:

I have read everywhere that Africa means sexual license. Perhaps it does. Most folk who talk sex frantically have all too seldom revealed their source material. I was in West Africa only two months, but with both eyes wide. I saw children quite naked and women usually naked to the waist—with bare bosom and limbs. And in those sixty days I saw less of sex dalliance and appeal than I see daily on Fifth Avenue. This does not mean much, but it is an interesting fact.[15]

So much of Du Bois is here in this brief African interlude: the elitist gratified by the rituals of power; the man drawn by deep full breasts; the daydreamer won by languor; the poet swooning on Africa's black bosom; the rhapsodist celebrating color, curve, and form; the aristocrat pleased by dignity, deference, order, and gentility; the Puritan alert to any nonpoetic license. But never submerged in any of these is Du Bois the race propagandist, always trying to carry his readers with him toward a better opinion of their past and present links to Africa and thereby toward a better opinion of themselves.

To this same end he also took the work done by various scholars and writers in history, art, and archeology to resurrect the African past, and in book after book, alongside his autobiographical fragments, his discourses on race issues and world politics, his exhortations and his polemics, he kept filling in and enlarging the tapestry of the Negro's remoter past, painting in great strokes of majestic achievement and prideful memory. In this work Du Bois was content to try to be the popularizer of

14. *The Crisis* (April 1924), 273.
15. *Dusk of Dawn*, pp. 127–128.

the most favorable findings of others. For his own preserve he took the intermingling of world politics, history, and race, and he entered upon it with full zest, wielding his pen like a field-piece, scattering his words like shrapnel over the whole range of the white man's depredations on the nonwhite world. For Du Bois the study of history was the study of the geopolitics of race.

In 1900, barely twenty years after he had raced, hurt, to that Massachusetts hilltop and strained his eyes toward farther horizons, W. E. B. Du Bois wrote one of his famous sentences:

The problem of the twentieth century is the problem of the color line—the relation of the darker to the lighter races of men in Asia and Africa, in America and the islands of the sea.[16]

He had by now taken into his widening view all the black men of America; he had explored their history and something of their present state. He had looked beyond them to the black men of Africa and to all the nonwhites in the rest of the world, and their common plight under the rule of the white master race, and in a deep lunge of intellect and intuition he had developed the issue to its full global dimensions.

When the First World War came, Du Bois saw it as a massive and bloody collision between rivals for the spoils of the earth. The issue was world power, and a major issue in power had become the distribution of colonies in Asia and Africa. Du Bois had already taken half a hold on the Marxist-socialist view which saw the fulcrum of affairs as economic and the main division in society running between exploiters and toilers. But he also saw that white toilers were just as committed as white capitalists to

16. These words are given here as they appear at the beginning of *The Souls of Black Folk,* first published in 1903. I am indebted to Professor Rayford Logan for a reference to Bishop Alexander Walters' *My Life and Work* (New York, 1917), p. 257, indicating that Du Bois first used this formula in 1900 at a conference in London where the slogan of Pan-Africanism was born.

the maintenance of the color line in all its brutishness, indeed often more so, and this kept him for years from coming closer to any of the forms of socialist doctrine professed by white politicians. On the world scene, as anyone could see, the exploiters were white and the toilers nonwhite. Around its world system of strategy, power, and political economy, Europe had draped an elaborate racist ideology, declaring, as Du Bois put it, that it was "the duty of white Europe to divide up the darker world and administer it for Europe's good." This was rationalized by the belief that the "darker peoples are dark in mind as well as in body" and are therefore "born beasts of burden for white folks." For their profitable toil they were to be paid what they—held nearly worthless—were worth, Du Bois wrote:

Such degrading of men by men is as old as mankind and the invention of no one race or people. Ever have men striven to conceive of their victims as different from the victors, endlessly different, in soul and blood, strength and cunning, race and lineage. It has been left, however, to Europe and to modern days, to discover the eternal world-wide mark of meanness—color! [17]

This marking of the color line gave Du Bois a hard and sometimes twisting path, but it also often led him to the heart of things:

This theory of human culture and its aims has worked itself through the warp and woof of our daily thought with a thoroughness that few realize. Everything great, good, efficient, fair, and honorable is "white"; everything mean, bad, blundering, cheating, and dishonorable is "yellow"; a bad taste is "brown"; and the devil is "black." The changes of this theme are continually rung in picture and story, in newspaper heading and moving picture, in sermon and school book, until, of course, the King can do no wrong—a White Man is always right and a Black Man has no rights which a white man is bound to respect. There must come the necessary despisings and hatreds of these savage half-men, this unclean canaille of the world—these dogs of men. All through the world this gospel is

17. *Darkwater*, p. 42.

preaching. It has its literature, it has its priests, it has its secret propaganda and above all—it pays! [18]

Of large events it gave him a much clearer view than most people had at the time, in 1920, when he wrote these prophetic
words:

> The World War was primarily the jealous and avaricious struggle
> for the largest share in exploiting darker races. As such it is and
> must be but the prelude to the armed and indignant protests of
> these despised and raped peoples. Today Japan is hammering on
> the door of justice, China is raising her half-manacled hands to
> knock next, India is writhing for the freedom to knock, Egypt is
> sullenly muttering, the Negroes of South and West Africa, of the
> West Indies, and of the United States are just awakening to their
> shameful slavery. Is, then, this war the end of wars? Can it be the
> end, so long as sits enthroned even in the souls of those who cry
> peace, the despising and robbing of darker peoples? If Europe hugs
> this delusion, then this is not the end of world war—it is but the
> beginning! [19]

Better vision, one must add, than a great many people had had
(or still have!) now that we have gone through so much that Du
Bois so clearly foresaw forty years ago.

Through his racial window on the world Du Bois saw some
things hard and clear, but some were out of focus, others out of
sight, and often his view was downright myopic. Like many
more common men, he built some of his prejudices out of his
vanity and out of scanty personal experience. His schooltime in
Berlin gave him a curiously affectionate view of culture in
Hohenzollern Germany. Because the French showed greater sub-
tlety in applying the color line both at home and in the colonies
and showed some greater readiness to recognize merit in black
men (even if it was only their merit in serving their white masters
or offering up their lives for the metropole in war), Du Bois

18. *Ibid.*, p. 44.
19. *Ibid.*, pp. 49–50.

took a much kindlier view of French whiteness than of most others. He was untiringly proud of his own Dutch and French ancestors, and especially of the suggestion of Huguenot nobility and wealth in the latter. He described himself as being born "with a flood of Negro blood, a strain of French, a bit of Dutch, but, thank God! no 'Anglo-Saxon'!" Du Bois had started out to be a social scientist, to accept the harsh discipline of the truth seeker in the belief that the truth would make men free. But when he felt driven to become a race propagandist, his truth seeking became more selective and his truths more supple. Negroness and blackness not only had to be made acceptable; they had to be romanticized. Race doctrine that was anathema when it was white became eloquent when it was black: "I believe in the Negro race, in the beauty of its genius, the sweetness of its soul . . ." The enslavement of black men by black and brown in the times before the white incursions into Africa became under his pen "the mild domestic slavery of the African tribes and of the Arabs and the Persians." The Moslem slave trade in black Africans was mitigated in his eyes by the thought that it was intended to supply soldiers and servants to a leisure class, not profit-making labor to a "commercial class." [20] And when virtual slavery was found still being practiced in modern Liberia, Du Bois brushed rather lightly over the facts as they were established in 1939 by a League of Nations commission of inquiry.[21]

Du Bois managed mainly not to notice either slavery past style or wage slavery modern style when they appeared in modern black Liberia. Perhaps the style of his bias will be illustrated best in two widely separated passages from his writings, both about the daughters of rich households. The first is imaginary:

. . . a lovely British home, with green lawns, appropriate furnishings and a retinue of well-trained servants. Within is a young woman, well-trained and well-dressed, intelligent and high-minded. She is

20. *The World and Africa* (New York, 1947), p. 77; *Black Folk Then and Now, An Essay in the History and Sociology of the Negro Race* (New York, 1939), pp. 130–131.
21. *Ibid.*, p. 292; cf. Broderick, *W. E. B. Du Bois,* pp. 134–135.

fingering the ivory keys of a grand piano and pondering the problem of her summer vacation . . . her family is not wealthy, but it has a sufficient "independent" income from investments to enjoy life without hard work. How far is such a person responsible for the crimes of colonialism? It will in all probability not occur to her that . . . her income is the result of starvation, theft, and murder, that it involves ignorance, disease, and crime . . . Yet . . . she is content to remain in ignorance of the source of her wealth and its cost in human toil and suffering.[22]

The second household is a real one, a mansion he visited upriver in Liberia:

A mansion of five generations with a compound of endless native servants and cows under the palm thatches. The daughters of the family wore, on the beautiful black skin of their necks, the exquisite pale gold chains of the Liberian artisan and the slim, black granddaughter of the house had a wide pink ribbon on the thick curls of her dark hair. . . . Double porches one above the other, welcomed us to ease. A native man, gay with Christmas and a dash of gin, danced and sang. . . . Children ran and played. . . . We sat at a long broad table and ate duck, chicken, beef, rice, plantain and collards, cake, tea, water, and Madeira wine . . .[23]

Du Bois might have noted the painful irony of the reproduction of the plantation manor of the old slave days in America. He might have asked whether these daughters, with the pale gold chains on their handsome black necks, had ever paused to think where the gold had come from, or all their comfort and plenty, including the "endless native servants"; and one wonders whether Du Bois would have found their ignorance, like the white girl's, "a colossal crime in itself." But if he did ask, he does not tell of it, and if he did wonder about it, we do not know, because he does not say.

Du Bois' color astigmatism appears even more strongly in the way he dealt over the years with the phenomenon of Japan.

22. *The World and Africa*, pp. 41–42.
23. *The Crisis* (April 1924), 250.

After exulting, like nonwhites all over the world, over Japan's defeat of Russia in 1905, Du Bois had wishfully seen Japan as the striking edge of the colored world against the white. He remained defensive about Japan's transformation into an aggressive imperialist power on its own terms. He saw its predatory assaults on China as part of colored Japan's resistance to the white West. He insisted that Japan's attacks on China were a prelude to a Japanese-Chinese bloc against the white world, and as late as the Manchurian invasion in 1931, he was seeing them as Japan's effort to save China from enslavement by Europe and America.[24] In his 1940 book, *Dusk of Dawn,* Du Bois managed to avoid any mention at all of Japan's ongoing war in China, and in 1947, in *The World and Africa,* he gave this remarkable capsule summary of the events just past: "Japan aroused Asia, and by attacking America thus furnished the one reason, based on race prejudice, which brought America immediately into the war." [25]

Du Bois poured his racial fantasies, his view of the world, his obsession with color, his public judgments and his secret hopes, and some of his own innermost dreams into a novel he called *Dark Princess,* published in 1928. It is one of the most forgotten of his many books, and as a work of literature deserves no other fate. But as a biographical item it is very much worth dwelling upon here for a bit, since it tells us much about our man and about our subject.

His story is of a young American Negro, frustrated by prejudice in his effort to become a doctor, who thereupon quits America for Europe. "I'm through," Matthew Towns writes his mother. "I cannot and will not stand America longer. I'm off." In Berlin he strolls into the Viktoria Café on the Unter der Linden, looking exactly as the young Du Bois himself has been described in his own Berlin days, wearing a new suit with "his newest dark crimson tie that burned with the red in his smooth dark face; he carried cane and gloves and he had walked into this fashionable café with

24. Broderick, pp. 133–135.
25. *The World and Africa,* p. 14.

an air." Here he encounters the Princess, whose color filled his eyes even before the rest of her beauty came into focus:

First and above all came that sense of color: into this world of pale yellowish and pinkish parchment, that absence or negation of color, came, suddenly, a glow of golden brown skin. It was darker than sunlight and gold; it was lighter and livelier than brown. It was a living, glowing crimson, veiled beneath brown flesh. It called for no light and suffered no shadow, but glowed softly of its own inner radiance.

He meets her by knocking down a white American who tries to annoy her. She turns out to be Her Royal Highness the Princess Kautilya of Bwodpur, India, who promptly invites him home for dinner. His fellow guests are a Japanese nobleman, two Indians, two Chinese, an Egyptian and his wife; all richly dressed, all obviously people of high status and importance. Matthew "could not keep his eyes from continually straying sidewise to his hostess. Never had he seen color in human flesh so regally set: the rich and flowing grace of the dress out of which rose so darkly splendid the jeweled flesh."

"You will note, Mr. Towns," she says, "that we represent here much of the Darker World. Indeed, when all our circle is present, we represent all of it, save your world of Black Folk."

The group turns out to be the executive committee of a world movement of the "Darker Peoples." They had just been debating whether to include American or African blacks, some of them questioning the "ability, qualifications, and real possibilities of the black race in Africa or elsewhere." Matthew hotly defends his race and proves its genius and its desire for freedom by suddenly singing the spiritual, "Let My People Go." The Egyptian, who had scornfully questioned the merit of "the black rabble of America," is silenced. "Pan-Africa belongs logically with Pan-Asia," decrees the Princess, "and for that reason Mr. Towns is welcomed tonight." So Pan-Africa, in the person of Mr. Towns-Du Bois, joins the circle.

Matthew goes back to America and there almost falls prey to

utter corruption when the Dark Princess appears to rescue him from this threatened suicide of his soul. He and the Princess then live a brief idyll in a Chicago slum. The Princess tells of her dream of the "substitution of the rule of dark men in the world for the rule of white, because the colored peoples were the noblest and the best bred." Matthew tries to broaden her view, arguing for the admission of "the masses of men of all races who might be the best of men simply imprisoned by poverty and ignorance." Indeed, throughout, Du Bois' hero valiantly tries to keep the broader human mass in view, just as he continues to argue for peaceful means as against violence; he has a hard time on both counts. He must also convince her that black men have their rightful part in the great times to come and were not, as her friends had charged, "only slaves and half-men."

In the end Kautilya's doubts are resolved and she writes Matthew, in language that oddly mingles the accents of Du Bois' global racism and the Communist party's doctrine, brand new in 1928, of "self-determination in the Black Belt," the idea of a Negro Republic across some part of the American South. Here is Kautilya's message:

You are not free in Chicago or New York. But here in Virginia you are at the edge of a black world. The black belt of the Congo, the Nile, and the Ganges reaches by way of Guiana, Haiti, and Jamaica, like a red arrow, up into the heart of white America. Thus I see a mighty synthesis: you can work in Africa and Asia right here in America if you work in the Black Belt. For a long time I was puzzled . . . but now I know. I am exalted, and with my high heart comes illumination. I have been sore bewildered by this mighty America, this ruthless, terrible, intriguing Thing. My home and heart is India. Your heart of hearts is Africa. And now I see through the cloud. You may stand here, Matthew, here, halfway between Maine and Florida, between the Atlantic and the Pacific, with Europe in your face and China at your back; with industry in your right hand and commerce in your left and the Farm beneath your steady feet; and yet be in the Land of the Blacks.

It develops that the Princess has not, as he thought, gone home to India, but to his mother's cabin in Virginia, to have Matthew's baby. He is summoned there by an East Indian courier in rich garb who bows low before him in his South Side tenement room. With her summons comes a prophecy:

The great central committee of Yellow, Brown, and Black is finally to meet. You are a member. The High Command is to be chosen. Ten years of preparation are set. Ten more years of final planning and then five years of intensive struggle. In 1952, the Dark World goes free—whether in Peace and fostering Friendship with all men, or in Blood and Storm—it is for Them—the Pale Masters of today— to say.

Matthew flies back to Virginia and walks up the long path to his mother's cabin, and there standing by the old black tree is the Princess, dressed in her royal robes and great jewels, blood rubies, silk, and gold, and in her arms is their baby, the new Maharajah of Bwodpur. In a wonderful touch that is like a sudden and unexpected chuckle from the author, Matthew's mother produces a local preacher to marry them "to make this little man an hones' chile." So there in the curve of a Virginia hill they are joined with a proper Christian knot, while from among the trees in the forest the royal retinue of Indians hails the pair and the princeling: "King of the Snows of Gaurisankar! Protector of Ganga the Holy! Incarnate Son of the Buddha! Grand Mughal of Utter India! Messenger and Messiah to all the Darker Worlds!"

Once again, much—if not all—of Du Bois appears in his book, his thoughts and fantasies about the world, and his dreams about himself, and about love and about fulfillment. Here are his angers and confusions, his color fixation, his racism, his belief in an aristocracy of talent and, more secretly, in an aristocracy of blood, really only the blood of dark-skinned men. Here too is his dream of liberation, a day of stern justice and reckoning but not—he struggles to believe—of vengeance. He dreams of it not as Armageddon but salvation, the rescue of the white world from self-destruction and the redirection of its energies—under the generous aegis of the new elect—toward true human advancement.[26] He presents it all with but small saving touches of a restraining intelligence and humanity and occasional flickers of prophetic insight. Written in 1928, his prophecy that the "Dark World" would go free by 1952 was not bad, not bad at all.

But in our present context the most striking thing about this whole fanciful construction is the virtual absence from it of *Africa.* It is included as a place name, but the only "African" who actually appears is an Egyptian, who has to be rapped to order for prejudice against black skins. The whole black race gets admitted to the circle of the Darker World only because young Towns-Du Bois, with gloves and cane, rescues a beauteous brown princess from a white American wolf in a Berlin café, and she, Pan-Asia, welcomes him, Pan-Africa, to her side. This singular personification was not an accident nor was it merely a literary convenience, for Pan-Africa was the other shape of Du Bois' dream, and while he dreamed it for Africa's fulfillment, what he really saw in it was his own.

Du Bois was a romantic racist, but through all the ups and downs and twists and turns of his thinking through the years

26. Du Bois liked to see himself as a cool human spirit with an icy mind contemplating squirming men from a high lonely seat behind the veil. But he has on occasion allowed himself the luxury of an outburst of good, hot hate, as in these lines from a 1920 poem:

Valiant spoilers of women
And conquerors of unarmed men;
Shameless breeders of bastards,
Drunk with the greed of gold,
Bating their blood-stained hooks
With cant for the souls of the simple;
Bearing the white man's burden
Of liquor and lust and lies . . .
      I hate them, Oh!
      I hate them well,
      I hate them, Christ!
      As I hate hell!
      If I were God,
      I'd sound their knell
      This day!

Who raised the fools to their glory,
But black men of Egypt and Ind,
Ethiopia's sons of the evening,
Indians and yellow Chinese,
Arabian children of morning,
And mongrels of Rome and Greece?
      Ah, well!
And they that raised the boasters
Shall drag them down again . . .
      —*Darkwater,* pp. 53–54.

he never got romantic enough to choose the ultimate option of urging Negroes to migrate en masse to Africa. Neither in his greatest anger nor in his deepest despair was he ever driven to the notion that there was an answer for Negroes in recrossing the ocean to resettle in the inhospitable homeland of their black ancestors. When he reverted in 1933 to the idea of Negro self-segregation, it never entered his mind that this self-containment would take place anywhere but right here in the United States. Du Bois had the imagination and intelligence to see, long before anyone else, that the meaningful slogan for beleaguered American Negroes as far as Africa was concerned was not *Back to Africa* but *Africa for the Africans,* and this is what he tried to promote with his Pan-African movement. He tried to win both the rulers of the white world and the Negroes of his own world to the self-serving good sense of his idea, and he failed with both.

Du Bois understood that the idea of going Back to Africa had appealed over time "not simply to the inexperienced and the demagogues, but to the prouder and more independent type of Negro . . . tired of begging for justice and recognition." [27] But from times past on down to the "crazy scheme of Marcus Garvey," Du Bois had simply found the idea impracticable. Negroes were not equipped to be pioneers, he patiently explained at the height of the Garvey movement, and in any case, Europe's expansion "made colonies in Africa or elsewhere about the last place where colored folk could seek freedom and equality." To would-be migrants moved by Garvey, Du Bois made sober answers:

No person of middle age or beyond should think of migrating. . . . Young and energetic people who want to migrate to Africa must remember [that] laborers are not needed in Africa . . . Skilled labor . . . is wanted, but even there the difficulties of remunerative work . . . are very great . . .[28]

Or again:

27. *Dusk of Dawn,* p. 195.
28. *The Crisis* (June 1924), 57.

Africa belongs to these Africans. They have not the slightest intention of giving it up to foreigners, white or black . . . They resent the attitude that assures that other folk of any color are coming in to take and rule their land. Liberia, for instance . . . is not going to allow American Negroes to assume control and to direct her government. Liberia, in her mind, is for Liberians. . . .[29]

No, Du Bois wanted to bend Africa otherwise to his designs. He had come strongly to believe, as we have seen, that the rise of the black man in America was linked with the rise of the non-white all over the world. He had real illusions in 1919 that the rulers of the white world, war weary and even frightened, might see the wisdom of beginning to change their ways. He saw that Japan and China were both seeking new voices for themselves in the postwar world. He thought that as far as the black men were concerned, the American Negro, rising steadily in education and attainment despite all obstacles, had to take the lead. He had to speak for the more slowly awakening masses of Africa, just as his hero did in *Dark Princess,* and, indeed, as Du Bois himself did when in Paris in 1919 he organized his first Pan-African Congress. He tried to bring Africans onto the world scene and to make their voices heard for the first time in the councils of power.

To American Negroes at home he tried to explain what he was up to:

This is not a "separatist" movement. There is no need to think that those who advocate the opening up of Africa for Africans . . . desire to deport any large number of colored Americans to a foreign and, in some respects, inhospitable land. Once for all, let us realize that we are Americans, that we were brought here with the earliest settlers, and that the very sort of civilization from which we came made the complete adoption of Western modes and customs imperative if we were to survive at all. In brief, there is nothing so indigeneous, so completely "made in America" as we. It is as absurd to talk of a return to Africa, merely because that was our home 300 years ago, as it would be to expect the members of the Caucasian

29. *The Crisis* (July 1924), 106.

race to return to the vastnesses of the Caucasus Mountains from
which, it is reputed, they sprang.

   . . . The African movement means to us what the Zionist movement must mean to the Jews, the centralization of race effort and the
recognition of a racial fount. To help bear the burden of Africa
does not mean any lessening of effort in our own problem at home.
Rather it means increased interest. For any ebullition of action and
feeling that results in an amelioration of the lot of Africa tends to
ameliorate the condition of colored peoples throughout the world.
And no man liveth to himself.[30]

This was Du Bois in 1919. He got nowhere. His attempt to be
sensible about migration was drowned in the din of the Garvey
movement and its alarms and diversions. His attempt to give
focus to the inner dynamic relating the American Negro to
Africa went unnoticed. His words remained without echo until
now, more than forty years later, when they ring in the air all
around us.

    Du Bois had first heard the word "Pan-African" at a confer-
ence he attended in London in 1900. It is odd, yet characteristic
of the man, that in his earlier autobiographical work he makes
no mention of this meeting. In a later book, in 1947, he refers
to it briefly, remarking that here is where the word "Pan-African" first appeared, but even then not mentioning his presence
there, perhaps because it was a meeting conceived and called
not by him but by a "black West Indian barrister, practicing in
London," whom he does not even name.[31] In 1911 Du Bois addressed a Congress of Races, held also in London under the
auspices of the Ethical Culture movement. Whatever sequel that
might have had was engulfed by the war. When Du Bois suddenly got the chance to go to Europe in 1919, he conceived the
notion of trying to dramatize his cause by calling a conference
of black men under the slogan of Pan-Africa. As he has re-

   30. *The Crisis* (February 1919), 166.
   31. *The World and Africa*, p. 7. The West Indian barrister was H.
Sylvester Williams. Cf. Walters, Chap. 2. The conference created an organization of which Du Bois was named as American vice president.

counted in several places,[32] he managed to assemble a Congress of fifty-seven individuals from fifteen countries, nine of them African. The Congress appealed to the Versailles Conference to give Africans a chance for free development under international auspices, starting with the African territories taken from Germany. Du Bois says that this was the origin of the mandates system.* Du Bois persisted and managed to assemble a second, larger conference in 1921, a third at Lisbon in 1925* and a fourth token gathering held in New York in 1927. Through almost all of this time Du Bois, to his great embarrassment, saw his Pan-African movement confounded in the world's press (and in many chancelleries) with Marcus Garvey's more flamboyant enterprise. It was, he wrote ruefully, a situation of "comedy and curious social frustration, but . . . real and in a sense tragic." [33] In the face of apathy and even resistance among his American associates and a large measure of indifference abroad, he made a last try to call another conference, this time in Tunis in 1929, but it failed to take place and the Pan-African movement fell into a coma. It was not revived until 1945 when the fifth Pan-African Congress was held at Manchester, England. It was organized by George Padmore, the ex-Communist West Indian writer who became father counselor to the colony of West African nationalist expatriates in London, and one of the most energetic members of

---

* Du Bois stated in his *The World and Africa* (pp. 7 and 8) that he landed in France in December, 1918. George Louis Beer, Chief of the Colonial Division of the American Delegation to Negotiate Peace in 1919, had prepared as early as 1917 a memorandum on the subject of a mandates commission. (See George Louis Beer, *African Questions at the Paris Peace Conference* [New York, 1923], pp. xix, 57–67.) On January 30, 1919, *The New York Times* speculated that it was not "beyond the bounds of probability to say that the principle of internationalizing the German colonies, with a future administration intrusted to governments designated by the [L]eague of [N]ations, will be recognized by the peace conference." The Pan-African Congress was held February 19–21, 1919 [ed.].

* London, Brussels, and Paris, 1921; London and Lisbon, 1923 [ed.].

32. *Dusk of Dawn,* pp. 260–262, 274–278; *The World and Africa,* pp. 9–12, 235–245.

33. *Dusk of Dawn,* p. 277.

that colony, a young man named Kwame Nkrumah. They invited Du Bois to serve as chairman. Nkrumah went on to become leader of the new Ghana and adopted the idea of Pan-Africanism as a central theme in his own vision of the African future. He invited Du Bois to the independence celebration in Accra in 1957, but Du Bois refused to sign the affidavit relating to Communist affiliation that was then part of the passport application, was refused a passport, and therefore did not go. In 1958, when Nkrumah convened the first All-African People's Conference at Accra, he again invited the aged Du Bois to come and witness the fruition of his early dreams. But this time Du Bois, who had received his passport when the affidavit requirement was dropped, was ill in Moscow and sent his wife to Accra to represent him. Opening the conference, Nkrumah paid tribute to Du Bois and to Marcus Garvey, linking their names, in a final ironic twist to this history, as the pioneers who had "fought for African national and racial equality." [34] Du Bois finally did get back to African soil to attend the Ghana Republic Day celebrations in July, 1069. He was much honored as the "father of Pan-Africanism," but he used the occasion mainly to warn Africans against Anglo-American capitalism and to extol the Soviet system. In the fall of 1961 he returned to Ghana, apparently this time to stay, even though by now the Communist empire far more than Africa had become the nonagenarian Du Bois' chosen spiritual home. His last act before leaving the United States was to apply formally for membership in the Communist party.[35]

When I was finally granted an hour's audience with Dr. Du Bois on a winter day not long before his ninety-second birthday,* I knew it would be impossible to re-explore much of all this past, that most of my questions would have to go unasked, that

* Since Du Bois would have been ninety-two on February 23, 1960, the interview took place in late 1959 or early 1960 [ed.].

34. St. Clair Drake, "Pan-Africanism, What Is It?" *Africa Today* (January–February 1959), 7.

35. *The New York Times,* November 23, 1961.

I would be lucky enough to catch a glimpse of how he now saw the future, of how the long story was ending. One wanted this glimpse, even knowing that for a quarter of a century what Du Bois thought had ceased to echo in the thinking of others, that he had passed from behind his famous veil to a new place behind an even more famous curtain.

In his half of a comfortable house in well-to-do Brooklyn Heights, I was shown into Du Bois' study, heavy with his life's accumulation of books, including his own on a long shelf. In spaces on the walls were the parchments of some of his recently acquired honors from Communist institutions in Eastern Europe. Over the mantel hung a portrait of what I took to be one of his prized ancestors, a handsome, fair-skinned patrician-looking man. Du Bois walked in slowly, short but of good carriage, fingering the gold chain across his gray waistcoated middle with a polished Phi Beta Kappa key gleaming upon it. With his small goatee, his high bald crown, his sharp and clear light eyes, his aquiline face, his tone and air of authority, he was the breakfast-table autocrat, only semiretired, calmly scornful of a world too unintelligent to accept the verities of which he was now the venerable guardian. But he was graciously willing to measure them out in quiet and genteel and clean sentences. His politeness, nearly punctilious, gave an odd contrapuntal effect to his words, especially when he was offering up, like verses out of scripture, bits of crude Communist hagiography.

He began by asking me what went on at the Center for International Studies, and when I spoke of its interest in world problems, he tapped his fingertips knowingly together and said: "I suppose this all has to do with investments." It became clear that what he pictured was a roomful of men with top hats, beaked noses, big bellies, and clawed hands grasping great big moneybags, drooling over the outlook for new profits in Asia and Africa. I murmured a small denial and changed the subject, but at first this did not help at all. When we began to discuss the impact of world affairs on Negroes, he said: "There is really no way for the young Negro to get to know about world affairs.

All the news here is suppressed and distorted. He has no way of learning what is going on in the Soviet Union or in China." Any young Negro traveling abroad, he went on, is "coached as to what to say. It means that a young man when he goes abroad has to be more or less a traitor to his people. He either keeps his mouth shut abroad or else he lies." When I opened the matter of his early recollections about Africa, he tapped a fat manuscript on the desk before him. "I have dealt with this in a new autobiography I have just finished," he said. "I will offer it for publication here, but I doubt that it will get published. Of course it *will* be published, in Russia, Czechoslovakia, and East Germany." * I looked over his head at the shelf of his own works, all issued here over the many years, and I thought that I might ask him if in all the Soviet Union or China he could find such a shelf of books, or even a single volume, written by anyone who was even in small part the critic, opponent, and rebel against the society that Du Bois had been all his life in America. But I pressed on to other things, and although Du Bois has never been a man lightly turned away from his obsessions, we did cover some small patches of new and higher ground, enough to show me that even in this latest and perhaps last of his outlooks an impressive intelligence survives.

It quickly became clear that Du Bois, who had despaired twenty-five years before of winning through to Negro integration in American life, was now concerned with the effects of integration, seeing its success as already assured. He had leapfrogged ahead to new problems: "The Negro child gets into a school which is integrated, and the chances are nine out of ten that he will have an unsympathetic teacher who won't know or care anything about the history of Negroes. How will he ever get to know anything about it?" He was worried much more by the fear that with

* This draft, somewhat revised by him in 1960, was published as *The Autobiography of W. E. B. Du Bois: A Soliloquy on Viewing My Life from the Last Decade of Its First Century*, Herbert Aptheker, ed. (New York, 1968). A shorter version, *An ABC of Color: Selections from Over a Half Century of the Writings of W. E. B. Du Bois*, was published in East Berlin, 1963 [ed.].

growing economic opportunity and well being, Negroes were getting to be just like whites: "Why, most of the Negroes who went to Ghana for the independence celebration or have gone there since have been interested in business and investments, in what money they could make . . . In Ghana there was a flood of Americans, Negro and white, who just wanted to make money. It was the same when Nkrumah was here." And the principal difference from the past was that "the Negro now assumes he has the same chance" as the white man to profit. "This is the sickness of the whole American civilization, money! The insidious thing is that Negroes are taking white Americans as their pattern, to make a life out of buying and selling and become rich, spending for show."

What were the alternatives for the Negro? I asked. Alienation? Migration? Integration?

Du Bois ruled out alienation, and he credited this to the Communist world. "The thing that will stop any new alienation of Negroes from whites will be the attitudes of the Soviet Union and China. The Negro gets more consideration in the Soviet Union and China than he ever got in England or France or elsewhere. You can't have another movement like Garvey's [*i.e.,* against whites] because you would have to include as whites the two hundred million Russians, Czechs, and so on. And now countries that can't get capital on satisfactory terms from the West can turn to the Soviet Union, and eventually to China, and get it at two percent."

Migration? He thought not. "Of course it is true that for a long time many Negroes had come to think that there was no hope of winning equality in the United States and that it was best to get out. But they were disappointed in Liberia and disappointed in Garvey and had to be content with the emphasis, sometimes the overemphasis, on Africa and race pride in books like Carter Woodson's. . . . But there will be no reproduction of any urge to migrate. Negroes now have the chance to go into business, opportunities are opening up. You now have Negro millionaires!"

Integration, then?

"The real question is: after there is no more discrimination based on race and color, what do you do? Where do you go? I have somewhere drawn the analogy of being on a train, and having a fight with my fellow passengers over my treatment on that train while I should be thinking: Where is this train going? We have fought down discrimination. There has been tremendous improvement. Negroes are becoming Americans. But then what are Americans to become?"

Well, what is the prospect, then, and what about Africa?

"I don't know," replied Du Bois. "The Negro is not working it out. He doesn't really see the problem yet. In the next ten to twenty years there will be a change of thought regarding the relationship of the American Negro to Africa and to the world. We used to think that because they were educated, and had some chance, American Negroes would lead Africans to progress. But the chances are now that Africa will lead American Negroes. But into what kind of world? And what kind of world will there be to be led into? I do not know where the American people will decide to move, but I am sure that the organization of Africa will have a decisive effect on what American Negroes will do and think about the future. I don't think they will leave the United States. Negroes will be more and more integrated. There will be more and more intermarriage. . . . But this will be a longtime development of a hundred years or more. The question even then is: What culture of Africa and what culture of the American Negro will succeed in surviving? What in general of the culture of the world? The question really is what will all human society be like? We prefer varieties. What will the varieties be? I don't think it is really important for the future of mankind what color skin men will have or what their racial characteristics will be. I don't think the issue of race is central, that the color of skin is the important thing. The Negro has been trying to unmake the situation in which this was important and he should not be drawn back toward it. I don't really care what the racial identity of people will be in the twenty-third century. I don't think the future of 'Negritude' is important. What will be important is what people will be thinking and doing by then."

This was Du Bois, at ninety-two, straining his eyes harder than ever from his lonely hilltop, and now, as at the beginning, glimpsing dreams and ideas far, far away, across a foreground pitted and barred by the grotesque shapes and distortions of the nearby reality. For him these were the enshrouding distortions of racism, and to fight debasement he made himself into a racist, genteel, intelligent, and literate, but still a racist. When he came, in his late age, to abandon the racist view—if that indeed is what he has really done—it has been to embrace as more humane the greater inhumanities of Communist totalitarianism. All his life Du Bois scornfully rejected the preachers of pie in the sky, believing that in heaven a man was nothing and had to win his freedom on earth, only in his last years to surrender to those for whom a man's freedom is nothing, neither in heaven nor, most of all, on earth.

Du Bois did not settle the Negro score. It is being settled by the great glacial pressures that do finally move human society. But he did make himself part of those pressures and the "settlement," as it comes, resembles much of what he wanted for black men in America and in Africa, and from this he must gather what satisfaction he can. But Du Bois did not settle his own score either. He wanted recognition, acceptance, eminence, a life among peers. When he was denied, he cut himself off. Today he still stands apart from all except the Communists, who cynically do him honor for his use as a symbol now, especially abroad, and some older Negroes who remember with respect what he did for them in a distant past. It is impossible for me to know whether all of Du Bois' unsatisfied urges and dreams for himself are gratified and realized in the recognition extended to him by the Communist world. He may insist that he sees Communist world power as man's last best hope; it is hard not to imagine that he also sees in it history's means for finally settling the white world's accounts with him and with his fellow nonwhites. Either way, he helps

explain the nature of his failure and leaves one only to guess
what a great man he might have become had he been able to set
himself resolutely all his life against *all* forms of tyranny over the
minds of men.

✪

The Historian*1

Dr. Du Bois was more a history-maker than an historian. The two were interwined, however; what interested Du Bois as a maker of History helped determine what he wrote, and what he wrote helped make history.

Du Bois was an agitator-prophet. He tore at the Veil; at the same time, behind that Veil, he had a particular perspective from which he saw this country and world, past, present, and future, differently—more truly, I think, but certainly in a manner different from the conventional and the dominant. His main formal training—fairly strong in mathematics, languages, psychology, philosophy and economics—was especially thorough in history.[2] As historian, dedicated to the most rigorous standards of integ-

* This paper, in abridged form, was read at the Annual Meeting of the American Historical Association, New York City, December 28, 1968 [ed.].

1. The author gratefully acknowledges the assistance of his wife whose help always has been important but in the preparation of this paper was quite indispensable. I wish to acknowledge also the kindness of Professor Otto H. Olsen for having read this paper and offering helpful suggestions.

2. The data are accurately presented in Francis L. Broderick, "The Academic Training of W. E. B. Du Bois," *The Journal of Negro Education,* XXVII (Winter 1958), 10–16.

rity, he remained, nevertheless, agitator-prophet; present was another fundamental ingredient in the man, namely, the poet. Professor Charles H. Wesley, in the course of producing perhaps the most penetrating review of Du Bois' *Black Reconstruction,* caught this aspect very well indeed when he referred to Du Bois as "the lyric historian." [3]

Du Bois' extraordinary career manifests a remarkable continuity. From his 1890 Harvard Commencement address[4] to his posthumously-published *Autobiography,*[5] the *essential* theme is the beauty, rationality, and need of service and of equality, and the ugliness, irrationality, and threat of greed and eliteism. Because of the especially oppressed condition of the colored peoples of the earth—and particularly of the African and African-derived peoples—Du Bois believed in their capacity for compassion and comradeship, or, as he put it in the 1890 speech, "for the cool, purposeful *Ich Dien* of the African." Keenly conscious of color and of consequent discrimination, convinced of his own capacities, and wedded to the idea of service—Du Bois never shed New England—he told himself as a graduate student in Berlin, on his twenty-fifth birthday: "The general proposition of working for the world's good becomes too soon sickly sentimentality. I therefore take the world that the Unknown lay in my hands & work for the rise of the Negro people, taking for granted that their best development means the best development of the world

3. Charles H. Wesley, "Racial Propaganda and Historical Writing," *Opportunity,* XIII (August 1935), 244–246, 254. The quoted words occur on p. 246. Wesley added that Du Bois was "the literary knight with the plumed pen."

4. The Commencement Address is entitled, "Jefferson Davis as a Representative of Civilization." Since Du Bois had ten minutes, the typed paper from which he read is less than 1,100 words long; a fuller version, hand-written (but in incomplete form) also is in the Du Bois Papers in this writer's custody. The Address has not been published.

5. [H. Aptheker, ed.,] *The Autobiography of W. E. B. Du Bois* (New York: International Publishers, 1968). For this sense of continuity, note also the striking similarity between Du Bois' "final word" in his *The Philadelphia Negro,* first published in 1899 and the Preface to his *Color and Democracy,* published in 1945.

. . . These are my plans: to make a name in science, to make a name in literature and thus to raise my race . . ." [6]

Our present task is to follow Du Bois as historian. How did he conceive of history? The basic answer comes, of course, from his writings, and an enormous—almost incredible—corpus they are.[7] While not all of it by any means represents history-writing, almost all of it—including the novels—does illustrate in one way or another Du Bois' view of history; to a few of these works we shall more particularly refer in subsequent pages. In addition, Du Bois did from time to time refer rather directly to his conception of history and historiography and to this we now turn.

For Du Bois, history-writing was *writing;* one who produces a book should try, thereby, to produce *literature*. He drove himself hard on this. All authors, I think, are anxious to see their work in print; crusading authors probably feel this anxiety more than others. . . . Yet, Du Bois wrote and re-wrote his massive *Black Reconstruction* three times; and after that, revised and revised and cut and cut (as much as 250 pages were cut by him in the summer of 1934).[8] In this connection he informed Charles Pearce—the person in charge of his manuscript at Harcourt, Brace—on July 10, 1933, that he had written his Reconstruction book a second time, but that it was not satisfactory for two reasons: "Its present length would require at least two volumes"; and: "It is not yet a piece of literature. It still resembles . . . a Ph.D. thesis, well documented and with far too many figures. I have clearly in mind the sort of thing that I want to do and I think I can accomplish it but that means writing the book again."

6. H. Aptheker, ed., *A Documentary History of the Negro People in the United States* (New York: Citadel, 1951), p. 753.

7. The present writer has completed what he hopes is a fairly definitive bibliography of Du Bois' published writings; it comes to several hundred pages. A selected bibliography, listing all his books and many of his most significant articles, is in the above-cited *Autobiography*, pp. 431–437.

8. Originally, Harcourt, Brace & Co., planned to issue the book in the spring of 1933 (Charles Pearce to Du Bois, August 15, 1932); it was then postponed to the autumn of 1934 (Alfred Harcourt to Du Bois, December 12, 1933); it actually appeared in May, 1935.

Somewhat later, explaining to his publisher why his galley corrections were so numerous, Du Bois wrote:[9]

My method of writing is a method of "after-thoughts." I mean that after all the details of commas, periods, spelling . . . there comes the final and to me the most important work of polishing and re-setting and even restating. This is the crowning of my creative process.

Du Bois was explicit in his belief that while living behind the Veil might carry the danger of provincialism, it had the great advantage of helping disclose truth or neglected aspects of reality exactly because its point of observation differed. There was something else, too; Du Bois not only held that a new vantage point offered new insights. He held also that a racist viewpoint was a blighted one; that it could not fail to distort reality and that an explicitly anti-racist viewpoint was not only different but better. Hence, he insisted that the view—or prejudice, if one wishes—which he brought to data would get closer to reality not only because it was fresh but also because it was egalitarian. One gets a somewhat different shading in at least one passage in Du Bois' writing where he suggests that possibly something "in between" may be nearer the truth. It occurs in *Black Folk: Then and Now* (New York, 1939, p. ix) and requires quotation in full:

I do not for a moment doubt that my Negro descent and narrow group culture have in many cases predisposed me to interpret my facts too favorably for my race; but there is little danger of long misleading here, for the champions of white folk are legion. The Negro has long been the clown of history; the football of anthropology; and the slave of industry. I am trying to show here why these attitudes can no longer be maintained. I realize that the truth of history lies not in the mouths of partisans but rather in the calm Science that sits between. Her cause I seek to serve, and wherever I fail, I am at least paying Truth the respect of earnest effort.

On this ground, too, he tended to justify—even excuse—his

9. Du Bois to Alfred Harcourt, November 17, 1934; see also Du Bois to F. P. Keppel of the Carnegie Corporation, same date.

practice of depending largely upon published sources and graduate papers rather than upon manuscript materials; he noted, in addition, particular discriminatory problems facing Negro scholars and authors and in his own case, problems of money and time—given his myriad activities.[10] In *Black Reconstruction,* after having told the reader in the Preface, that he meant to retell the history of the years from 1860 to 1880 "with especial reference to the efforts and experiences of the Negroes themselves," he added that he was "going to tell this story as though Negroes were ordinary human beings, realizing that this attitude will from the first seriously curtail my audience." And in the body of the text (p. 724) he apologized for having "depended very largely upon secondary material," named collections of Papers that he was sure would contain relevant materials, acknowledged that the "weight of this work would have been vastly strengthened" had they been consulted—for which he had had neither "time nor opportunity." Nevertheless, he wrote that, standing as he did "literally aghast" (p. 725) at what racist historiography had done in this field, his own effort certainly must represent a significant and needed corrective.

A generation earlier, in the preface to his *John Brown* (1909), Du Bois made a substantially similar point and added a thought which still awaits comprehension by most in the historical profession:

After the work of Sanborn, Hinton, Connelley, and Redpath, the only excuse for another life of John Brown is an opportunity to lay

10. For example, in the midst of writing *Black Reconstruction,* Du Bois also—during a single year—taught two seminars and two classes at Atlanta University, conducted a housing-survey in an Atlanta area destined for slum clearance, lectured in Texas, Louisiana, Missouri, Ohio, Indiana, Illinois, and Iowa, had general charge of the editing of *The Crisis* (and wrote its editorials), spoke twice at chapel at Morehouse, and—as head of the University's Department of Sociology—held "six or eight" conferences with the two other members of the Department!—Du Bois to President John Hope of Atlanta University, March 28, 1934. (It should be added that Du Bois also was a conscientious and devoted husband and father.) See also Du Bois' Preface to his *Black Folk: Then and Now* (New York: Holt, 1939).

new emphasis upon the material which they so carefully collected, and to treat these facts from a different point of view. The viewpoint adopted in this book is that of the little known but vastly important inner development of the Negro American. John Brown worked not simply for Black Men—he worked with them; and he was a companion of their daily life, knew their faults and virtues, and felt, as few white Americans have felt, the bitter tragedy of their lot.

Du Bois saw the neglect of, or prejudice against, the Negro in American historiography as an aspect of a prevailing eliteism in dominant history-writing in general. Du Bois felt that the assumption linking the well-born with the able was no more than an assumption; that to insist the poor's incapacity was demonstrated in their poverty was, at best, elliptical argument. His ironic response to the way in which dominant history deplored the suffering of the elite in periods of decisive social change or challenge—as Reconstruction—and its blithe ignoring of or apologizing for the age-long crucifixion of the poor reminds one of the celebrated passage in Mark Twain's *Connecticut Yankee*; Du Bois' image, too, comes from the French Revolution: "In all this," he wrote in *Black Reconstruction* (p. 353), "one sees the old snobbery of class judgment in new form—tears and sentiment for Marie Antoinette on the scaffold, but no sign of grief for the gutters of Paris and the fields of France, where the victims of exploitation and ignorance lay rotting in piles." (See also, p. 206.)

Sometimes Du Bois made this aspect of his philosophy of history perfectly explicit; thus: "We have the record of kings and gentlemen *ad nauseam* and in stupid detail; but of the common run of human beings, and particularly of the half or wholly submerged working group, the world has saved all too little of authentic record and tried to forget or ignore even the little saved." [11]

Du Bois in practice resolved the difficult problem of objectivity and partisanship, of truth and justice, of the moral and the scientific by affirming—perhaps assuming would be more exact,

11. This is from Du Bois' Preface to H. Aptheker's *Documentary History*.

for the argument is never quite explicit—that separating morals from science caricatures the latter, that the just is the true, and that while objectivity in the sense of utter neutrality in any meaningful matter is absurd this does not rule out the describing of reality—of "telling it like it is"; that, rather, the solution to the apparent paradox has a paradoxical twist: it is intense partisanship—on the side of the exploited and therefore on the side of justice—that makes possible the grasping of truth. Or, at least, that such partisanship is the highway leading to that accumulation of knowledge which brings one closer and closer to the real but not reachable final truth.

At times, Du Bois does separate the function of description and interpretation even to affirm—in a way reminiscent of his late nineteenth-century German training—that it is necessary (and possible) for an historian to "make clear the facts with utter disregard to his own wish and desire and belief," that "we have got to know, so far as possible" the "things that actually happened in the world" and then "with that much clear and open to every reader, the philosopher and prophet has a chance to interpret these facts" (*Black Reconstruction*, p. 722). Yet, in practice, he combines the philosopher and the prophet with the historian; else the latter will become a clerk rather than a scientist; indeed, few writing in the area of American history have accomplished this combination so effectively as did Du Bois.

In a book review that Du Bois published in the *American Historical Review*, in lamenting what he thought were failures, he illuminated his own views on historiography; the succinctness necessary to the review form leads to a certain clarity of expression. Du Bois regretted that in the study in question he could find,

. . . no sense of unity or growth, no careful digestion or arrangement of his material, no conception of the inner reactions of this changing and developing group of human beings, and no comprehension of the drama involved.

In connection with "drama" Du Bois added: "Some social scientists seem to think that because the scientist may not be emotional he has, therefore, no call to study emotion. This, of course, is a ridiculous *non sequitor*." [12]

In *Black Reconstruction* (pp. 714–715) a few paragraphs devoted to the Beards' *Rise of American Civilization* illuminate Du Bois' concept of history and offer penetrating criticisms of the Beards' work. Reading it, said Du Bois, one had "the comfortable feeling that nothing right or wrong is involved." Two differing systems develop in the North and the South, Du Bois continued, and "they clash, as winds and waters strive." The "mechanistic interpretation" failed because human experience was not mechanistic. Furthermore—and here we get again Du Bois' insistence on "drama" as the heart of history—in such a presentation,

. . . there is no room for the real plot of the story, for the clear mistake and guilt of building a new slavery of the working class in the midst of a fateful experiment in democracy; for the triumph of sheer moral courage and sacrifice in the abolition crusade; and for the hurt and struggle of degraded black millions in their fight for freedom and their attempt to enter democracy. Can all this be omitted or half suppressed in a treatise that calls itself scientific?

Du Bois had a towering sense of the Right, of the Just, a basic faith in reason and a passionate commitment toward achieving the just through the use of reason. Indeed, all this together is what Du Bois meant by that word which to him was most sacred: Science. And in his lifetime and in his experience the central lie was racism; this, therefore, received the brunt of his blows. "As a student of science," he wrote (in *Black Reconstruction,* p.

12. Du Bois' review of Robert A. Warner, *New Haven Negroes* (New Haven: Yale University Press, 1940), in *American Historical Review,* XLVII (January 1942), 376–377. Du Bois, feeling that the author—a white man—had failed to *comprehend* his subject, added this comment: "I do not say that the only person who can write of England must be an Englishman, or that only Japanese should write of Japan; but I would insist that if a person is writing of a group to which he is socially and culturally alien, he must have some extraordinary gifts of insight."

725), "I want to be fair, objective and judicial; to let no searing of the memory by intolerable insult and cruelty make me fail to sympathize with human frailties and contradiction, in the eternal paradox of good and evil." What, he asked, should be the object of writing history—the history of Reconstruction, for example?

Is it to wipe out the disgrace of a people which fought to make slaves of Negroes? Is it to show that the North had higher motives than freeing black men? Is it to prove that Negroes were black angels? No, it is simply to establish the Truth, on which Right in the future might be built.

With all this one understands that Du Bois could never accept the idea that cause and effect was nothing but a man-made myth; he caustically rejected this idea which attracted much attention early in the 1940's, especially with Charles Beard's abandonment of causation. He labelled this, indeed, "asinine frivolity" and thought it "must cease if the decadence of the age is not to become definitive and irreversible." In this same essay, Du Bois, again decrying a mechanistic outlook, insisted that for the historian causation must be "conceived in truly humanistic, dynamic terms." He repudiated the heritage of Ranke only insofar as it had "become so exaggerated as to tend to dehumanize it." The historian, Du Bois held, must believe "that creative human initiative, working outside mechanical sequence, directs and changes the course of human action and so history . . . it is man who causes movement and change. . . ." [13] Du Bois did not mean here that man functioned independently of his circumstances; rather he was created by and created them. Thus, Du Bois' work is filled with the pressure of such circumstance, notably, but by no means solely, the economic. An example from his first professional history paper—that delivered before the Annual Meeting

13. This is from an instance—unique, I believe—where Du Bois was the joint author of an essay—with the late Professor Rushton Coulborn, of Atlanta University—"Mr. Sorokin's Systems," *Journal of Modern History*, XIV (December 1942), 500–521; quoted material from pp. 507, 511, 512, 517.

of this Association in this same city, back in 1891—must suffice: [14]

If slave labor was an economic god, then the slave trade was its strong right arm; and with Southern planters recognizing this and Northern capital unfettered by a conscience it was almost like legislating against economic laws to attempt to abolish the slave trade by statutes.

As historian, Du Bois' first concern—and one he never lost—was the rigorous study of the American Negro's past. The preface to his first book (published in 1896) before its paragraph of acknowledgments, closes with this thought: ". . . I nevertheless trust that I have succeeded in rendering this monograph a small contribution to the scientific study of slavery and the American Negro." [15]

Somewhat later he articulated another basic working hypothesis in his approach to history; he began his *Black Reconstruction* (p. 3) by offering its reader the opinion that the experience of Negro people "became a central thread in the history of the United States, at once a challenge to its democracy and always an important part of its economic history and social development."

His penetrating observation, first offered in 1900 and twice repeated in a significant article published the next year[16]—"The problem of the twentieth century is the problem of the color line"—was fundamental to his vision of the unity of all African peoples (to grow, as Du Bois advanced in years, to the idea that

14. Du Bois, "The Enforcement of the Slave-Trade Laws," *Annual Report, American Historical Association, 1891* (Washington, D.C.: U.S. Government Printing Office, 1892), Sen. Mis. Doc. 173, 52nd Cong., 1st Sess.

15. Du Bois, *The Suppression of the African Slave-Trade to the United States of America, 1638–1870* (Cambridge, Mass.: Harvard University Press, 1896; reprinted New York: Social Science Press, 1954).

16. Du Bois, "To the Nations of the World," statement issued by Pan-African Conference, London, 1900, reprinted in Du Bois, ed., *ABC of Color* (Berlin: Seven Seas Press, 1963), p. 20; Du Bois, "The Freedmen's Bureau," *Atlantic Monthly* LXXXVII (March 1901), 354, 365; reprinted as Chap. 2, "Of the Dawn of Freedom," in *Souls of Black Folk* (1903).

this itself was preliminary to the unity of all the darker peoples of the earth and *that* was part of the process of the worldwide unification of all who labor) and was, indeed, first enunciated as the Call of the original Pan-African Conference. This insight forms the inspiration for and thesis of his *The Negro* (London: Home Library, 1915), *Black Folk, Then and Now* (New York: Holt, 1939), *Color and Democracy: Colonies and Peace* (New York: Harcourt, Brace, 1945), *The World and Africa* (New York: Viking, 1947); most completely in the enlarged edition of that volume published two years after his death.[17]

How shall we sum up Du Bois' conception of history? There is the facile technique of labels, normally unsatisfactory and in the case of a man as polemical, radical, and productive as Du Bois, bound to be, I suggest, especially unsatisfactory. This does does not mean the labelling has not been done, of course—and not simply by a berserk government that said Du Bois was—of all things—an "unregistered foreign agent!"

Thus, two historians were not only convinced that Du Bois was a Marxist; they felt able to tell their readers just when his baptism occurred. Harvey Wish wrote that Dr. Du Bois went to the Soviet Union in 1927—which is true—and that he "emerged a confirmed Marxist." Carl Degler puts the conversion seven years later, affirming that "by the time" Du Bois wrote *Black Reconstruction* "he had become a Marxist." On the other hand, Rembert W. Patrick writes that Du Bois was "not a Marxian" when writing that book; while Howard K. Beale suggested that "perhaps it would be fairer to Marx to call Du Bois a quasi Marxist." [18] Having found Du Bois described as a confirmed

17. This edition appeared in May, 1965. It contained almost ninety additional pages consisting of selections—made by the present writer—from Du Bois' writings on Africa from 1955 through 1961.

18. Wish, *The American Historian* (New York: Oxford University Press, 1960), p. 259; Degler, *Out of the Past: The Forces That Shaped Modern America* (New York: Harper, 1959), p. 441; Patrick, *The Reconstruction of the Nation* (New York: Oxford University Press, 1967), p. 306; Beale, "On Rewriting Reconstruction History," *American Historical Review*, XLV (July 1940), 809n.

Marxist, a plain Marxist, a quasi Marxist, and not a Marxist we have perhaps exhausted the possibilities.

Du Bois was a Du Boisite. His political affiliations or affinities varied as times changed, as programs altered, and as he changed: in his twenties no doubt a reform Republican (like Douglass); prior to World War I a Socialist; in 1912, however, urging Wilson's election; in the post-War period often voting—at least in national elections—for Thomas; in the early thirties a leader, along with John Dewey and Paul Douglas and others, in a movement for an Independent politics; after World War II, favoring the (Henry) Wallace movement and Progressive party efforts; in the 1950's running for U.S. Senator on the American Labor party ticket (and getting a quarter of a million votes); and at the nadir of the political fortunes of the Communist party, with its illegality apparently affirmed by the U.S. Supreme Court, choosing that moment to announce his decision to join the party.

These were, however, political choices and not defining marks of his philosophical approaches. All his life Du Bois was a radical democrat; this was true even with his "Talented Tenth" concept which held that mass advance depended upon leadership and service from a trained minority, and insisted that such a goal and such service were the duty of such a minority and if not accepted and performed spelled the vitiation of the minority itself.[19]

This sketch of Du Bois' political biography and the account in the preceding pages of his views of history surely do not add up to the term Marxist in any meaningful sense. Du Bois certainly was significantly influenced by Marx and Marxism which is to say—as C. Wright Mills did say under somewhat analogous

19. Du Bois' "The Talented Tenth," appears in the illuminating book of essays (no editor given) by several Negro authors called *The Negro Problem* (New York: Pott & Co., 1903), pp. 33–75. Significant in this volume was Charles W. Chesnutt's "The Disfranchisement of the Negro"; it contains a powerful attack on the pro-Bourbon version of Reconstruction. The relationship of Albion W. Tourgee to this—and to Du Bois—is noticed in Otto H. Olsens' fine biography *Carpetbagger's Crusade* (Baltimore: Johns Hopkins University Press, 1966), pp. 297–354.

circumstances[20] that Du Bois was an educated man; this influence, however, came in concentrated form only toward the last third of his life. For this lateness Du Bois was severely self-critical (as he was, by the way, for a neglect of Freud);[21] he certainly did conclude that no other system of thought was as revealing as Marxism but to the end of his days he remained an idealist—philosophically speaking—in key areas of his thinking. It may be added that while he found Marx rather late in his life, he seriously concerned himself with Lenin's views even later; as late as October, 1934, he remarked in a letter:[22] "I have a fair library of Marx, but only one or two of Lenin's works." Had this neglect not existed it is difficult to see how Du Bois could have persisted in using the term "dictatorship of the proletariat"— even in the very limited way in which he did use that term (something on which more will be said below)—as pertains to the Radical Reconstruction governments. He did affirm views on capitalism as a system and colonialism as a phenomenon that were strikingly similar to—though not fully identical with— those of Marx and of Lenin, but his attitude toward the working class, the State, Communist parties, mass initiative and toward the entire materialist outlook were not those of Marx nor of Lenin, though again marked similarities appear. If one insists on shorthand perhaps the careful Howard Beale came closest with his term, "quasi Marxist"; given, however, Du Bois' own genius and the monumental scope of his interests and his output and the dynamic quality of his thinking I would myself prefer the term of Du Boisite;* what this lacks in imagination and in illumination it makes up for in—accuracy!

Du Bois, while personally shy and remarkably objective about

---

* Aptheker meant that Du Bois was unique [ed.].

20. See a letter from Mills in *Commentary* (June 1957), quoted in my *World of C. Wright Mills* (New York, 1960), p. 7.

21. Du Bois' self-criticism on both counts will be found in his "Fifty Years After" note to the 1953 Blue Heron Press edition of his *Souls of Black Folk*, and in the "Apologia" to the 1954 edition of his *Suppression of the African Slave Trade* (cited in note 15, above).

22. Du Bois to Benjamin Stolberg, Atlanta, October 1, 1934.

himself, never suffered from self-effacement or an excessive hu-
mility. At a very early age he was persuaded—as were his neighbors and associates, black and white—that his powers were
considerable. Of all his books, he knew the first was the most
scholarly—in the conventional sense (he even saw this as one
of its limitations).[23] The volume which—as he once told this
writer—was his favorite was his biography of John Brown, based
altogether upon rather easily accessible secondary works. But in
the area of historiography, he knew, as he said in a letter written[24] while in the throes of creating it, that his "magnum opus"
was *Black Reconstruction*; that book he said, in applying for
funds to assist in its final revision, "will not sell widely," but "in
the long run, it can never be ignored." [25] Du Bois was right on
both counts.

Black Reconstruction deserves a book in its own right: how
it came to be written, its sources, the people participating in its
creation, how it was funded, examining its revisions, analyzing
its contents, estimating its critical and popular reception, observ-
ing its impact upon black and white opinion, upon the scientific
community, upon the making of history and the making of history books and texts. Obviously this is not the occasion for the
presentation of such an effort.

For purposes of brevity we choose as a theme the remarks of
one among the many more recent commentators on Reconstruction; this is Professor Staughton Lynd and I select him for both

23. Du Bois meant that the detailed monograph tended to abstract its
subject from the larger world and that such abstraction meant distortion;
it "sets a man to segregating from the total flow of history. . . ." He
thought his own first book suffered from this—see his "Apologia," as cited
above in note 21.

24. Du Bois to Ruth Anna Fisher, Atlanta, March 26, 1934.

25. Du Bois to F. P. Keppel, of the Carnegie Corporation, Atlanta,
November 17, 1934. The request was approved. Though the book was
quickly, widely, and well reviewed, it did not, at first, "sell widely." During
the entire year of 1936—the first full year following its publication—376
copies were sold, according to royalty statements sent Du Bois by Harcourt, Brace & Co.

what he says and what he omits.[26] Lynd pays generous tribute to Du Bois' pioneering in denying that enfranchising the Negro after the Civil War was a "great mistake"; and in showing that the Reconstruction governments had been slandered by the profession generally. Lynd says that "liberal historians of the last generation who have sought to correct the traditional image of cigar-smoking Negro legislators voting themselves gold-spittoons have added very little," since Du Bois' paper of 1909.*

Lynd writes that the main problem now and for the future should be "what strategy of planned social change might have succeeded?" He thinks that the futility of legal and military force "to coerce deep-seated attitudes" is plain; that those who hold that such efforts stopped too soon offer little real help; and that a third alternative is sounder, namely: "the fundamental error in Reconstruction policy was that it did not give the freedman land of his own . . . Congress should have given the ex-slaves the economic independence to resist political intimidation."

* This statement by Lynd, endorsed by Aptheker, is incorrect. For contrary views, see Francis B. Simkins and R. H. Woody, *South Carolina During Reconstruction* (Chapel Hill: University of North Carolina Press, 1932); J. G. Randall and David Donald, *The Civil War and Reconstruction*, rev. ed. (1961), pp. 535–701; John Hope Franklin, *Reconstruction After the Civil War* (Chicago: University of Chicago Press, 1961); Kenneth M. Stampp, *The Era of Reconstruction, 1865–1877* (New York: Alfred A. Knopf, 1965); and David Donald, *The Politics of Reconstruction, 1863–1867* (Baton Rouge: Louisiana State University Press, 1965 [ed.].

26. S. Lynd, ed., *Reconstruction* (New York: Harper & Row, 1967); quotations from Lynd's Introduction. He reprints in this volume Chap. 2 of *Souls of Black Folk* and Du Bois' 1909 paper before the American Historical Association, "Reconstruction and Its Benefits," *American Historical Review*, XV (July 1910), 781–799. In his *Dusk of Dawn* (New York, 1940), pp. 318–319, Du Bois states that this paper troubled U. B. Phillips very much but that "Dunning of Columbia and Hart of Harvard" seemed pleased. Wharton comments that the paper "received little attention"; certainly in terms of impact the profession was utterly unready.— Vernon L. Wharton, "Reconstruction," in Arthur S. Link and Rembert W. Patrick, eds., *Writing Southern History: Essays in Historiography in Honor of Fletcher H. Green* (Baton Rouge: Louisiana State University Press, 1965), p. 308. Wharton's own summary of Du Bois' work in this essay is markedly inadequate.

It is unclear to this writer that alternative number three should be distinguished from alternative one and/or two; giving land to the freedmen surely would have required legal action and in all likelihood rather considerable military action, too; and to see that such a transformation in the socio-economic nature of the South was actually maintained as well as begun would have surely required alertness lest both legal and military measures be terminated too soon.

Professor Lynd goes on to point out that Du Bois in his 1901 article on the Freedmen's Bureau saw the consequence of this kind of land policy. I want to add that this is one of the central themes of his *Black Reconstruction* and that in the book it is developed and documented with infinitely greater care and depth than in the limits of the 1901 essay; Lynd's failure to make this clear is noted because in the estimates of *Black Reconstruction* this significant feature of its content is normally omitted.[27]

27. Lynd observes that this awareness of the significance of the land question was "not new" even with Du Bois, for it had been emphasized by contemporaries—as Julian Stevens and Douglass. Lynd moves from them and Du Bois to the 1960's; unfortunately he omits any reference to what I suppose is the "Old Left"—as James S. Allen's *Reconstruction: The Battle for Democracy* (New York: International, 1937); Manuel Gottlieb's "The Land Question in Georgia During Reconstruction," *Science & Society,* III (Summer 1939), 356–388; H. Aptheker, *To Be Free* (New York: International, 1948), pp. 136–187; and relevant documents in my *Documentary History,* indexed under "land, desire for."

There is a very clear summation of certain basic concepts later to be developed in *Black Reconstruction* in an appeal "To the People of Russia" which Du Bois wrote sometime in 1925 (probably in the latter half of that year—the manuscript is undated but from its contents there is no doubt of the year, for one of its purposes was to appeal for support in the Sweet Case then being conducted by the NAACP). The relevant sentences appear as Du Bois commences a treatment of the Civil War period: "In this war nearly 200,000 Negroes fought for their own freedom and perhaps 300,000 others helped as laborers and servants so that their freedom was not given to them, it was earned. However, the emancipation of the Negroes was not complete. They received no land, no tools, no capital. Most of them were compelled to remain on the same plantations as wage earners and usually their wages were paid in food and clothes sold at exorbitant prices. Those who ran away and went to the cities got a

Many other areas of Reconstruction—some of them beginning to receive treatment only in our own day—are in *Black Reconstruction*.

The point made by Professor C. Vann Woodward—that the political rights of the Southern black population were quite tenuous, given dependence upon a single party, the political and economic motivations of Republican leaders for extending those rights, with the possibility (and, as it happened, the reality) of the motivations changing and so the attitude toward those rights changing—also is in Du Bois' book.[28]

The relationship between the possibilities of the exploitation of the resources and labor of the South by a rising industrial capitalism and the impact this was bound to have upon Reconstruction politics also is in his work; so is the suggestion that much of the alleged corruption in Reconstruction governments would be found to originate in one or another mode of enriching the masters of that rising industrial capitalism—a central theme in Horace Mann Bond's penetrating study.[29]

While Du Bois' book is weak insofar as it tends to ignore the former nonslaveholding whites who were landed—*i.e.,* the yeomanry—and who therefore had class as well as racist differences with the black millions, and is weak, too, insofar as it accepts the concept of a monolithic white South from the pre-Civil War period to Reconstruction, it pioneered in a related area, for it

chance to work as laborers and to receive money wages. Naturally the working conditions of the Negroes were much worse than those of white laborers and they were exploited to the last degree." Du Bois Papers.

28. C. Vann Woodward, "The Political Legacy of Reconstruction," in his *The Burden of Southern History* (Baton Rouge: Louisiana State University Press, 1960); originally in *The Journal of Negro Education,* in 1957. See *Black Reconstruction,* pp. 210, 212, 216, 584.

29. Horace Mann Bond, *Negro Education in Alabama: A Study in Cotton and Steel* (Washington, D.C.: Associated Publishers, 1939); Bond notes on p. 309 that Du Bois "hints" at this. Du Bois in his review of Bond's book comments upon its confirmation and documentation of his earlier "unproved contention" and adds that this is a "most important contribution"—*American Historical Review,* XLV (April 1940), 669.

called attention very forcefully to the neglect, then, of the history of the poorer whites in the South.[30]

The momentous impact upon the nature of U.S. society and therefore upon world history of the failure of the effort at democratizing the South—which is what the defeat of Reconstruction meant in Du Bois' view—is emphasized in *Black Reconstruction*. The consequent turn toward an imperial career, to which Woodrow Wilson pointed with delight, was a development which Du Bois denounced and concerning which he warned in prescient terms.[31]

Du Bois also sought to make clear that Reconstruction was an episode in the entire—and worldwide—struggle of the rich versus the poor; in this connection he emphasized not only the specifics of the land question in the South but the whole matter of property rights; indeed, he called one of the most pregnant chapters in his volume, "Counter-Revolution of Property." He saw— as had Madison a century before him—that the right to and control of property was central to problems of the state and therefore of all forms of state, including that of democracy. Indeed, Du Bois—as Madison—emphasized the special connection between democracy and property insofar as the principle of universal enfranchisement meant political power in the hands of the majority and that majority normally had been and was the nonpropertied.

In this sense, Du Bois saw the story of Reconstruction—especially as it concerned the millions of dispossessed blacks—as an essential feature of the story of labor; not labor in the sense of industrial and/or urban working people, but labor in the more generic sense of those who had to work—to labor—in order to make ends meet. I think, too, that Du Bois' use of the term proletariat was more classical than Marxian; *i.e.,* the proletariat, the lower classes, as the dictionary says, and from the Latin

30. On the call for historians to treat the poorer Southern whites, see *Black Reconstruction,* p. 721.

31. See *Black Reconstruction,* pp. 368, 602, 631. Wilson's essay appeared in the same volume of the *Atlantic Monthly* as Du Bois' on the Freedmen's Bureau—"The Reconstruction of the Southern States," LXXXVII (January 1901), 1–15.

proletarius, a citizen of the lowest class. (In this connection, let it be recalled that Du Bois began his teaching career as Professor of Greek and Latin and that throughout his life he would lapse into Latin phrases at frequent intervals.)

Du Bois states in *Black Reconstruction* (p. 381n.) that he had originally entitled Chapter ten "The Dictatorship of the Black Proletariat in South Carolina," but that he had changed it to "The Black Proletariat in South Carolina" because "it has been brought to my attention that" the former would be incorrect. Obviously, since he made the change, he agreed with the criticism (which came from Abram L. Harris and Benjamin Stolberg and probably others). But here is the reason which he gave for the original title:[32]

My reason for this title is that in South Carolina, beginning in 1867, there were distinct evidences of a determination on the part of the black laborers to tax property and administer the state primarily for the benefit of labor. This was not only a conscious ideal but it would lead to heavy taxing on land, to the buying of large tracts of land to be distributed among the poor, and to many direct intelligent statements of the object of these policies.

In this same letter, Du Bois himself went on to remark that this manifested petty bourgeois influences "both among white and colored, and in a strict Marxian sense, the state and country was not ready for that dictatorship of the proletariat which might have come in a later development and on [*sic*] other surroundings."

When this meaning that Du Bois had in mind and when his purpose is comprehended, then perhaps one will be less apt than both contemporary and later commentators have been to simply dismiss all this out of hand. Certainly, in the Marxian sense, Radical Reconstruction represented an effort to bring a bourgeois-democratic order to the South and in this effort—given the formerly slave-based plantation economy—the idea of "land to the landless" was fundamental; this meant not the elimination of

---

32. Du Bois to Stolberg, Atlanta, October 1, 1934.

the private ownership of the means of production—a basic aim
of the dictatorship of the proletariat—but rather its wider distribution. From this point of view Du Bois' choice of words and
expressions was confusing—and erroneous; but his perception of
the relationship of particularly exploited black masses to any effort at making democracy real and to any secure advance of the
deprived of all colors—which is what he was bringing forward—
was a profound one and remains a challenging one for today, not
only in terms of history-writing but also in terms of history-
making.

In this connection it is relevant to note that Du Bois' original
title for his book was *Black Reconstruction of Democracy in
America.* At the urging of the publisher the title was shortened;
nevertheless, with the shortened title, Du Bois insisted that the
title page (and the original dust jacket) carry this subtitle: "An
Essay toward a History of the Part which Black Folk Played in
the Attempt to Reconstruct Democracy in America, 1860–
1880."

While spelling out the full subtitle, notice is to be taken of the
dates Du Bois offered, and his book does start with the Civil War.
This represented not only Du Bois' insistence upon the decisive
role Negroes had played in preserving the Union and in emanci-
pating themselves—quite new ideas in the 1930's, and still un-
reported in most U.S. history texts—but also his conception of
the unity of the whole struggle against slavery, of the War, and of
the Reconstruction effort. This, too, has been urged by some
later commentators (as Howard K. Beale[33]) who have failed to
note Du Bois' attempt at it decades ago. It should be added also
that in *Black Reconstruction* Du Bois denied that with its defeat,
struggle and activity on the part of black people ceased for a
generation; on the contrary, he pointed out that it continued and
even had some successes in the late 1870's, 1880's, and 1890's:[34]
this theme, too, has only recently been "discovered."

33. H. K. Beale, pp. 811–812.
34. For Du Bois' remarks on post-Reconstruction history, see *Black
Reconstruction,* p. 692.

It will be well at this point to allow Du Bois himself to state the basic theme of *Black Reconstruction*; presumably he is good authority for this. He stated this, in differing ways, several times; we shall for reasons of space, quote only one and that extremely brief:[35]

To me, these propositions, extreme as they may sound, seem clear and true:

1. The American Negro not only was the cause of the Civil War but a prime factor in enabling the North to win it.

2. The Negro was the only effective tool which could be used for the immediate restoration of the federal union after the war.

3. The enfranchisement of the freedmen after the war was one of the greatest steps toward democracy taken in the nineteenth century.

4. The attempts to retrace that step, disfranchising the Negro and reducing him to caste conditions, are the deeds which make the South today the nation's social problem Number One.

Du Bois added that involved in the reality of Reconstruction was "the question of the equal humanity of black, brown, yellow and white people." And then he flung this question—in his prophetic way tossing out a generation ago today's most urgent problem: "Is this a world where its people in mutual helpfulness and mutual respect can live and work; or will it be a world in the future as in the past, where white Europe and white America must rule 'niggers'?"

Certain critical comments on Du Bois as an historian have been offered above and perhaps the most cogent were made by himself, as we have indicated. There remain certain other failings, really of a quite minor nature.

35. Du Bois, "Reconstruction, Seventy Years After," in *Phylon*, IV (3rd Quarter 1943), 205–212. In September, 1931, Alfred Harcourt expressed interest upon learning of a Rosenwald grant to Du Bois for a study of Reconstruction (the grant was publicized in the press that summer). On October 21, 1931, therefore, Du Bois sent Harcourt a four-page, typed manuscript dealing with "the thesis of this book"; publication of this document must await another opportunity; it does constitute the earliest and fullest expression on its subject that I have seen.

In the enormous body of Du Bois' writings, errors of fact will be found; almost always these are of a minor—even picayunish —nature. I think it is true that their occurrence is probably somewhat less uncommon than among historians of analogous scope. It is worth adding that reviewers often made a point of calling attention to these failings or slips. These range from apparent slips in proofreading, as dating a Governor's message of 1875 as 1865; to confusing David Walker with his son, Edwin; or occasionally misspelling the name of Henry Highland Garnet; or consistently misspelling the name of Martin R. Delany; or confusing General William T. Sherman with General Thomas W. Sherman and placing him in Port Royal, South Carolina, in October, 1861, rather than in November; or spelling the name of the leader of the Boer Rebellion in 1914 as Martiz, rather than Maritz. In only one book, however—and that the only one Du Bois ever wrote "to order" as it were—is the carelessness really excessive, but Du Bois himself confessed that this had been "too hurriedly done, with several unpardonable errors." [36] Let those in a stern mood look up these errors; as for others, they are so inconsequential that I shall not waste footnotes upon them.

Somewhat more serious was a kind of literary tendency on Du Bois' part which took the form of rather exaggerated assertions or a kind of symbolism that in the interest of effect might sacrifice precision. Professor Wesley in his already cited review in *Opportunity* (1935) gave several examples of this tendency; he called it "a tendency to dismiss the explanation of some events with all too brief a wave of the hand." Exaggerations for effect would lead Du Bois to ascribe the Seminole Wars *purely* to the problem of fugitive slaves, or U.S. acquisition of the Louisiana Territory *solely* to the rebellion of Haitian slaves. A kind of poetic license would lead Du Bois to place John Brown's hopes as centering on the Blue Ridge Mountains—which was probably

---

36. The book referred to was done for the Knights of Columbus as part of a series it was supporting on "minority" peoples; its title was *The Gift of Black Folk* (Boston: Stratford Co., 1924). Du Bois' comment on it occurs in his *Dusk of Dawn*, p. 269.

true—but he would add that it was in those same mountains "where Nat Turner had fought and died, [and] where Gabriel had sought refuge," which is simply not true; but probably this objection reflects the weaknesses of a pedestrian plodder before the canvases of an inspired poet-historian.

With such nitpicking I am reminded of Du Bois' "Forethought" to his immortal *Souls of Black Folk*: "I pray you, then, receive my little book in all charity, studying my words with me, forgiving mistake and foible for sake of the faith and passion that is in me, and seeking the grain of truth hidden there."

His grains accumulated to a vast monument and precious heritage. It was Du Bois who began the scientific study of the Negro's history, who saw that it constituted a test of the American experience and dream, that it was a basic constituent in the fabric of United States history, that it was part of the vaster pattern of the colored peoples who make up most of Mankind.

Even in detail, it was Du Bois who pioneered the study of the slave trade, who first offered new insights into the Freedmen's Bureau, who first pointed to the significance of the Negro in the Abolitionist movement, who contested the stereotype of the docile and contented slave, who helped illuminate the meaning of John Brown, who transformed approaches to the Civil War and Reconstruction, who pioneered in writing the history of African peoples, whose studies of Southern agriculture and of Northern cities—in particular Philadelphia—remain massive and—again —pioneering efforts in historiography.

In view of all this we must respectfully dissent from Professor George B. Tindall's conclusion: "He [Du Bois] became himself a historical figure whose writings constitute an important source for historians of the Negro, but his own career as historian was somewhat limited." [37] Only in the sense that, as I have stated,

---

37. Tindall, "Southern Negroes Since Reconstruction: Dissolving the Static Image," in Link and Patrick, eds., p. 344. I wish to take note of four previous essays which deal with Du Bois as historian or with a particular aspect of his historical writings: Jessie P. Guzman, "W. E. B. Du Bois—the Historian," *Journal of Negro Education*, XXX (Fall 1961),

Du Bois was more history-maker than historian may one properly speak of his performance in the latter as "somewhat limited." For any person not of Du Bois' monumental stature his achievements in history-writing would make of him an outstanding practitioner of that art in the record of American historiography.

One may note that of all major publications only the *American Historical Review* failed to review Du Bois' *Black Reconstruction*; this may have been due to some accident unknown to the present writer but it strikes me as unforgivable, though with the state of American historiography in 1935 the absence of a review in that journal may well have been a service to its author.[38]

More bothersome is the one-sentence notice of Dr. Du Bois'

377–385; Daniel Walden, "Du Bois: Pioneer Reconstruction Historian," *Negro History Bulletin* (February 1963), 159–160, 164; Charles H. Wesley, "Du Bois the Historian," *Freedomways*, V (Winter 1965), 59–72; William Leo Hansberry, "Du Bois' Influence on African History," *Freedomways*, V (Winter 1965), 73–87.

38. As fate would have it, at the very period of the appearance of Du Bois' *Black Reconstruction*, the *American Historical Review*, XL (April 1935), 438–449 published Theodore Clark Smith's "The Writing of American History, 1884–1934," which was an attack upon any departure from orthodoxy (Smith had in mind some recent heresies announced by Charles Beard). Smith offered as prize exhibits of "rigidly accurate, impeccably documented" history-writing that was "absolutely without prejudice"—"the general onslaught on the Reconstruction period which took place at Columbia under the guidance of our former honored associate, Professor Dunning. . . ." Another among Smith's prize exhibits of unprejudiced history-writing was that by U. B. Phillips, whose "works . . . substituted direct observation and analysis for propaganda or emotional treatment."

It was of the 1930's also, that L. D. Reddick, at that time a professor at Dillard University, wrote: "The American Historical Association has on occasion allowed such men as Professor Munroe [*sic*] Work, of Tuskegee, to appear. On the other hand, when one member of the committee on programs and arrangements suggested the names of Dr. Carter G. Woodson and Dr. Charles H. Wesley (both Harvard Ph.D.'s and authors of several volumes), who happen to stem from a more aggressive tradition, the committee was immediately reshuffled and this member was promptly dropped." (Quoted by V. F. Calverton, "The Negro," in Harold E. Stearns, ed., *America Now: An Inquiry into Civilization in the U.S.* [New York: Scribner's, 1938], p. 488.)

passing that the *Review* managed to spare in its issue of January, 1964 (LXIX, 602); in the same issue the death of Charles Seymour received fifteen times as much space, Ralph Flanders' four times more, and Ernst Kantorowics' five times as much. I begrudge nothing to these other estimable mortals but I was and am mortified by the judgment behind such allocations of space.

Perhaps this session, in his Centennial Year, represents the Association's way of publicly acknowledging error—to use no harsher word; if this is so and if this also reflects a real concern to study the life and work of W. E. Burghardt Du Bois then—if for no other reason—the 1968 Meeting of the AHA will be memorable.

✪

A Black Messianic Visionary[1]

As far as I have been able to gather, Du Bois never referred to himself as a "Negro Nationalist," and indeed on one occasion he cautioned against his views being placed in that category. But his very need to raise the word of caution is a hint in itself: it reminds us that there were many points in his life and work when his thought could have been identified with a variety of nationalist ideologies.

Nor should this be surprising. Du Bois was born into a time of nationalism—a time when men believed in progress (with a capital P), and he later admitted that in his youth that chief of nationalists, Otto von Bismarck, was his hero. Of *that* fascinating relationship Du Bois wrote:

Bismarck was my hero. He had made a nation out of a mass of bickering peoples. He had dominated the whole development with his

1. This paper, except for the Epilogue, was delivered at the opening session of the American Historical Association, December 28, 1968. This is part of a longer essay on the Messianic elements of Du Bois' life and thought.

Reprinted from *Freedomways: A Quarterly Review of the Freedom Movement*, 9, No. 1 (1st Quarter 1969), 44–58, by permission of Freedomways Associates, Inc. Copyright © 1969 by Freedomways Associates, Inc. Originally published under the title "W. E. B. Du Bois and the Black Messianic Vision."

strength. . . . This foreshadowed in my mind the kind of thing that American Negros must do, marching forth with strength and determination under trained leadership.[2]

For the practitioners of many nationalisms it is obvious that all the painful, exhilarating acts of gathering a scattered people and stamping them with identity are seen as ends in themselves. For others the establishment of physical and spiritual homelands and states becomes the ultimate goal. Some of these views were shared by Du Bois, others obviously not, but even that is not the main burden of this paper.

Rather, I should like to suggest that while Dr. Du Bois was obviously concerned—often obsessed—with the ultimate destiny of black people in America, that dark, compelling destiny was almost always defined by him as fulfilling the national vocation. Indeed, he did not limit himself to that level; but for much of his life Du Bois saw the black people of the nation as critical transformers and redeemers of the destiny of the world. We understand Du Bois best, I would suggest, if we see him beyond the perimeters of nationalism, beyond even the dreams of Pan-Africanism. I think we are most faithful in our recording if we define his deepest hopes and convictions as those of a Black Messianism stretched over the boundaries of humanity. This, in his thought, was the calling of Africa's rejected children; and those of us in the American diaspora were to be in the vanguard of that awesome hope.[3]

To fulfill that Messianic role, as Du Bois grew to sense it, there was an absolute necessity for black people here to develop economic, political, cultural, and moral force, strength—let us call it power. As both paradox and reinforcement of this need for black solidarity, it was clear to Du Bois that such power and fulfillment could not be achieved unless the bonds imposed by

2. W. E. B. Du Bois, *Dusk of Dawn: An Essay Toward an Autobiography of a Race Concept* (New York, 1940).
3. St. Clair Drake, unpublished manuscript prepared for delivery at Roosevelt University, Chicago, Illinois, summer 1963.

America on its black people were broken. So, for the task of breaking bonds and of convincing men that they needed to be broken, black people again had to organize, sometimes with whites (but often without them, according to Du Bois); *always* they had to organize *within* the race to prepare a broken people for its destiny. Often, he saw that inner organization as a form of black communalism, inspired by the African past, informed by the socialism rising all around him.

So neither power, solidarity, civil rights, nor aspects of nationhood were ends in themselves, even though Du Bois often tended to glory in their appearance. They were consistently put forward as means toward a new humanity. It was not until the end of his life that this Messianic vision of the vocation of Africa's children in America was transferred to the homeland itself. But that moves ahead of the story.

Within the limits set by time and patience, we cannot possibly tell the full story of Du Bois' thought and action toward Black Messianism, but some particulars will be necessary. First, of course, it must be clear that this aspect of the thought of Dr. Du Bois did not develop in a vacuum. Its roots went back into Afro-American thought at least as far as the anguished *Appeal* of David Walker, and included the scholarly sermons, essays, and books of Alexander Crummell, a man known and loved by Du Bois.[4] Men like Walker and Crummell, in different ways, saw redemption coming forth from black America. W. E. B. Du Bois was born into a time when men, both black and white, still believed in redemption.

He was born, too, into the bosom of the North, and his experiences with the subtle color line of Great Barrington must enter into the bill of particulars when we try to understand sources. As with all other aspects of the man's intellectual and ideological life, this one had deeply personal fountains. They were located not only in the quiet rebuffs of his school days, but in occasions

4. W. E. B. Du Bois, *The Souls of Black Folk* (New York, 1965). See essay, "Of Alexander Crummell."

like his first hearing the Hampton quartet, and being moved to tears as he "seemed to recognize something inherently and deeply my own." Thus, in spite of the fact that black Fisk was not his first choice of college, he was likely right when he recalled that he was "beginning to feel lonesome in New England," and looked forward with anticipation to the black world of Fisk.[5] *

The genius of Du Bois is that he was able to take his personal responses to the color line and turn them into matters of ultimate significance—matters of personal, racial, and human destiny. So Fisk was not only the place where he gloried in the opportunity to meet more beautiful black women than he had ever seen in all his seventeen years, but it was also the occasion for him to declare publicly:

> I am a Negro; and I glory in the name!
> I am proud of the black blood that flows
> in my veins . . . [I] have come here . . .
> to join hands with my people.[6] †

His people included the poor blacks of the Tennessee countryside, as well as the middle class sons and daughters of the University, so he went out during his two summers in the state to teach and learn. Later when he remembered those days the Messianic commitment surely colored his memories, but he said that it was at Fisk and in the black rural areas of Tennessee that he "accepted

---

* Like some other writers today, Harding generally prefers *black* to *Negro* or *colored*. The passage in the *Autobiography* to which he refers in his footnote 5 reads as follows: "Fisk University, a college for Negroes. . . . I was going into the South; the South of slavery, rebellion and black folk; above all, I was going to meet colored people of my own age and education, of my own ambitions." Here as in numerous places, Du Bois uses *Negroes, black,* and *colored* [ed.].

† Du Bois did not write this in poetic form [ed.].

5. W. E. B. Du Bois, *Autobiography of W. E. B. Du Bois: A Soliloquy on Viewing My Life from the Last Decade of Its First Century* (New York, 1968), pp. 105–106.

6. Francis L. Broderick, *W. E. B. Du Bois: Negro Leader in a Time of Crisis* (Stanford, 1959), p. 8.

color caste and embraced the companionship of those of my own color," then quickly added:

This was, of course, no final solution. We Negroes were going to break down the boundaries of race; but at present we were banded together in a great crusade and happily so.[7] *

FROM FISK TO HARVARD

To break down the barriers of race in a lifetime was surely a divine vocation for any people—especially those who lived behind the barriers, within the Veil.

After three years, he went on to Harvard and was away from the warmth of Fisk's inspirational environment. Nevertheless, Du Bois said:

I was firm in my criticism of white folk and in my dream of a Negro self-sufficient culture even in America.[8]

Of course, there was never Du Bois without paradox, so even while convinced of the need of a self-sufficient Negro culture, he was excitedly producing and directing a performance of Aristophanes, *The Birds,* in a black church in Boston.

Du Bois was never afraid to admit that dividedness in his own being, a dividedness which sometimes made it difficult for him to affirm with consistent intensity his sense of black vocation. Certainly that is why his years in Europe were filled with evocations of the greatness of German culture, with at least one love affair with a blue-eyed damsel, and with those "friendships and close

---

* This passage reads as follows in the *Autobiography:* "This was, of course, no final solution. Eventually with them and in mass assault, led by culture, we Negroes were going to break down the boundaries of race; but at present we were banded together in a great crusade and happily so" [ed.].

7. Du Bois, *Autobiography,* p. 135.
8. Du Bois, *Autobiography,* p. 136.

contacts with white folk [which] made my own ideas waver.[9] (Beware of close contacts with white folk!) *

It was especially in Germany that the outpouring of nationalism and patriotism which he often witnessed drove him relentlessly up against a series of agonizing questions concerning his own ultimate vocation and that of his black people in America. Du Bois later wrote:

> I began to feel that dichotomy which all my life has characterized my thought; how far can love for my oppressed race accord with love for the oppressing country? And when these loyalties diverge, where shall my soul find refuge? [10]

Whatever the ultimate answer to that question, it was also in Germany that Du Bois made his well-remembered dedication of his life to his "oppressed race." The ceremony on his twenty-fifth

* Du Bois made no reference to the "blue-eyed damsel" on pp. 101–102 of *Dusk of Dawn*. On p. 46 of that book, Du Bois wrote: "I had already told the daughter, Dora, with whom I was most frequently coupled, that it would not be fair to marry her and bring her to America. She said she would marry me 'gleich!' [at once] but I assured her that she would not be happy; and besides, I had work to do." It is in Du Bois' essay "My Evolving Program for Negro Freedom" (Logan, ed., *What the Negro Wants*, p. 46) that he referred to "blue-eyed" Dora. The rest of the reference to this episode is substantially the same as that in *Dusk of Dawn*. But Harding's parenthetical warning is not supported by what Du Bois wrote immediately after his explanation of the episode in "My Evolving Program for Negro Freedom."

In the immediately ensuing paragraph he wrote

> From this unhampered social intermingling with Europeans of education and manners, I emerged from the extremes of my racial provincialism. I became more human; learned the place in life of "Wine, Women, and Song"; I ceased to hate or suspect people simply because they belonged to one race or color; and above all I began to understand the real meaning of scientific research and the dim outline of methods of employing its technique and its results in the new social sciences for the settlement of the Negro problems in America.

Aptheker repeats on p. 160 of the *Autobiography* the paragraph cited above but places the Dora episode, considerably expanded, on pp. 161–162 [ed.].

9. Du Bois, *Dusk of Dawn*, pp. 101–102.
10. Du Bois, *Autobiography*, p. 169.

birthday must not be set aside simply because Du Bois later called it "rather sentimental," for one of his friends was right to call him a marvelous combination of the romantic and the rationalist. Indeed, one must add, too, that he also tended to combine all the strengths and weaknesses of the mystic and the materialist. So the dedication must be taken seriously, especially within the context of the present examination.

Significantly enough he began that ceremony by dedicating his library to his dead mother—calling on history, on the ancestors, at the moment of profound decisions for the future. Then he went on to make this vow, as he records it:

I will seek [the Truth] on the pure assumption that it is worth seeking—and Heaven, nor Hell, God nor Devil shall turn me from my purpose till I die.

From the concern for Truth he turned to the world, and said,

I am firmly convinced that my own best development is not one and the same with the best development of the world and here I am willing to sacrifice. That sacrifice to the world's good becomes too soon sticky* sentimentality. I therefore take the world that the Unknown lay in my hands and work for the rise of the Negro people, taking for granted that their best development means the best development of the world. . . .[11]

Here, for our purposes is the central, tripartite dedication: to truth, to the world's good, and to the good of his people. Du Bois came to manhood when men believed such things possible, and for all of his life—with significant periods of doubt—he seemed to believe it too. In Germany, he began where he was, on the black and inner ground of his own life, hoping against hope that there was no basic incompatibility among these ultimate commitments he had made.

We shall not attempt here to delineate the development of Du Bois' life when he returned to America. Let it suffice to say that

---

* In the original, "sickly" [ed.].

11. Du Bois, *Autobiography*, pp. 170–171.

he gave every evidence of holding fast to the resolves made in North Germany. Indeed, the familiar, bloody, American ground seemed to carry him even more deeply into the Messianic understanding of the nation's black aliens. This was surely the burden of the essay published by the American Negro Academy in 1897, "The Conservation of the Races." [12] *

It deserves careful examination, for in this essay we find much of the Black Messianism that Du Bois would carry with him in one form or another, at one level of intensity or another, until he was buried in the land of his forefathers.

In the essay, after having defined race in terms of common heritage, language, blood, tradition, and impulses, he adds that members of such a racial group are also "striving together for the accomplishment of certain more or less vividly conceived ideals of life." Out of that setting he continued: "Some of the great races of today—particularly the Negro race—have not as yet given to civilization the full spiritual message which they are capable of giving." In order to do this, Du Bois called for black solidarity and originality. He writes:

> For the development of Negro genius, of Negro literature and art, of Negro spirit, only Negroes bound and welded together, Negroes inspired by one vast ideal, can work out in its fullness the great message we have for humanity.

As Du Bois saw it, black people in America were "the advanced † guard of Negro people," and had to remember that "if they are to take their just place in the van of Pan-Negroism, then their destiny is *not* absorption by the white Americans." Rather, he proclaimed that if blacks were faithful to their calling, America could become the place where it could be demonstrated that blacks "are a nation stored with wonderful possibilities of culture." If this was to begin, he said, then black destiny "is not a servile

* The correct title is *The Conservation of Races*. Instead of p. 485, read pp. 483–492 [ed.].

† In the original, "advance" [ed.].

12. Howard Brotz, ed., *Negro Social and Political Thought: 1850–1920* (New York, 1966), p. 485.

imitation of Anglo-Saxon culture but a stalwart originality which shall unswervingly follow Negro ideals."

Afro-Americans had "a distinct mission as a race" according to Du Bois. Put somewhat mystically, it was to be "the first fruits of this new nation," of an Africa reborn, "the harbinger of that black tomorrow which is yet destined to soften the whiteness of the Teutonic today." Obviously intoxicated with hope, Du Bois went on to say, "it is our duty to conserve our physical powers, our intellectual endowments, our spiritual ideals; as a race we must strive by race organization, by race solidarity, by race unity to the realization of that broader humanity which freely recognizes differences in men, but sternly deprecates inequality in their opportunities of development."

So Du Bois called upon black people to have faith in themselves, in their past and in a glorious Messianic vocation. His peroration—and in spite of himself he *was* a preacher—included these words: "we must be inspired [he wrote] with the divine faith of our black mothers that out of the blood and dust of battle will march a victorious host, a mighty nation, a peculiar people, to speak to the nations of the earth a Divine truth that shall make them free." *

Of course, it takes no special wisdom or insight to see that Dr. Du Bois in this essay had grasped an Old Testament understanding of the Messianic people and nation. That is, those who have a sense of common encounter—experience with the acts of God in their history and who are called by their prophets to a common vocation on behalf of all men. Not until sixty years later, after a lifetime of basic faithfulness to this vision, did W. E. B. Du Bois move in another related, but significantly different direction. Even as he moved though, he still believed that history defines both present and future.

---

* The quotation on p. 489 of Brotz reads: "No people that laughs at itself, and ridicules itself, and wishes to God it was anything but itself ever wrote its name in history; it *must* [italics in the original] be inspired with the Divine faith of our black mothers," to the end of the quotation [ed.].

Returning to the earlier period, it should be apparent that Du Bois' program for the Talented Tenth grew naturally out of his Messianic vision of the role of the black people in America, out of his nineteenth-century German-American-Old Testament understanding of leadership, and out of his mistrust of white leaders for black hosts. Whites, he said, could not be trusted "to guide this group into self-realization and to its highest cultural possibilities." [13] Therefore, the specially trained black minority was also part of his Messianic commitment.

In an important sense, much of Du Bois' scholarship came out of the same Messianic context, out of the same tripartite commitment to truth, the world, and his people. He saw his trust was not betrayed. Later he would constantly chastise and encourage black schools in the task of scholarship on the Afro-American experience as part of their role in building their people's sense of self as well as contributing to the broader truth.

Such an attitude was especially evident in his comments about his commitment to the clarification of African history. In his autobiography he wrote, "I am not sure just when I began to feel an interest in Africa." But he said he knew that he became tired of "finding in newspapers, textbooks and history, fulsome lauding of white folk, and either no mention of dark peoples, or mention in disparaging and apologetic phrase."

RECLAIMING THE PAST

It was at that point, Du Bois remembers, that "I made up my mind that it must be true that Africa had a history and a destiny, and that one of my jobs was to disinter this unknown past, and help make certain a splendid future." [14]

The insistent theme of black solidarity was somewhat toned down in *The Souls of Black Folk* (1903), but the profound love of black people came out in many of the essays, especially, for

13. Du Bois, *Dusk of Dawn*, p. 70.
14. Du Bois, *Autobiography*, p. 343.

instance, the memoir of Alexander Crummell and the meditation on "The Sorrow Songs." Of course, Du Bois could not write for public consumption without the Messianic theme being stated on one level or another, and it was present—though muted—in that most famous of his writings. It was recognizable near the closing of the first essay, when Du Bois wrote:

> Work, culture, liberty—all these we need . . . each growing and aiding each, and all striving toward that vaster ideal that swims before the Negro people, the ideal of human brotherhood, gained through the unifying ideal of race . . . that some day on American soil two world-races may give to each other those characteristics both so sadly lack.[15]

It was in *The Souls of Black Folk,* too, that there appeared for the first time—as far as I can tell—the suggestion of a fear that remained with Dr. Du Bois all his life, a fear that Afro-Americans might betray their own Messianic vocation. In the essay "Of the Wings of Atlanta," he asked these questions:

> What if the Negro people be wooed from a strife for righteousness, from a love of knowing, to regard dollars as the be-all and end-all of life? Whither, then, is the new-world quest for goodness and Beauty and Truth gone glimmering? Must this, and that fair flower of freedom which . . . spring from our fathers' blood, must that too degenerate into a dusky quest of gold? [16] *

By the time a half-century had passed, Du Bois thought he had the answer, and it transformed his hope as well as his final days.

But in 1904 Du Bois still had much ground for hope. He shared it with his students and with young persons wherever he found them, challenging them to become leaders of the black Messianic vanguard. In his "Credo," published that year, he continued to

---

* In this quotation, there should be three dots after "life?" to indicate the omission of several lines. *Goodness* should be capitalized. The last sentence should read: "Must this, and that fair flower of Freedom which, despite the jeers of latter-day striplings, sprung," to the end of the quotation [ed.].

15. Du Bois, *Souls of Black Folk,* p. 22.
16. *Ibid.,* p. 69.

affirm the creative tension of his convictions. Thus he proclaimed a belief in the brotherhood of all men, as well as a special belief "in the Negro Race; in the beauty of its genius, the sweetness of its soul, and its strength in that meekness which shall inherit the earth." * So, too, he could believe "in pride of race" and also in "Liberty for all men." [17] Throughout his life the task was continually to keep these beliefs in tension. His record in accomplishing that task was mixed with success and failure, but I think the success clearly dominates the scene.

The Niagara Movement was, of course, an attempt to sustain the tension, to put action behind the creed, to gather together a black vanguard for the struggle. That story cannot be told here, but it must be seen in the context of the commitment to black solidarity and hope.

On the other hand, Du Bois often admitted that it was hard for him to trust whites, even those he knew were theoretically his allies in the building of a kingdom beyond caste. The raw nerves of his blackness and the long memories of racial pain made it difficult to know how to put together his hope for a new brotherhood beyond race with his sense of need for a committed black brotherhood. Later he wrote, for instance, about those first two decades of the twentieth century:

I was bitter at lynching, but not moved by the treatment of white miners in Colorado or Montana. I never sang the songs of Joe Hill, and the terrible strike at Lawrence, Massachusetts, did not stir me, because I knew that factory strikers like these would not let a Negro work beside them or live in the same town. It was hard for me to outgrow this mental isolation.[18] †

This suggests, of course, that it was often difficult for Du Bois to

* "this turbulent earth." In the next sentence, *pride* should be capitalized [ed.].

17. W. E. B. Du Bois, *Darkwater* (New York, 1920), pp. 3–4.

18. Du Bois, *Autobiography,* p. 305.

† The view of Du Bois on this crucial point would have been clearer if Harding had placed a comma after "isolation" and continued: "and to see that the plight of the white workers was fundamentally the same as that of the black, even if the white worker helped enslave the black" [ed.].

live up to the socialism that he and Niagara proclaimed—difficult because of his commitment to black people and his experience with whites. (It was in this context that he left the Socialist party in 1912, believing that his devotion to blacks would not allow what he considered the luxury of wasted votes on a socialist Presidential candidate.)

Du Bois' ever-deepening sense of commitment to black solidarity held profound implications for his relationships with the white-dominated NAACP. It is already apparent that one of his most important reasons for taking an executive position with the organization was the opportunity it afforded to have his own forum in *The Crisis*. Early in the game the founding editor began to use the pages of the periodical to put forward his own convictions, suggestions, and intuitions for the building of black solidarity— often at the expense of the Association's stated goals and methods.

So by 1915 Du Bois was writing words which may have surprised others, but which grew out of the days of Fisk and Germany, and "The Conservation of the Races." He said:

The Negro must have power; the power of men, the right to do, to know, to feel and to express that knowledge, action and spiritual gift.

Besides, he repeated, "the first article in the program of any group that will survive must be the great aim, equality and power among men." His program for this empowerment included political, educational, and cultural organization among blacks. Finally he said:

I thank God that most of the money that supports the National Association for the Advancement of Colored People comes from black hands; a still larger proportion must so come, and we must not only support but control this and similar organizations and hold them unwaveringly to our objects, our aims and our ideals.[19]

One of the natural products of his position was his call within a year for a black political party.

19. Francis L. Broderick and August Meier, eds., *Negro Protest Thought in the Twentieth Century* (Indianapolis, 1965), p. 60.

Du Bois' position was reaffirmed in his slim but significant book, *The Negro*. In addition to the immeasurable service it performed in introducing many black persons to their African roots, it continued the theme of Black Messianism, in a way that surely made the Spingarns and the Villards even more uncomfortable. Near the end of the work, Du Bois wrote:

> Instead of being led and defended by others, as in the past, American Negroes are gaining their own voices, their own ideals. Self-realization is thus coming . . . to another of the world's great races.[20]

POST WORLD WAR I ATTITUDES

This was, of course, the time of the European holocaust, and the war had a significant effect on Du Bois' sense of the role of black people and all of what he called "the darker races." For instance, in 1916 he stated his conviction that the European struggle had vividly illustrated the bankruptcy of Western civilization. There fore, he said it was time for black people to reassess old ideals— from the African past.

> Old standards of beauty beckon us again . . . not the blue-eyed, white-skinned types . . . but rich, brown and black men and women with glowing dark eyes and crinkling hair. . . . Life, which in this cold Occident stretched in bleak conventional lines before us, takes on a warm golden hue that harks back to the heritage of Africa and the tropics.

Then, predictably, the Messianic word was spoken again. Du Bois wrote, "Brothers, the war has shown us the cruelty of the civilization of the West. History has taught us the futility of the civilization of the East. Let ours be the civilization of no *man,* but of *all* men. This is the truth that sets us free." [21]

It is obvious, too, that Du Bois' angle of vision from the black

20. W. E. B. Du Bois, *The Negro* (New York, 1915), p. 231.
21. W. E. B. Du Bois, *An ABC of Color* (Berlin, 1963), pp. 87–88.

side made it possible for him to see new aspects of the world through the carnage of the War, especially the significance of the Second Coming of the non-white peoples of the world. As a result of the war he was also able to develop new approaches to his long-standing interest in Pan-Africanism, a topic purposely slighted here, but surely important for our full understanding of Du Bois.

In America, "after the war" meant the riots of 1919 and a general resurgence of black suffering. It meant the rise of Marcus Garvey, and Du Bois had to come to terms with *that* variety of black solidarity—another issue that we must slight at this time. Almost predictably, the post-war period found Du Bois responding to the intensified problems of black people with more extended attempts to spell out his concerns for the inner organization of the black community. None of the institutions in that community escaped his scrutiny, and as we might expect, the colleges were especially exposed. For instance, when in 1926 Tuskegee and Hampton received multimillion dollar endowments, Du Bois wrote of his hope that the funds would make them independent enough to "say to all whites: This is a Negro School." Tell them, he counselled:

> In the long run we can imagine no difference of interest between White and Black; but temporarily there may be, or men may imagine there is; in such case we stand flatly and firmly for Negroes. This school is not a sanatorium for white teachers or a restaurant and concert hall for white trustees and their friends.[22]

His constant demand of black schools was that they be faithful to their role—or, perhaps, that they first understand their role—in the struggle for survival and for fulfillment in which black persons were involved.

By 1929 Du Bois was proposing that the future road for black people lay in the direction of consumer and producer's cooperatives. As the Depression began he urged the development of "an

22. *The Crisis*, XXXI (March 1926), 216.

economic General Staff" for black America which would help chart the way ahead.[23]

As we approach 1934, the year that his black solidarity program and his criticism of the NAACP finally provided the occasion for his departure from *The Crisis,* several issues should be clearly stated. First, Du Bois' emphasis on the organization of the black community was not new to the depression period. Its roots went back in his own life to the nineteenth century. The pronounced emphasis on economics was more recent, and had been influenced by many factors, not the least of them being the brutal experience of blacks during the Depression. Du Bois had also watched the success of Garvey for a period and could observe the economic achievements of Father Divine and his strange form of religious communalism. The socialist-communist movements had their effect. (Du Bois had visited Russia and was deeply impressed with what he saw.) At least as important as any other single factor was Du Bois' own conviction that blacks were still faced with a struggle of several generations before racial prejudice would be overcome.

So he called for what might be labelled "Black Socialism" or black communalism, from cooperative farms to urban communities, to socialized medicine—all in the hands of black people. He proposed that many of them be underwritten with federal funds.[24] He refused to run from the term segregation, and used it almost as a goad, saying that since it existed and would continue to exist until deep levels of change came in the white psyche, that blacks should use it for their own good. He recognized the sense in which this might compromise his ultimate vision for blacks, and, March, 1934, published this brief summary of the dilemma:

1. Compulsory separation of human beings by essentially artificial criteria such as birth, nationality, language, color and race, is the cause of human hate, jealousy and war, and the destruction of talent and art.

23. *The Crisis,* XXXVI (November 1929), 392; XL (July 1932), 242.
24. *The Crisis,* XLI (January 1934), 1; XLI (February 1934).

On the other hand, he put this proposition up for consideration:

2. Where separation of mankind into races, groups and classes is compulsory, either by law or by custom, and whether that compulsion be temporary or permanent, the only effective defense that the segregated and despised group has against complete spiritual and physical disaster, is internal self-organization for self-respect and self-defense.[25]

By then it was clear that his concern for the continuation of black spiritual life was equal to that of his concern for the physical, and he desired self-respect at least as much as self-defense. This was a natural response for one who sought to maintain a Messianic hope for black people. They must endure, but they must endure with integrity, not as wards of the white society, Du Bois said, not as beggars at white doors.

He was even ready to face the possibility of black emigration if the nation made it impossible for this black solidarity and selfhood to develop. In several instances he compared the black situation in America to the Jewish predicament in Europe. But he never gave up his ultimate concern for the Truth of black people in America. In the last issue of *The Crisis* which he edited, he refused to back down against the NAACP's opposition and said:

In this period of frustration and disappointment, we must turn from negation to affirmation, from the ever-lasting "No" to the ever-lasting "Yes." Instead of drowning our originality in imitation of mediocre white folks . . . [we] have a right to affirm that the Negro race is one of the great human races, inferior to none in its accomplishment and in its ability.[26]

When he was attacked on the grounds that he now seemed to be changing his position, Du Bois said, "I am not worried about being inconsistent. What worries me is the Truth." He said he saw more segregation in the North in 1934 than in 1910 and

25. *The Crisis,* XLI (March 1934), 85.
26. *The Crisis,* XLI (June 1934), 182.

wondered how black men would keep their souls while battling against the walls.

Interestingly enough, the following month, June, 1934, Du Bois showed some concern for both consistency and truth when he inserted in *The Crisis* several paragraphs from "The Conservation of the Races," dated 1897. They ended with the familiar issue of the distinct mission of black people versus "self-obliteration." Then he added a note, saying: "On the whole, I am rather pleased to find myself still so much in sympathy with myself." [27] In the light of the present mood of black America, it appears that Du Bois now has many more sympathizers than he could then imagine. But none of them was on the Board of the National Association for the Advancement of Colored People at the time, so the resignation of W. E. B. Du Bois was accepted—for reasons only partly related to black socialism.

Referring to the black communalistic emphasis of his Messianic vision, Du Bois later wrote:

I shall not live to see entirely the triumph of this, my newer emphasis; but it will triumph just as much and just as completely as did my advocacy of agitation and self-assertion. It is indeed a part of that same original program; it is its natural and inevitable fulfillment.[28]

Du Bois did not live to see our own black-conscious age arrive in America. Indeed, before he died he often appeared to despair of its borning. But we see it, and remembering his words, some of almost a century ago, we can do no less than stand in awe before this giant of a man.

What more we can do depends, I suppose, upon whether we still believe in fulfillment, redemption, new men, and new societies. Or—perhaps more importantly—what more we can do depends on whether we are convinced that a man can, in *this* age, still say without shame:

27. *Ibid.*, 183.
28. Du Bois, *Dusk of Dawn*, p. 311.

I will seek [the Truth] on the pure assumption that it is worth seeking—and Heaven nor Hell, God nor Devil shall turn me from my purpose till I die.

EPILOGUE

When it is complete, the last portion of this essay will attempt to establish several clarities. First, and perhaps most obvious, is the fact that in the wilderness of the Western black diaspora W. E. B. Du Bois was likely the most significant voice to prepare the way for this current, newest age of blackness. He is the proper context for an adequate understanding of Malcolm, of Fanon, of Stokely Carmichael and Martin Luther King.*

The last section will also examine the significance of legal desegregation in America for Du Bois' vision of the Messianic role of black people here. I will suggest that by the 1950's he became convinced that his beloved people were "being bribed to trade equal status in the United States for the slavery of the majority of men." Many events—including the frightened response of black leadership to his own time of McCarthyite trial —reinforced that conviction. Black Americans were being led to a betrayal of their Messianic calling.

Within that setting, finally, we understand more fully his decision to return to the land of his forefathers near the end of his life. Among the many other factors involved, W. E. B. Du Bois had evidently transferred his black Messianic hope to the brothers in the homeland, especially those under Kwame Nkrumah's leadership. This was surely apparent in the words he spoke when he became a citizen of Ghana—just six months before his death, just six days before his ninety-fifth birthday. Du Bois said then:

My great-grandfather was carried from the Gulf of Guinea. I have returned that my dust may mingle with the dust of my forefathers. There is not much time for me. But now, my life will flow

* See Introduction, p. xiii [ed.].

on in the vigorous, young stream of Ghanaian life which lifts the African personality to its proper place among men. And I shall not have lived and worked in vain.[29]

Thus, at this next to the last moment of his life, the past, the present, and the future were joined as one in the thoughts of Du Bois and in his undying hopes for the glorious destiny of the peoples of Africa, wherever they may be found.

29. William Branch, New York *Amsterdam News,* Saturday, September 7, 1963. Accra, Ghana, dateline.

Bibliographical Note

The writings of Du Bois include a dozen important books, the fifteen useful Atlanta University Publications, the last three with the assistance of A. Granville Dill, more than a hundred pamphlets, articles in scholarly journals, editorials and other comments in *The Crisis* (1910–1934), essays, public addresses, novels, and poems.

The best known of his poems, "A Litany at Atlanta," written following the race riot there in 1906, has been described by the editors of *The Negro Caravan* (New York: The Dryden Press, Inc., 1941) as "one of the earliest poems by a Negro in free verse . . . the author's impassioned prose at its most typical, prose that has crossed the tenuous line dividing it from poetry." His novels are not masterpieces of literature; on the other hand, as revelations of his personality and views about the events depicted, they deserve careful study by historians and psychologists. In *Dark Princess: A Romance* (New York: Harcourt, Brace and Company, 1928), the principal male character, Matthew Towns, as Harold Isaacs pointed out, is in many respects the personification of Du Bois and a spokesman for his dream of a Dark World. Hugh Gloster in *Negro Voices in American Fiction* (Chapel Hill: The University of North Carolina Press, 1948) agreed with the general view that *Dark Princess* revealed Du Bois as "more of a

propagandist than a realistic painter of folk and the social scene";
on the other hand, Gloster placed *The Quest of the Silver Fleece*
(Chicago: A. C. McClurg & Co., 1911), a sociological study of
the Southern cotton industry, in the tradition of Frank Norris'
The Octopus (1901) and *The Pit* (1903). But *The Quest* was
also propagandistic in its glorification of Negro characters designed to instill race-pride in Negroes. *The Black Flame* trilogy
(New York: Mainstream Publishers)—*The Ordeal of Mansart*
(1957), *Mansart Builds a School* (1959), and *Worlds of Color*
(1961)—is as Du Bois said in *Mansart* (p. 316) a fictional
interpretation of history since Reconstruction. Written during the
last years of his life, they are probably his worst books as fiction
and history.

Of his public addresses, the almost forgotten *The Revelation of
Saint Orgne the Damned* (Nashville?: The Hemphill Press, 1938)
is probably the most significant. This Commencement Address at
Fisk University, 1938, the fiftieth anniversary of his graduation,
reveals the mystic and the pragmatist. Orgne (Negro) revealed
the meaning of life as "the fullest, most complete enjoyment of
the possibilities of human existence." However, Du Bois said,
Negroes could not enjoy this kind of life, partly because of inadequate education, especially in the South. While demanding at least
nine months a year of good education for every Negro child
between the ages of five and fifteen, he placed the main responsibility upon the family for uplifting the Negro. "It is in vain that
the University seeks to cope with ill-bred youngsters, foul-mouthed
loafers and unwashed persons who have happened to pass the
entrance examinations." This is hardly the "racist" Du Bois who
did not hesitate in the same address to say that in the American
democracy, "With few exceptions, we are all today 'white folks'
niggers." In the *Revelation* there are judgments from on High,
Delphic oracular pronouncements, and proposals for solving
major problems.

The better-known *The Conservation of Races* is one of his
best separate essays, notable for his early exposition of the dilemma which still perplexes many American Negroes: "Am I

an American or am I a Negro? Can I be both?" This essay, the second *Occasional Paper* of the American Negro Academy (Washington, D.C., 1897) presented a temperate seven-point manifesto to the Academy calling for the "earnest and long continued efforts" of Negroes to cure the socials ills, aided by the "earnest efforts of the white people" of the United States.

The Souls of Black Folk (Chicago: A. C. McClurg & Co., 1903) is the most valuable of Du Bois' collected essays. In addition to the one on "Of Mr. Booker T. Washington and Others," three in particular help to make *The Souls* a classic. "Of the Passing of the First-Born" reveals his poignant grief on the death of his son. It concludes: "Sleep, then, child—sleep till I sleep and waken to a baby voice and the ceaseless patter of little feet—above the Veil." Du Bois renounced the ministry as a career and liked to tell about the time he was called upon to lead the Wilberforce faculty and students in prayer, and he responded, "No, he won't." On the other hand, "Of Alexander Crummell" tells how this Episcopal priest, one of the most learned Negroes of the nineteenth century, overcame Doubt, Despair, and Hate. The editors of *The Negro Caravan* (1941) considered "Of the Sorrow Songs" the first essay on the spirituals by a Negro "and in many respects still one of the best."

In his editorial and other comments in *The Crisis,* notably "As the Crow Flies" and "Postscripts," Du Bois continued to "protest and assail the ears of America," as he said he would do at the second meeting of the Niagara Movement, Harpers Ferry, August 15, 1906. Under his editorship, *The Crisis* was not only one of the foremost polemical magazines but also an indispensable source for the study of American life and thought. While some of his articles in other magazines were also polemical, many of them were scholarly, especially those in *American Historical Review, Atlantic Monthly, Independent, Dial, Annals of the Academy of Political and Social Science, Harper's Weekly, American Journal of Sociology,* and *Foreign Affairs.* His articles published in the *Bulletin of the Department of Labor* and the *Bulletin of the*

Department of Commerce, Bureau of the Census were largely factual studies.

While Broderick concluded (p. 41) that a tight budget prevented Du Bois from making his Atlanta University Publications "substantial, scholarly" reports, Du Bois stated in *Dusk of Dawn* (pp. 64–66): "Between 1896 and 1920 there was no study in America which did not depend in some degree upon the investigations made at Atlanta University; often they were widely quoted and commended." And Broderick stated (p. 43) that the well-known Southern sociologist, Howard W. Odum, in 1951 "listed twelve of Du Bois' titles at the top of a chronological list of American sociological works in the area of race, ethnic groups, and folk."

The fact that *The Suppression of the African Slave-Trade to the United States of America: 1638–1870* (1896) was the first book in the Harvard Historical Series establishes it as a "creditable" volume to "American historical scholarship," to quote the view of an anonymous reviewer in *The Nation* (December 31, 1896), pp. 499–500. While Broderick was ambivalent in his evaluation (pp. 37–39) of *The Philadelphia Negro* (Philadephia: For the University of Pennsylvania, 1899), especially toward Du Bois' portrayal of the role of the Negro elite, Broderick praised the "patience and honesty revealed on every page" and added: "It was undoubtedly this aspect of the work which, forty-five years later, led Gunnar Myrdal, the Swedish economist and sociologist, to regard [in *An American Dilemma*] *The Philadelphia Negro* as a model study of a Negro community."

An evaluation of *John Brown* (Philadephia: George W. Jacobs, 1909) depends in large measure upon the reader's philosophical view about the right to revolution against the government. In this frame of reference, it is difficult to describe Brown as a fiend or maniac while proclaiming Robert E. Lee a great hero and defender of "The War for Southern Independence."

The slim volume *The Negro* (New York: Henry Holt, 1915) is still valuable as a brief summary of the subject. *Black Folk Then and Now: An Essay in the History and Sociology of the Negro Race* (New York: Henry Holt, 1939) incorporated some of *The Negro* and attempted to refute a widespread belief that "the Negro has no history" (p. vii). *Black Folk Then and Now* was inspired also in part by the failure of the Phelps-Stokes Fund to obtain financial support for a proposed Encyclopedia of the Negro, one of the great disappointments of Du Bois' life. As Secretary of the Board of Directors for the project, I know that the support was denied because a white consultant warned that Du Bois was a "racial chauvinist." Instead of the multivolume Encyclopedia, there was published the *Encyclopedia of the Negro: Preparatory Volume with Reference Lists and Reports* (New York: The Phelps-Stokes Fund, Inc., 1945). It would be useful as a starting point for an updated Encyclopedia of the Negro.

Broderick (p. 156), not the most kindly of critics, found in the "hastily written survey of the Negro's contribution to America," *The Gift of Black Folk: Negroes in the Making of America* (Boston: Stratford Company, 1924), "unmistakable strength" in at least one passage, comparable to that in "Of the Passing of the First-Born."

The most widely discussed of Du Bois' histories is *Black Reconstruction in America: An Essay Toward a History of the Part Which Black Folk Played in the Attempt to Reconstruct Democracy in America, 1860–1880* (New York: Harcourt, Brace, 1935). A strained and slanted Marxist interpretation of Reconstruction, it would have been a better book if some of the tediously long quotations had been reduced or summarized. This volume, which is the major subject of Aptheker's analysis of Du Bois as an historian, is a signal contribution to American historiography for several reasons. The chapter on Andrew Johnson, "The Transubstantiation of a Poor White" into a rabid racist, still refutes Columbia Professor Eric L. McKitrick's defense, *Andrew Johnson and Reconstruction* (Chicago and London: University of Chicago Press, 1960). While many histories of Reconstruction still attribute its "evils" to Southern state conventions and legislatures supposedly controlled by Negroes,

Du Bois pointed out that only in the South Carolina constitutional convention did Negroes outnumber whites—seventy-six to forty-eight—and that only in the Louisiana constitutional convention was there an equal number of colored and white delegates. He also stressed, as perhaps no previous writer had done, some admirable provisions in the constitutions and laws: the liberalization of the suffrage and the enlargement of the rights of women; the abolition of dueling, imprisonment for debt, the whipping post, the branding iron, and penal stocks; the repeal of the labor laws in the 1865 and 1866 "Black Codes." As Professor Arthur M. Schlesinger, Sr. had already written in his *Political and Social History of the United States, 1829–1925* (New York: The Macmillan Company, 1925), p. 243, none of these measures was "more laudable perhaps than the mandatory provisions for the inauguration of free public-school systems." In retrospect, the greatest value of *Black Reconstruction* resides perhaps in its emphasis on the failure of the federal government to provide land for rural freedmen, even though there was not enough confiscated land to give them an acre apiece.

Du Bois' two books on Africa—*Color and Democracy: Colonies and Peace* (New York: Harcourt, Brace, 1945) and *The World and Africa: An Inquiry into the Part which Africa Has Played in World History* (New York: The Viking Press, 1947) —expressed the hope in the first volume that the end of World War II might mean a new day for the liberation of colonies but, after a very good history of Africa from the earliest times, concluded in the second volume (p. 252): "America invests in colonies—British, Dutch, and French; and colonies are slums used to make a profit from materials and labor." Except for Du Bois' recollections of the Pan-African Congresses in 1919, 1921, 1923, 1927, and 1945, *The World and Africa* repeats much of the material in *Black Folk Then and Now.*

Dusk of Dawn: An Essay Toward an Autobiography of a Race Concept (New York: Harcourt, Brace, 1940) is really an autobiography, the source for much of the information about his life up to 1940. One of the most important tasks of a biographer today is to find in *The Autobiography of W. E. B. Du Bois: A Soliloquy on Viewing My Life from the Last Decade of Its First Century,* Herbert Aptheker, ed. (New York: International Publishers, 1968), the sources of *Dusk of Dawn.* Since there are practically no footnotes, this is an arduous task. I have found several instances in which Aptheker followed in part portions of *Dusk of Dawn* and Du Bois' "My Evolving Program of Negro Freedom"; the latter Aptheker does not list in his "Selected Bibliography." Since he has possession of the Du Bois Papers which were closed to authors as of 1910, it is also difficult to determine how accurately the *Autobiography* reproduces them.

An adequate biography must await the granting of unrestricted access to the Du Bois Papers to scholars, preferably those who knew him during a considerable part of his long life.

The literature about Du Bois, in addition to that included in this book, is so voluminous that only the most significant can be summarized here. Booker T. Washington's writings, which might have been the most important, unfortunately contained almost nothing about his principal adversary. Some twelve books, in considerable measure repetitious, numerous speeches and magazine articles rarely mentioned him by name. Washington did refer, in *Up from Slavery* (1900), p. 270, to a meeting in Boston in 1899, at which "Dr. W. E. B. Du Bois read an original sketch." In *The Story of My Life and Work* (1901), p. 271, this "original story" was "well received." *The Story of the Negro,* 2 vols. (1909), had two footnotes to Du Bois' writings: *The Suppression of the African Slave-Trade* (I, 95) and "The Freedmen's Bureau," *Atlantic Monthly,* March, 1901 (II, 13); they did not identify the author. Nor did the reference in the text (II, 256) to Du Bois' estimate of the value of Negro-owned property in Philadelphia in 1899 identify him.

Washington's only fairly long comment about Du Bois, *The Future of the American Negro* (1901), p. 230, read as follows:

The Negro should be taught that material development is not an end, but simply a means to an end. As Professor W. E. B. Du Bois puts it,

"The idea should not be simply to make men carpenters, but to make carpenters men."

I believe that this virtual silence was a calculated ploy, designed to avoid directing readers' attention to Du Bois. This belief is reinforced by the failure of Emmett J. Scott, Washington's confidential secretary for eighteen years, and of Lyman Beecher Stowe, another warm admirer, to mention Du Bois in *Booker T. Washington, Builder of a Civilization* (1916).

"Rough Sketches, William Edward Burghardt Du Bois, Ph.D." by John Henry Adams in the anti-Washington *Voice of the Negro,* II (March 1905), 176–181, contained rare photographs of Du Bois in his high-school graduating class, 1885, and in the group of six speakers at his Harvard College Commencement, 1890. They support Adams' statement that Du Bois was "clean and neat," a little below average height, and weighing about 145 pounds. (In later life, he was considerably heavier.) "His face is oval, tapering toward the chin, and the richness of its brown color, together with the evenness of his features makes him rather impressive and attractive." He showed little patience with those who simply wanted to be seen in his company.

Of the writers discussed in this section, James Weldon Johnson, John Hope, and Walter White knew Du Bois best. (I, who worked with him intermittently between 1921 and 1958, doubt that anyone *really* knew this complex personality.) Johnson, a graduate of the first Atlanta University, 1894, was one of the better exemplars and practitioners of the "Talented Tenth." As field secretary, 1916–1920, and as general secretary, 1920–1930, of the NAACP, he was well acquainted with Du Bois professionally and personally. His comments about him in *Black Manhattan: The Story of the Negro in New York* (New York, 1930) show neither adulation for a kindred spirit nor the acrimony which often arises between two close associates. While generally favorable to Du Bois, Johnson agreed with the observation in 1929 of Robert Russa Moton, Washington's successor at Tuskegee: "In truth, they are working for the same thing in different spheres and by a different approach" (p. 139), a conclusion with which I disagree. Johnson is more accurate in his evaluation of Marcus Garvey, "a supreme egotist, his egotism amounting to megalomania. . . . As he grew in power, he fought every other Negro rights organization in the country, especially the National Association for the Advancement of Colored People, centring his attacks upon Dr. Du Bois" (pp. 256–257). Edmund David Cronon's comprehensive, authoritative *Black Moses: The Story of Marcus Garvey and the Universal Negro Improvement Association* (Madison, 1962) throws valuable light on the Du Bois-Garvey controversy. As early as December, 1920, Du Bois published in *The Crisis* a severe indictment of Garvey's Black Star Steamship Line, "based on a shrewd analysis of its financial reports" (p. 97). Four years later the editor of *The Crisis* wrote: " 'Marcus Garvey is, without doubt, the most dangerous enemy of the Negro race in America and the world. He is either a lunatic or a traitor' " (p. 190). Garvey called Du Bois " 'purely and simply a white man's nigger,' " and blamed the light-skinned members of the NAACP for his failures (pp. 130–131). On the other hand, Cronon agreed (p. 204) with Du Bois' assertion in *Dusk of Dawn* (p. 277) that Garvey's Back to Africa Movement "was a grandiose and bombastic scheme, utterly impracticable as a whole." Yet, as Cronon pointed out, Du Bois admitted "it was sincere and had some practical features; and Garvey proved not only an astonishing popular leader, but a master of propaganda. Within a few years, news of his movement reached Europe and Asia, and penetrated every corner of Africa." (This is not true as far as Africa was concerned.) Cronon added, however: "Despite Garvey's triumph as an unparalleled propagandist and organiser of the Negro masses, his success proved ephemeral, and his vaunted Universal Negro Improvement Association turned out to be only a transient, if extremely colorful, phenomenon" (p. 220). In recent years Negro Americans who seek to identify with a romantic interpretation of "Black African" history and civilization deride this point of view. To them, Marcus Garvey is the precursor of self-government and independence in "Black Africa." Du Bois and his Pan-African Congresses are generally ignored or derided by these advocates of négritude.

One of the more perceptive remarks about *Black Reconstruction* was made by Howard K. Beale, late Professor of History at the University of North Carolina and the University of Wisconsin, in his article "On Rewriting Reconstruction History," *American Historical Review* (July 1940). After criticizing the book for its unscientific Marxist views, Beale praised it for its emphasis on economic problems and "its mass of material, formerly ignored, that every future historian must reckon with" (p. 809). His admonition has not been unheeded.

The personal reminiscences of Miss Mary White Ovington contained gleanings that are particularly valuable because of her association with Du Bois from 1904 to 1932. In *Portraits of Color* (1927), she observed: "Among the distinguished Negroes in America, none is so hated as Burghardt Du Bois. And for excellent reason. He insists upon making them [white people] either angry or miserable. . . . He is a master of invective" (p. 78). She once heard a young white man attempt to read "Of the Passing of the First-Born" in *The Souls of Black Folk*. Finally, he exclaimed, sobbing: " 'No man . . . should dare to write like that' " (p. 86). She saw a cruel [I prefer sardonic] look in Du Bois' sensitive poet's face. "It lurks somewhere near the mouth—a half-sneer, a scorn" (p. 86). While caste still ruled, "no man in this country has done more to secure the white man's reluctant gesture of respect for the Negro's attainments than Burghardt Du Bois" (p. 91).

In her later volume *The Walls Came Tumbling Down* (1947), this white "Mother of the New Emancipation" revealed the courage of Dr. and Mrs. Du Bois, who received her in their Atlanta apartment and drove her through the streets of the city in 1904, two years before the Atlanta riot (pp. 55, 56). Du Bois was not afraid to have her attend the 1906 Harpers Ferry Niagara Movement meeting as a reporter for the New York *Evening Post* (p. 101). Her comments about Du Bois—the allusions to Du Bois' courage are mine—must be considered within the context of her long association with him. She and Du Bois were among the sixty prominent Americans who signed *The Call,* February 12, 1909, which led to the creation of the NAACP in 1910. Unabashedly terming herself one of the "anti-Washingtonians," she was, especially as chairman of the organization's board, 1919–1932, one of the staunchest supporters of Du Bois during his stormy career with the NAACP. It may be her admiration for him that led her to write that his editorial page in *The Crisis* was "always scholarly in his effort to tell the truth" (p. 108).

An American Dilemma: The Negro Problem and Modern Democracy, 2 vols. (New York and London, 1944), by Gunnar Myrdal, with the assistance of numerous competent Americans, is rightly considered one of the most important publications about the Negro in the United States. Contrary to Du Bois' attempt to demonstrate in *Black Reconstruction* the solidarity between landless Negroes and poor whites, this work concluded: "the Negro's friend—or the one who is least unfriendly—is still the upper class of white people, the people with the economic and social security who are truly a 'noncompeting group' " (p. 69). Another valid conclusion rejected Du Bois' advocacy of a cooperative Negro industrial system in the United States (*Dusk of Dawn,* pp. 208, 231) because "Americans in general have been weak in their cooperative endeavors" (p. 802).

An American Dilemma made an odd editorial mistake. In *Dusk of Dawn* (pp. 130–131), Du Bois emphasized the difficulty of seeing "the full psychological meaning of caste segregation," because "some thick sheet of invisible but horridly tangible plate glass" was between Negroes and the world. In Myrdal's work (p. 724), "plate glass" was rendered as "glass plate." There was agreement as to the result, however: "*Negroes and whites in America deal with each other through the medium of plenipotentiaries* [emphasis in the original]." There was agreement also with Du Bois' description of the Negro preacher as "a leader, a politician, an orator, a 'boss,' an intriguer, an idealist" (p. 940).

The Philadelphia Negro, "all but forgotten," met the highest requirements for the study of a Negro community (p. 1132).

One of the outstanding present-day intellectual heirs of Du Bois and contemporary American historians is Professor John Hope Franklin. His *From Slavery to Freedom: A History of American Negroes* (New York, 1947, 1956, 1967—*Negro Americans* in place of *American Negroes* in the 1967 edition) is the most widely used and a most distinguished text on the subject. More severe in his conclusion about Washington than was James Weldon Johnson, Franklin agreed (3rd ed., p. 393) with Du Bois' criticism in *The Souls of Black Folk* (p. 50) of Washington's preaching "a gospel of Work and Money to such an extent as apparently almost completely to overshadow the higher aims of life." By clear implication Franklin also approved Du Bois' stricture that under modern competitive methods it was not possible for Negro artisans, businessmen, and property owners to defend their rights and exist without the suffrage. However, "Washington ignored or winked at the South's reduction of the Negro's political and civil status" (p. 395).

Especially revealing is Franklin's frequently overlooked point, namely that some of the weaknesses in Washington's doctrines "are perhaps more obvious today than they were sixty years ago" (p. 395). But, after enumerating some of these flaws—for example, what is today called "Black Capitalism," the outmoded curriculum for industrial training, and the hostility of organized labor—Franklin rightly concluded that Washington was "the central figure—the dominant personality—in the history of the Negro down to his death in 1915" (p. 397).

The feud between Du Bois and Walter White, Acting Secretary of the NAACP, 1918–1928 and Secretary from 1928 until the former's second appointment, 1944–1947 (and later), was even more acrimonious than that between Washington and Du Bois, who fought at long range. Since White and Du Bois had adjoining offices, there were more opportunities for clashes between these superegotists in their struggle for power. White's reticence about Du Bois in *A Man Called White: The Auto-biography of Walter White* (New York, 1948) is therefore even more disappointing than Washington's. White stated briefly that at the London session of the Second Pan-African Congress, 1923, Du Bois tried in vain to obtain some definite statement from Prime Minister Ramsay McDonald about what the Labour party would do to correct glaring evils in the colonies (p. 61). Du Bois and others addressed meetings in 1928 that opposed the Senate confirmation of Judge John J. Parker of North Carolina as Associate Justice of the United States Supreme Court (p. 107). (This successful campaign was frequently mentioned during the opposition that led to the Senate's rejection, 1970, of Judges Clement E. Haynsworth, Jr. and G. Harrold Carswell as Associate Justices.) White made other minor references to Du Bois. His longest comment briefly narrated Du Bois' persistent but unsuccessful efforts to gain permission to present *An Appeal to the World!* (New York, 1947) to Trygve Lie, Secretary General of the United Nations. It did gain acceptance by the office of the UN Human Rights Commission (pp. 358–359).

Du Bois was less circumspect than White. While in Atlanta during his second appointment, Du Bois refused several invitations by White to attend meetings of the NAACP "because I did not like Mr. White's methods nor did I trust his personal attitude toward me" (*Autobiography*, p. 328). But he did not hold White entirely responsible for his dismissal in 1947 (p. 335).

John Hope, like James Weldon Johnson, was a contemporary intellectual heir of Du Bois. A graduate of Worcester Academy, 1890, and Brown University, A.B. 1894, he taught Greek and Latin at Atlanta Baptist College, 1896–1906, and became its first President in 1906. Born in the same year, 1868, as Du Bois, he was the only colored college president who dared to attend the 1906 Niagara Movement conference at Harpers Ferry. As Ridgely Torrence observed in *The Story of John Hope* (New York, 1948): "One of Hope's most intimate and enduring friendships" was with Du Bois who began teaching at Atlanta University the year after Hope began teaching at Atlanta Baptist College

(p. 332). "They were united in their doubts as to Booker Washington's program, though neither of them had any desire for a personal contest with him and both recognized him as a great man" (p. 133). It was Hope as President of the new Atlanta University who after several years persuaded Du Bois to come to the university in 1933, shortly before his separation from the NAACP (p. 342). While I was professor of history at Atlanta University, 1933–1938, President Hope told me that he wanted Du Bois to sit on Mount Olympus and survey, as he wished, the problems of the Negro.

One of the most moving passages in Torrence's volume depicts the pilgrimage to John Brown's fort in Harpers Ferry, August, 1906. Torrence, a poet and an author of plays about Negroes, wrote (p. 149):

High on a magnificent promontory, out of a mist, a hundred people gathered at early dawn. They formed and moved forward with evident purpose. The light grew and shone upon their faces. They were Negroes. They were on a solemn pilgrimage. They were barefooted in sign of their reverence and profound dedication. Du Bois was among them, and John Hope. . . . There was majesty in the scene, and there was majesty in the spirit of the pilgrims and in their cause. Their cause was to find justice in their native land.

Southern-born C. Vann Woodward, one of America's most scholarly historians and President of the American Historical Association in 1969, wrote: "The picture of the Niagara adherents marching barefooted . . . to the scene of John Brown's raid offered a bold contrast to the spirit of the Atlanta Compromise" (*Origins of the New South, 1877–1913* [Baton Rouge, 1951], p. 368).

But Samuel R. Spencer, Jr., another Southern-born historian and one of the more adulatory biographers of Washington, lampooned the scene as bordering on the "burlesque" in *Booker T. Washington and the Negro's Place in American Life* (Boston, 1955), pp. 157–158. Upon his return from Europe in 1894, "Du Bois was almost a caricature of what Washington despised: a highly educated but penniless man, indulging in the affectation of gloves and cane while traveling in the steerage" (p. 146). While Du Bois did wear gloves and sport a cane like his fellow students in Germany and at Wilberforce after his return to the United States, evidence is lacking to validate Spencer's allegation. He took delight in stating that Du Bois' application for a teaching position at Tuskegee began "President Washington, Sir" (p. 147). Though the essay "Of Mr. Washington and Others" in *The Souls of Black Folk* was "measured and restrained," during the last twelve years of his life, Washington was "pursued relentlessly by his self-appointed gadfly, Du Bois" (p. 151). Perhaps unaware of Du Bois' concept of his "two-ness" (see pp. ix–x), Spencer asserted that "Washington was first and last an American, Du Bois first and last a Negro" (p. 152). While Spencer concluded that "the challenge of the NAACP was never great enough to shake the foundations of his [Washington's] influence" (p. 177), Professor George B. Tindall, also Southern-born, was convinced: "If Du Bois alone could not speak with the authority of Washington and if he lacked Washington's contact with the masses of the Negro people, before a decade had passed [after 1910] there could be little doubt that the organization he represented stood as the most influential in Negro leadership" (*The Emergence of the New South, 1913–1945* [Baton Rouge, 1967], p. 158).

One of the proposals advanced in the 1930's and later by Communists and recently by black militants is the creation of a separate "black state," nation, or republic in several Southern states. While negative evidence is not conclusive, there is no indication in one of the most comprehensive books, Harry Haywood's *Negro Liberation* (New York, 1947), that Du Bois supported the idea. Wilson Record's authoritative *The Negro and the Communist Party* (Chapel Hill, 1951) likewise presents no positive evidence on this point. To the contrary, the Communist-controlled League of Struggle for Negro Rights condemned in 1933 Booker T. Washington, the NAACP, Walter White, and Du Bois for not supporting its program, including the establishment of the "Black Belt." Record, one of the most trenchant critics of the American Communist party, alluded to its shifting tactics with respect to such moderate organizations as the NAACP and said that in 1950: "Of course, Du Bois is no longer included on the list of traitors, since he has become a contributing editor of *Masses and Mainstream* and a prominent figure in the 'Partisans for Peace' " (pp. 80–81).

One of the longest and most heated *causes célèbres* in United States history involved the "Scottsboro Boys." In early 1931, eight of nine young Negroes were convicted by the Alabama Supreme Court of raping two young white girls who were riding on a freight train with them and some white male itinerants. The American Communist party endeavored to use the convictions as a part of its attacks upon the American "ruling class." Du Bois wrote in *The Crisis* (Tindall, p. 314): " 'If the Communists want these lads murdered, then their tactics of threatening judges and yelling for mass action . . . is calculated to insure this.' " Since the NAACP also denounced the Communists, the party in 1934 charged that Walter White, Du Bois, and others " 'carried through treacherous activities in connection with the Scottsboro campaign, and sabotaged the mass movements against the Scottsboro verdicts' " (quoted by Record, p. 92). The United States Supreme Court in 1932 and 1935 ruled that the verdicts were unconstitutional. Two years later the International Labor Defense, the legal arm of the American Communist party—which at times worked with, without, and against the lawyers of the NAACP and other "reformist" organizations—abandoned direction of the case to the Scottsboro Defense Committee, a coalition of Northern and Alabama organizations. Between 1937 and 1950, the Committee obtained the release of the Scottsboro Boys. Few maneuvers by the American Communist party alienated such a large number of American Negroes. The party's attacks upon Du Bois did not prevent him, however, from applying, in *Black Reconstruction,* some of the views of Karl Marx to Reconstruction.

An interesting critical evaluation of Du Bois is Earl E. Thorpe's *Negro Historians in the United States* (1958), especially pp. 56–83. The author, Ph.D., Ohio State University, 1954, pointed out that, like George Washington Williams, the ablest of the early group of Negro historians, Du Bois wrote in part to redress ignorance about Negroes based upon prejudice. (Some writers today, especially black militants, believe that they are pioneers in this undertaking.) But Du Bois also wrote in *What the Negro Wants* (1944), p. 49: "My long-term remedy was truth: carefully gathered scientific proof that neither color nor race determined the limits of a man's capacity or desert." Between the date of publication of Thorpe's book in 1958 and Du Bois' death in 1963, his growing conviction that communism was the salvation of Negroes made him more of a propagandist than an "objective" historian.

Thorpe rightly concluded (p. x) that Du Bois and Carter G. Woodson were the two Negro historians of "greatest stature" of the twentieth century. (John Hope Franklin would have to be added to the list in 1971.) Woodson, who earned his Ph.D. in History at Harvard University in 1912, also wrote propagandistic and scholarly books. My agreement with Thorpe that "of the two, Woodson was probably more balanced and objective" (p. 55) is based largely upon the fact that Woodson did not become a Marxist. In my judgment, Woodson's pedestrian writings were inferior to Du Bois' polished and at times elegant and brilliant style.

Thorpe's assertion that "throughout his life, Dr. Du Bois viewed the question of slavery in the United States as essentially a moral problem" (p. 63) is wrong. In fact, Thorpe quotes in part a sentence from *The Suppression of the African Slave-Trade:* "The history of the slave trade after 1820 must be read in the light of the industrial revolution through which the civilized world passed in the first half of the twentieth century" (p. 65). The pages devoted to brief summaries and remarks about Du Bois' books—extended for *Black Reconstruction*—quotations from book reviews, and copious footnotes are valuable even today.

Agreeing with *An American Dilemma*'s praise of *The Philadelphia Negro* and regretting that it is "all but forgotten" (see above, p. 305), E. Digby Baltzell, Professor of Sociology at the

University of Pennsylvania, gave detailed reasons for his encomium in a long Introduction to a reprint, 1967, of the 1899 edition. The reviews at the time of publication, he wrote, "invariably praised the book and remarked on the objectivity of the author. In fact, between the lines, one has the impression that most of the white reviewers were rather surprised that a Negro author could have been capable of a work of such careful scholarship and objectivity." I think that the review in the *American Historical Review* (1900–1901, p. 163) was oddly contradictory. On the one hand, the review stated that Du Bois "is perfectly frank, laying all *necessary* [my italics] stress on the weaknesses of his people." On the other hand, the reviewer stated that the Negro's plight "is due *chiefly* [my italics], in Dr. Du Bois' judgment, to a color prejudice." Baltzell observed that the "ultimate truth" about the hereditarian or racial as against the environmental or cultural approaches to the causes of the differences between Negroes and whites lies in a "both/and" rather than an "either/or" approach (pp. xxiii–xxiv). His most important conclusion stated that "the origins, in both method and theoretical point of view" of several significant studies, "are to be found in *The Philadelphia Negro*." Among the books inspired by this work he listed, notably (pp. xxv–xxvi) Franz Boas' *Mind of Primitive Man* (1911) and W. I. Thomas' and Florian Znaniecki's *The Polish Peasant in Europe and America* (*1918–1921*). I am not competent to voice an opinion on this point. I disagree, however, with Baltzell's comment (pp. xxvii–xxviii) that Du Bois' criticism of the Philadelphia Negro middle class was valid and anticipated E. Franklin Frazier's more comprehensive assertion in *Black Bourgeoisie* (1955): "The *single* [my italics] factor that has dominated the mental outlook of the black bourgeoisie has been its obsession with the struggle for status" (pp. 235–236). Neither Du Bois nor Frazier, to name only two, was thus obsessed.

A brief evaluation of Francis L. Broderick's *W. E. B. Du Bois: Negro Leader in a Time of Crisis* (1959), Elliott M. Rudwick's *W. E. B. Du Bois: Propagandist of the Negro Protest* (1968), and Peter Shaw's "The Uses of Autobiography," *The American*

Scholar, 38, No. 1 (Winter 1968–1969), pp. 138–150, provide a sharp contrast with Leslie Alexander Lacy's recent biography of Du Bois (see below, pp. 316–317). Professor Broderick stated as his goal: "My intention has been neither to exalt nor to demean Dr. Du Bois; it has been to understand him in the context of his time" (p. vii). Not until scholars have unrestricted access to the Du Bois Papers after 1910, when he closed them to outsiders, will it be possible to offer more than tentative conclusions about the degree of the author's fulfillment of his contract. The following necessarily brief evaluation is based upon his concluding chapter, "The Man behind the Myth."

Broderick rightly believed that the myth, to which Du Bois himself "sedulously contributed" and which several writers, notably Henry Steele Commager, Jay Saunders Redding, and William Stanley Braithwaite, promoted, needs revision (pp. 227–228). There will be little need, however, to revise Broderick's judgments that no single scholarly work by Du Bois "except *The Philadelphia Negro,* is first class" and that, as for his *belles lettres,* "Du Bois never surpassed the month-to-month prose of his editorials on social, political, and economic topics in *The Crisis*" (p. 229).

On the basis of evidence available to Broderick on November 1, 1958, when he completed his manuscript, I disagree with two of his conclusions. One, he stated that the turning point in Du Bois' career was not, as is generally assumed, 1934, the year he broke with the NAACP and recommended Negro separatism, but 1952, "when he abandoned the struggle for Negro rights to concentrate on world movements for peace and socialism" (p. 229). Du Bois did not *abandon* the struggle for Negro rights in 1952; he *continued* it within the framework of world movements for peace and socialism.

Two, Broderick wrote that by 1933 "Du Bois was being rejected, by-passed by a new generation with ideas of its own." In support of this view he cited (pp. 218–219) the refusal of large numbers of Negroes to stand by Du Bois when he was under indictment on a charge of being an unregistered agent of the

Soviet Union. Du Bois' *In Battle for Peace* (1952), which Broderick discussed (pp. 216, 218–225, 227), refuted in part this assertion. It is true that many prominent Negroes (and whites), cowed by Senator Joseph McCarthy's witch-hunting, were so afraid to support Du Bois that they did not attend a testimonial dinner in New York on his eighty-third birthday, February 23, 1951. However, even after the hotel at which the dinner was to be held cancelled its contract, E. Franklin Frazier presided and spoke at the dinner which was then held elsewhere; Attorney Belford Lawson, Jr., General President of the Alpha Phi Alpha Fraternity, of which Du Bois was a member, "made a fighting speech; Paul Robeson spoke courageously and feelingly. A strong letter from Judge Hubert Delany was read." There were about $6,557 in dinner fees and donations (*In Battle for Peace,* pp. 62–65). Moreover, some moderate Negroes supported Du Bois until, during, and after his acquittal (*ibid.,* pp. 65–159). Broderick probably did not know that, despite considerable local opposition, the Division of Social Sciences of Howard University presented Du Bois to an overflow crowd in Rankin Memorial Chapel on March 31, 1958. I presided and Dr. Mordecai W. Johnson, President of the university, sat in the front row (Logan, *Howard University: The First Hundred Years, 1867–1967* [Washington, D.C., 1969], pp. 408–409, 541).

Broderick's final paragraph stated: "In performing these two functions, propagandizing for equality and inspiring younger Negroes, Du Bois achieved enough significance for one lifetime. It is not necessary to gild the lily with myths" (p. 231). His conclusion is as valid in 1971 as it was in 1959, and will perhaps still be when the Du Bois Papers after 1910 are not as restricted as they now are.

Rudwick completed in September, 1960, his manuscript of *W. E. B. Du Bois: A Study in Minority Group Leadership,* published in 1968 as *W. E. B. Du Bois: Propagandist of the Negro Protest,* with a new Preface by Louis R. Harlan and an Epilogue by Professor Rudwick. My tentative evaluation of the author's biography as a whole is based upon his final chapters,

"The Recent Years: An Epilogue" and "Conclusions." Like
Broderick, Rudwick exaggerated the extent of Du Bois' alienation
"from the thinking of American Negroes." It is not true that "only
the far left continued to claim this man whom one observer described as a 'Prophet in Limbo' " (p. 291). Rudwick's comments
on the March on Washington for Jobs and Freedom disproved this
assertion. The vast assemblage at the Washington Monument
Grounds "stood bowed in silent tribute" when the news of Du
Bois' death was announced (p. 295). Moreover, I still recall my
satisfaction when Roy Wilkins, Executive Secretary of the
NAACP, hardly a member of the far left, gave a brief but moving
eulogy at the Lincoln Memorial ceremonies of the March. In addition, the October 1963 issue of *The Crisis* (pp. 428–473) reproduced a photograph of Du Bois, gave a brief laudatory biography,
and printed excerpts from his resolutions at the Harpers Ferry
Niagara Movement Meeting, August 15–19, 1906, preceded by the
sentence: "They still express the aspirations of Negro America."
This issue of *The Crisis* also included the full text of the resolution
adopted by the NAACP Board of Directors on September 9, 1963,
one paragraph of which read (p. 473): "His contributions to the
ageless struggle for human rights are imperishable. His passing
leaves a great void which there is no immediate prospect of filling."
The NAACP Board of Directors did not consign him to limbo.

Nor did Professor John Hope Franklin. In his address at the
Du Bois Memorial, Carnegie Hall, 1964, he deplored the fact
that "one of the great learned journals [the *American Historical
Review*, he told me on September 26, 1970] "merely reported
that he had died, thus indicating its own inability or unwillingness
to comment on the impact of Du Bois on the field represented by
that journal." Franklin summarized his evaluation of Du Bois
as follows:

He will be remembered wherever people take inventory of those who
have contributed significantly to the improvement of the lot of mankind. He will be remembered by all of us who find in his own words a
pattern of thinking and an approach to our problems that will move
us closer to their solution. All of this remembrance will be with the

deepest gratitude, for without souls such as that of Du Bois the world would not only be drab and dreary but intolerable as well. Even in moments of despair and discouragement we who have the security that comes from knowledge that our cause is just will never stop fighting—not merely for our own sake but for the sake of the world.

One of Rudwick's debatable conclusions stated that Du Bois had been "too stern in assigning to Washington 'a heavy responsibility' for Negro disfranchisement, the poverty of Negro colleges, and the entrenchment of the caste system in the country." Washington's responsibility was lessened by his limited powers with whites; he was only "their spokesman" (p. 304). I believe that for this very reason Washington's responsibility was indeed "heavy." Less debatable and more significant is Rudwick's conviction that, even before Booker T. Washington died, he " 'moved considerably towards his opponents' because of societal changes and Du Bois' propaganda" (p. 306).

On the vital point of the time of the zenith and decline of Du Bois as a leader, Rudwick placed the zenith during the period preceding and immediately following World War I and fixed the turning point in 1934 (p. 306, 312). At the very end, Rudwick's conclusion is not unlike that of Broderick (to whom he acknowledged in his Preface his indebtness for "scholarly studies" in Negro leadership): "There can be no doubt that in the field of race relations, W. E. B. Du Bois, despite his individualism, was the dean of the protest advocate leaders during the first half of the twentieth century" (p. 318). This view, also, may be valid when the Du Bois Papers after 1910 are opened to scholars.

Peter Shaw, on leave from the State University of New York at Stony Brook, wrote a trenchant review of *The Autobiography of W. E. B. Du Bois: A Soliloquy on Viewing My Life from the Last Decade of Its First Century* (1968), Herbert Aptheker, ed. As may be expected, this review in *The American Scholar,* an organ of the United Chapters of Phi Beta Kappa, attempts a balanced view of the *Autobiography* and of Du Bois. For instance, his "perspective of his most broadly conceived involvement . . . brought his autobiography so close to the historical pole that one begins to read it more as a document of the Negro struggle than as the story of a personality" (p. 136).

Shaw's major criticism of the *Autobiography*—which like those of other famous writers "has not usually found its success in the perfection of form"—is crucial. "The body of the work," he stated, "was not written from late perspective, but reproduces passages written twenty or even forty years earlier—something the editor, Herbert Aptheker, misleadingly omits from his introduction" (p. 138). Aware of this shortcoming, I suggested to one of my graduate students that his research find the original sources of the passages and that his dissertation compare them with Aptheker's rendition. The student reported that the research and writing would require too much time. I am, therefore, all the more convinced that this contribution is necessary and can be done only by a mature scholar able to devote considerable time to the problem.

With one of Shaw's summations I disagree in part, however. It stated (p. 144):

If history took away from Du Bois the chance to lead a quiet life by emphasizing his race, it also gave him, as he early discovered, a special insight. And just as he learned that the problem of his minority was *the* central problem of the country, and came to believe that the exploitation of the darker races was *the* key to the history of the twentieth century, his life of rejection, disappointments, constant hope and final exile seems an epitome of the American Negro experience [my italics].

Professor Shaw would have been less vulnerable if he had substituted "a" for the words that I have italicized. My more important basis for disagreement stems from the inclusion of Du Bois' "final exile" as a part of "an epitome of the American Negro experience." At no time has a sizable number of American Negroes sought exile as an escape from their experience.

The death of Du Bois, August 27, 1963, naturally led to many publications about him. One of the most recent is Leslie Alexander Lacy's *The Life of W. E. B. Du Bois: Cheer the Lonesome*

Traveler (New York, 1970), a biography that is "primarily . . . for the young" (p. 9). Especially for this reason, the author's grievous mistakes are regrettable. The Fifteenth Amendment sought to protect the right of Negroes to vote, not to assure "that law and justice would prevail" (p. 16). Du Bois voiced his demands for full equality for Negroes at the Harpers Ferry Conference, 1906, not at the 1905 conference (pp. 53–54). *The Negro* was not "a study similar in quality to his earlier book *The Philadelphia Negro*" (p. 62). Du Bois was not "tall" (p. 31) but below average height. *The Encyclopedia of the Negro* is not a "historical chronicle" (p. 175) but a list of references and reports on sources for the writing of an encyclopedia.

Lacy's biography is marred also by his following the semantic nonsense of some more mature authors. He did not commit their aberration of using indiscriminately "blacks" when referring to groups. On the other hand, labeling individuals such as Dean Horace Mann Bond of the Atlanta University School of Education, Booker T. Washington, and Du Bois as "black" (pp. 41, 43, 22, respectively) is catering too much to the cliché "Black Is Beautiful."

Some of Lacy's comments show better judgment. His treatment of Marcus Garvey is on the whole good, but the author erred (p. 68) when he wrote that "Du Bois did not retaliate in kind" against Garvey's personal attacks. He concluded his discussion of the Du Bois-Washington controversy with this interesting anecdote (p. 49): "One evening in Ghana, Du Bois summed up the controversy: 'I think that maybe the greatest difference between Booker T. [*sic*] and myself was that he felt the lash, and I did not.' " I agree. The chapter on "The Du Bois I Knew" is, however, disappointing, for Lacy had met Du Bois briefly in the United States and talked with him only once, for about an hour, in Ghana. Nevertheless, two of the author's comments are valuable: "Du Bois' mind was clear; his words lucid" (p. 133); he believed that "one could be for peace in Vietnam, . . . but must support all the violent efforts of the South African freedom fighters." This inconsistency on the use of violence, voiced almost on the eve of his death, repeats a pattern that characterized most of his adult life.

Lacy also published the message of President Kwame Nkrumah to the people of Ghana on the evening of the funeral. It ended: "Dr. Du Bois is a phenomenon. May he rest in peace." It appears that his peace in Atlanta was oblivion. *Phylon,* the magazine which he founded, 1940, and edited until 1944, carried no obituary; it did not even mention his death.

The thirty-four contributors to the "W. E. B. Du Bois Memorial Issue" (Winter 1965, First Quarter) of *Freedomways, A Quarterly Review of the Negro Freedom Movement* did not measurably enlarge knowledge about him. Some of the pieces were brief tributes; others, personal reminiscences; still others spoke with little authority. Worthy of more than cursory reading are Professor Eugene Holmes' "W. E. B. Du Bois—Philosopher"; Herbert Aptheker's "Some Unpublished Writings of W. E. B. Du Bois"; and Elinor D. Sinnette's account of a monthly magazine which Du Bois edited from January, 1920, to December, 1931: "The Brownies' Book: A Pioneer Publication for Children." The most significant theme of the issue is the intellectual influence of Du Bois upon such diverse writers and personalities as Professor John Hope Franklin, Langston Hughes, and Horace Mann Bond, on the one hand, and Paul Robeson and James E. Jackson, editor of *The Worker,* on the other hand.

This theme is repeated in John Oliver Killens' Introduction to the paperback reprint, 1969, of Du Bois' *An ABC of Color,* originally published in East Berlin, 1963. On the eve of the August 28, 1963 March on Washington for Jobs and Freedom, the novelist and essayist was with James Baldwin and Sidney Poitier when they were informed: "The old man died." No one needed to tell them that the old man was Du Bois, for, "To some of us he was our patron saint, our teacher and our prophet" (p. 9). This, I believe, is a fitting valedictory.

Contributors

HERBERT APTHEKER, one of the most prominent theoreticians of the American Communist party, is also a well-known historian and editor. Born in New York City, July 31, 1915, he received his B.S., M.A., and Ph.D. degrees from Columbia University in 1936, 1937, and 1943, respectively. He served in the United States Army, 1942–1946, and was discharged with the rank of major. Dr. Aptheker was a Guggenheim Fellow, 1946–1947, a grantee of the Social Science Research Council, 1961, and of the Rubinowitz Foundation, 1965. Perhaps his best-known books on Marxism are *Marxism and Democracy,* which he edited in 1965, and *Marxism and Alienation,* 1966. In addition to other works, especially his *Documentary History of the Negro in the United States* (1962 and 1964), he edited *The Autobiography of W. E. B. Du Bois: A Soliloquy on Viewing My Life from the Last Decade of Its First Century* (1968), and has written many magazine articles.

A Director of the New York School of Marxist Studies since 1960 and of the American Institute of Marxist Studies since 1964, Dr. Aptheker received the honorary degree of Doctor of Philosophy from the Martin Luther University of Halle (West Germany), 1966. In 1970 he was appointed Professor of History, Bryn Mawr College.

FRANCIS LYONS BRODERICK was born in New York City on September 13, 1912. He received his A.B. degree, with high honors, from Princeton University, 1943; his M.A. and Ph.D. degrees from Harvard University, 1947 and 1950, respectively. After serving as a first lieutenant in the United States Air Force, 1943–1945, he taught at Princeton University, 1945–1946, State University of Iowa, 1948–1950, and Philips Exeter Academy, 1951–1963. He was Director of the Peace Corps in Ghana, 1964–1966, when he became Dean of Lawrence and Downer Colleges as well as Gordon R. Clapp Professor of American Studies, Lawrence University, Appleton, Wisconsin. He was a Woodrow Wilson Fellow, 1945–1946, and President of the American Catholic Historical Association, 1968. Professor Broderick is the author of *Right Reverend New Dealer: John A. Ryan* (1963) and coeditor with August Meier of *Negro Protest Thought in the Twentieth Century* (1966). With John Tracy Ellis he published *The Life and Times of James Cardinal Gibbons* (1963) which won, 1964, the National Catholic Book Award. His *W. E. B. Du Bois, Negro Leader in a Time of Crisis* (1959) is one of the two full-length biographies that have been written about Du Bois.

WILLIAM H. FERRIS was born on July 20, 1874, in New Haven, Connecticut. After graduating from Hillhouse High School, New Haven, in 1891, he entered Yale University where he received special honors in philosophy and English, and ranked among the top men in Professor William Graham Summer's class in sociology. He received his baccalaureate degree in 1895 and his M.A. degree from Yale in 1899. He studied for a year in the Harvard Divinity School and received another M.A. degree in 1900. During the spring of 1901, Ferris taught mathematics, science, religion, and Latin at Florida Baptist College, Jacksonville, until fire closed the school.

A correspondent for the Indianapolis *Freeman* while in high school, he wrote an article for the Boston *Transcript,* 1901, the *Literary Digest,* 1904, and the Springfield *Republican,* 1912. He was Associate Editor of *The Champion,* Chicago, 1916–1917; General Literary Assistant, A. M. E. Book Concern, Philadelphia, 1917–1919. From 1919 to 1923, he was the Literary Editor of *The Negro World,* established by Marcus Garvey as the organ of his Universal Negro Improvement Association. Ferris served briefly in 1920 as Acting Chancellor of the UNIA; at the Second International Convention for Negroes in New York, August, 1921, he was elected Assistant President General of the Association, and served for one year.

Except for *The African Abroad,* his only other known publication is *Alexander Crummell, An Apostle of Negro Culture* (Washington, D.C.: American Negro Academy, 1920). Ferris died in 1941.

VINCENT HARDING was born in New York City, July 25, 1931. He received his A.B. degree from City College, New York City, in 1952; his M.S. in Journalism from Columbia University in 1953; his M.A. in History from the University of Chicago in 1965. After serving as Supply Associate Pastor, Seventh-Day Adventist Church, Chicago, 1955–1957, he became Lay Associate Pastor, Woodlawn Mennonite Church, Chicago, 1957. Since then, he has been an active participant in the activities of the Mennonite Church. A Kent Fellow of the Society for Religion in Higher Education, he was Professor of History and Sociology at Spelman College, Atlanta, Georgia, and Chairman of its Department of History and Social Sciences. He was also Director of the Martin Luther King, Jr., Memorial Library Project in Atlanta until August, 1970, and was Director of the Institute of the Black World, Atlanta. He is the author of *Must Walls Divide?* (1965), and has contributed articles, short stories, and sermons to several journals.

HAROLD ROBERT ISAACS was born in New York City, September 13, 1910, and received his A.B. degree from Columbia University in 1930. During the years 1928–1931 he served as a reporter for *The New York Times,* the *Shanghai Evening Post,* and the *China Press,* and between 1931 and 1940 was a reporter for the *Agence Havas,* Shanghai and New York City. He was a correspondent for the Columbia Broadcasting System, New York City and Washington, 1940–1943, a war correspondent in the China-Burma-India theater, and an Associate Editor of *Newsweek,* 1943–1950. A Guggenheim Fellow in 1950, he was Research Associate at the Center for International Studies at the Massachusetts Institute of Technology, Cambridge, Massachusetts, 1953–1965, and since then Professor of Political Science. His books include *The Tragedy of the Chinese Revolution* (1938), *Scratches on Our Minds: American Images of China and India* (1958), and *Emergent Americans, a Report on Crossroads Africa* (1961). *The New World of Negro Americans* (1963), a chapter of which is included in this volume, won in 1964 the Anisfield-Wolf Award for the best book on race relations. Professor Isaacs has contributed articles to magazines, notably *Public Opinion Quarterly, Phylon,* the *Atlanta University Quarterly, The New Yorker, Commentary,* and *Foreign Affairs.*

CHARLES FLINT KELLOGG was born October 28, 1909, in Pittsfield, Massachusetts, not far from the birthplace of W. E. B. Du Bois. He received his A.B. degree from Columbia University, 1931; his M.A. degree from Harvard University, 1933; his Ph.D. degree from Johns Hopkins University, 1963. He was a Scholar at the General Theological Seminary, New York City, 1933–1936, and at the Massachusetts State Hospital for Mental Diseases, 1935. He has been an administrator and a member of the faculty at Dickinson College, Carlisle, Pennsylvania, since 1946, rising from the rank of Instructor in History to Boyd Lee Spahr Professor in History in 1968. He is the author of *NAACP: A History of the National Association for the Advancement of Colored People, Volume I, 1909–1920* (1967), and has written the Introduction to a new edition of Mary White Ovington's *Half a Man* (1969). Bard College, Annandale-on-Hudson, New York, conferred upon him the honorary degree of Doctor of Humanities in 1960.

BASIL JOSEPH MATHEWS was born in Oxford, England, in 1879. After graduating from Oxford High School and Oxford University, he resided in London for many years and served the British Missionary Societies as editor, writer, and press representative. In 1924 he became Literature Secretary of the Boys' Work Division of the World's Alliance of Young Men's Christian Associations with headquarters in Geneva. For a number of years he edited *The World's Youth,* a magazine published in several languages for leaders of boys, and carried on an extensive correspondence with missionary agencies in Europe and America in behalf of youth throughout the world. For more than a decade prior to the publication of *Booker T. Washington* (1948), he taught at Boston University and at Andover Newton Theological School. Some of the books he wrote are *Black Treasure: The Youth of Africa in a Changing World* (New York: Friendship Press, 1928); *Consider Africa* (New York: Friendship Press, 1936); *Livingstone, the Pathfinder* (New York: Missionary Education Movement of the United States and Canada, 1912; rev. ed., London: A. & C. Black, 1960). In addition, he wrote many books for young people. Mathews died in 1951.

AUGUST MEIER was born in New York City on August 30, 1923. He received his A.B. degree from Oberlin College in 1945; his M.A. and Ph.D. degrees from Columbia University in 1949 and 1957, respectively. He was Assistant Professor of History, Tougaloo College (Mississippi); a research assistant to President Charles S. Johnson of Fisk University, 1953; Assistant Professor of History, Fisk University, 1953–1956; Assistant, then Associate, Professor of History, Morgan State College, Baltimore, 1957–1964; Professor of History, Roosevelt University, Chicago, 1964–1967. He is now University Professor of History and Senior Research Fellow at the Center for Urban Regionalism at Kent State

University. In 1952 he was awarded a fellowship from the American Council of Learned Societies. Professor Meier is the author of *Negro Thought in America, 1880–1915* (1963), and has published with Elliott Rudwick *From Plantation to Ghetto* (1963, rev. ed., 1970) and *The Making of Black America*, 2 vols. (1969). With Francis Broderick, he was coeditor of *Negro Protest Thought in the Twentieth Century* (1966). He has written numerous magazine articles about American Negroes, and is a prominent revisionist interpreter of Booker T. Washington. Since 1966 Professor Meier has been a consulting editor to Atheneum Publishers for the Studies in American Negro Life series.

ELLIOTT M. RUDWICK was born in Philadelphia on July 19, 1927. He received his A.B. degree from Temple University in 1949; his M.A. and Ph.D. degrees in Sociology from the University of Pennsylvania in 1950 and 1956, respectively. He has taught at Florida State University and Southern Illinois University (Edwardsville). Since 1968 he has been a Professor of Sociology and Senior Research Fellow at the Center for Urban Regionalism, Kent State University. During the 1960's he was a Consultant to the United States Commission on Civil Rights, the Kerner Commission's *Report of the National Advisory Commission on Civil Disorders* (1968), and the National Commission on the Causes and Prevention of Violence (Eisenhower Commission).

Professor Rudwick is coauthor with August Meier of *From Plantation to Ghetto* (1963; rev. ed., 1970), and coeditor with Meier of *The Making of Black America*, 2 vols. (1969). He has published with John Bracey, Jr., and Meier, *Black Nationalism in America* (1970).

Rayford W. Logan, Professor of History at Howard University, knew Du Bois over a period of thirty-seven years, having first met him in 1921 in Paris, where Logan served as Secretary and Interpreter of the Second Pan African Congress. They were colleagues at Atlanta University from 1933 to 1938. They were also associates on the Encyclopaedia of the Negro project. Dr. Logan received his A.B. (Phi Beta Kappa) from Williams and his M.A. and Ph.D. from Harvard. He received the L.H.D. from Williams College in 1965. Logan is the author of numerous articles and books, his most recent being *Howard University: The First Hundred Years, 1867–1967* (1969) and *Diplomatic Relations of the United States with Haiti, 1776–1891* (1969).

✪

Aïda DiPace Donald holds degrees from Barnard and Columbia and a Ph.D. from the University of Rochester. A former member of the History Department at Columbia, Mrs. Donald has been a Fulbright Fellow at Oxford and the recipient of an A.A.U.W. fellowship. She has published *John F. Kennedy and the New Frontier* and *Diary of Charles Francis Adams.*